# The Time of the Monkey, Rooster, and Dog

Also by Charles A. Hobbie: *Buffalo Wings*

Geoje Island, Korea, June 1969

Countryside near Daegu, Korea, July 1969

Train Station, Samnangjin, Korea, August 1969

Village in South Gyeongsang Province, Korea, August 1969

Sobaek Mountains, Korea, October 1970

Street in Busan, Korea, June 1969

# CHARLES A. HOBBIE

# THE TIME OF THE MONKEY, ROOSTER, AND DOG

A Peace Corps Volunteer's Years in Korea

iUniverse, Inc.
Bloomington

# The Time of the Monkey, Rooster, and Dog
## A Peace Corps Volunteer's Years in Korea

iUniverse books may be ordered through booksellers or by contacting:

iUniverse
1663 Liberty Drive
Bloomington, IN 47403
www.iuniverse.com
1-800-Authors (1-800-288-4677)

ISBN: 978-1-4620-3494-9 (sc)
ISBN: 978-1-4620-3492-5 (e)
ISBN: 978-1-4620-3493-2 (dj)

Library of Congress Control Number: 2011912165

Printed in the United States of America

iUniverse rev. date: 7/29/2011

Dedicated to the love of my life and best friend—my wife, Shin Young-ei—and our families; the Korean and American Peace Corps staff in Hawaii, Korea, and Washington DC; my Korean family in Daegu—Na Chae-woon, his wife, and children; Kyungpook National University faculty and students; other Korean, Hawaiian, and American friends, especially John and Jean Sibley; and to the people of Korea, especially the citizens of Daegu.

*　*　*

With great thanks to my sister, Cecilia Pehle, for her help editing this memoir.

*　*　*

And in grateful memory of Choi Hwa-wook, Han Jae-chul, Chauncey and Margaret Allen, Kim Young-hee, Lee Woo-gun, Na Eun-shin, Alix and John Hobbie, and Sargent Shriver.

*Peace requires the simple but powerful recognition that what we have in common as human beings is more important and crucial than what divides us.*—Sargent Shriver

주 한 미 평 화 봉 사 단

Peace Corps Korea

# CONTENTS

Flooded Rice Paddies near Daegu, Korea, May 1969

Girls Playing the *Kayageum* (Korean Zither) at School Performance,
Daegu, Korea, November 1969

# FOREWORD

There are two hundred thousand memoirs stored in the hearts, minds, and lives of the Peace Corps Volunteers who have served in the past fifty years. If only they all could be compiled, what a profound addition they would make to America's understanding of the world and of the lives of some of our nation's most dedicated and adventurous citizens. Added now to the several hundred who have written books about their experiences is Chuck Hobbie, with this deeply personal account.

Other former volunteers who read his book will most likely be envious of the details Chuck has retained about friends and daily experiences. Letters home that captured his work and cultural growth guide the book's deep insight into a rapidly changing Korea. How lucky his parents must have felt as they followed their son's challenges and maturation.

Older Koreans who read the book will find details of a life they have largely forgotten over the last forty years. Younger Koreans can hardly comprehend such a life. All will be pleased by the genuine affection Chuck shows for Korea and its people.

War and peace are emotive themes of the era Chuck describes. Korea was emerging from its war with a little help from Peace Corps Volunteers, while in Vietnam other young Americans fought and died.

A simple sentence that captured my attention early in the book was, "I had never seen a rice paddy." He was to see so much more, as will the reader, about a culture, life, hopes, and dreams. In leaving Korea, he wrote, "My personal journey through and past Korean rice paddies in the Peace Corps was a path on which I had passed into the community of the world."

Dig deeply into the details of this fine and very personal exploration, and you will have joined his vibrant community.

Jon Keeton

President

Friends of Korea

Returned Peace Corps Volunteer/Thailand 1965–67

Peace Corps/Korea Country Director 1973–76

Peace Corps Regional Director

North Africa, Near East, Asia Pacific Region 1984–89

Downtown Seoul, Looking toward *Namdaemun* or South Great Gate,
July 1969

Islands in the Korean Archipelago, July 1970

# INTRODUCTION

For the past fifty years, a small, poorly funded federal agency has sent Americans abroad on two-year missions. The work of these Americans is not well publicized. In fact, this agency's work is virtually unknown in this country. Each American sent abroad pursues three goals: helping the people of interested countries in meeting their need for trained men and women; helping promote a better understanding of Americans on the part of the peoples served; and helping promote a better understanding of other peoples on the part of Americans. Of course I am referring to the Peace Corps.

More than two hundred thousand American volunteers have served overseas in about one hundred and forty different countries during this fifty-year period. Approximately 1 percent, or about two thousand Americans, served in Korea from 1966 until 1981, when the program in Korea ended. I was one of those volunteers from 1968 to 1971, which was a time of awakening for Korea and for me. This is my attempt—before the prism of forty years rends the light of that time into too many fluttering ribbons of color—to tell the story of those unforgettably challenging years of transformation.

All volunteers in the Peace Corps ask themselves at some point whether or not their service was of any value to anyone, whether they realized the three Peace Corps goals in any part at all, and whether the considerable efforts of the host people and their government and of the American government were worthwhile. At the time of my experiences in Korea, I doubted that Korea, Koreans, my own country, or I were benefiting in any significant way from the Peace Corps program in the "Land of the Morning Calm." When I clambered up the steps of the Pan American plane at Busan airport in January 1971, on the first leg of my long trip home, I reflected that, despite the many wonderful Korean friends, American colleagues, and experiences of my Peace Corps service, I would not have joined the Peace Corps program in Korea had I known in 1968 what I knew about isolation, culture shock, job frustration, and material deprivation almost two and a half years later.

By the time I arrived home in Buffalo, New York, seven weeks later, my reflection on the Busan runway had totally changed. As I thought about the years in Korea, memories of the hardships and loneliness paled in comparison to the positive recollections of the Koreans I knew and of their incredible country and culture. I began to appreciate the Peace Corps experience as a turning point in my life and perhaps the single most important factor shaping me as an adult. I realized that I had achieved a kind of enlightenment in Korea. Peace Corps and Koreans taught me that what matter in life—besides the all-important love, family, and friendship—are humility, nurturing persistence, faith in the future, and self-discipline, all to be cultivated with an abiding awareness of the world as a community. As the years passed, my appreciation for these lessons has deepened, with my deep affection and admiration for, and gratitude to, the people of Korea.

Recent events have renewed memories and friendships, which had begun to fade. More than a quarter of a century after the last Peace Corps volunteer left Korea, the Korea Society in New York—at the suggestion of the Korean government—honored former Peace Corps volunteers in 2008 with the following words and individual awards:

> Many Americans have dedicated themselves to the cause of US–Korea friendship over the years. Few Americans have done more for this cause than the approximately twenty-five hundred men and women who served as Peace Corps volunteers in Korea from 1966 to 1981. Answering their country's call, these Americans gave two years of their lives to work in Korea during an era when the idea of Korea as a modern democracy and a world-class economy was only a dream in the minds of visionaries.

The Peace Corps Korea volunteers shared with Koreans from all walks of life their skills and their spirit of sacrifice. Traveling to a foreign land, they were determined to contribute to its development and did so in a way that is still remembered and appreciated on both sides of the Pacific. The volunteers shared their talents and knowledge with newfound friends in Korea, and in doing so they developed a deep appreciation for Korea's culture and language, as well as a strong affection for the Korean people.

Today, many Koreans speak of the profound educational and personal impact the Peace Corps volunteers had on them. And today, those volunteers continue to distinguish themselves in government, academia, and business, carrying with them and spreading to others the deep feelings for Korea that have helped make fast the bonds that link our two peoples. The Korea Society is pleased to honor the selfless dedication these Americans showed in support of US–Korea relations by bestowing a 2008 James A. Van Fleet Award on the veterans of the Peace Corps Korea program. It is a special honor to have the Honorable Kevin O'Donnell, the first country director of the Peace Corps Korea program, accept the award on behalf of all those who served America—and Korea—so well as Peace Corps Korea volunteers.

The Korean Government subsequently invited all former volunteers to come to Seoul, as its guests, to "revisit" their former Korean colleagues, students, friends, and families by participating in a weeklong visit filled with seminars, receptions, cultural events, and visits to the volunteers' former work sites. The program also included meetings with Koreans heading overseas in Korea's overseas voluntary service program. Hundreds of former volunteers have responded to this gracious invitation. Former Peace Corps/Korea Country Director Jon Keeton has coordinated these events stateside. Four such revisits took place in 2008–2010, under the skillful auspices of the Korea Foundation, and more are planned for the next several years.

My wife, son, and I took part in the first of these revisits in October 2008, with about sixty other former volunteers. We reunited with beloved Korean friends, whom I hadn't seen for thirty-five years, marveled at the incredibly modern, friendly, democratic country that Korea has become, and rejoiced in meeting the officials and volunteers of Korea's own overseas volunteer program (modeled in many ways after the American Peace Corps). Our feelings during the revisit may only be characterized as overwhelmingly ecstatic!

That initial revisit program serendipitously coincided with the arrival of the new American Ambassador to Korea, the Honorable Kathleen (Kathy) Stephens, who is the first female American Ambassador to the "Hermit Kingdom" and the first to speak Korean. When I first met Kathy, she was departing to become a Peace Corps Volunteer in Korea (1975–1977), where she taught English at Yesan Middle School in Chungcheong Province, as a member of the thirty-fifth Peace Corps Korea group to serve in Korea. She is undoubtedly among the finest examples of a volunteer who successfully pursued Peace Corps' three goals (mentioned earlier). It is not surprising, and a blessing to former volunteers, that her posting to Korea renewed the Korean government's and Korean people's interest in the decade and a half of Peace Corps' presence there so long ago.

Ambassador Stephens's first official function as the new American envoy was a reception for high-level Korean government officials—many of whom had been English students of former volunteers, three to four decades before—and for former volunteers then revisiting Korea. She asked the volunteers to bring pictures with them of their experiences in Korea, as members of the Peace Corps. Hundreds of pictures poured forth. Many were posted for viewing at the reception. As a result of the heartwarming response to these pictures and memories by Koreans and Americans alike, a group of former volunteers decided to publish a book of their pictures, depicting Korea and their experiences decades before. Acting on behalf of this group—organized formally as the Friends of Korea (an organization primarily consisting of former Peace Corps Volunteers and staff in Korea)—former K-35 volunteer William Harwood spearheaded the publication of this book in 2009: *Through Our Eyes: Peace Corps in Korea, 1966–1981*.

One look at *Through Our Eyes* leaves no doubt of the love and respect for Korea engendered in the hearts of former volunteers. At one of the revisit programs recently, the observations of former Peace Corps

Volunteer Dick Christenson articulated how all of us, who lived and worked in Korea, feel:

> We former Peace Corps Volunteers all agree on one point: that the Korean people gave us much more than we gave them. The Korean people helped us understand the world and our shared humanity. They taught us the truth of Buddha's teaching that to seek enlightenment, one must travel to far-away places. They shared with us their homes, their way of living, their way of thinking. They taught us to appreciate, to understand—to talk less and listen more. So we count ourselves lucky that we were assigned to serve in Korea, a country that made the most of whatever small things we were able to contribute, and whose people appreciated our sincerity, even when sincerity was all we could offer—when the work we did was not of much help. Our gathering here now is proof that Korea is indeed a country that generously appreciates those who come sincerely. Of the 139 countries the Peace Corps has served in, none but Korea has invited all its volunteers back to say thank you. But it is we, more than Koreans, who owe gratitude. To the Korean people … we say simply this: "Thank you for all you have given us. We are lucky to have known you, and to know you now, anew."

(Dick was a volunteer in the third group of volunteers to arrive in Korea and subsequently served as the American Deputy Chief of Mission in Seoul.)

This memoir is intended to convey my deepest thanks to the Korean people. It is based on the dozens of letters I wrote home to my parents and other relatives and friends—letters returned to me over the past thirty-five years. The descriptions and stories of these letters were once fresh in my memory. With their aid, the joys and tribulations of that time are rekindled in these pages, together with my deepest admiration for Koreans and my gratitude toward them.

To this appreciation, I add only two things: my thanks to the American government and to the American people for permitting a young man to join the Peace Corps more than four decades ago, and my fervent hope that the future foreign policies and resource allocations of my country may more closely reflect the ideals upon which the Peace Corps was founded more than fifty years ago.

Ferryboat between Geoje Island and Chilcheon Island, Korea, July 1969

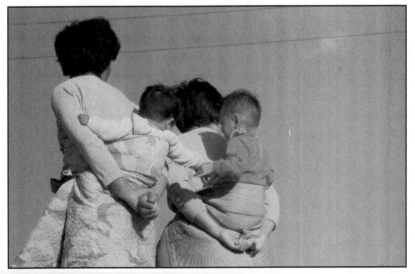

Two Mothers and Two Friends near Daegu, Korea, September 1969

Summer Sunset from the Geoje Island Rural Health Project,
July 1969

A Newly Married Couple in a Park in Daegu, Korea, June 1969

Women Washing Clothes near Gumi, North Gyeongsang Province,
Korea, July 1969

*Kwanghwamun* and former Japanese Governor-General Building,
Seoul, Korea, July 1969

# The Year of the Monkey

# CHAPTER ONE—PROLOGUE IN MADISON, WISCONSIN

As Dickens would have said, it was the coldest of times. It was the warmest of times. It was a season of war. It was a season of peace. It was the Year of the Monkey. I stumbled through the tear gas on Wisconsin's campus, past the armed forces of the national guard, eyes brimming in tears, and I had no idea what I was doing or where I was going in 1968.

I was trying to be a poet in those days. The shocks of assassinations, the outrages in Vietnam, and rising racial violence filled us with distaste and disillusionment. My friends and I took the graduate courses, struggled to become immersed in writing poetry and to cope with the horrific events swirling around us, and watched our country betray its ideals. It is difficult, in retrospect, to convey the depths of my despair that year. The first seven months of 1968 saw several events of which even the retelling shades the many joyous remembrances of that time in darkness.

January was a brutally cold month in Madison. In Vietnam, it was hot and sultry. On January 10, the one thousandth US warplane was lost in Vietnam.

Eleven days later, on January 21, a group of thirty-one North Korean commandos trudged undetected through the snow for about forty miles from the border to the presidential Blue House of South Korean President Park Chung-hee in downtown Seoul. Twenty-eight North Koreans and thirty-four South Koreans were killed in the fighting. The same week, on January 23, North Korean patrol boats captured the USS *Pueblo*, a US intelligence gathering ship, and its eighty-three man crew, charging that *Pueblo* and its crew had violated North Korea's twelve-mile territorial limit.

Several thousand miles to the south of the Korean peninsula, on the eve of the lunar new year, the North Vietnamese initiated what became known as the Tet Offensive in Vietnam, launching major coordinated attacks for the first time on South Vietnam's supposedly well-secured urban centers. As the Year of the Monkey began, these attacks belied the assurances of the White House of President Lyndon Johnson that victory was imminent for the American and South Vietnamese forces.

We read in amazement that the American Embassy in Saigon had been seized and held by the Vietcong (a political and military organization that fought the South Vietnamese and American forces) for six hours on the same morning. Although we did not realize it at the time, these events finally would mark a turning point in American public opinion regarding the war, but to my friends and me, the new Year of the Monkey held little promise of any change in the drumbeat of tragic news from Asia.

In February, we saw on the front pages of the *Capital Times* of Madison the sickening, Pulitzer Prize-winning photograph of a South Vietnamese official summarily shooting a Vietcong prisoner in the head with his revolver. The Valentine's Day week saw the highest American weekly casualty toll of the Vietnam War: *543 killed and 2547 wounded.* Shortly afterward, an American Army major informed the world that it had been necessary to destroy an entire Vietnamese village in order to save it. An Orwellian world had become manifest sixteen years earlier than George Orwell predicted.

As New York Senator Robert F. Kennedy (former attorney general and brother of President John F. Kennedy) decided to join the presidential race in mid-March, rumors from Vietnam—substantiated years later—hinted of unarmed Vietnamese villagers being massacred by American soldiers. In My Lai—a farming village—more than half of the village's five hundred non-combatant inhabitants were reportedly killed by US Army Lieutenant Calley and the men of Company C. Accounts of such atrocities became regular reading fare in the *Capital Times*. My friends and I viewed the American government's initial denials of such events with the same skepticism and outright disbelief as the previous three years' weekly optimistic reports of the progress of the war.

Amid our despair, there were Americans we considered heroes. Robert Kennedy promised to end the war, if elected president. Another brave man, African-American Baptist minister and civil rights leader, Martin Luther King Jr., was eloquently decrying the immoral war while he battled for black equality. Dr. King led a march in Memphis in the name of peace and racial equality on March 28. Like so many such events, it turned violent, as police intervened. After King himself had been led from the scene, one sixteen-year-old black boy was killed, sixty people were injured, and more than one hundred fifty people were arrested.

That week, on the way to classes one rainy morning, we walked past hundreds of small crosses in cemetery rows on the sloping lawn of Bascom Hall. The March 29, 1968 issue of *Time* noted the four hundred thirty-five crosses and the cortege of mock mourners who shuffled past, chanting, "Pray for the dead and the dead will pray for you; pray for the dead." We saw the sign posted near the crosses. "BASCOM MEMORIAL CEMETERY, CLASS OF 1968."

For senior students and graduate students, the sign and funeral procession were shocking reminders that death in Vietnam was a possibility, if a student deferment ended. To my surprise, the crosses and the sign were still on the lawn in the evening, untouched by university officials, who seemed to sympathize with the protesting students and to approve of the dignified and nonviolent antiwar demonstration.

Several days later, seven friends and I gathered at the apartment of another graduate student on the evening of March 31 to listen to a speech by President Lyndon Johnson. In his "Address to the Nation Announcing Steps to Limit the War in Vietnam and Reporting His Decision Not to Seek Reelection," President Johnson announced the first in a series of limitations on bombing by American forces, promising to halt these activities above the twentieth parallel. I rejoiced in the president's pledge as the first official indication of American intent to wind down the war and to negotiate an honorable end, as newscaster Walter Cronkite had advocated in his historic report in February.

Then came the president's words that brought my friends and me to our feet, dancing and shouting. Johnson announced that he would not seek reelection in November. The Vietnam War had claimed its most prominent American political casualty, and we were ecstatic. We hugged each other exultantly. (In later years I have come to appreciate tremendously the many great accomplishments of President Johnson, but in 1968 the Vietnam War was our foremost measure of the man.)

Our joy was short-lived. Four days later, on April 4, Martin Luther King Jr. was killed in Memphis, where he had been planning his Poor People's March on Washington to take place late in the month. Robert Kennedy, hearing of the murder just before he was to give a speech in Indianapolis, delivered a powerful, extemporaneous eulogy in which he pled with the audience "to tame the savageness of man and make gentle the life of this world."

The King assassination sparked rioting in Baltimore, Boston, Chicago, Detroit, Kansas City, Newark, Washington DC, and many other cities. Across the country, forty-six deaths resulted from the riots. Our despair increased daily.

My circle of friends at graduate school was a valuable support group during this dark period. Four couples had come together by chance. We picnicked, sailed, drank, studied, and smoked marijuana together (although I was an infrequent smoker, because the pungent smoke hurt my eyes, if I was wearing contact lenses, which was almost all the time). Two of the circle I had known before Wisconsin. Hans Krichels had been one class ahead of me at Dartmouth College and my student advisor when I was a freshman.

Besides Hans, our group of close friends consisted of his girlfriend, Debbie; my roommate, Bob Jacobs (who was a longtime friend from elementary school and high-school days in Buffalo); Bob's girlfriend, Michelle; Ingvi Jonsson (a young Icelandic student studying journalism at Wisconsin, who lived across the hall from Bob and me); Ingvi's wife, Hrefna (who was a flight attendant for Icelandic Airlines); my girlfriend, Dariel Lynn Rousar (who was an undergraduate student in Scandinavian Studies at Wisconsin); and me. Hans, Bob, Michelle, and I were in the English department. All of us were strongly against the war and in support of civil rights. It is a gross understatement to say that we were all also extremely depressed and cynical during this difficult period.

Dariel and I clung to each other and to our friends during those bitter months. Fortunately, Madison and the campus of the University of Wisconsin are beautiful in any season, nestled among four frozen lakes in winter and caressed by warmer winds off the lakes in spring, summer, and autumn. Despite the grim reminders of reality—in the form of the national guardsmen standing guard on the campus and the occasional student protest with its incense of tear gas—we endured, celebrating nature, partying with our friends, writing poetry, and loving each other. Tough times on the world and national scenes somehow generated inner spiritual warmth that in the Year of the Monkey kept us going.

I recall one trip across the frozen wasteland of Lake Mendota in January, with the wind whistling across the ice and our faces white with cold. When the darkness fell on us late in the afternoon, as we skated back across the ice, the lights of the student union on the shore glowed warmly as our beacons.

In the gray light of another Wisconsin winter afternoon, we walked through the university arboretum in February, after a massive snowstorm, rejoicing in the grandeur of the snow-covered trees and bushes, and laughing at the plumes of snow that dropped on our heads from overhanging boughs. The arboretum was a favorite place—unearthly quiet, exquisite in its barren, leafless silhouettes on all sides, and intriguing in its snow-cast trails of the deer, foxes, and other animals there. Dariel and I shared a love of the outdoors in all seasons.

I first saw Dariel at a holiday party of the student Scandinavian Club—a New Year's Eve party, as 1967 ended. My Icelandic neighbor across the hall in the apartment house, where Bob Jacobs and I shared a two bedroom, comfortable apartment, had become a good friend, often sleeping on our couch, when his wife kicked him out of their apartment after arguments. Ingvi knew of my love for Sweden and Swedish culture, engendered by my summer work in Uppsala, Sweden, and Lapland during the summers of 1964, 1965, and 1967, so he persuaded me to join the Scandinavian Club on campus. There were lots of Swedes, Danes, and Norwegians in the club, of course, as well as a few students from Iceland and Finland, and I became friends with several of them.

Ingvi, Hrefna, and I went to the club's party, which featured a hilarious skit performed by about a dozen student club members. I don't remember much about the skit, except that it was a bit ribald, reminded me of Chaucerian stories, and starred a lovely, saucy, dark-haired girl as the flirtatious French maid in a skimpy costume. I was very interested. In fact, I was struck by the "thunderbolt," as my Sicilian neighbors on Buffalo's west side would have put it. The student's throaty laugh and earthiness, and captivating brown eyes, particularly attracted me. As I was trying to figure how to get introduced to the French maid after the skit was over, the cast members retired after the club's party to her house, where she lived with her mother, to continue the party. I tagged along as a mixture of rain and snow began to fall.

I am usually not a very devious person. That morning, however, as the party wound down at the French maid's house, I decided to slip my umbrella into a corner of the living room at Dariel's home and to conveniently leave it there when I left the party. Several days later, when I returned to retrieve it, Dariel and I sat down and talked over hot cocoa. I discovered that she had studied in Copenhagen, was the youngest of three children (like me), was athletic, had summered during her childhood at a cabin on a lake, and had been a member of the Peace Corps Club in her school days in Madison. We were similar in many ways. That was the beginning of a wonderful relationship, which, like all of the best things in life, seeded incredible joy and some pain at its end.

As Madison and the university blossomed in April with thousands of daffodils and tulips, Dariel moved in with me. She was working as a dental assistant (her father had been a dentist before his death and had trained her well) and was in her junior year at Wisconsin. Besides being warm, sensitive, and beautiful, I soon discovered Dariel was very smart, cared deeply for her widowed mother, Grace, loved adventure in life and the outdoors, and appreciated weird, pop culture, such as that spring's surprise hit, "Tiptoe Through the Tulips" by Tiny Tim.

My friends and I were working as research assistants at the university, helping the famous linguist, Frederic Cassidy, compile the *Dictionary of American Regional English* (*DARE*). We worked as so-called "pre-editors," compiling information furnished by field workers across the country about American word usage—from conversations with older people, publications, and surveys. Some of the words were hilarious! For example, Americans have many names for the kind of sandwich that includes meats, cheeses, lettuce, tomatoes, and other condiments served in a long bun. What *DARE* was trying to accomplish was to inform (and often illustrate through the use of maps based on fieldwork) *where* the words "hero," "hoagie," "grinder," "sub," "torpedo," and "Cuban" are the local terms for this sandwich. When some word or phrase usages were quite rare, a map depicting the location of their use revealed how a particular word or phrase had migrated across the country, as members of a village or family had dispersed. Needless to say, many of the terms we dealt with were not as innocuous as kinds of food. We were in stitches much of the time, particularly with the usage of sexual terms.

Professor Cassidy had a fine sense of humor and joined us in laughter while trying to maintain a semblance of order and decorum in the pre-editors' room. A distinguished looking older man, he delighted in listening to a person speak for a few minutes, and then, like Henry Higgins in *My Fair Lady*, telling the person, based on word pronunciation and usage, where they had been born, grown up, and gone to school. He was a fantastic boss. I am still thankful for the laughter and positive, intellectual nourishment my editing work and Fred Cassidy provided me that difficult year.

In April, Dariel and I visited my family's Buffalo home, Niagara Falls, Dartmouth College, and New Hampshire's White Mountains in the incredible beauty of a northern spring, borrowing my parents' old Dodge. We camped at the Dartmouth Outing Club cabin on the summit of Mt. Moosilauke in New Hampshire, still surrounded by snow, danced through the Canadian gardens at Niagara Falls, and walked the beaches and woods of Holloway Bay on Lake Erie in Canada. We saw the only flock of rose-breasted grosbeaks that I have ever seen, near my family's cabin on the northern shore of the lake. The world and my heart were warming. I told my parents that I might marry this amazing woman.

June in the university arboretum was a perfume heaven in the lilac garden. Dariel and I spent rapturous afternoons in the lilacs, picnicking among the fragrant blossoms of every color imaginable. With her in my arms in the sunshine and my senses overwhelmed by the warmth, smells, and beauty of her and the Earth all around us, those moments for me hid for a time the world that otherwise buffeted us emotionally and intellectually. On June 5, we returned to the apartment to learn that Bobby Kennedy had been shot in a hotel earlier that morning. He died the next day.

Our anguish over Kennedy's death was a prelude to another death. On July 28, a Dartmouth classmate, Bill Smoyer, was killed with eighteen other members of Kilo Company, Third Battalion, Seventh Marines, in an ambush while crossing a rice paddy at An Hoa, Vietnam. Bill had just arrived in Vietnam two days earlier. When I heard of his death, I realized that the war had now taken a life I knew. The horrible abstraction had resonated personally. I thought of Bill's family and what they must be going through. I had never seen a rice paddy.

The seemingly constant barrage of sad news was counterpoised with the daily joy of a beloved companion. What I liked best about Dariel was that she was always full of surprises. I remember a touch football game at Picnic Point on Lake Mendota. At some point in the game Dariel asked if she could be quarterback. The men in the huddle smiled to themselves but agreed. On the next play Dariel took the snap, started around the right end, and then stopped suddenly to rifle a twenty-five yard pass to me. Ingvi Jonsson almost fainted on the spot. Dariel turned out to be a very strong and accurate passer, as well as a formidable wide receiver, on our pickup team.

On another occasion we were telling each other secrets about ourselves that we usually didn't reveal to others. I told her about my geographic tongue and my embarrassment at having had it coated with a purple medicine, called Gentian Violet, when I was very young. (When my childhood pediatrician discovered that I had a condition called geographic tongue or benign migratory glossitis and treated it by painting my tongue with an antifungal agent, my tongue was bright purple. I refused to let my mother paint my tongue each week, as prescribed, unless my sister also had her tongue painted. So both of us had purple tongues for several months. My sister was enormously grateful for this opportunity to have a purple tongue. I later learned that the condition occurs in up to 3% of the general population. Geographic tongues are ridged and furrowed and often have areas of strange and wonderful coloration. I kept the secret of this disfigurement from all my friends and never told anyone until I confided in Dariel.)

She told me how hard, when she was growing up, she had prayed to

God to give her big breasts. When I commented that I guessed he had listened, she laughed her comfortable laugh and kissed me.

In the midst of the joy of my life with Dariel, there was always a small voice reminding me that my deferment from military service was temporary and pretty much at the whim of the Selective Service board in Buffalo. In six months I might be walking through rice paddies in Vietnam. My best friend in high school, Bob Ramage, was at that moment training to be a second lieutenant in the Marine Corps, destined for Vietnam, just as Bill Smoyer had been. Other classmates and friends had moved to Canada to avoid being drafted. In Buffalo, that option meant merely moving two miles west, across the Niagara River, for my hometown friends. I had spent so much of my childhood in Canada that this option was not unattractive. Still, I felt that I was an American and had an obligation to my country, although I felt that this obligation did not include killing Asians, who posed no threat to my country.

About this time, I was told by my faculty advisor that I had completed the coursework necessary for my master's degree in English Literature, and that, to my great surprise, my 1966 term paper of about eighty pages, written in French at Dartmouth, on Honoré de Balzac's *La Comédie Humaine*—a product of my studies at the University of Montpellier in France—would be an acceptable substitute for a master's thesis. This was wonderful news, because I was now relieved of the considerable burden of writing the usual thesis. At the same time I was suddenly confronted with the fact that my student deferment would soon end, probably by summer's end, unless I continued for a PhD in English. After almost nineteen straight years of studying, at the age of twenty-three I was in no mood to continue my formal education.

While I was tormented with trying to decide how my life should play out, or perhaps terminate, Dariel and I escaped together on sailboats on Lake Mendota and on my small motorcycle on Wisconsin's back roads. The jewels of the Madison area are the four lakes—Kegonsa, Waubesa, Monona, and Mendota—that hug the city's lawns, parks, and residential neighborhoods. Lake Mendota is the crown jewel. In a small boat with Dariel on Mendota, beneath a taut sail and billowing clouds, I could forget the world and fill my thoughts with the oval face on my lap as we silently glided past the red tile-roofed dormitories on campus, Picnic Point, and Governor's Island. On other days we took quiet routes out of the city to the nearby farms and woods of southern Wisconsin, with the wind in our hair and the joy of speed and danger that only riding a motorcycle can impart. Dariel's arms around my waist and the warmth of her behind me on the bike were reassuring and blissful.

My love for Dariel and fondness for the university and Madison had persuaded me to stay in Madison one more year, while she finished her studies, at least until I was forced to make another decision by my draft board, when quite unexpectedly a letter arrived from Washington DC. It was a summons that forever changed my life.

Dated July 27, 1968 (on Dariel's twenty-second birthday), and received by me via Buffalo on August 10, 1968, the letter stated:

Dear Mr. Hobbie:

Congratulations! I am happy to inform you that you have been selected to train for Peace Corps service in Korea, as a teacher of English in a university or teacher training college.

Out of a large number of applicants for the Peace Corps, only a few are invited to enter training. You are among this group because there is a need for individuals with your background and because your personal qualifications for overseas life seem to be of the highest caliber. We believe that Peace Corps Volunteers *can* make a difference—a difference that may create a condition for peace.

The work will be difficult, for this kind of job is never an easy one. It will test some of your strongest convictions and utilize abilities, which might otherwise lie dormant. Serving as a Peace Corps Volunteer is a rare opportunity to derive great personal satisfaction from using your skills where they are most needed.

Specific details on your assignment are being forwarded to you. I sincerely hope that you will accept this invitation and that your service in the Peace Corps will be both rewarding and successful.

Sincerely,
Jack Vaughn
[Director]

Application Number 225533

I had applied to the Peace Corps in the spring of 1967, as I was finishing my senior year at Dartmouth. A young recruiter had handed me an application one morning at the Hopkins Center, near Dartmouth's student mailboxes. She and I spoke for a few minutes, and I sat down and completed the application—a totally impulsive action. In my mind at that moment were the repeated admonitions of Dartmouth's then president, John Sloan Dickey, that we are citizens of the world and must behave as such, because, as he often stated in conversations, "There is nothing wrong with the world that better human beings cannot fix."

Six months later I was invited to train for a program going to the West African, French-speaking country of the Ivory Coast, presumably because I spoke French pretty well in those days. I had declined the invitation then because I felt, rather selfishly, that I should get a master's degree before I left academia, and I was looking forward to an academic experience at a large university in an urban setting—a contrast to my four great years at a small college in the countryside.

Also, I had spent the summer term of 1966 on campus, studying German and working three jobs. One of those jobs had been as a part-time French language assistant in the Dartmouth language laboratory for a small group of Peace Corps trainees, who were preparing to go to West Africa. I had learned something about the Ivory Coast and several other French-speaking West African countries then. As a result, I was more interested in serving in a country where I could learn a new language and about a totally new culture. After I declined the invitation to the Ivory Coast program, I had completely forgotten about Peace Corps in the past half year.

The letter from the Peace Corps director turned my world upside down. My friends and I rushed to a world map to find the Republic of South Korea. It took a while. We finally located the Korean peninsula, surrounded by Russia, China, and Japan. Much of the information available to us about Korea focused on its harsh climate, its war-torn physical and economic conditions, its denuded mountains, its extremely difficult language, and the nationalism of its people, who were historically xenophobic (not surprising, in view of its neighbors, I thought), according to the encyclopedia. Great! Other information emphasized that South Korea was legally and, in a very real sense, still at war with North Korea, and that the demilitarized zone between the two countries was a mere thirty miles from South Korea's capital city, Seoul. I thought that the encyclopedia must be mistaken. *Thirty* miles? Then I remembered the USS *Pueblo* and its captive crew and the North Korean attack on the presidential mansion in Seoul earlier in the year.

I turned this information over and over in my mind. On the one hand, it seemed almost crazy to accept an invitation to spend two years of my life in a harsh climate, among treeless mountains and xenophobic people, struggling with a tough language, and with the North Korean army less than an hour away. Perhaps I would get another Peace Corps invitation to a more hospitable country.

On the other hand, in South Korea I could possibly make "a difference that may create a condition for peace," as Jack Vaughan had written, or help to "make gentle the life of this world," as Bobby Kennedy had urged. My prior experiences had taught me at least one thing: facing difficult circumstances often makes people stronger and happier in the end. Korea seemed to have some potential in this light. It also had rice paddies.

The prospect of being separated from Dariel dismayed me. I lay awake at night, worrying that I would lose her if we were separated. She said that she would join the Peace Corps too, but we were informed that she had to finish her undergraduate degree before Peace Corps would even consider her. Dariel felt that I had few alternatives, that it sounded like a great adventure, and that our future together was unpredictable at this point, anyway.

I also discussed the invitation with my parents, sister, and brother, and with my Aunt Kate Hobbie, who was always a reliable voice of reason. All of my friends and family encouraged me to accept the invitation. Aunt Kate, in particular, felt that I would love the experience in Korea. One dissenter, Art Markwardt, our long-time mailman in Buffalo, voiced his opinion that the Peace Corps was a great endeavor but that Korea was not a place he would wish to go back to (he had had a terrible experience there during service in the Korean War).

The information from Peace Corps that soon arrived about the program to which I had been invited painted a positive picture. The three page description stated as follows:

PEACE CORPS KOREA
*UNIVERSITY ENGLISH TEACHING AND
TEACHER TRAINING 1968*

If you would like to devote the next two years to one of the most challenging opportunities for service, then the Peace Corps has a job for you in the Republic of Korea.

You are invited to teach English at a teacher's college or a university in the Republic of Korea. Your students will be English majors and prospective English teachers.

In November 1967, the Korean Ministry of Education requested that Peace Corps expand its TESOL (*T*eaching *E*nglish to *S*peakers of *O*ther *L*anguages) program in Korea. As a result of this, a Peace Corps survey team was sent to Korea in January 1968. The purpose of the team was to evaluate and clarify the request and to suggest approaches for implementing it through programs suited to both Korea's educational needs and volunteer capabilities. Conclusions drawn from this evaluation provide the basis for the program to which you are being invited to train.

Most Koreans look upon English as a world language, and thus, as an essential means toward helping their country to progress and prosper. It is a medium of international communication, which can be used to develop markets abroad and as a tool for research and development. Moreover, Koreans look to English as a way of projecting the many cultural achievements of their long four thousand-year history into the world scene.

In general, you will be teaching approximately fifteen classroom hours per week. This will include working as a native language informant, as well as working with your students on reading and composition. In addition to classroom teaching, you may also expect such varied activities as acting as a consultant to Korean English teachers, working on improving language laboratory materials and usage, handling student extracurricular activities (e.g., English conversation clubs, speech contests, drama clubs), working with faculty English conversation clubs, and working on developing materials for use by prospective English teachers.

The Korean school year has two long vacation periods—winter (approximately late December to late February) and summer (approximately mid July to late August). During this time, you may expect to participate in workshops for the retraining of English teachers who are already teaching in the Korean school system. You may also find yourself joining some of your students from the university on field trips and work camps.

As a Volunteer, you will be an English teacher, but more importantly, you will be a member of the community in which you live, and your actions and relationships should reflect this. To be an effective teacher, you must become involved in Korean society; to understand and communicate with your students, you must have contact with Korean people and culture outside of the classroom professional relationship. The totality of the Peace Corps Volunteer experience rests on this premise of interaction and involvement on the part of the Volunteer and the host country people with whom he lives and works.

Training for this program will be at the University of Hawaii and will begin on or about October 7, 1968, extending for sixteen weeks. The training program will provide an intensive preparation in the theory and methods of TESOL as appropriate to Korea, an intensive study of Korean language, history, and culture, and an introduction to community analysis.

This program will also provide an opportunity to earn potential credit towards an MA in TESOL while training as a Peace Corps Volunteer for Korea. The technical component of training will consist of some of the courses offered in the regular TESL graduate program of the University of Hawaii. You will study basic TESL methodology before going overseas. It is hoped that your two-year service as a teacher in Korea will build upon the work in the training program so that, for those who are admitted as graduate students in the English Language Institute of the University of Hawaii, the remainder of coursework and degree requirements may be completed in a shorter time after finishing your Peace Corps tour and returning to the university as a full-time student. Not all of you will be interested in this, but for those who are, further details will be available after you arrive at training.

Your tour of service, including training, will be twenty-seven months, with a termination date in December 1970.

When you arrive in Korea, you will find approximately 234 Volunteers already working there. Of these, 137 will be working TESOL at junior and senior high schools. The other 97 Volunteers work as health auxiliaries in rural health sub-centers in five of Korea's nine provinces. Peace Corps Volunteers have been in Korea since September 1966. You will be a member of the eighth group of Volunteers assigned there.

Peace Corps needs Volunteers with sensitivity, flexibility, competency and a desire and ability to work with people. We think you have these qualities—we hope you will accept the challenge of this important new program.

I noticed in particular the reference to the training in Hawaii for almost four months. This was a positive development. In the "worst-case" scenario I could always participate in the training program, check out Hawaii, and then withdraw if necessary, depending on the circumstances and my feelings at the end of training in January 1969. Hawaii did not sound like a bad place to spend four months. The program itself also seemed worthwhile. With many misgivings, including a feeling of overwhelming guilt that I was deserting a kind and wonderful woman, I accepted the invitation.

Bob Jacobs, Ingvi Jonsson, and Hans Krichels arranged a fine farewell party. They had all been my good friends at Wisconsin. Bob Jacobs had also been a tolerant and wise roommate. Bob and Hans were to continue to work at *DARE* with Professor Cassidy. Ingvi was to get a master's degree in journalism.

After the party, Dariel and I spent our last weeks together, preparing to lose each other—at least that was how I felt—although we did not talk much about it. We spent a wonderful week in August in the north woods of Wisconsin at her family's summer cabin on South Turtle Lake in Winchester. The beauty and calmness of the lake were bewitching. I will never forget that week.

In mid September, Dariel moved back home with her mother, and I packed up to leave Wisconsin. I left part of my heart with her and thought about her every day for the next five years, until another dark-haired woman—from Germany with a Korean smile—came into my life. The only time we ever met again, in Buffalo briefly more than ten years later, Dariel was married, had two handsome boys, and, coincidentally, was living at 406 Linwood Avenue, not far from my parents' house on Buffalo's west side. I will always be grateful to her for making the coldest of times sometimes the warmest of times, and making a season of war, at least at moments, a season of serene peace during my one year in Madison. Although the beauty of the Wisconsin campus and the charm of the city of Madison captivated me that year, I have never returned there.

Mom, Dad, and I celebrated their thirty-fifth wedding anniversary several weeks early together in Buffalo, just before I left for Hawaii. We had a simple dinner together at the Jafco Marina restaurant on the Niagara River. Their anniversary was on October 14. Dad was sixty-four years old. My mother was fifty-nine. I told them that I hoped we could celebrate their thirty-sixth anniversary together next year in Korea. (Coincidentally, as I begin this memoir in 2010, I am sixty-four years old, and my beloved Korean wife and I celebrated our thirty-fifth wedding anniversary last year.)

The Girl I Left behind with Part of my Heart, Dariel Lynn Rousar,
Madison, Wisconsin, June 1968

Arrival of Peace Corps Korea Group VIII Trainees in Hilo, Hawaii,
October 1969

Rainbow Falls, Hilo, Hawaii, October 1968

Assistant Language Director Ahn Hee-ja Playing the *Kayageum* on
Korea Night, Hilo, Hawaii, October 1968

# Chapter Two—Peace Corps
# Training in Hilo, Hawaii

On October 7, 1968, Mt. Kilauea erupted on the island of Hawaii in the area known as the east rift-zone of Kilauea. More than 6.6 million cubic meters of lava spewed from the mountain—one of the world's most active volcanoes—during the fifteen days of the eruption. The plane, carrying more than one hundred twenty-five young Americans from Los Angeles to Hilo, Hawaii, that day was approaching the "Big Island" from the east when the mountain exploded into a fiery furnace before our eyes. Welcome to Peace Corps training! How the training staff arranged for that pyrotechnic display upon our arrival is a mystery to this day.

I left Buffalo on Sunday, October 6, spent a fine day in Los Angeles with my sister-in-law's family, and boarded the flight to Hilo on Monday morning. It was a deluxe flight in honor of Aloha Week in Hawaii. We sipped wine and champagne with our dinner. During the flight, I met and talked with dozens of my co-trainees, finding three other Dartmouth students from the class of 1968 on the flight, including one (Jon Moody) who was a good friend from Glee Club. It seemed like a fine group.

Ten minutes after we first spotted the Hawaiian Islands out of the plane's windows, Mt. Kilauea began to belch steam and flames. We landed at Hilo's tiny airport, our eyes still round with wonder at the volcano's display of fire, and were greeted by local Hawaiian girls and female training staff members, with fragrant leis, which they placed around our necks. (This elaborate, ritualistic greeting was forever thereafter, unfortunately, described in the stories of our group by the male trainees as "getting leied" (translation of this innuendo: "having sex") at the airport on the first day of training. We had an uncanny, cross-cultural sensitivity already.)

After posing for a picture next to the Pan American plane in our floral leis, we were driven in creaky buses from the airport to the Peace Corps Training Center, about one and a half miles from Hilo's center, on Waianeuneu Avenue. The center was located in an old, wooden, former hospital complex, surrounded by coconut palms and huge banyan trees. A couple of outlying smaller buildings were to be our dormitories and classrooms.

Several of these ancient buildings were connected by narrow walkways covered by tin roofs. The covered walkways were supposed to provide shelter from the tropical rainstorms that swept through the center's grounds every day in the afternoon. However, you took your life into your hands if you ventured onto these walkways during a storm, for the roofs leaked, the wind blew sheets of water sideways onto anyone on the sheltered walkways, and lightening threatened to strike the tin roofs at any moment in these tropical storms. I stayed off those walkways during storms, for, besides not wanting to be completely soaked, I could anticipate the unfortunate headline in the Hilo newspaper: "Peace Corps trainee who escaped volcanic eruption is fried by lightning strike at training center." Happily, the daily storms seldom lasted more than about ten minutes, and, in fact, lightning storms were a rare occurrence.

In front of the main building, which was the training center administration building, was a small monument commemorating the first three Peace Corps groups that had trained at the center in 1963. On its face were carved the following words from John F. Kennedy's inaugural speech:

> AND SO, MY FELLOW AMERICANS,
> ASK NOT WHAT YOUR COUNTRY
> CAN DO FOR YOU, ASK WHAT YOU
> CAN DO FOR YOUR COUNTRY.
>
> —John Fitzgerald Kennedy
> Saba/Sarawak III, Thailand VII, Indonesia II

I wondered how many hundreds of groups, like the three Asia-bound groups mentioned on the memorial, training for countless Peace Corps countries' programs, and how many thousands of Americans had gone through the training that I was just beginning.

Behind the dormitory to which I was assigned was the Wailuku River—a small but lovely river with a magnificent waterfall known as Rainbow Falls. Water dropped more than eighty feet into a pool or lagoon formed by the rocky riverbed, assuring a constant and calming background of the sounds of cascading water. From my dormitory I could see the falls, and its roar was audible everywhere on the campus of the training center. At the back of the falls was a large cavern, which Hawaiian legends claim is the home of Hina, the mother of the demigod Maui. On most days, two narrow cascades of water combined just below the lip of the falls to form the main part of the waterfall. Just after the daily downpour the falls quadrupled in size, covering most of the edge of the cliff over which it plunged, and dropping an enormous volume of water into the lagoon.

As soon as we arrived at the center late on Monday afternoon, we met the Peace Corps training director, Phil Olsen; the training center director, Al White; our training program director, Scott Duncan; and the ten American staff members and twenty-one Korean language teachers who would be our trainers for the next almost-four months. There were also several Hawaiians, who were training center permanent support staff, such as the administrative director of the center, Mary Matayoshi, and her assistants, kitchen workers, and groundskeepers.

The American training staff—two thirds men and one third women—seemed clean-cut for the most part and a few years older than most of us. They were casually dressed, many in Hawaiian shirts and skirts, and mostly fairly conservative looking, although one girl— Jackie Tanny—had long blond hair, reaching well below her waist, and a deep tan, suggesting southern California origins. One of the American training staff—Lindsay Pollock—was actually from Hawaii, I remember.

The Koreans were all well dressed and intimidating to me, at first. The thirteen men ranged from average height to quite tall. Some were more than six feet tall and thin with muscular arms. Several were short but looked tough. They seemed military in appearance, with their crew-cut hairstyles, straight posture, white short-sleeve shirts, and dark trousers—except for one man, who wore Bermuda shorts. The eight women were short, pretty, bashful, and even more nervous than the trainees, I thought. They wore almost no makeup, covered their mouths with their hands when they laughed or smiled, and were dressed in conservative, knee-length dresses. It was hard to guess the age of any of the Koreans, but they all seemed roughly our ages, between twenty-two and twenty-six.

As a group, the American trainers impressed me as generally friendly, but they were also a little bit diffident; it seemed as though they regarded the trainees with suspicion and a slight sense of superiority. At the same time, they seemed socially awkward. They were all members of the first group of Peace Corps Volunteers to Korea in 1966, and most had come to Hawaii from Korea directly. I think, in retrospect, that some were still suffering from "reverse culture shock," as they tried to adjust to being back in an American life and culture that was totally different from what they had become accustomed to over the past two years, living primarily with Koreans. There was one couple: Rick and Jan Laylin. Two other women—Marilyn McMeekin and Jackie Tanny—and six men—Dave Bachner, Griff Dix, John Keller, Ed Klein, Lindsay Pollock, and Terry Reeve—completed the American staff of returned volunteers. Over time, I got to know the single men pretty well during countless hours of discussion about their experiences in Korea. (Several of the American staff have remained my good friends for more than four decades.)

When I first took a quick glance at the Korean staff, I was a bit shocked. They all looked similar in facial features as well as attire. The higher cheekbones, smaller noses, heavy lidded eyes, and somewhat flatter faces were quite strange-looking to me, although also attractive. I thought to myself that I would never learn to distinguish one from another or get used to their different appearance. (I had met perhaps half a dozen Asians in my life before this time, and I had had a Chinese-American fraternity brother at Dartmouth, with whom I had been fairly close. But I could not recall having seen more than a couple of Asians *together* before now.) I reflected initially that they were probably equally shocked by our appearances and numbers. There were about one hundred twenty-five trainees, constituting the combined seventh and eighth group of volunteers headed for Korea.

Many of the Hawaiians who comprised the center's permanent staff seemed to be Asian Americans of Japanese background. They were very friendly, dressed in colorful clothes, and had quite long hair, compared to the short hair of most of the American training staff. From the beginning, they all seemed anxious to be helpful and to share Hawaiian culture with us.

The trainees in the combined groups—about 30 percent of whom were women—were all white, except for one Japanese American named John Kumabe. All were college graduates and seemed to be primarily middleclass. They were generally attractive, well spoken, pleasant, and looked determined. The single women were serious, intellectual looking, and a bit uptight. The single men appeared generally clean-shaven, with relatively short hair and conservative clothes. (We had been told to get rid of facial hair and to get haircuts before training began.) Several of us had sideburns. The married couples seemed more friendly, more at ease, and more outgoing than the rest of us. Several couples were obviously newlyweds.

I was struck by our geographical diversity. We seemed to have come from all over the United States, and from rural and urban areas alike. I surmised that eventually some of our future Korean students, when they spoke English, would have unmistakable Texas and Carolina drawls, and others would surely have New England twangs.

The names of the members of our two groups—the K-VII group and the K-VIII group, as we were called forever thereafter—who started training reflected the different nationalities that you would expect in any American college's graduating class. The K-VIIs were Peter Michael Adams; Michael Mohr Carlson; Donald Bruce Cochran; Jonathan Condit; Brian Evans Copp; Margot Joyce Diltz; Donald (Don) Owen Diltz; Virginia Kathryn (Ginger) Douglas; Clyde Michael Douglas; Lawrence K. (Rusty) Driscoll; David Allen Eger; Margaret (Peggy) Condon Eger; Fred James Evans; John A. B. Fagei Jr.; Mary Elizabeth Frantz; James Nickerson Gahn; Thomas George Gulick; Andrew Steven Hess; George Starr Humphrey; John Edward Johnson; Julie Ann Joyce; Richard Stanton Kennedy; Edward W. Kloth; Elizabeth Mariue Koscielny; Kathleen Mary Kowalczyk; Robert Thomas

Kowalczyk; Michael William Kramer; Frederick Andrew Krehely; John Kumabe; Howard Marsden Lamont; Maria A. Lanteri; Gloria Marli Levin; Norman David Levin; Dwight Les Linsley; Paul Michael Luchessa; Donald Robert Meyer; Virginia Louise Meyer; Peter Paul Mikuliak; Jonathan Corwin Moody; Christine Louise Murphy; Marion Wolsey Murphy; Kenneth Thomas Nickele; Robert Louis Oakley; Mary Kathryn Ostenson; Thomas James Quinn; James Larry Reid; Michael E. Robinson; Sally Sue Schooler; Janis Lee Shannon; Steven Alan Singer; Louis John Spaventa; John Kenneth Steffen; Susan Marie Steffen; Howard Mark Tarnower; Eileen Lois Tarnower; Donald Mclean Thompson; Thomas Shahan Ulen; James Douglas Vick; Margaret Brock (Rachel) Wenz; Peter Samuel Wenz; and Scott Warren Williams. (Among the K-VIIs were the three other Dartmouth graduates, as I have mentioned: Kloth, Moody, and Ulen.)

In my group (K-VIII), the trainees were Ellen Kay Bacon; Thomas Jason Bacon; Frederick Armour Beardsley III; Richard Lewis Burke; Morrison Griffin Cain; William Howard Cantrell; Diane Rogers Casselberry; Samuel Howard Chernoff; Sharon Elizabeth Desrosiers; Gennaro (Jerry) Anthony Diiorio; Patricia (Pat) Mary Donegan; Richard Raymond Dow; Carter J. Eckert; James Joseph Eros; Mary Clare Eros; Gary Randall Esarey; Karen Jean Farr; Gary John Fedota; Russell Joseph Feldmeier; Ruth Warren Flaherty; Robert Paul Gardella Jr.; Aaron Samuel Gurwitz; George Edward Hall; John Earl Hiles; Charles Arthur Hobbie; Judith Collings Hudson; Stanley George Hudson; Jan Sullivan Justice; John Keith Justice Jr.; Bryna Meryl Kaitz; Merrill Arnold Kaitz; Kenneth Karmiole; Steven Lance Keller; Raymond I. Korona; Gordon George Korstange; Charles Donald Kuhn; Clyde Ray List; Richard Peter Magurno; Philip A. Melzer; Victoria Elise Melzer; Gary Edward Mintier; Mary Ann Mintier; William Thomas Moore; Margaret Mary Peters; Leo Harold Phillips Jr.; John Joseph Podgurski; Richard Hamilton Rettig; Lenore Jaye Rich; Hugh Barnes Rogers Jr.; Ruth Blackwell Rogers; Barry Edward Rosenstock; William Edward Ryan; Richard Mosby St. Clair; Eugene Raven Severens; Kathleen Marie Severens; Stephen Arthur Shakman; Susan Curtis Shakman; Richard Skala; Bernard Joseph Smith; Roger Kent Snodgrass; Nadine A. Strahle; Cathy Bjorklund Tollefsen; Thomas Arthur Tollefsen; and

Gerald Gross Workinger Jr. I recognized only one member of my group: Carter Eckert, whom I had met at Wisconsin.

After dinner in the cafeteria in the main building, the evening sky above our training center was incredibly beautiful from the reflection of the distant lava fountains—reds, yellows, and oranges, with purple plumes. There were so many new sights, sounds, and smells stimulating my senses upon arrival, I was in a state of overwhelmed shock (to say nothing of so-called jet lag). But I still was able to appreciate, from the moment of arrival, the overwhelming loveliness of Hawaii.

The center was situated on the side of Mt. Mauna Loa—one of the five volcanoes forming the island of Hawaii—amid lush, tropical vegetation on all sides. Several large red and yellow hibiscus bushes were scattered around the center's campus, shaded by dozens of coconut palms and several enormous banyan trees. Along the riverbanks were many kinds of exotic, tropical plants, including several varieties of gorgeous orchids. From the top floor of the three-story main building you could see the ocean in the distance on one side and Rainbow Falls on the other side. The center's location was a naturally lovely site, although it had a tired, poorly kept-up feel about its buildings. The overpoweringly strong smell of ripe vegetation and moist soil permeated everything. I sensed that a lot of people had died at this old former hospital, probably of tropical diseases. Hopefully not too many had been Peace Corps trainees.

Our sleeping accommodations were in the outlying dormitories with two trainees to each quite small room. My roommate was a very smart and personable guy from Long Island—Robert Oakley, who had graduated from Cornell. Men and women were on the same floors and shared the same bathrooms, which in those days was quite an unusual arrangement. The dozen or so young married couples in training were housed in the same dormitories as the single men and women, and the walls were pretty thin! My roommate and I flipped a coin to determine who would get the top bunk in our room; I won. You could see the falls from the top bunk, and it was marginally quieter and more private.

There was a general meeting on the first evening, where we learned that we were the first group of volunteers in Korea who were to be trained to be English, or TESOL (Teaching English to Speakers of Other Languages) instructors, at universities and colleges. Most of the American training staff had taught English as members of the first group in Korea, as I have mentioned, and had been trained to be secondary level (middle school and high school) teachers. Some of them had ended up eventually teaching at colleges or universities during their final year, when their initial placements had not worked out. We learned to refer to the first group of volunteers in Korea as K-Is, or K-1s. The number designating the order of each subsequent group's arrival in Korea identified that group. While we were in training, Peace Corps/ Korea groups II through VI were in Korea as current Peace Corps Volunteers.

Approximately half of the trainees at the center in Hilo with me were to be K-VIIs, or K-7s. The other half were to be K-VIIIs, or K-8s. As I have mentioned, I was a K-VIII. The groups were to follow identical training curricula. The differences between the two groups were that the K-VIIs had Bachelor's degrees in varying subjects, and the K-VIIIs had either Bachelor's degrees in English or a further graduate degree (several had law degrees). The K-VIIs were to teach at teacher colleges and the K-VIIIs were to teach at universities, we were told. We were all to focus on teaching the *methodology* of teaching English, so as to teach future Korean teachers how best to teach English.

In the first meeting we learned some common Peace Corps acronyms and terms. Returned Peace Corps Volunteers, such as our American training staff, were called RPCVs. Current Peace Corps Volunteers were PCVs. Peace Corps trainees were PCTs. The Korean training staff members were "Host Country Nationals," or HCNs. PCTs who failed to satisfy expectations and were sent home were delicately referred to as "deselectees," or sometimes "terminees." I felt that "terminee" seemed a bit ominous, suggesting that the person had been thrown over Rainbow Falls, or tied up and left to fry in a lightning strike on the tin-roofed walkways in a storm. Until this moment, I hadn't contemplated the possibility of termination. I had naively thought that it was my decision as to whether or not I stayed. This information cast a new light on the program.

We were told that the training would focus on developing Korean language skills, teaching skills, interpersonal skills, and cross-cultural skills, and that we would be periodically tested in each area, including psychiatric evaluations. I went to sleep in my bunk that first night with acronyms whirling around in my head and dreamed of the outrageously demanding language tests, cross-cultural hurdles, psychiatric exams, and teaching evaluations that I expected to confront. Most of us were slightly paranoid by morning.

I have always been an early riser. My East Coast, inner time clock had not yet reset, so I was up and walking around the center's grounds by three o'clock in the morning, which was nine o'clock EST. There was a lot of mist on the river, shrouding the falls in the moonlight. In the stillness and soft light it was easy to believe that the cavern behind the falls was the home of Hina, who was known as the Hawaiian Moon Goddess, according to the Hawaiian staff at the center. I wished Dariel were with me to share the beauty of that pre-dawn moment.

As the sun's rays finally began to lift the mist, rainbows played and danced over the lagoon and around the falls. It was a spectacular first morning in Hawaii! I have always loved rainbows and felt that their Biblical association with new beginnings, hope, and future promise was justified. I took the glorious sight next to our center that morning as an auspicious sign that this experience, called Peace Corps service, would be a good one.

The rainbow's promise did not extend to the breakfast food at the center, however. Breakfast, which was served promptly at six o'clock, consisted primarily of a lot of overripe fruit, such as papaya, pineapple, mangos, oranges, grapefruit, and bananas—not much to my liking. I got used to it quickly, though, and even began to like it, never anticipating that the abundant fruit during the training in Hawaii would later become an obsessive desire in Korea.

After breakfast, we began language instruction and started a routine that was fairly consistent for the next two months. That first day, and on most days thereafter, we generally followed an intense schedule of instruction and activities—twelve hours per day, six days a week. From seven until ten o'clock in the morning we learned Korean in small classrooms, with seven to eight trainees and an instructor in each class. Only Korean was spoken in the classes.

During the first week, intelligent communication—if you can call repeating nonsensical sounds "communication"—was almost nonexistent in those classes, as the instructors struggled to overcome their own shyness in teaching some very strange Americans, and we tried to understand what they were trying to communicate and to overcome our reticence to put our minds, mouths, and tongues around some very odd sounds, many of which I had never heard before. "Listen and repeat" was the first phrase we learned to say in Korean, since our instructors probably said it a thousand times a day to us. I couldn't ever recall having been in a situation before quite like that classroom, trying to memorize a series of sounds—many of which were impossible to pronounce—and at the same time to comprehend what in the world the instructor was attempting to explain. Well, if success in training meant memorizing gibberish, then I was going to do it, I resolved.

Following a coffee break, we had two hours of lecture and discussion about Korean culture. We were told that the Korean staff was putting on a "welcome show" for us that evening, featuring various aspects of Korean culture that were previewed in the lecture's brief overview of the role in Korean life of song, dance, musical instruments, and martial arts. Later such lectures were on Korean history, teaching methodology, health hazards in Korea, and similar topics.

Around eleven o'clock each morning, the stifling heat and humidity began to be quite oppressive. In our classrooms (with no air conditioning or fans), not a breath of air stirred, even though the windows were wide-open most of the time. We sat and repeatedly mumbled the sounds we heard from the teachers, and we sweated until little pools of water formed under our chairs. Our clothes were often soaked by mid afternoon.

We ate lunch at noon. Soup, salad, and sandwiches were the usual luncheon fare. From one until three o'clock we had more Korean language instruction, and then group discussions, for about one and a half hours, regarding our motivation (Why did we come? What did we hope to get out of the Peace Corps service? What did we find disturbing about the training?), problems we could anticipate (lack of privacy, lack of sanitary facilities, alcoholism, sexually transmitted diseases), and how to deal with some common issues that troubled past volunteers in Korea (food, Korean military state, toilets, practicing religious beliefs, avoiding political discussions, social and sexual behavior). In the group discussions, the Korean staff was conspicuously absent. Two psychologists from Honolulu also participated in these sessions. Their presence somewhat dampened the openness of what we talked about, I felt. It always rained hard in the afternoon during these discussions.

At four thirty the male trainees had group lessons in *taekwondo*, the Korean martial art and the national sport of Korea. By the time we began our class on the lawn, the afternoon deluge had ended, and the hot sun had dried the grass completely. Several Korean language instructors, as well as three of the RPCVs, were black belts, so the martial arts instruction was excellent. Each of us was fitted for a taekwondo uniform and belt. For one hour, under the banyan and palm trees, we did push-ups, leg lifts, jumping jacks, and other exercises, as well as rudimentary taekwondo punches, kicks, and blocks, all apparently designed to exhaust us, which they did. We soon learned that in Korean *tae* means "to strike or break with foot"; *kwon* means "to strike or break with fist"; and *do* means "way, method, or art." Taekwondo, as a result, may be loosely translated as "the way of the foot and fist" or "the art of kicking and punching." If the North Koreans attacked, the K-VIIs and K-VIIIs would be ready.

Those of us who could still move after the taekwondo lesson turned to swimming, volleyball, touch football, or Frisbee on the center's vast lawn, and the rest of us returned to our dorms to relax. With more than one hundred fifty combined staff and trainees, there were lots of participants in each kind of activity. On that first day it seemed the Koreans were most interested in volleyball. With an eye toward getting to know them better, I joined the two dozen or so staff and PCTs playing volleyball.

One of the other PCTs on the volleyball court was wearing a purple T-shirt with the letters "MMVSP" on the front. I had such a shirt myself and returned to the dorm to put mine on. The letters stood for Mt. Madison Volunteer Ski Patrol, which was an organization I had helped found in New Hampshire's White Mountains during the summer of 1962. I had worked several summers as a so-called "hutman" for the Appalachian Mountain Club (AMC) at its Madison Spring Hut on the shoulder of Mt. Madison. At the instigation of the head of the crew, of which I was a part, we started a ski patrol, although there was no skiing then, and never has been any skiing, on Mt. Madison. Except for me, in fact, most of the crew couldn't even ski very well. The MMVSP became an elite kind of club. The purple shirt wearer was surprised to see my shirt.

As it turned out, the PCT with the purple shirt was Brian Copp.

He had worked for the AMC in 1967, and in 1968, he joined the MMVSP. Brian was tall and wiry, had a great sense of humor, and loved hiking. As former AMC hutmen and members of the MMVSP, we shared a special bond and immediately became good friends. (Later we planted the MMVSP flag on the summits of several of Korea's highest mountains.)

Volleyball became one of my favorite activities in the training program. The Korean men were extremely athletic and excellent players. The Korean female instructors were not, but their giggling and earnest attempts to play started to break down the cultural barriers between us.

Swimming was another favorite recreational activity. Above Rainbow Falls in the Wailuku River were a series of large, deep pools in which we swam almost daily. The wonderfully refreshing water was our only relief from the high humidity and stifling heat that enveloped us almost every day.

Dinner was served from six until seven. The menu usually featured white rice or pasta, a salad, a meat dish of some sort, something called *kimchee*, and the omnipresent fruits. Kimchee is a generic name for a host of Korean vegetable and fruit dishes featuring garlic and red peppers in prodigious amounts as the common denominators. It was always spicy, and the degree of its red pepper-based hotness varied according to the kind of kimchee. There were radish, turnip, lettuce, cabbage, and cucumber kimchees, to name only a few. We were encouraged to sample it, at least, at every dinner and admonished that kimchee would be a staple of our diet in the next two years. Most of us did not particularly like it at first, but within a week, all the trainees smelled of garlic, onions, and red peppers! According to our Korean instructors, our body odor was much more pleasant in class in the morning, now that we reeked of garlic instead of the sour, rancid butter smell that most Americans give off (which we couldn't smell then but understood when our noses recoiled from this American scent upon our return home two years later.)

The last daily hour of language instruction—usually in a large group—was from seven until eight in the evening, followed by concluding announcements of changes in the next day's program. Each day seemed slightly different enough from the days before—with varying amounts of work in each subject, changing hours, teachers, and classrooms, and different events planned for each subject area—that we were seldom bored.

On that first evening of the formal training program, the Korean staff treated us to a superbly entertaining, two-hour performance of Korean songs, traditional classic dances, taekwondo, music on traditional instruments, and a skit that depicted Korean life. All the women and some of the men wore traditional Korean clothes, generically called *hanbok*. The women were dressed in exquisite dresses, which initially looked to me like high-waisted ballroom gowns in lovely colors. We learned that the top of the ensemble is called a *jeogori*. It is blouse-like with long sleeves. The men's version was longer, stretching down to the waist. Below the jeogori, the women wore gorgeous, embroidered skirts called *chima*, while the men wore baggy pants called *paji*. Several of the women also wore fancy hairpins and diadem-like hair ornaments. I was totally entranced. I thought that in these costumes the women were magically transformed into some of the most beautiful women I had ever seen.

We later learned, first in our classes and then by experience in Korea, that people in the cities, and especially in Seoul, now predominantly wore Western-style clothing. But hanbok was still commonly seen as everyday dress in the smaller cities and in rural areas on older men and on women, especially at churches and temples, parties, festivals, and special occasions, such as weddings, or at expensive restaurants. This style of clothes had its roots from more than two thousand years ago. *Two thousand years ago!* Images came to my mind of the Bible and how the contemporaries of Jesus, or the Romans, had dressed. For the first time I became acutely aware of the truly ancient origins of the marvelous culture that we first briefly glimpsed that evening—a culture that turned out to be more than *four thousand* years old.

Some of the male instructors wore their taekwondo uniforms—loose fitting, pajama-like, and white—and performed astonishing feats, such as breaking boards and bricks with their bare hands and feet. I still recall the ferocity and gracefulness of Choi Seuk-ho, one of the black belts in taekwondo, when he demonstrated his skills.

As a group, the instructors sang several traditional Korean songs, as well as the Korean national anthem, which we would later all learn and be prepared to sing after our arrival in Korea. I was struck by the high quality of the singing. Either these Koreans had been handpicked for their lovely voices or the entire Korean race was genetically programmed with musical ability. We soon discovered it was the latter.

Several of the other Korean instructors—Jeong Jin-oak, Kim Hwa-won, and Sung Sook-ja—performed graceful, Korean court dances to traditional music. Another, the assistant director of the language program, Ahn Hee-ja, played several pieces on the Korean twelve-stringed zither, or *kayageum*. One of the RPCVs, Lindsay Pollock, also played the kayageum beautifully during the program.

Additionally, five of the instructors performed a skit that featured a common theme of our discussions during Peace Corps training and a common theme of everyday life in Korea: marriages arranged by matchmakers. The sadness of unfulfilled love between two young people, whose parents have arranged other spouses for their future or otherwise blocked a union because of the unsuitability of one or the other of a young couple, seemed to be an age-old issue. I still recall instructor Kim Hae-shik, as the tragic, disappointed lover, pretending to cry during that performance. (We later discovered that two of the instructors themselves were actually in that situation, having fallen in love with each other during our training, but being unable to get married because their marriages to others had been arranged by their parents. The unconfirmed story later was that they had eventually eloped, after the completion of the training program, and settled in Toronto.)

We ended our first full day of training on a high note, congratulating the Korean training staff on their fine performance and celebrating the beginning of training with a beer party. The Korean men drank prodigious quantities of beer, although some of them quickly turned beet red. I went to sleep thinking of swirling Korean dresses and lilting melodies. Indeed, as we were told that first day, Koreans did not seem to be at all the stereotypical Asian of quiet, self-effacing, and consummately polite demeanor, but rather could be called the "Irish" of Asia.

The next morning we were each presented with the following letter from an Irishman we would come to know well—the Peace Corps/Korea director, Kevin O'Donnell:

Dear Korea Trainee:

Kipling only said, "Ship me somewhere East of Suez." We hope you are saying, "Ship me somewhere East of China, but West of Japan, and more specifically, to the Republic of Korea."

Congratulations on having been invited to train for our Peace Corps/Korea Program. Let me give you a quick rundown on what to expect:

First and foremost—Korean is a jaw-fracturing language that is considered one of the most difficult to learn for an English speaker.

Next, Korea is a country with hot, humid summers, and cold, cold winters.

Expect also a dual Peace Corps role as both a teacher and as a person. In Korea, teaching is still valued on the Confucian set of scales. A great deal of competency, as well as sophistication, will be required—no, demanded—of you. And you'll be living and working in a culture steeped in the intricacies of Oriental personal relations.

In addition to the above, however, you can also expect a feeling of warmth and excitement as you gradually realize you can communicate in Korean.

You can look forward to the invigorating spring and fall seasons in Korea, which wipe away other memories and replenish body and soul: the joy of seeing brown, rural Korea come to life, as the rice seedlings and spring crops appear; the prolonged autumn, when every day is ideal and Korea proves her claim to high, blue skies.

In short, Peace Corps/Korea offers you an opportunity to truly be a Peace Corps Volunteer who, while working under hardship conditions, can have that inner satisfaction—that feeling of serving, of doing something tough and important.

We don't have Moulmein Pagodas, but we do have pagodas galore, plus a lot of other interesting items and places that only a four-thousand-year-old culture can generate.

If you're ready, we're looking forward to having you.

Sincerely,
Kevin O'Donnell
Director
Peace Corps/Korea

The letter from Director O'Donnell was the first of many communications from Korea during our training program, which made us feel from the beginning that there would be challenges ahead, such as a harsh climate, difficult language, and cross-cultural issues, and that Korea and Peace Corps/Korea truly welcomed us. We had the reassurance from the letter that the Peace Corps staff who awaited us in Korea wanted us to succeed and would do almost anything to help us. The O'Donnell letter increased my expectation that the experience in Korea would be a worthwhile one.

After the first day of training we settled into a daily routine that focused primarily on learning Korean, with cross-cultural and teacher training important, but secondary, concerns. The Korean language instructors—most of whom spoke little English—were truly wonderful teachers, engaging our interest and spurring our learning in every possible way, with humor, role-playing, and numerous teaching devices.

For example, throughout the training center were little signs in Korean identifying objects or places. Virtually everything was marked with a little sign: Banyan and palm trees, bamboo, volleyball court and equipment, bathrooms, eating utensils, food, beds, doors, windows, toilets, toilet paper, entrances, exits, waterfalls, rivers, walkways, buildings, classrooms, blackboards, chalk, desks, chairs—if you could see it, there was a little sign attached to it. The writing was strange, reminding me a little of cuneiform.

One teacher had us play a game—a kind of competition, sending us out from the classroom to copy these signs in our notebooks. Whoever copied the most signs in the allotted time won a prize. This focused us on the signs and got us to thinking about the structure of the writing and its meaning. We learned that the native alphabet of the Korean language—probably the most scientifically designed system of written communication ever devised—is called *hangul*, which means "great script" or "Korean script" in Korean (*han* means "great" or "Korean"; *gul* means "script" or "writing"). It was created in the mid-fifteenth century, through the graces of an enlightened ruler—King Sejong—who promoted universal literacy, and hangul is now the official script of both North Korea and South Korea.

What makes hangul so special is that it is an almost perfectly phonemic alphabet organized into syllabic blocks. Each block consists of at least two of the twenty-four hangul letters, with at least one each of the fourteen consonants and ten vowels. These syllabic blocks can be written horizontally from left to right or vertically from top to bottom in columns from right to left. Because the alphabet is so perfectly phonetic, if you memorize the twenty-four letters and corresponding sounds, you can read each syllable and easily string the syllables into words, and thus into sentences, pronouncing the syllables and ultimately words with intelligible accuracy. Most importantly, it is relatively easy to read and write. Once you have mastered the alphabet, it is so quickly shaped into words that it used to be called *achimgul* (*achim* means "morning"), or literally, "script you can learn in a morning."

The Korean alphabet looked like the symbols set forth below, taken from our training materials. In writing each symbol of the alphabet, you usually started the stroke of your pen at the top and proceeded downward, or on the left side, proceeding to the right, as appropriate for each letter of the alphabet.

Consonants:

| ㄱ | ㄴ | ㄷ | ㄹ | ㅁ | ㅂ | ㅅ | ㅇ | ㅈ |
|------|-----|-------|-------|-----|-------|--------|------|--------|
| (k,g) | (n) | (t,d) | (r,l) | (m) | (p,b) | (s,sh) | (ng) | (ch,j) |

| ㅊ | ㅋ | ㅌ | ㅍ | ㅎ |
|-------|-------|------|--------|-----|
| (ch') | (k') | (t') | (p',f) | (h) |

Vowels:

| ㅏ | ㅑ | ㅓ | ㅕ | ㅗ | ㅛ | ㅜ | ㅠ | ― |
|-----|------|------|-------|-----|------|-----|------|------|
| (a) | (ya) | (eo) | (yeo) | (o) | (yo) | (u) | (yu) | (eu) |

| ㅣ |
|------|
| (ee) |

Of course, first we had to learn the sounds of Korean, many of which are quite difficult (even after two years in Korea, speaking Korean, most PCVs cannot correctly pronounce all of the sounds of the Korean language). Our teacher would say a sound, and the seven or eight trainees in the class would repeat the sound. "Listen and repeat." After perhaps one hundred repetitions, the single sound would be combined with another or others to form a syllable. After another hundred repetitions, the syllable would be combined with another—and so forth, until we had a word consisting of several syllables. The words then formed phrases. Finally, often through our teacher's pantomime, we would discover what outlandish thing we had learned to say in Korean.

Each of us was given a Korean-English/English-Korean dictionary that soon became an extension of our bodies. We learned to look up words quickly and to view with great skepticism some of the too literal or archaic translations and definitions in that dictionary. For example, "speaking with another" translated to "oral intercourse." There were lots of similar pitfalls too risqué to mention here. We slept with those dictionaries under our pillows, hoping that some of their contents would seep into our brains during the night.

As the Korean instructors taught us, utilizing repetition drills, substitution drills, role-playing, and other teaching tools, we learned how to be a good teacher from them. Each instructor had a carefully organized and well thought out lesson plan. Classes were extremely lively, and the teachers conveyed energy and enthusiasm in their body language, as well as in their spoken language.

Whether intentionally or not, we learned about Korean culture from their performances in the classroom. We switched instructors almost every day. Over time we found that each instructor had come from a different part of Korea and that some had come from the urban centers, while others were from smaller cities or towns in the rural areas. Each teacher's accent and word usage were slightly different from another teacher's. Each teacher's cultural behavior and background were different as well. In this way we were exposed to many different kinds of Koreans, accents, and points of view. As a group, we found that when we got to know them, the Koreans were generally outgoing, emotional, extremely intelligent, eager to find out about the United States, and fun to be with.

The only initial problem we had with respect to our teachers was their names. It took us a while to discover that in Korea, the last or family name is placed first, while the given name (usually two syllables) is second. During training, we called our instructors by their last names, followed by the honorific form in Korean of teacher. Thus, Kim *sunsaengnim* meant Kim honorable teacher. But there were several Kims and several Chois. Among ourselves, we distinguished between those with the same family names by adding a nickname, such as Grandfather Choi (because he was three years older than the other Chois), short pants Choi (because he always wore shorts), and Taekwondo Choi, because of his skill in this martial art. One Kim became Daegu Kim, because he was from the city of Daegu and was proud of it!

The PCTs in my language class seemed to have been assigned randomly to the class in the first week. Each week thereafter, the class composition changed, probably based upon the relative language ability and speed of language acquisition of each student in the class. After the third week, trainees began to leave and the classes became smaller in size. Over the more than three and a half months of training, our combined Korea VII and Korea VIII groups decreased in number from more than one hundred twenty-five to about ninety, as close to thirty-five trainees were deselected or left voluntarily. Classes correspondingly decreased in size to only four or five in each class by the end of our training.

During the second weekend of training, all the trainees were kicked out of the center and ordered to stay away for two and a half days. We were told to explore the island of Hawaii and to learn about its culture and people. A bus dropped us off individually at about two mile intervals around the island, one PCT or one PCT couple at each drop. I decided to hitchhike around the entire island on the coastal highway, which was a narrow, two-lane road that wound through small towns, past lovely beaches, and over the shoulders of the volcanoes forming Hawaii. We were each given ten cents to cover the cost of a telephone call to the center, in case we needed help. Additionally, most of us had saved several dollars from the dollar and a half daily living allowance we were allotted in training to cover the cost of toothpaste, shampoo, and such minor essentials.

The first car that came along the road stopped to pick me up.

The Japanese-American family inside asked if I was a Peace Corps trainee (because the training center and its trainees had been a part of Hawaiian life in Hilo since 1963, the Hawaiians were very familiar with seeing trainees), and they were very interested that I was going to Korea. They invited me to share their dinner and to stay with them at their campsite on Hapuna Beach that night, almost a third of the way around the island. It was a delightful encounter and demonstrated what I already suspected—Hawaiians are a very kind and welcoming people. I remember a fine dinner, a pleasant evening of discussion with the family about their life in Hawaii, and a great day of swimming the next morning at Hapuna Beach, which is one of the world's best beaches!

Brian Copp and I had planned to meet up at one of the state parks along the route. After rendezvousing, we continued around the island, visiting Volcanoes National Park and Black Sand Beach, as well as several historic sites. Except for the daily afternoon deluge, which forced us to seek refuge in a few churches and pavilions at coastal parks, we had no problems, easily surviving through the tremendous generosity of the people we met.

Among the Hawaiians who picked us up on the highway were the island's director of water, and later on the same day, the director of power. Both explained to us how their respective departments worked and the issues involved in each area. These meetings were serendipitous encounters that gave us an excellent overview of Hawaiian government.

I was especially intrigued by the mixture of races in Hawaii, which seemingly coexisted in harmony, although the Japanese-American family told us about the race-based class distinctions and ethnic discrimination on the island. Hawaiians of Japanese, Filipino, Indonesian, Chinese, and Korean descent, as well as "pure" Hawaiians, picked us up— all of whom insisted on feeding us and driving us to whatever our next destination was. We found that most of the people we met had never been to the mainland and that all were intensely curious about mainland life and about us. We were equally curious about them. Long conversations ensued in the cars that picked us up. The people on the Big Island could not have been more friendly and hospitable.

As we hitchhiked around the island, particularly fascinating for me were the amazing changes in climate from one side of Hawaii to the other. At our training center in Hilo, on the east side of Hawaii, as I have already described, it was very wet and humid, with tropical vegetation and fauna, due to one hundred fifty inches of precipitation per year. Hilo is known as the American city with the most annual rainfall. In contrast, on the west side of the island it was dry and like a desert, with fewer than thirty inches of rain per year, and correspondingly totally different birds, animals, and vegetation from the east side. As the road climbed over the shoulder of the volcano from one side to the other, the delineation between the climatic zones was clear, so that within a mere hundred feet or so, on the border of the two zones, the difference in vegetation became quite obvious.

Back at the training center, it was interesting to hear the other trainees talk about their experiences during the weekend away from the center. Many had the same kind of delightful experience that Brian and I had. Others had had relatively unpleasant experiences and were angry that the unstructured weekend away, fending for themselves, had been planned by the staff. There was a lot of speculation as to why we had been sent out as we had. I secretly hoped that the negative feedback to the staff from some of the trainees about the weekend would not hurt the possibility that we could do it again. I thought that the two and a half day adventure was a worthwhile exercise in adapting to a totally foreign situation and in gathering information through intellectual pursuit, particularly on the beach at Hapuna.

In the third week of training we began the program called HILT, or High Intensity Language Training. Korean language instruction was the primary focus, and classes were extended so that we spent almost eight hours per day with the Korean language instructors. The most difficult thing about Korean for most of us was the "form" of addressing different people, according to their position relative to our own status. Another way of saying this is to refer to levels of speech—higher level and lower level. In French, I had learned the formal and familiar forms of address—the *vous* and *tu* forms, both meaning "you," for example, with their corresponding verb forms—to be used as appropriate, depending on the individual to whom you were speaking and your relationship to that person. In Korean there are at least fifteen different levels of address, each with its own corresponding verb endings and different vocabulary.

Which level of speech to use depends on a host of factors—primarily your status relative to the person or thing being spoken to.

We were being taught, essentially, one of the more common, formal levels of speech, as well as a common familiar level, and a very low form (to use with children and animals). When in doubt, we were told, use the more formal level! (Of course, if you use one level of speech to address a dog, and then use the same level of speech to address a person, you have grossly insulted the person by indicating that the person is as low as a dog! You are probably also insulting the dog. I did this repeatedly, I am afraid, as it took me a long while to become used to using the multiple forms of speech.)

Apart from the problems of the correct level of speech, the multiple changes in verb conjugation and vocabulary that accompanied different levels, and the difficult sounds of Korean, there was some good news: Korean seemed to be a highly schematic and consistent language, at least at the relatively low level of fluency we had attained.

During the HILT program, we were supposed to only use Korean at the center, so in the cafeteria and dormitories, as well as in the classrooms, we were struggling to communicate. Each of us was given a Korean name, which was supposed to be used instead of our American names. Mine was *Haw Chung* (family name *Haw*), which was the name of a former prime minister of Korea, I was told, and quite unusual in having only two syllables, instead of the normal three-syllable Korean name. As to my name's origin, I was informed only that Prime Minister Haw lasted three months in office, during the Second Korean Republic (June–August 1960), and I didn't dare ask what happened to him after that! Later, I discovered that the former prime minister's name was Haw Jeong—not Chung—similar sounding but not the same, to my relief.

I am not sure why we were given the names that we were, but I suspect that "Hobbie, Chuck" may have sounded slightly like Haw Chung to the Korean who devised our Korean names. To this day many of my Korean friends from my Peace Corps days know me as Mr. Haw.

In the middle of the HILT program, Hilo held its annual county fair. It was just like any other county fair that I had been to, except that some of the produce on display was different (e.g., huge pineapples), and the people strolling around the grounds were beautiful Hawaiians and

Asian Americans, for the most part. None of the Korean training staff had ever been to a county fair, of course. What they knew about county fairs they had gleaned from the movie *Picnic*, they told us. So a group of trainees took the Korean instructors to the fair to introduce them to this icon of American life.

We had a fantastic time with them, screaming on the small roller coaster, carousel, and other rides; eating cotton candy, hot dogs, and cracker jacks; laughing as we failed to win prizes at the various skill games; and watching the enchanted faces of the children and the excited eyes of the lovers we encountered there. Any cultural barriers that still may have existed between the PCTs and the Korean staff tumbled that night, as we clung to each other and gasped together, on the roller coaster at the Hilo fair. Afterward, I thought to myself that a county fair should be a planned component of any important activity in which it is imperative to build bonds of trust between culturally different people, such as peace negotiations with North Vietnam, and that riding together on a roller coaster should be mandatory for all participants.

The last week in October I received notification from my draft board in Buffalo that I had been given an occupational deferment and classified 2-A. That was a relief! Several of the other men in the training program were engaged in ongoing disputes with the Selective Service system, which in some cases was refusing to recognize Peace Corps service as a valid reason for postponing military service. At least the draft board in Buffalo seemed to be reasonable. My military service would wait until after I had completed my Peace Corps service. My 2-A status took a big load off my mind. The draft board, however, had not given me permission yet to leave the United States, which was a final hurdle to overcome.

On Sunday, October 27, three of us PCTs—Brian Copp and Bruce Cochran, who were good friends in training, and me—and my best friends among the American training staff—Ed Klein, Griff Dix, and Terry Reeve—took several of the Korean language teachers down to the harbor at Hilo to visit three US Navy ships docked there. The ships were open for public inspection—a sleek attack submarine, a minesweeper, and a rescue ship. As most of our Korean teachers had served in the Korean military, anything of a military nature fascinated them. They were very impressed by the ships but extremely taken aback by the fact that these military ships were open to the public. Such openness did not happen in Korea, we were told. Afterward, the teachers accompanying us—Lee Han-il, Chang Hae-ung, Kim Hae-shik, and Yim Chun-bin, who were the teachers I was becoming good friends with—were so effusive in thanking us for the harbor expedition and the trip to the county fair that we resolved to include them in any future such diversions. We realized that the high-pressure language training we were engaged in during the HILT affected the teachers in a stressful way just as much as it affected the trainees.

About this time, we spent a lot of time learning and practicing Korean songs after our Korean language classes. Each of the eighteen language classes prepared several songs for a singing contest held late in October. All of us first learned Korea's most famous folksong—"Arirang"—Korea's unofficial national song.

There was an amazing level of musical talent among the PCTs. Guitars, recorders, and many other instruments were brought out to accompany the singing, and we had a tremendous amount of fun. At the contest our class of six came in second overall, singing "Gohyang Pom" ("Hometown Spring") and "Doraji" (flower name). (I liked the second song—about a white flower—so much that forty years later my license plate in Virginia reads DORAJI.) Although I enjoyed the singing a lot, it was tough to learn those songs—it was like learning eighty nonsense syllables and then trying to remember to sing them in order to an unfamiliar tune!

On Halloween, about thirty of us dressed up in old clothes and costumes, with bags or stockings over our heads, and surprised the Korean staff, or should I say, terrorized them, before persuading them to come trick-or-treating with us in Hilo. Most of the Koreans—especially the men—had made a pretense of great dignity much of the time, except when they were screaming with us on the county fair's roller coaster. But that night of great indignities—as they donned strange masks and costumes—brought us all a lot closer. We ended up walking around Hilo together, serenading the local Hawaiians with Korean songs. I was especially amused that evening at some of the Korean songs we were taught, with familiar tunes like those of "Greensleeves" and "It Came Upon a Midnight Clear," which the Koreans swore were traditional Korean folk melodies.

During the first week in November, we had a distinguished visitor: the Korean consul general from Honolulu. We made a banner in Korean welcoming him, which several PCTs held high in front of the training center when he arrived. For his entertainment several of the PCT women presented some lovely Korean dances they had learned, four classes sang Korean folk songs, several classes sang, in a kind of chant, Korean odes (accompanied by drums and garbage can tops), and four of us sang a barbershop version of a Korean folksong we had learned. We were pretty impressive!

The first month of Peace Corps training was an extremely intense, stressful, and fun period of learning for me. Studying a language in such a concentrated manner—especially during the HILT period of language class for eight hours each day—was immensely satisfying. You could see real progress on a daily basis. Every moment my mind was barraged with information. Even in language class, while my mouth was making sounds, my eyes, ears, and mind were busy assimilating information about the Korean instructors—how they talked, dressed, laughed, taught, and walked.

Outside our language classes we learned English phonology and morphology, how to prepare lesson plans, and teaching techniques. As an undergraduate English major with a master's degree in English, I was quite surprised by how little I knew at the beginning of the training program about my own language's structure, sounds, and other characteristics.

Our daily lectures and demonstrations of Korean culture were fascinating in every way. This component of the training program was called area studies. Each week we had a different professor of Asian studies from the University of Hawaii in Honolulu come to the center to teach us about their particular area of focus involving Korea. We learned about Korea's geography; history; relationships with China, Japan, and the West; mythical origins; holidays; government; religions; educational system; economy; and arts. We discussed Korean ideals, interpersonal relationships, etiquette, and public relationships.

A US Army general spent an evening with us, giving a military account of the Korean War with emphasis on the size of the current North Korean military machine and on the fact that North and South Korea were still at war, although an armistice was in place. He told us that there were about sixty-two thousand US military personnel in Korea at that time, which was quite surprising to most of us. I thought to myself that, with so many American soldiers in Korea, they must be swarming everywhere. We paid special attention to this lecture, particularly when the general mentioned that en route to Seoul's Kimpo Airport, when we headed for Korea in January, we would be flying extremely close to both Soviet and North Korean air space.

On other evenings in the area studies program we practiced how to bow (there are at least five kinds of bows), how to exchange business cards, how to buy tickets, how to drink various kinds of alcoholic beverages, and how to handle hundreds of other practical situations we would encounter. We learned, for example, that Korean friends of the same sex often hold hands in public, but that Koreans of different sexes almost never do so. This custom had initially caused some confusion among the PCTs, when we observed our male language instructors holding hands.

We also learned a number of other Korean mannerisms that were quite surprising. For example, when counting something using one's fingers, Americans start with a closed hand and extend a thumb and then a finger each time a number is counted—one, two, three, four, and five—until the thumb and four fingers are extended, signifying five. As with so many little mannerisms, Koreans do exactly the opposite. Koreans begin counting with an open hand (all four fingers and the thumb extended) and, beginning with the thumb, gradually close the fingers as each number is counted, resulting in a closed hand that represents number five. It is easy to misinterpret what is happening (in this example, how many) unless you are aware of the difference in custom. This was a valuable lesson applicable to almost everything.

Despite the thirteen books on Korean culture and history we read during the course of the four months of training, and the hundreds of hours of lectures and discussions, my overall impression of our area studies program was that it was providing a minimal sampling only of the society, culture, and people of the country we would be living in for the next two years. The short time available during training could give us merely a taste of the excitement and obstacles we would experience and help us to identify the aspects of Korea that we might like most to pursue, once we had begun our service there. The amount of information we had been given, however, was overwhelming. I wished I had been able to receive comparable information, before I had lived in France and in Sweden in past years.

One aspect of life in Korea was particularly emphasized by the staff and by the psychologists during the area studies program: the total lack of privacy in Korea, resulting from the small living quarters (compared to American homes), the primitive toilet and washing facilities, and the overall population density. We were told that Korea's population—about thirty-one million people—crammed into a country slightly smaller than the state of Indiana, was the second densest in the world, only surpassed by the Netherlands. The per capita gross national product was about $165 in 1968, ranking among the poorest countries of the world, compared to about $4,500 for the United States. Korea's poverty had been shaped by almost half a century of exploitive, Japanese occupation and by a devastating three-year-long war that had ravaged the entire peninsula. The fighting had ended only fifteen years before, in 1953.

Apart from the American and United Nations military presence, there were only about six hundred foreign diplomats, missionaries, and others in Korea in 1968, we were advised. So no matter where you were in Korea, it was pointed out, you will stand out as a foreigner. No matter what you do, your actions will be known, either by the Koreans of your community or by the Korean police, which has informants everywhere. The message, of course, was that we were expected to act at all times in a manner consistent with the highest standards of conduct. But, as we were still learning what those standards entailed in Korea, judging what to do and what not to do could be a tricky exercise.

Then one of the psychologists told us a story about another Peace Corps country, and the arrival there of a new Peace Corps staff member, so as to drive home the point about a lack of privacy and differing cultural norms. I was shocked by the following story:

> The new Peace Corps official arrived unexpectedly at the country in the south Pacific several days ahead of schedule. When there was no one at the airport to welcome him, he called the Peace Corps office in the country to advise of his arrival. He was told to check in to the airport hotel, because a big welcome was being arranged for his arrival by the host

country government and American embassy staff, and all would be spoiled if he arrived ahead of schedule. So the Peace Corps official settled in to the hotel for a couple of days, glad for the opportunity to rest after the long, two-day flight from the United States.

On the day of his scheduled arrival, there was a big, boisterous crowd of people at the airport. He was escorted to a place of honor in front, where he sat for several minutes while all awaited the arrival of government dignitaries. During this interlude of waiting, a young boy in the front of the crowd started to talk in a loud voice in the local language—which the official could not yet understand—with much gesticulating. His impromptu narrative elicited a warm response from the crowd, which cheered and laughed. Minutes later the formal welcoming ceremony began, and the official was amazed at the crowd's friendliness and standing ovation when he was introduced. The warmth of his welcome there and at the following reception was overwhelming.

In thinking about his wonderful welcome several days later, the official thought about the boy and wondered if what the boy had talked about to the crowd had had anything to do with the crowd's mood and enthusiasm. He asked one of the Peace Corps staff what the boy had said. The staff member refused to tell him at first. Only after much cajoling did the staff member tell the new official that the boy had been describing to the crowd the different ways that the official had masturbated in his hotel room.

There was silence for several moments upon the completion of the story. We all squirmed uneasily. Living in Korea would be like living in a glass bowl, with every action scrutinized by Koreans, in addition to other hardships, which we were just beginning to appreciate.

With the intense assimilation of information we were undergoing, we experienced an acute need to really get away from the classroom on Sundays and to do something totally different from the training routine. The training staff had recognized this and planned for it. One of the planned activities was a group climb of one of the volcanoes.

Mauna Kea is one of five volcanoes that together form the island of Hawaii. The center staff told us that *Mauna Kea* means "white mountain" in the Hawaiian language, a reference to its summit being regularly covered by snow in winter. The peak of Mauna Kea is 13,803 feet above mean sea level, about 100 feet taller than neighboring Mauna Loa and about 33,000 feet above its base on the floor of the Pacific Ocean. By this measurement, the Hawaiians told us, Mauna Kea is the world's tallest mountain, taller than Mount Everest, which is the highest mountain *above sea level*. When we heard that the world's tallest mountain was on our doorstep and could be climbed in a day, our anticipation of the ascent planned by the training staff grew each week. After several postponements due to predicted adverse weather conditions, the big day arrived on the first Saturday in November.

The staff drove us in a bus up the narrow, dirt Saddle Road, which traverses the shoulder and divide separating Mauna Loa from Mauna Kea. There were about forty in the climbing party—an equal mix of Korean staff, American staff, and PCTs. After leaving the bus, we struggled up, past the observatory, to the summit at the top of the cinder cone called *Pu'u Wekiu*, traditionally known as *Pu'u o Kukahau'ula*, which is the highest of the numerous cinder cones on the summit plateau. It is also the highest point in the state.

I do mean *struggled*. Although I had done a lot of climbing in my prior life—in New Hampshire's White Mountains, in the Colorado Rockies, in Alaska's Brooks Range, and in the mountains of northern Sweden and Norway—the ascent of Mauna Kea was an ordeal. It took us fourteen hours to get up to the top and back to the bus. At that altitude, the lack of oxygen gave us tremendous headaches and other symptoms of altitude sickness. We probably would have been all right, except that the climb soon turned into a contest between the Koreans (five tough, ex-army officers) and five of us Americans to see who could get to the summit first. Most of us had also quaffed a few beers the night before. We all underestimated the difficulty of walking for hours on a dusty road (leading to the Keck Observatory), lava flows, and volcanic ash, which was like coarse sand, as well as the bad effects of the altitude. We ended up helping each other, for three of the Koreans became quite sick, and the rest of us were pretty beat by the time we got to our objective.

It was worth the trouble. There was a fantastic view of the entire island from the summit! Brian Copp and I took our MMVSP T-shirts out from our backpacks and waved them at the top. (We would have worn them, but the temperature dropped steadily as we climbed, and at the summit our sweatshirts and parkas were needed in the stiff wind.) Despite the exhilaration of reaching the top of the world's "highest mountain," I don't think that I would make that climb again. The entire hike was like walking, hour after hour, mile after mile, through a desert area that had been bombed—all rock and ash, cinder cones, and dust, dust, dust!

The next morning, those of us who had climbed Mauna Kea had a really tough time concentrating in language class, due to lingering headaches. We also ached all over. That evening, several of the male Korean instructors asked me if I would guide them to the movies in Hilo. They had heard, they said, that one theater showed sex movies, and they wanted very much to experience such movies. In Korea, they told me, you never could even see kissing in a movie. American movies, such as *Picnic*, or other romances, were so heavily censored that you could hardly tell that romance was involved in the plot. I checked the local paper. Sure enough, on Wednesday evenings, the Busy Bee Theater in Hilo showed X-rated movies. So we made plans to meet in front of the center after the evening lecture, and to walk together to the movie theater, which was only about one and a half miles away. Several of the other male trainees and American staff indicated that they wanted to go too.

We assembled at the appointed place and time. There were about fifty people, to my great surprise, including all of the Korean instructors—even the shy and dainty female instructors. I was totally taken aback. I was even more shocked to discover, upon entering the Busy Bee, that it seemed as though this was a "family night out" affair for the Hawaiians in Hilo, who brought their entire families, including grandparents and young children! The Koreans watched the movie attentively, without expressions on their faces. Afterward, all thirty-one of them thanked us for an enjoyable evening. I wasn't sure what their true reaction to the movie was, but I noticed that on subsequent Wednesday evenings many of the instructors—males and females—disappeared from the center. I wasn't particularly anxious to take the credit for their introduction to this aspect of American culture and hoped that the psychologists would not find out about my role.

By the end of the fifth week of training, we had all been to the dentist and to the eye doctor in Hilo for checkups. My eyes and teeth were just fine, so the medical staff at the training center decided to cripple me with immunizations. Right after the Veteran's Day holiday, a series of seven inoculations were administered to us in rapid succession. Most of them had after-effects, especially the cholera shot, which made me quite sick for twenty-four hours. We were warned that before we left Hilo, we would have to have a total of eighteen inoculations, so I had an additional eleven shots to go! This process was a necessary evil, but it sure was unpleasant at the time, and I wondered if there wasn't a better way of administering all these shots. The RPCVs, seeing our distress, were terribly helpful in mentioning that the shots don't do much good anyway—all of the RPCVs from the Korea I group had been sick in Korea with everything from typhoid to hepatitis!

The BIG TEST followed the shots. Peace Corps required all trainees to take the Foreign Service Institute's language test (FSI test), and all PCVs to take the test at six-month intervals. The FSI test was the official test given to all US government personnel overseas to measure their oral language proficiency, and improvements in language proficiency, during their overseas service. Tested individuals are rated on a scale of 0 to 5, with 0 being no proficiency and a score of 5 being perfect fluency. (Not even Koreans themselves, we were told, get a 5 on the test. No American had ever scored higher than a 4 when tested in Korean.) During the twenty-minute oral test, the test administrator is supposed to take into account everything pertaining to the way we speak, comprehend, and use Korean.

It was quite a frightening experience to walk into a room, meet the examiner, and then try to field a barrage of questions in Korean. (For sheer terror I would rate the experience a 5 on the Hobbie terror scale of 0 to 5, comparable to my first Supreme Court argument fifteen years later.) Happily, during the several weeks before the test I had a reciprocal teaching arrangement with one of the Korean instructors—Yim Chunbin. I taught him English, and he gave me special tutoring in Korean in preparation for the test. Mr. Yim taught me several key polite expressions and greetings—not taught to other trainees in class—which I dropped strategically into the conversation with the test examiner during the test, and thus bluffed my way through. I was horribly nervous.

At the end of the week we were given our scores. Twenty of us were lucky enough to score S-1, while most of the other trainees scored between S-0 and S-0+. I heard that at least one PCT had a negative score, although I have no idea how that could be accomplished. (Perhaps the trainee used the lowest form of speech while addressing the examiner and thereby grossly insulted him, we speculated.)

When we received our scores, we were also shown the results of a study, conducted for the US government several years before, which placed all foreign languages into four groups, according to the degree of difficulty an English speaker has in learning each language. The hardest languages to learn for English speakers are placed in the fourth group—Arabic, Japanese, Chinese, and Korean, which was the hardest of all. I think that we were informed of this to encourage our rather deflated egos, which had taken quite a pounding from the Korean language instruction and low test scores. We also learned that Korean belongs to a kind of unique language group that includes Hungarian, Finnish, and Turkish, and is not closely related to either Japanese or Chinese.

After six weeks of English teacher training, phonology, and morphology, we began practice teaching using our Korean language instructors as pupils. I enjoyed this part of training immensely! It was quickly evident that, although the Koreans had a tremendously broad, latent knowledge of English grammar and vocabulary, they were reluctant to use this knowledge in oral conversation. We knew what that feeling was like. So a big part of our challenge as teachers was to get the students speaking English, by repetition drills, role-playing, and other teaching devices, which we had just been subjected to ourselves during the past six weeks in the Korean language classes.

As we taught individually in these practice sessions, we were videotaped. It helped a lot to watch yourself teaching in front of a class. Some of the mannerisms and nervous habits each of us evinced as a teacher became quite obvious on the tape—picking your nose, jingling coins in your pockets, swaying from side to side as you speak, rubbing your ears or your crotch, running your hands through your hair, not looking at your students, pointing at individual students, voicing "um" or "er" as space fillers while formulating words, and other bad teaching habits.

During the third week of such practice teaching we each had to prepare for, and teach, a class in a foreign language (not Korean), speaking only that language. The students, again, were our Korean language teachers. All PCTs were required to watch each class. The class was supposed to last thirty minutes and to be conducted entirely in the selected foreign language—no English was allowed. For me, this was not much of a challenge, due to my having had a French minor at Dartmouth and having studied at the University of Montpellier in France just two years earlier. My class was in French. It went pretty well.

The next day, another trainee from Dartmouth, Tom Ulen, taught a class in "Magno-Croatian," which seemed like a complicated language and one whose sounds were very strange. He did very well at first, I thought. Then I grew increasingly suspicious as I watched Tom teach and examined the words he was writing on the blackboard. "Tihsllub," "kcuf," "tinmaddog," and "nmad," among others, were very strange and difficult to pronounce. It couldn't be a coincidence that many of the words in the exotic language he was teaching, when spelled backwards, were English obscenities. Slowly, most of us caught on to what he was doing, and the classroom observers dissolved into laughter, to the bewilderment of the Korean "students," who didn't know what was going on. All this was in preparation for the real thing in the near future, we were told, when we would begin to teach, as part of our training, at the East-West Center of the University of Hawaii in Honolulu, as well as in the Honolulu high schools.

In mid-November, the PCTs started planning an elaborate "American Night," as a thank you to the Koreans for the wonderful "Korea Night," which they had presented to welcome us in October to the start of the training program. We had several planning meetings to discuss what we should do. Finally, we decided to present as many tastes of American traditional entertainment as we could. For the next two weeks, each evening saw groups of PCTs retreat to remote parts of the training center to practice their contribution to the big event, which was to take place during Thanksgiving week.

Four of us got together and formed a barbershop quartet. We called ourselves the "Hilo *Esos*," which translates literally as the "Hilo Ins," or the quartet "In Hilo." Our chosen name was kind of a strange name, but the Koreans understood. Brian Copp sang first tenor, Jon Moody (from the Dartmouth Glee Club) sang second tenor, Jim Gahn sang baritone, and I sang bass. We found an old deserted operating room in the main training center building (formerly the main building of the hospital) for our practice room. It was walled with tile and had wonderful acoustics, so it was like singing in the shower. In that operating room we sounded fantastic! We had sung together before, during the training program, when we had presented several Korean songs on different occasions, such as the visit of the Korean consul general, which I have already mentioned. Now we would sing traditional, American barbershop quartet songs and dress in vests and bow ties. We also planned a "visit" from a new ukulele strumming popular singer of 1968—Herbert Khaury, a.k.a. Tiny Tim, who had had a very distinctive hit song earlier in the Year of the Monkey.

As the preparations were well underway for American Night, a mystery unfolded at the center. For one week, just at sunset, we had a blackout at dinnertime, affecting all of Hilo. We had just started to eat dinner every evening in the Korean traditional manner—at low tables, sitting cross-legged on the floor, and using chopsticks. Now we had to eat in candlelight, which was delightful. The blackout usually lasted two hours or so, and then, just as suddenly as the electricity had gone out, it would reappear. I felt like contacting the director of power, who had picked up Brian Copp and me when we were hitchhiking more than a month earlier, to thank him for blacking out all of Hilo. You could see hundreds of stars in the nighttime sky, without the interference of Hilo's city lights. We never found out why those blackouts happened that one week.

The food at the center continued to be quite good. For the most part, we ate Hawaiian food now—lots of fruit, chopped up meats, fish, rice, and vegetables—and different kinds of kimchee. The funny thing was that despite eating more and more of the spicy, garlic charged Korean dish, we could no longer smell the garlic on each other's breath. Our noses had changed, without changing size.

The two psychologists, who were married to one another, periodically met with each of the trainees to discuss how we felt about the training program and about ourselves. I had many talks with them on an alternating basis—although I can't remember their names—and they seemed like normal, decent people. Many of the other PCTs voiced the opinion that the psychologists were crazy. They both told me early in the program that I was in good shape with the staff assessments and should make it through the training, barring something unforeseen (such as introducing the Korean staff to X-rated movies). I was reassured to be told by both psychologists that I was pretty stable, due mainly to what they called an unusually good home environment. They never discovered how neurotic I was.

Several of us made reciprocal arrangements with our friends on the Korean staff for extra tutoring. We helped them with English, and they juiced up our Korean vocabularies. Instructors Kim Hae-shik, Lee Han-il, Yim Chun-bin, and Chang Hae-ung and I became quite close over time. They were tremendously helpful in assisting me to improve my spoken Korean, as well as to learn some Chinese characters, which we had begun to study in November. Our goal was to learn the five hundred most common Chinese words by the end of training, since Chinese characters were still in use in Korea. Especially in reading train and bus schedules, it was important to know Chinese numbers and other common words.

One thing drove me especially crazy: Koreans use pure Korean numbers for counting some things and Chinese numbers for counting others. So we had to learn two systems of numbering. For example, in telling time, the hour is identified by the Korean number, while the minutes are identified by Chinese numbers. Depending on what you are counting, you use one or the other language's numbers, and you just have to learn what things are counted with which system.

Even more important than the assistance of the instructors with Korean and Chinese, however, was the intimate look at many of their attitudes and beliefs that spending so much extra time with them afforded me. With them I encountered the opposite end of the political and moral spectrum that I had met in Sweden. Politically, morally, and socially I received a perspective from them that I never before had grappled with. I started to question a lot of my previous beliefs.

For example, my Korean male friends were staunchly anti-Communist. All had served in the Korean military, which was mandatory for all Korean men. Some had served in the Korean forces in Vietnam. They strongly favored the American effort there and could not comprehend my opposition to the war. In talking with them about Vietnam, my mind was not changed, but I began to understand better the perspective that supported the war. For the Koreans, of course, the 1950 invasion by the Communist North Korean forces was still fresh in their minds.

We also discussed a subject—much debated among the PCTs— that I will refer to as "cultural imperialism," which we defined as spreading American influence—economic, cultural, religious, and governmental—around the world with the unspoken but real objective of domination. The Vietnam War, and the American military presence in so many countries around the world, smacked to some of us as cultural imperialism in its most heavy-handed form. The Peace Corps programs around the world could also be viewed as a more sophisticated—even more insidious—form of American cultural imperialism.

When we brought this issue to the Koreans' attention, they understood clearly what we meant—having relatively recently suffered under Japan's attempts to impose its culture on Korea during Japan's occupation of Korea for almost half a century. But they were shocked that we would think of the American military presence in Korea or of Peace Corps in this way. From their perspective, Americans had intervened militarily during the Korean War and were continuing a substantial presence in Korea to protect South Korea from an evil North Korea, which had attacked them in 1950. Peace Corps, they argued, was a sincere attempt to help Koreans restore their country, after a devastating war, by working in health programs, in other educational programs, and in English education—English being the language of world trade, world diplomacy, and technological development. As English teachers, our trainee groups would really be helping Koreans improve their lives, they insisted.

Another example involved the appearance of American women, including the female PCTs and RPCVs. Many wore makeup and short skirts or shorts, especially in Hilo's heat and humidity. Additionally, on our weekend visits to the bars and tourist hotels in Hilo, my Korean friends met local women from Hilo and from the University of Hawaii's

Hilo campus nearby, most of whom were beautifully made up and suggestively dressed.

In Korea, they explained, women made up and dressed like the American women all around us would be viewed as pleasure women, bar girls, or even prostitutes. For them it was very confusing to engage these women as students, teachers, and marriageable women, when the signals they received—based on the women's appearance—told them otherwise. I began to understand that appearance, including dress, hairstyle, and makeup (or lack thereof), was a much more important identifier in establishing status in Korean culture than in multicultural America.

While our friendships developed, and the Koreans became convinced that we were not members of the American Central Intelligence Agency (such outspoken, language challenged, crazy people could not possibly be CIA agents), the pace of activity in the training program became more and more frenzied. In a matter of weeks the PCTs in Korea VIII would be leaving for Honolulu to focus on practice teaching. The rest of the PCTs would follow soon thereafter. Language study, area studies, TESOL study, Chinese study, and even the taekwondo sessions became more intense. More and more trainees were deselected; about thirty had left the program by mid-November, causing concern that our production in honor of the Koreans might have no trainees left to stage.

The grand performance took place on Thanksgiving eve. Named "How the West Is Run," it was a combination of literary readings (part of Dylan Thomas' *Under Milkwood*); a musical play; a blue grass/ Country and Western group (two banjos, two guitars, and a violin); a jazz group; a one-man acrobatic show; a barbershop quartet with "Tiny Tim" in "Tiptoe Through the Tulips," featuring Brian Copp on the ukulele (with a mop on his head); a choir that sang several spirituals; several modern and folk dance routines; and a multitude of guitar and banjo strummers, violin players, recorder players, and folk singers, as well as a one-man parody of life at the Peace Corps Training Center! Several of the trainees were hilarious masters of ceremony. The entire performance took about four hours and exhausted all of the performers and audience. The following program best shows the eclectic nature of the performance, which was quite bewildering to the Koreans:

Choir (James Reid, Director):
    "America the Beautiful"
    "Go Down, Moses"
    "Swing Low, Sweet Chariot"

"Consider Yourself at Home" (Married Couples)

Folksongs (Sharon Desrosiers, Pat Donegan, Jim Gahn):
    "Scotch and Soda"
    "Edelweiss"
    "He's Got the Whole World"
    "All My Trials"

Square Dance and English Country Dances (Wales) (Bob Oakley, Director)

Country/Western Music (Howie Tarnower, Lou Spaventa, George Humphrey, Stan Hudson, and Bruce Cochran)
    "My Heart Skips a Beat"
    "Love's Gonna Live Here"
    "Are You Washed in the Blood"

*Under Milkwood* [excerpted] by Dylan Thomas (Jerry DiIorio and Maria Lenteri)
    Voices: Gay Garland, Christy Murphy, Gary Fedota, Jerry DiIorio, and Ray Korona

"The Old Songs" (Brian Copp, Jim Gahn, Chuck Hobbie, and Jon Moody):
    "Jeanie with the Light Brown Hair"
    "In the Evening by the Moonlight"
    "Tiptoe Through the Tulips" (Brian Copp as Tiny Tim)

A Mauna Kea Victim (Jerry DiIorio) (gymnastic free exercises)

Songs (Howie Tarnower and George Humphrey)
   "Mr. Bojangles"
   "Urge for Going"

Two Hamlet Soliloquies (Bill Ryan)

Flamenco Guitar Solo (Scott Williams)

An American Pioneer (Dick St. Clair)

Our Norman Heritage (Janis Shannon, Bill Cantrell, Bob Oakley, and Aaron Guritz, playing recorders):
   "Summer Is Icumen In" (thirteenth century)
   "Dulcina" or "Pills to Avoid Melancholy" (seventeenth century)
   "Drink to Me Only with Thine Eyes" (eighteenth century)

Two Russian/American Folksongs (Peter Mikuliak)

The training staff had arranged a fine picnic of hot dogs and hamburgers beforehand, and afterward we had a beer party in honor of the Korean staff. It was a wonderful night!

The next day was Thanksgiving. Whether it was a post-performance letdown or merely missing Thanksgiving with my family that made me very sad on Thanksgiving, I don't know. I missed my parents and other family; I missed Dariel; and I missed the cool, autumn weather—even snow—of Buffalo, Wisconsin, and New Hampshire in late November. I think I realized for perhaps the first time that I would not see these beloved people and places again for more than two years. In my heart I also suspected that I would never see Dariel again—which made me very blue.

The residents of Hilo were generous in opening their homes and families for all of us on the Thanksgiving holiday. Each of us received multiple invitations to Thanksgiving dinners. I was invited, with several Koreans, to the home of the owner of the local bookstore in Hilo, with whom I had struck up a friendship while searching for barbershop quartet music in Hilo. Nine of us had a fine dinner and a great Thanksgiving celebration with Mr. Haritani's family. Despite my mood, it was a pleasant holiday.

During the first week in December, we spent five days in Waipio Valley—an incredibly lovely, secluded valley on the northeastern coast of Hawaii. The valley itself is about four miles deep, running from a beautiful black sand beach back into the side of the Mauna Kea volcano, and about one mile wide. Two-thousand-foot cliffs surround the valley on three sides, and a river twists down the middle of the valley floor, fed from several impressive waterfalls that drop more than fifteen hundred feet off the cliffs. An extremely steep, dirt road led down into the valley from the main highway. We were dropped off on the rim, walked down the road a mile into the valley, and then hiked over another mile or so to the small village in the heart of the valley that had been constructed to acclimate PCTs training for south Asian countries with tropical climates.

We lived in grass huts, slept on mats under mosquito netting, and coped—for the first time during training—with a total lack of electricity and running water. Our camp consisted of six small wood and grass thatch structures constructed on stilts about ten feet off the ground and accessible by wooden ladders. We speculated that the houses were built off the ground in case a tsunami struck, as it had eight years earlier, but we doubted that their flimsy construction would withstand such a catastrophe. The valley looked as though it would be a tsunami death trap.

Unfortunately, there was a lot of water from a different source the entire week. It rained hard every day in a steady downpour that soaked us to the skin in minutes. We explored the valley thoroughly anyway, finding several small Filipino farms further up the valley. Except for the farmers and a few million voracious mosquitoes, we were the only inhabitants in the entire valley.

Although I loved the beauty and isolation of Waipio, the heat, humidity, and insects confirmed my instinctive—but until now untested—misgivings about a primitive, tropical environment. Our last day there the sun finally came out as we trudged up the road and out of the valley in our soggy clothes and boots. We were all relieved that, from what we had learned to this time about Korea, it would not be like Waipio Valley, but we remembered the days in Waipio fondly, two months later, when we were slogging through deep snow in Seoul.

On the Sunday evening after Pearl Harbor Day, following our return to the training center in Hilo from our adventure in Waipio Valley, I arranged a square dance for the training program. We had a professional square dance teacher and caller come from Hilo. The whole dance went very well. It gave us all a chance to relax with the Korean women, especially, in a social setting that brought smiles to their faces. Just before going to Waipio, several of us had taught the Korean instructors some of the fundamentals of square dancing, so they were able to enjoy it as much as we did.

That same week saw the end of the taekwondo classes. I was sorry that this activity was over, because it was just beginning to get exciting. We had begun to make physical contact with each other, and the exercises had been getting more and more difficult. I think that some of our Korean instructors were trying to show us how tough they were, for they had us doing incredibly hard backbends, as well as dozens of pushups each morning on two knuckles on the pavement of the center's driveway. Nobody had yet been hurt in taekwondo; it was just a matter of time, for volleyball and touch football games had already produced several broken fingers, a couple of blown-out knees, and a half dozen sprained ankles.

On Friday, December 13, as it poured rain on my last full day at the Hilo Training Center, I spent most of the day packing for the move to the island of Oahu the next day. As I prepared to leave the Hilo Training Center and Rainbow Falls, I reflected on the development of my friendships with the Koreans. In a matter of months my feelings about them had completely changed. Every week I had gotten to know them better—at least the Korean men. The Korean women had become quite friendly and had gotten over their shyness, but my discussions with them were about such topics as the weather or other innocuous subjects. They seemed so innocent and delicate somehow. It was difficult to talk with them in depth, perhaps because they didn't drink and seemed to be at a level of social experience on a par with American high-school girls.

With the Korean men it was a different story. After their initial reserved demeanor had been cracked, I found them to be almost exactly like my American or Swedish friends in many ways. Based on my friendships with them, I tentatively concluded that the picture they presented of Korean culture, as young, Korean men, whose very presence in Hawaii as Peace Corps instructors set them apart from more traditional Koreans, clashed hugely with the more historically based picture we were being shown in the area studies program to date. I had a feeling already that Korean culture and social customs were in a state of tremendous transformation, hesitantly moving from the traditional oriental culture and norms toward the Western versions introduced by the American and United Nations military presence in the past fifteen years, since the cessation of the fighting. So I would have an exciting, challenging time in Korea, I thought, trying to figure out what I was seeing and experiencing, which would undoubtedly be evolving rapidly in the turbulent, Korean society.

The next day, the remaining K-VIII PCTs boarded buses for the Hilo airport. I sadly said goodbye to the training center staff, who had been wonderfully supportive, and to the beautiful Rainbow Falls, which had provided such a lovely backdrop to many, happy weeks of language, TESOL, and cross-cultural training. I was especially glum to leave my closest PCT friends—Brian Copp, Bruce Cochran, Jon Moody, and Jim Gahn—all of whom were members of the K-VII group that would remain in Hilo for one more week.

The flight from Hilo to the island of Oahu was awesome, as we flew directly over the spectacular volcanoes of the island of Hawaii (although this time none was erupting) and had gorgeous views of Waipio Valley, as well as Hapuna Beach. It would be forty years before I saw the Big Island again.

I was reluctant to leave the routine and environment in Hilo to which I had become accustomed after many weeks. I guess I like the familiar. At the same time, I knew that the remaining four weeks of training in Hawaii would be exciting and present new challenges on Oahu. I was firmly committed to Peace Corps by this time. Despite the lingering ache in my heart for my beautiful Dariel—which I tried to shake off every day—any thought of voluntarily leaving was gone. I was in this for the long run—Peace Corps, my draft board, and God permitting.

Korean Language Instructors, Jackie Tanny, and Lindsay Pollock,
Korea Night Cast, October 1968

Trainees' Chorus in How the West is Run, Hilo, Hawaii,
November 1968

Country and Western Singers Howie Tarnower, George Humphrey, Lou Spaventa, and Bruce Cochran, Hilo, Hawaii, November 1968

Married Couples' Musical Fascinates Lee Han-il and Choi Seung-deuk, Hilo, Hawaii, November 1968

# CHAPTER THREE—PEACE CORPS TRAINING ON OAHU, HAWAII

On Christmas Eve and Christmas Day it rained heavily. Somehow, in the rain on the island of Oahu, with temperatures in the high seventies, it didn't seem like Christmas. I missed being home. For me, Christmas in Buffalo had always been a special occasion. You could always count on lots of snow for a white Christmas at home.

To call family on the mainland on the holiday you had to make a reservation with the telephone company for a specific time. I made mine three weeks before Christmas and was able to talk with my parents in Buffalo and other relatives on a conference call by phone for about three minutes, precisely at noon, Hawaii time. How wonderful it was to hear their voices! PCTs who hadn't made a telephone reservation forlornly tried to get through to Honolulu on jammed telephone lines all day, without success. There were two telephones at our new training site. On the day after Christmas I tried all day, without success, to get through to Dariel.

After relocating to our new training site, we found ourselves at a YMCA camp on Kaneohe Bay—Camp Kokokahi—about as isolated as you could get on Oahu. The camp was ten miles northeast of Honolulu, with no connecting bus or public transportation. Approximately sixty staff and PCTs were crammed into eight small primitive cabins with open, screened windows on all sides and overhanging roofs—just like being at camp. Each cabin was about sixteen feet square, had four to six bunk beds, and featured three bare lightbulbs hanging from the ceiling. The sleeping arrangements were less than comfortable for most of the PCTs—especially for the married couples, who were crammed into their cabins, three couples to a cabin, with no privacy. There were outdoor communal restrooms and showers.

Because it was overcast and rained for most of the first week at the camp, my initial impression was fairly negative. The soaking rains, humidity, bugs, and mud everywhere were very depressing, especially because it was the pre-holiday season. The female PCTs, especially, suffered in the dampness, many with colds, flu, and allergy problems. I characterized it as a Godforsaken place in a letter to my parents.

As often is the case, first impressions were misleading. Camp Kokokahi turned out to be situated in one of the most stunningly beautiful places I have ever lived in. We were right at the water's edge on Kaneohe Bay, a large, shallow bay—eight miles long by three miles wide—with the knife-edged, cliff-ringed Ko'olau Mountains to the southwest, forming a magnificent backdrop. From the camp you could see several islands in the bay. One was called "Chinaman's Hat Island." Another was "Coconut Island." A large pier, several hundred feet long, jutted out into the bay from our camp, affording a fantastic view of the entire area from its end.

When the sun finally came out after a week of rain, I spent a lot of my free time out on that pier, admiring the sweeping view of the bay and mountains, reading, writing, and watching all the young local boys fish. Periodically, fighter jets in the distance would land at the Kaneohe Marine Corps Air Base, located several miles to the north. Except for the roar of the occasional fighter plane, our training site was a peaceful, idyllic spot.

We arrived on the island of Oahu on Saturday, December 14. Our group was driven by bus from the airport up the Nu'unau Valley in the mountains to the east of Honolulu, through the Pali Tunnels, which cut through the Ko'olau Range, and down into Kaneohe. We were told, during the drive, that we were passing the place where the forces of Kamehameha the Great fought their final battle to conquer all the Hawaiian Islands, cornering the Oahu army here, and then pushing the survivors off the high cliffs. It was surprising for me, as it had been on Hilo, to learn that in the past the incredibly peaceful islands had been the scene of so much bloodshed, a century and a half before the attack on Pearl Harbor. During the construction of the highway, more than eight hundred skulls were found—presumably the remains of the fallen warriors of that time. It was a beautiful drive, even in the rain.

At Camp Kokokahi our routine consisted of the usual five hours of morning language study, followed by lunch. Our language classes were held in a building that housed a recreation hall, dining hall, and lounge on the twenty-acre campground. We also enjoyed a fine, outdoor swimming pool (there was no swimming in the shark-infested Kaneohe Bay). There were also several smaller rooms in the main building on the shore of the bay, where we held classes. With our smaller number of PCTs—about forty-five trainees were left in Korea VIII—there were fewer classes. About half of the training staff had accompanied us, while the remainder was with the Korea VIIs, who had remained in Hilo for a week and flown to Oahu on December 21. The K-VIIs were now living with Korean host families in Honolulu, while we were at Camp Kokokahi. The two groups would later switch living arrangements.

The language study at Kokokahi was even more intensive than in Hilo. One of the best Korean language teachers, Sul Sang-soo, kept admonishing us that there were only a few weeks left of training, so we had to learn Korean "harder and faster." (Mr. Sul and I became good friends many years later when we both worked together as staff of the Korea XIX training program at the School for International Training in Putney, Vermont.)

Each afternoon we rode in buses back through the Pali Tunnels to the University of Hawaii on the leeward side of Oahu for lectures and classes at the English Language Institute there—part of the East-West Center. I was impressed by the University of Hawaii campus, as well as by the university students. The campus was modern, large, neat, and filled with attractive male and female students from all over the world, most of whom were Asian. After one week, the members of the Korea VII group joined us in these lectures and classes, although they had begun to live with Korean families in Honolulu. I was very happy to be reunited with my best friends among the trainees, many of whom were in the K-VII group that arrived on Oahu one week after the K-VIIIs' arrival. Just before dinner, when classes were over, the members of K-VIII hopped on the buses and returned to Camp Kokokahi. Area studies continued each evening at the camp.

On the Monday of Christmas week, the Korean community in Honolulu threw a stupendous party for all of us at the Korean consulate. It was a blast, complete with free drinks to loosen our reluctant tongues, more than two hundred Korean residents and students to speak Korean with, and a delicious Korean dinner. We had already learned that most Korean parties feature wild singing, usually by individuals (whose singing is greatly improved by the consumption of alcohol), and this one followed suit, finally turning into a singing contest of sorts. Our barbershop quartet was persuaded to sing several Korean songs, and despite many drinks beforehand—or perhaps because of the drinks— we performed fairly well and won the evening's prize—a bottle of after-shave lotion to split four ways. It was a lot of fun, and I was pleased to be able to talk with strangers in Korean and actually have them understand me.

After the party at the Korean consulate, I wondered if the warmth, gratitude, and concern toward us, expressed by virtually every Korean with whom I talked that evening, were typical of the peoples of all of the countries where Peace Corps Volunteers were serving. I was deeply moved by what I had experienced that evening. It seemed incredible that these complete strangers could care so much about us. Certainly, in my experiences in France and Sweden I had found the people friendly and helpful for the most part. What I was now experiencing was at a totally different level of intense feeling. The Koreans in Hawaii were genuinely and deeply happy to meet us, extremely pleased that we were going to Korea, and prepared to help us in whatever way possible. This initial experience was repeated again and again in Korea, when Koreans became aware that we were volunteer teachers.

The next evening—Christmas Eve—we had another huge party at the East-West Center for the entire combined groups. After lots of drinking and singing, late that night I found myself in Honolulu, bar hopping with several other trainees, about fifteen miles from Camp Kokokahi. Christmas morning I woke up on the couch of one of the students I had met. I was then faced with the problem of getting back to Camp Kokokahi, in the pouring rain, with no transportation available. The problem of Camp Kokokahi's isolated location was probably the biggest issue we faced on Oahu. As I have already mentioned, no buses or other transportation connected Honolulu with Kaneohe, and hitchhiking on Oahu, we were told, was strictly forbidden—probably because of all of the servicemen in Honolulu's vicinity.

I ended up taking a city bus as far as I could and then hitchhiked in the rain with amazing success. The first car that came along, at about nine o'clock in the morning, stopped to pick me up, and the woman who was driving not only invited me to her house for Christmas dinner that night but drove me all the way back to Camp Kokokahi. As it turned out, she and her husband were originally from Madison, Wisconsin, and had attended the University of Wisconsin. They were fellow Wisconsin Badgers! I spent a delightful evening with her family of seven, plus a German girl, a French girl, a Colombian boy, and a Hawaiian girl—all the last being students at the university. It was a wonderful social event, and of course, I was especially happy to meet several lovely girls in Honolulu. After two Christmas dinners (one at camp in the early afternoon), on Christmas night I waddled into bed quite bloated and full of good cheer!

Although it was possible to get news from the outside world during the training program, for me it was as though the rest of the world had almost disappeared during our intensive language study, area studies, and TESOL training. I did manage to follow the World Series, which was the last "pure" such event prior to the start of so-called divisional playoffs in 1969. We watched the final game in Hilo, as Detroit finally completed its comeback, from having been down three games to one, and beat St. Louis. And of course, 1968 was an election year. I was very upset that Richard Nixon prevailed over Hubert Humphrey. Even my father—a staunch Republican—did not vote for Nixon, because he thought he was dishonest.

On the day after Christmas we heard a bit of interesting news, for which we were all grateful. The crew of the USS *Pueblo* had been released by the North Koreans on December 23 and had walked across the so-called Freedom Bridge at Panmunjom to liberty shortly thereafter. The newspapers were full of accounts of their capture, imprisonment, and release. One story mentioned the food they had been given in captivity. Apparently, while we were munching on kimchee in Hilo and growing to like it, the members of the crew of the USS *Pueblo,* as they later recounted, were forced to exist in their North Korean prison on a diet of rice and what they described as "rotten, foul-smelling, highly spiced and inedible fermented cabbage and turnips"—all part of the torture they endured on a daily basis, according to the account. I guess context is important as to whether or not you like kimchee.

During the week between Christmas and New Year's day, the members of K-VII continued their living arrangements with Korean families in Honolulu, joining the K-VIIIs for language classes, TESOL training, and area studies at the East-West Center each day. The K-VIIIs stayed on at Camp Kokokahi, still complaining about the cramped quarters and isolation at the YMCA camp. I was so frustrated on Oahu by the tight schedule of language classes and classes at the University of Hawaii that just before New Year's Eve I took several hours off on three days, skipping some afternoon TESOL classes in order to visit Pearl Harbor, climb Diamond Head, and catch some sun on Waikiki Beach. I knew that once we began our practice teaching in the new year there would be no time for such diversions. I felt guilty about missing some of the training, but I felt a real need to get away by myself, and the staff gave me permission to be truant. I appreciated their flexibility and understanding.

While on my several excursions, I took a lot of pictures. My camera was an old East German-made Exacta, which I had been given by my brother years before when we worked together in Alaska's Brooks Range. On my visit to Pearl Harbor, the shutter became stuck. I spent several hours on the phone the next day, trying to find a camera store in Honolulu that could fix an Exacta. I was finally successful, but as I had no money, I had to borrow thirty dollars from Ed Klein, one of the American training staff, to pay for the repairs. Fortunately, the camera worked fine after I retrieved it from the store. My parents repaid Ed for my loan. That camera was perhaps the most important thing I had brought with me to take to Korea.

One afternoon, after having returned from a full day of classes in Honolulu, I was exploring the grounds at Camp Kokokahi and stumbled upon the boat building, which housed several canoes and sailboats. These were used at the camp, as part of the recreational program, when the YMCA camp was in session. Words cannot adequately express my excitement at finding those boats. I soon obtained permission to use the boats in my spare time and started to sail on Kaneohe Bay at every opportunity. The camp, however, required that there always be two persons in a boat, so my first task was to persuade some reluctant Korean and American staff friends, or other trainees, to accompany me. None of them had ever sailed before, and the sharks in the bay posed enough of a potential threat that I had some difficulty convincing anyone that I could sail competently. I think that the Koreans, especially, thought to themselves that, if my poor competency in Korean was any reflection of my other abilities, they would soon be shark food if they joined me.

The sailing was unbelievably superb! There was always a stiff breeze off the ocean, but the bay was protected from the open ocean by reefs, so the bay's surface was generally pretty calm. The boats were small dinghies, with a single sail—not the best, but adequate to get me out into the bay. I took a boat out over a dozen times in the remaining weeks at Kokokahi, and always took Ed Klein, or one of the Koreans or trainees, with me. We had a fantastic time, but the occasional shark made me a bit nervous and cautious. It was a bittersweet experience. I have never sailed in a more spectacular place, with the beautiful, blue bay beneath the sculptured cliffs of the Ko'olau Mountains, but at the same time, sailing brought the ache of my longing for Dariel, reminding me of the special moments we had had together in Madison on Lake Mendota.

On New Year's Eve we had a lively party. Everyone seemed to release all the pent-up emotions generated by thoughts of home during the holidays and by the stress of the past year. My group had been mostly separated from the other group since mid-December. This party was a kind of reunion, as well as being the last occasion in training that the combined groups (K-VII and K-VIII) could party together before K-VII's departure for Korea at the end of the first week in January. As with so many events of the next two years, I had mixed feelings of joy and sadness. While I enjoyed the party a lot, I was also sad to think of saying goodbye to so many Korean and American staff friends, many of whom I would not see again after another week. Although in all likelihood I would be seeing most of the K-VIIs in Korea, some of them would be deselected soon. Even for those I would meet again, once our service began, of course, it would not be the same as our training experience together.

The year 1969 started out on a promising note. I was placed with a delightful Korean family in Honolulu, with whom I would live for the next two weeks. I continued the area studies program at the East-West Center, as well as TESOL classes, and began to "practice-teach" at a Honolulu high school. In a typical day I would teach three morning classes at the high school, take a bus to the university for afternoon Korean language and TESOL classes, and then take a bus to my Korean family's home, arriving there about five o'clock each afternoon.

My family was the Chung family. I had an older "sister," Anna, who was about thirty years old—the same age as my real sister—and very attractive. I was extremely impressed by her. She was a doctor of optometry, single, and a member of the board of directors of the East-West Center (and 1968's chairman of the board). My Korean "mother," Mrs. Chung, who insisted that I call her *eomoni* (which means "mother" in Korean), spoke Korean with me all the time, although she was fluent in English. She was a widow—warm and very kind—who had come to Honolulu from Korea with her husband about 1930. They lived in a lovely, split-level house, rather high up in Manoa Valley, above the university campus, in a suburb of Honolulu that climbs beautifully up the side of a mountain. The view from their home was spectacular.

Anna was very interested in and supportive of the Peace Corps programs, especially in Asia and, of course, in Korea in particular. We had many long talks together. Mrs. Chung was a fine cook. We had delicious Korean meals every evening—my first exposure to home-cooked Korean food. Besides eating a lot of excellent Korean dishes, such as *bulgogi* (marinated, barbecued beef), *kalbi* (marinated, barbecued ribs), and *kimchee chigae* (a spicy soup), and speaking Korean in a family setting, I learned a tremendous amount about Korean art, since the Chungs had an extensive collection of old Korean art works, especially pottery.

My friend Yim Chun-bin, who had worked as a regional director in the Ministry of Cultural Preservation in Korea before joining the Peace Corps language staff, was astounded at the age and excellent condition of the pieces of art the Chungs showed him one evening. Dr. Chung had brought most of the collection from Korea in 1962, before the Korean regulations that prohibited the removal of art treasures. It was quite an education for me, knowing as little as I did then about artistic works, especially Korean art.

The Chungs were amazing. They had apparently left Korea without many resources, settled in Hawaii, and in one generation had become prosperous, intellectual leaders of the community. They were the first Korean-Americans I had ever met and gotten to know. I thought to myself that, if all Korean immigrants to the United States were like the Chung family, these people—as a race—were indeed very special.

During the two weeks that I lived with the Chungs, I taught English to newly arrived foreign students from Samoa, Korea, Japan, China, and the Philippines at several high schools in Honolulu. After some initial nervousness on both sides, all of my classes were responsive and engaging. We had lots of fun together. My classes averaged about twenty students. The students were of such mixed backgrounds and experience in English that it was almost impossible to plan something relevant to each of the levels of ability in English. I also found that many of the students spoke a kind of Pidgin English, which they used to communicate effectively by using English words but completely torturing pronunciation and syntax. It was difficult to teach the students who spoke this Pidgin English, because they had to unlearn so many bad speaking habits. Those students who spoke almost no English at all picked up correct pronunciation and grammar quickly, by comparison.

After two weeks of teaching, I must admit that I saw almost no improvement in my students' ability to speak English. Despite this frustrating fact, the teaching in Honolulu was one of the best experiences of my life. I thoroughly enjoyed the interaction with the students and getting to know them, and I think they found my classes stimulating and fun. My high-school students also provided a unique window into the world of Asian immigrants and their issues. I was fascinated and upset every day by what my students told me. I wish, in retrospect, that more of the Peace Corps training had been devoted to the invaluable practice teaching component at the high school, which turned out to be an effective, cross-cultural training element, as well.

I look back on the weeks with the Chung family, teaching in the high schools, and studying at the East-West Center as probably the most enjoyable part of the Peace Corps training program, probably because it was the most comfortable. The Chungs' home was luxurious by any standard, and every moment there I learned something from Mrs. Chung and Anna about Korean life, culture, and kindness. I enjoyed English teaching a lot and looked forward to every class. My students were friendly and needed me. Korean language classes continued for several hours each day at the University of Hawaii, which was a wonderful place to study. I enjoyed the cool weather—about sixty degrees and sunny with a soft breeze—and the lovely long muumuus and very short miniskirts on the coeds. The girls of the University of Hawaii compared favorably in appearance with the students at Wisconsin and Uppsala, Sweden—a different type of beauty but extremely appealing with their slim figures, oval eyes, and long, dark hair. I wished that those weeks could have continued indefinitely.

In October, upon the start of training, I had written to my Selective Service board in Buffalo to request permission to leave the United States. Such permission was required for all draft-age men in those days. Several trainees were in disputes with their draft boards regarding this permission, and mine was taking a long time to make up its mind. Although I had previously been granted a deferment based on my Peace Corps service, I could not leave the United States without formal permission from the Selective Service system. Finally, as I neared the end of my family stay in Honolulu and approached the last weeks of training before the planned departure for Korea, I received permission from my draft board to go to Korea. One more hurdle had been overcome.

On January 13, the K-VIIs left for Korea. Six were deselected at the last minute—one of my good friends got the axe unexpectedly, as did several other very good people and friends. I was quite shocked and sad when I heard the news. My group was told that the verdict on each of us would be given at the end of the third week in January. We waited anxiously.

In the meantime, there were lots of discussions among the training staff and the trainees as to which cities in Korea would be the best to live and work in. Being somewhat superstitious, I tried not to participate in these discussions. I didn't want to jinx my chances of surviving training by prematurely thinking about where I would be assigned. I also felt in my gut that no matter what information I received about potential assignment sites in Korea, there was no way I could even speculate in an informed manner about where I might be happiest as a volunteer in Korea, until I had actually spent time at the site, met co-teachers and students, and lived for a period with the family with whom I would be placed.

Others, however, seemed to revel in the banter about potential assignments. There were rumors that all of us would be placed in universities in Seoul. A week later, the opposite story was making the rounds. It seemed to most of us, based on advice from the Korean language staff, that it would probably be better to be working and living outside of Seoul somewhere, perhaps in a city that was a provincial capital, where life would be at a slower pace and the people and culture would be less Westernized and more authentically Korean. Several trainees were strongly hoping for a placement somewhere along Korea's southern coast, with its relatively warm climate. Others were hoping to be on Jeju Island—a volcanic island off the south coast with a semi-tropical climate and lovely beaches. Still others—the hikers and skiers in our group—opined that the spectacular mountains of the northeastern corner of Korea would be a delightful home for the next two years. When asked by the Korean staff about my preference, I always responded that I had no idea, which was absolutely the truth!

Several days after the departure of the K-VII group, we were called to a meeting, after our classes at the East-West Center. There the staff outlined the schedule for the remainder of the training. We were about to move back into the cabins at Camp Kokokahi for the last week of training in Hawaii. Then, on Monday, January 27, after getting the verdict on whether we were to become volunteers or be sent home, we would depart either for home or for Seoul.

Because of the proximity of Kimpo Airport, where we would be landing, to the border with North Korea—or more precisely, with the so-called Demilitarized Zone—night landings were not permitted, necessitating an overnight stay in Tokyo en route. Our arrival in Korea was planned for Wednesday, January 29 (we would lose a day when we crossed the dateline). On the very first weekend in Korea, we were advised, we would travel individually to our assigned university or college for a brief visit and to make contact with the institution's officials. Then we would return to Seoul for an additional two weeks of training, before joining our university or college to begin our two years of teaching.

Events did not quite work out as planned. On January 17, we said fond farewells to our high-school students, who had provided so much fun and satisfaction to our practice teaching, as well as to the regular teachers at our schools, who had been so kind in helping us to adjust to

Hawaiian schools. On the following Sunday we profusely thanked our Korean families in Honolulu for their wonderful hospitality during the past two weeks and assembled at the East-West Center to be driven by bus over to Camp Kokokahi. I was moved when Mrs. Chung began to cry as I said goodbye. It would be almost five years before I returned to Honolulu to thank the Chungs again and to tell them about my volunteer service in Korea.

Some of our group hated to return to the YMCA camp. For me, there had been good and bad experiences there during our initial stay. Certainly after the luxury of the Chungs' beautiful home, Mrs. Chung's delicious meals, and a certain degree of privacy, it was difficult to readjust to bunkroom living and cafeteria food. On the other hand, beautiful Kaneohe Bay and the mountains were still there, and the sailboats awaited me. During the remaining days in the United States, I spent several gorgeous afternoons on the bay, with the sail taut above me, the only sounds those of the water rushing by the bow, the wind snapping the lines, and the calls of the coots on the water.

The last week in Hawaii went extremely fast. We continued our Korean language classes for five or six hours each day, met repeatedly with the two psychologists, and tried to prepare—mentally and practically—for the upcoming departure for Korea. Each of us had been provided with a big black trunk during training—a kind of footlocker, with a locking top. We were told to pack the trunk with the clothes and other personal effects we wouldn't need for about three weeks, until we had settled into the living arrangements at the universities and colleges to which we would be assigned.

In our suitcases—limited to two each—which would accompany us to Seoul, we were to pack the clothes we would need for the first three weeks in country, including lots of warm winter clothing. The training staff had advised us that good winter boots were very cheap in Seoul, so most of us decided to forego any such purchases in Honolulu (where we probably couldn't find them anyway). I bought lots of film and packed it in my suitcases. In the trunk went much of the TESOL training material and area studies books, as well as clothes for the rest of the year. After three days of careful packing, including a list of what was packed where, I was ready.

In the last several days at Camp Kokokahi I wrote dozens of letters to family and friends at home, giving them the names of my new Korean friends, many of whom hoped to stay on in the United States to study, or at least to sightsee for a month or so. Buffalo would be a popular destination, due to its proximity to Niagara Falls, and I wanted my family to be prepared to host the Koreans, who had been so kind to me for the last four months in Hawaii. One of the youngest of our Korean language teachers—Chung Ho-jung—was secretly engaged to be married to a Korean man in Eggertsville, New York—a suburb of Buffalo. I knew Eggertsville well and was very familiar with the street (Cambridge Drive) where she would be living. Two other friends—Kim Hae-shik and Chang Hae-ung—were hoping to study in North America and expected to visit Buffalo. (Hae-shik ended up at the University of Illinois, and Hae-ung settled in Toronto.)

At the direction of the training staff, we wrote home to advise our families how best to contact us in an emergency. Telephone service to Korea was almost nonexistent, and what existed was very expensive. We told our parents and friends to call Peace Corps' Office of Special Services (OSS) in Washington DC in an emergency. That office could reach us quickly through the American embassy in the event of a death at home or some other emergency. (As I wrote home with this information, I didn't suspect that almost four years later I would be an officer in OSS at Peace Corps headquarters for one year and then the Korea desk officer for the next five years.)

On my last weekend in Hawaii I had a fine lunch with a distant, older cousin—Professor Margaret Ayrault—who was a librarian and educator at the University of Hawaii. I had promised my father and my Aunt Kate that I would visit her while in Hawaii. She was a fascinating person, a well-known professor of library science, and lots of fun to talk with over lunch. I wished that I had been able to meet her sooner. I had just been told in the morning by the training staff that I had successfully completed the stateside part of training and would be going to Korea, so I was in a happy, excited mood, and my cousin and I celebrated with glasses of wine.

I told her, while we ate lunch, how amazed I was at the warmth and hospitality of Hawaiians in general, and of Korean Hawaiians especially. During our Peace Corps training program, the people of Hilo and of the Big Island, and more recently the people of Oahu, had opened their homes and their hearts to the Peace Corps trainees in our groups. This was such an unexpected outpouring of affection and support that most of us were still in a state of shock. I thought about this aspect of our training a lot, wondering why we were the beneficiaries of such fond attention. My cousin felt that part of what we were experiencing came from Hawaiians' natural hospitality, part from the economic reality that Peace Corps' training programs were good for local economies, and part from the respect that most people had for the Peace Corps itself, for its ideals, and for people who volunteered their service. In any event, on that last Saturday in Hawaii I was overwhelmed with gratitude for the emotional and physical support furnished by the people of Hawaii—especially the Korean Hawaiians—over the past almost four months.

On Sunday, January 26, I finished packing the trunk and my suitcases and went for a last sail on Kaneohe Bay. In the late afternoon I joined my Korean family at their home in Manoa Valley for a lovely dinner. The next morning, the Chungs and many other Korean families were at the airport to see us all off, together with the Korean and American members of the training staff. Only one of the K-VIII group had been deselected at the last minute, which compared favorably with the K-VII group, which had lost six at the last minute. Our group now had forty members left of the original sixty-seven at the start of training almost four months before.

The weather that day was unusually cool for Hawaii—about fifty degrees, with sunny skies. Mrs. Chung could not remember it having been that cool before. As we said goodbye, she told me to give her love to her homeland, and she cried. We all sang the Korean national anthem at the airport together. I was too excited to be sad. I looked for Dariel's face in the airport crowd—by now an old, wistful habit whenever I saw a crowd—as the plane taxied away from the terminal.

Then the sadness hit me. Our group's official song was John Denver's "Leaving on a Jet Plane," sung by the group known as Peter, Paul, and Mary. I whispered it to myself, as I thought of Dariel: "So kiss me and smile for me, tell me that you'll wait for me, hold me like you'll never let me go. 'Cause I'm leaving on a jet plane, don't know when I'll be back again, oh baby, I hate to go ..."

We arrived in Tokyo on Tuesday night in the midst of a snowstorm. Korea and Japan were reeling under a major storm with high winds and lots of snow that stranded us in Tokyo for two days and two nights. We were told that in order to land safely at Kimpo Airport, the weather had to be clear with calm winds. No one wanted to be blown inadvertently across the Demilitarized Zone!

In Tokyo we stayed at the Prince Takanawa Hotel, which was perhaps the most luxurious hotel I had ever stayed in. We had beautifully appointed private rooms, delicious meals in the hotel's elegant restaurants, and marvelously cold weather, with lots of gorgeous snow! Downtown Tokyo astounded us with its crowds of bundled-up people, modern buildings, neon lights, scintillating nightlife, and winter beauty. It seemed a bigger, more crowded version of New York City, and we loved it as we roamed for two days without classes.

On Thursday morning we were told that the weather had cleared in Korea, after dumping the most snow on Seoul since weather recordings had started in 1907. About twenty-six centimeters of snow had fallen (just over ten inches). Only ten inches of snow? A blizzard? For a guy raised in Buffalo, where we routinely had snows each year of well more than one foot, it was hard to understand that for Seoul the storm had been such a big deal, closing the airport for two days. On the other hand, it was certainly a blessing to have had several days in Tokyo to recover from the long flight from Hawaii and to begin to get accustomed to the crowded cities of the Far East.

We boarded the Pan American plane for Seoul on January 29, two days behind schedule, but not terribly upset about the brief vacation in Japan. It was a short flight of just less than two hours to Seoul, Korea. We looked down on Korea's snow-covered mountains with eager anticipation as the staff members who were accompanying us gently reminded us that the less said to Koreans about our positive impressions of Tokyo the better. (As we had learned in training, Japan and Korea had been historic enemies for centuries. Moreover, Koreans had not forgotten the murder of the Korean Empress in 1895 by Japanese officials and the brutal Japanese occupation of Korea from 1910 to 1945, both of which had left a burning hatred of Japan on the part of all Koreans.)

From the plane's window I saw my first terraced rice paddies, which looked like inviting steps, chiseled into the snow by some gigantic shovel, up the sides of Korea's beautiful mountains.

"Hilo Esos" Brian Copp, Jim Gahn, Jon Moody, and me, Hilo, Hawaii, November 1968

Taekwondo Students, Hilo, Hawaii, November 1968

Seoul, January 1969

American Military Escort near the Demilitarized Zone (DMZ),
Korea, January 1969

Sign at Freedom Bridge near Panmunjom, Korea, January 1969

Freedom Bridge, DMZ, Korea, January 1969

Buildings at Panmunjom, DMZ, Korea, January 1969

PCT Jan Justice Sitting in North Korea at the Negotiations Table,
Panmunjom, DMZ, Korea, January 1969

# Chapter Four—Arrival in Seoul

We landed at Kimpo Airport late on Thursday afternoon. The airport building and runways were covered in fresh snow. The sun was shining brightly under clear skies. I have always loved snow in January. My family's house in Buffalo usually had a six- to twelve-foot pile of snow next to the front porch and front sidewalk most of the winter. My first impression of Korea was of lots of snow. It was a good, homey feeling. Seoul reminded me immediately of a wintry, larger version of Rutland, Vermont, surrounded as it was by low mountains, located next to a frozen river, and covered by cleansing whiteness, like Rutland. The below zero temperature and biting wind also felt like New England in winter, as we exited the plane and headed for the terminal.

What shocked me at the airport were the bunkers, with their anti-aircraft guns everywhere, the tightly guarded, camouflaged, fighter plane hangers, and the tough-looking Republic of Korea (ROK) soldiers with automatic rifles and submachine guns slung over their shoulders. Soldiers stood at crisp attention at each door and at intervals of about thirty feet throughout the terminal—hundreds of soldiers everywhere. This was definitely not Vermont but a nation at war. I didn't expect this display of military strength.

Although we were somewhat prepared to encounter evidence of both extreme poverty and a tremendously militarized state in Seoul, it was equally shocking to see so many modern military jeeps, tanks, and other military vehicles sharing the roads with oxcarts, old buses, pushcarts, ancient trucks, horse-drawn wagons, and bicycles laden with huge loads of every conceivable type of cargo. It was a strange mix of new and old, wealth and poverty.

As we drove from Kimpo Airport to downtown Seoul, we saw hundreds of small houses and tiny shops lining the major thoroughfares, as well as the narrower side streets and alleys that led into the main streets like so many crooked streams feeding into congested rivers. An occasional building of up to ten floors high stuck up like an intruding pinnacle from the sea of tile-lined roofs, many of which were slightly raised at each end, and partially covered with snow, giving an overall wavy effect to the rows of black, single level snow-splotched roofs marching up the sides of the hills. The taller buildings became more and more numerous as our buses neared the downtown area. Few buildings, however, were higher than ten stories. Mixed in with the newer, bland Western-style buildings was an occasional old building with heavy-lidded swooping tile roofs.

Thousands of people were in the streets. Some were well dressed with warm coats. Others wore little more than rags. Feet wore boots, a tremendous variety of shoes, or what looked like thin, rubber slippers with slightly pointed toes. Groups of people warmed their hands around barrels with fires in them that lined the sidewalks, giving off clouds of black smoke and the acrid smell of burning kerosene. Vendors seemed to be on all sides, selling foods and merchandise of every type.

Our buses slowly made their way through the congested streets to a place called Shin Chon Rotary, near Yonsei University. We were housed in Korean-style small hotels, or *yogwans*, located on Shin Chon Rotary, which was a large confluence of several major streets, or traffic rotary. "Korean style" meant that we slept two to a room, in small rooms, approximately nine feet by nine feet, on a very comfortable, thin mattress called a *yo*, beneath a warm comforter called an *ibul*. The floor of the room was heated from beneath at night. A room with such a heated floor was called an *ondol pang*, as the subfloor heating system was known as *ondol*, and the word for room was *pang*. There was no other furniture in the room, and during the day there was so little heat, especially with the outside temperature below zero, I could see my breath. But at night, on the heated floor, I was toasty warm. A single fluorescent light fixture in the middle of the ceiling gave us a cool light at night. We removed our shoes at the entrance to the room.

The toilet was down the hall and consisted of a porcelain fixture in the floor, over which you squatted to do your business. You pulled a chain to flush. There was no toilet paper. Sometimes you could use a torn up newspaper to clean your bottom, but that could leave ink stains on your rear end. I soon learned to carry a packet of Kleenex wherever I went in Korea. Although I didn't know it during that first week in Seoul, while I was fussing to myself about how uncomfortable and smelly these squatting facilities were, in the future I would be grateful to have *any indoor toilet*, since most of my future stays in yogwans outside Seoul featured outdoor facilities with a smell that made your eyes water.

One good thing about Korean toilets was increased efficiency—you were in no mood to read while you were doing your business because the position was so uncomfortable. The goal was to squat, complete what you were about, and get up and out as soon as possible, saving countless hours that most Americans waste, comfortably resting on sit-down toilets and reading magazines or catalogues.

For food, we were pretty much on our own. Our ears still rang with the training staff's cautionary admonitions to be very, very careful what food we ate, to eat only cooked foods (no raw fish), and to drink only boiled liquids (with no ice under any circumstances). We had a meager daily allowance with which to buy meals. There were lots of small restaurants of many types on the narrow alleys and broader boulevards that connected to the rotary. These were of many types and levels of quality. Most were small restaurants with ten tiny tables or so and corresponding chairs in a plain, unadorned room, where you came in, sat down, ordered, and ate. These restaurants had potbellied stoves in the midst of the tables. Patrons crowded around the tables closest to the stoves to stay warm.

Other restaurants were more traditional in style, where you removed your shoes in the vestibule, stepped up onto an ondol floor, sat cross-legged on the floor at low tables, and were served by friendly women, eager to help you select a delicious meal. Such restaurants were often beautifully decorated with Korean art. Peace Corps had armed us with several mimeographed pages of the names of food that we would find in Seoul's restaurants and of explanations of exactly what the food was. These pages were helpful, particularly in avoiding the restaurants that featured *poshintang*, or cooked dog.

Most restaurants had the same food for the morning, lunchtime, and evening meals, largely based on rice, noodles, bean curd, vegetables, and meats. Each meal featured *banchan* (side dishes) that accompanied steam-cooked, short-grain rice, often with several kinds of kimchee. The cuisine invariably involved rich seasoning with sesame oil, *doenjang* (fermented soybean paste), soy sauce, salt, garlic, ginger, and *gochujang* (red chili paste). After several days of sampling a lot of spicy foods, my stomach told me to slow down, so I started to frequent Chinese restaurants, with their blander fried rice, noodle, or dumpling dishes. I began to miss fresh fruit, fruit juices, eggs, bacon, hamburgers, milk, Coca Cola, ice cream, and a lot of other American foods that I had previously appreciated in my life, which were difficult to find in Seoul.

We spent almost three weeks in Seoul for our final training and orientation. Each morning we had three hours of Korean language classes at the Korean Language Institute (KLI) of Yonsei University, with some of our former teachers and some new teachers. Every afternoon we practiced teaching at Myongi University, with volunteer Korean university students as our victims. In the evening we had time to explore Seoul's beer halls, nightclubs, and tearooms, with an occasional evening lecture at Yonsei regarding Korean culture, history, and economic development.

Among my favorite lecturers during these weeks was a brilliant, tall, handsome professor at Yonsei named Hahm Byung-choon, who salted his lectures about Korea with humorous stories of his student days at Harvard and pleas for understanding of Korean etiquette and beliefs. I got to know him quite well. (Professor Hahm, who was obviously a great friend and admirer of Peace Corps and the United States, subsequently went on to become the Korean Ambassador to the United States and, still later, Chief of Staff to Korea's President Chun Doo-hwan. Tragically, North Koreans assassinated him during an official visit in Rangoon, Burma, in 1983.)

Another favorite lecturer was Father Terry Doyle, who was a Catholic priest teaching at Sogang University in Seoul. Father Doyle struck me, at first, as a typical Irish priest who loved to laugh and drink. He also clearly loved Korea and Koreans, spoke excellent Korean, and, over the course of several lectures, told us of his perceptions and experiences of Korean culture in a frank and humorous way that immediately endeared him to all of us. (Father Doyle left the priesthood in later years and became a Peace Corps official in Washington DC, where we became good friends.)

To get to our classes at Myongi and to sightsee in Seoul, we learned to navigate the city's amazing bus system, which featured three distinct classes of buses (with young girls as conductors)—ranging from standing only to roomy seating, and the wildest drivers in the universe. Needless to say, we traveled by the most crowded and cheapest kind of bus, more often than not sharing the bus with twice as many passengers as the bus could reasonably hold, assorted chickens, and every kind of produce that you can imagine. The fare was twenty-five *won* (the Korean unit of currency), or about eight cents, and you could use a transfer to continue your trip in one direction. The price was unbeatable! I came to admire the young female conductors, called *chajang*, who were experts at packing passengers onto the buses with broad smiles and good humor, as well as at helping the drivers maneuver out of outrageous traffic snarls by leaning out of the back doors, with their hands thumping on the buses' sides and calls of *ohri ohri* (all right, all right) to guide the drivers.

We soon found that Korean social life for students and teachers centered around the ubiquitous tearoom, or *tabang*, where you could get an assortment of beverages—from coffee and tea to Korean soft drinks and more exotic concoctions, depending on the tearoom. I still recall being asked by one lovely tearoom hostess one morning if I would like some morning coffee. She was speaking to me in Korean, but I clearly understood the words "morning coffee," even with Korean pronunciation. That sounded good to me, so I ordered a cup. She returned with a cup of steaming coffee and a raw egg, which, as I watched in disbelief, she broke into the cup of hot coffee. Raw egg in coffee, I found out, is morning coffee. It was the last time I ordered morning coffee in Korea.

Everyone hung out in tearooms. In most, friendly tearoom ladies or girls—hostesses—welcomed you as you entered with cries of *ososayo* ("welcome," or literally "come"), seated you in comfortable chairs around small tables, and took your order while making small talk about the weather, how nice you look, how sad they have been because of the infrequency of your visits, and when you will return. Most tearooms also featured good music: Korean or Western classical music, jazz, pop songs, and other musical genre, depending on the tearoom. For the equivalent of about fifteen cents you could spend an entire evening in a tearoom, talking with friends and with the hostesses, listening to excellent music, and warming yourself near the charcoal stoves inside. Tabangs became a favorite hangout of mine. There was one on almost every block, and they had interesting names, such as "Pine Tree Tearoom," "Beethoven Tearoom," "Doraji Tearoom," or "Peace Tearoom."

They also had telephones. Since almost no Korean had a telephone at home, the neighborhood tabang served as a public telephone, where messages could be left for friends and neighbors and where social or business telephone calls could be made. The tabang ladies would frequently canvass the tearoom for a customer, for whom a telephone call was waiting.

One very interesting aspect of Koreans' use of telephones was their telephone voices. All Koreans shouted into the telephone, as though the person on the other end was deaf. Women tended to raise the pitch of their voices to a much higher level than used in ordinary conversations. As a result, every patron in the tabang could hear all of the telephone conversations quite clearly.

Our Myongi University students made sure that we visited several tearooms a week with them to practice English conversation. The tearooms also provided a quiet refuge from the crowded streets and sidewalks of Seoul. From the end of the military curfew each morning at about four o'clock until the curfew sirens went off at midnight, the streets were jammed with vehicles, and the sidewalks were cheek to jowl with people. I had never before seen crowds of people like this, except perhaps as people exited from Dartmouth football games in Hanover or from Bills' games in Buffalo. New York City's sidewalks at rush hour had about one third of the congestion of Seoul's sidewalks.

Koreans were aggressive walkers. I had often in the past been amused by watching what I called "contact avoidance" strategies by pedestrians in cities, such as Stockholm, Copenhagen, Amsterdam, London, and Paris. In those cities people walking on sidewalks could easily be seen to alter their paths—sometimes quite far in advance of an encounter—to move around groups of people in the way or to avoid contact with on-coming pedestrians. Not so in Seoul! If you were in the way of an oncoming Korean pedestrian, the person would bump right into you, try to walk through you as if you didn't exist, or elbow their way through, without a second thought or hint of apology. In the marketplaces the degree and severity of contact was ratcheted up several notches—almost to the level of Canadian hockey.

I have always liked to walk and to move with long strides, if possible. To walk several blocks in Seoul—a distance of perhaps one-quarter mile—took half an hour sometimes, because of the crowds and the detours across overpasses or through pedestrian tunnels under the major intersections. Few streets had traffic lights or any semblance of pedestrian crosswalks. Those that did were not places where pedestrians dared to cross, since a red light seemed to be a signal to taxicabs and buses to speed up, rather than stop.

On the positive side, you were almost always within several steps of a tearoom. These were often located on the second floor, above retail shops, on the main thoroughfares, or nestled cozily up little alleys, away from the noise, dirt, and bustle of the streets. When you opened the door to the tearoom, it was like entering another world, where sanity, politeness, and relaxation ruled—except for the noisy telephone calls.

On our first Sunday in Korea—Groundhog Day—there was a surprise announcement early in the morning. For security reasons we had not been told beforehand, but right after breakfast we boarded buses at Shin Chon Rotary and drove north to the Demilitarized Zone (DMZ). This would be a very special trip. The area of the DMZ had been closed to visitors for the past year, because 1968 had seen more than one hundred eighty serious incidents at or around the DMZ, making the previous year the most violent in Korea's border areas since the armistice in 1953.

It was a cold, clear sunny day with no wind. The bright light from the reflection of sunlight on the deep snow hurt my eyes. The temperature was ten degrees below zero. As we drove north along a highway from Seoul, we passed hundreds of so-called tank traps on all sides of the road. These were fortifications, apparently designed to keep tanks and other armored vehicles out of certain areas and concentrated in other areas. Some of these traps looked like a set of strange teeth from a distance. Our guide, who was a young American army captain, called them "dragon's teeth." There were rows and rows of them. We also passed other concrete fortifications and miles of barbed wire and concertina wire designed to deter infantry. Sometimes the buses passed between concrete structures, which were pre-wired to be blown up in case of an attack from the north, so as to prevent the use of the road, we were told.

The terrain we drove through reminded me of the green mountains of Vermont in winter. On both sides were lovely—though treeless—mountains. We snaked through valleys, across small bridges (all wired to be blown up), and past several military camps. All were exquisitely draped in dazzling snow. Every other mile, it seemed, we went through a checkpoint, sometimes manned by United Nations Command soldiers in blue helmets, sometimes by ROK army soldiers in white helmets, and sometimes by American military personnel in dark green helmets. As we drove, the chatter on the buses, which had started out at a high volume, grew quieter and quieter. The small isolated villages that we passed through became fewer and fewer until they disappeared completely after half an hour. It was a surreal experience—incredibly bleak winter beauty on all sides, punctuated by the presence of war machines and personnel.

As we neared the DMZ, we were told that on the day of the arrival of the K-VIIIs in Seoul last week, North Korean Radio broadcast our names from Pyongyang (the capital of North Korea), calling us CIA agents and enemies of the Korean people. I wondered if they used our American names or our Korean names in the broadcast. North Korea lay just ahead.

For the final several miles we were escorted by several jeeps and by a truck bristling with American soldiers. They were all really tall and strapping young Americans. One reminded me of my Dartmouth classmate Bill Smoyer, whose death I have already mentioned. I didn't see anyone shorter than about six feet four inches tall! They wore heavy parkas, huge gloves, and sunglasses, and every soldier carried an automatic rifle. On the warm bus, I thought that these soldiers must be extremely cold in the open jeeps and the truck as we crawled up a very narrow road, paralleling the frozen Imjin River just to our north, through open fields and pockets of pine and hardwood trees. Finally, we came to a one-way, single-span bridge called Freedom Bridge, which crossed the Imjin River and linked the village of Panmunjom with South Korea. We were reminded that only six weeks before, the crew of the USS *Pueblo* had walked to freedom across this bridge.

The buses drove down what was called Liberty Lane, between Freedom Bridge and the site of ongoing negotiations between the United Nations Command and North Korea, in the so-called joint security area at Panmunjom. The buses parked some distance from a cluster of low buildings, painted blue. We walked on crunchy snow for about one hundred yards to the main building, walked inside, and inspected the room and table where negotiations occurred. There was a line drawn through the room, indicating the division between the North and the South. Jan Justice—one of our group—and I nervously crossed the line into North Korea with one step and quickly retreated. Justice was not a welcome presence, we sensed, in North Korea. Some of us sat down at the table—the shape of which had been the subject of arduous negotiations—where so many lengthy and momentous talks had taken place.

Through the windows of the building to the north we could see North Korean guards standing at attention in their olive-green uniforms and red-starred hats. They seemed both curious and ferocious. The United Nations soldiers were friendly but tough looking. There was no doubt that the guards on both sides had been handpicked for their size and fierce appearance. In talking with our military escorts, I discovered that they considered duty at the DMZ both a privilege and somewhat pleasant. They said that the countryside was lovely, that they enjoyed special food and comparatively good living arrangements, and that morale there was the best in Korea, despite the dangerous proximity to North Korea.

On the return trip to Seoul, we stopped at the United Nations compound and were treated to a magnificent, lavish dinner of American food. It had only been six days since we left Hawaii, but already I was starved for food from home! The personnel of the United Nations Command were very kind and gracious. We unknowingly continued a well-established Peace Corps/Korea tradition of completely pigging out on the buffet set before us. I think we ate on that February 2 with such ferocity that any groundhogs in the area—regardless of any appearance of a shadow—would have immediately retreated into their burrows, fearful of being eaten by us, guaranteeing another six weeks of winter.

Every day in Seoul, after our return from the DMZ, brought new sensations and sights. Our daily classes were generally enjoyable. The students were fun and dedicated to learning English, but the classrooms were cold—often heated by a single, small stove, around which the twenty or thirty students tried to keep warm with us. Regular university classes were not in session.

In Korea, the schools closed from Christmas until early March— the coldest part of the year—and from July until early September, the hottest months of the year—because the school buildings were neither heated nor air-conditioned. Our students at Myongi University were volunteers, helping us in our practice teaching in exchange for the chance to learn English. Seeing them shivering in my classes made me appreciate their generosity and their desire to learn—qualities I invariably found in my Korean students over the next two years.

Language classes continued at the KLI every morning for several hours. Yonsei University had central heat! Of course, being surrounded by Korean speakers, we were immediately able to practice in the streets of Seoul what we learned each day in the classroom. I sensed that my Korean language ability, which had leveled off after reaching a kind of plateau about two weeks before we arrived in Korea, began to improve slowly once again.

One example of my new horizons in language was my experience in a bathhouse. We spent several days in language classes at KLI, learning what to say and what to do in order to take a bath in Korea. Korean homes and most Korean-style hotels did not have showers or other bathing facilities, except for simple washbasins. Sometimes hot water was available, for shaving and washing, from large kettles in which water was heated on small stoves. Often there was no hot water. To cleanse their entire bodies, at least once a week, Koreans go to a bathhouse, where there is usually lots of hot water, a pool of very hot water for soaking, and, sometimes, even showers.

Bathhouses were identifiable by their tall chimneys. Men bathed on the men's side of the building; women bathed on the women's side. For a small fee you were provided with a locker or box in which to place your clothes and with a large towel and washcloth. You draped yourself in the towel and entered the public bathing room itself, taking off your towel and sitting on a stool or squatting in the area for cleaning yourself, soaping up, and shampooing. This area was quite separate from the large, heated pool for soaking, which you entered only after thoroughly cleaning and rinsing yourself. Most of the men in the bathing area were scrubbing every inch of themselves with the washcloth, in silence, as though they intended to remove all of their skin. This process took fifteen or more minutes. Then, basins of water were used to rinse their bodies, or they moved to showers along one wall, so as to remove all soap and dirt, before stepping into the heated pool. The water in the pool was extremely hot—almost scalding hot. I could barely stand it! After several minutes of being boiled alive, you got out of the pool, dried yourself off, and exited to the locker room to dress and cool down.

Although I enjoyed the bathhouse experience in Seoul, where the presence of dozens of foreigners seemed to be taken for granted by the Korean men there, I enjoyed even more each evening's activities, which during the entire first week quite spoiled us. Almost every night there was a reception or dinner of some sort where we met Korean education ministry officials, American embassy officials, and Peace Corps/Korea officials. At one of these we were fortunate to meet the Nobel Prize- and Pulitzer Prize-winning author Pearl Buck, who was visiting the foundation she created to support Korean children of mixed blood.

The most important people we met during this first week were the Peace Corps director, Kevin O'Donnell, and his wife, Ellen, and the deputy director, Wayne Olson, and his wife, Yvonne. Both wives were friendly, attractive, and like big sisters or mothers to the volunteers. In our meetings with Director O'Donnell and Deputy Director Olson, we were told what their expectations of us were, what the next few weeks would involve, and what we could expect of them. Both men, I felt, were people I would be delighted to serve under. They were warm, smart, and tolerant, with outstanding people skills. You could immediately tell they were both respected and loved by the Peace Corps staff and current volunteers.

We found the rest of the staff of the Peace Corps—Americans and Koreans—also extremely helpful. Our contact with them was limited to a couple of meetings in these first weeks in the country. During my entire Peace Corps service, in fact, with a couple of notable exceptions,

I hardly ever met them again. But they administered the entire program and did so with great energy and expertise. I never had a complaint about the staff in Seoul or in the regional Peace Corps offices and felt that all of them were very tolerant of the gripes and problems raised by the approximately three hundred volunteers then in Korea.

Despite the friendly students, Peace Corps staff, and KLI teachers, I felt quite depressed at moments during the first several weeks in Korea. It was exciting to experience so much that was totally foreign, and I enjoyed all of the attention and the receptions. At the same time, the grinding poverty all around us—beggars and small children with hardly any clothes or footwear in the sub-zero temperatures—and the presence of so many police and soldiers everywhere—literally on every block and at the doorways of every public building—were together very disturbing. Combined with the difficulty of keeping warm in the unheated classrooms and the generally unfamiliar food, the poverty, and the military state slowly began to unnerve me. I found myself wanting to stay in my room at the yogwan, and write letters and read instead of taking the long walks around the city that I had usually enjoyed in foreign surroundings in the past in France, Sweden, and Denmark. I was experiencing culture shock, I realized after several days. We had been taught during training that one of the symptoms was a desire to withdraw from the unfamiliar. Well, that was happening to me, in my second week in Korea, and it took me a while to understand what was happening.

In the middle of my first bout with culture shock, we were advised of our future assignments and told to prepare for a quick visit to the schools where we would be teaching. That snapped me out of my funk. I was assigned to teach at the Language Institute of the English Department in the Liberal Arts College of Kyungpook National University. Kyungpook was located in Daegu. I was extremely happy with my assignment. One of my best friends during training was language teacher Kim Hae-shik, who was from Daegu and had told me a lot of wonderful things about the city and the province—North Gyeongsang Province—where it was located. I was ready to go to Daegu, home of Daegu Kim.

Between Groups VII and VIII, there were eight volunteers assigned to colleges and universities in Daegu. Three K-VIIIs were assigned to Kyungpook National University. Moe Cain and Russ Feldmeier would be teaching in the English department of the Teachers College. I would be the sole PCV teaching at the Liberal Arts College. Rachel and Peter Wenz, K-VIIs, would be teaching English at the Kyungpook University Medical College. I would have company for the next two years, although the four other volunteers at Kyungpook would be teaching in different colleges of the university, and I would hardly ever see them at the university, as it turned out. Mary Franz, K-VII, was assigned to teach in the English department of a small, Catholic women's college, Hyosung Women's College. K-VIIIs John and Jan Justice were assigned to teach at a Presbyterian college: Keimyung College. All of us were pleased with the assignment to Daegu.

The reaction of my students and faculty colleagues at Myongi University was, without exception, shock that I was going to be assigned outside of Seoul, in Korea's hinterland. They expressed great concern that I could never live for two years in Korea anywhere outside of Seoul and survive. The food and water will be dangerous, and the people will not accept foreigners, they warned; Daegu is the hottest place in Korea in the summer, and the coldest in winter, they fretted. All were sure I would be extremely unhappy in Daegu.

On our second Saturday in Seoul, those of our group who had been assigned to schools outside Seoul headed to the Seoul Station with an overnight bag. At the station each of us put our language training to good use, buying our own ticket to our destination cities on the local train, which stopped at every small city along the way but was much cheaper than the express train. We had practiced buying train and bus tickets hundreds of times in Korean language class. Happily, the ticket tellers seemed to know that a lot of Americans, who spoke poor Korean, were in desperate need of help. I still recall, when I began my memorized request for a ticket, that the teller quickly responded by complimenting me on my good Korean—a response that was not in the script and totally unexpected. That stopped me in my tracks.

It was a compliment, thereafter, that we all heard over and over from virtually any Korean with whom we tried to strike up a conversation. If we could get over the first hurdle—communicating that we were actually trying to speak Korean, despite our abominable pronunciation—the reaction on the part of the Korean to whom we were speaking was always surprise, and then a gracious, profuse (and wholly unjustified) compliment. I was not expecting that Koreans would be so surprised and pleased at our poor attempts to speak Korean. I thought of the contrast between the Koreans' attitude and that of the French people, especially in Paris, who were always so disdainful of anyone speaking poor French.

With our tickets in hand, the next challenge was boarding the train and finding a seat. It seemed as though thousands of people were trying to board the train to Daegu and would do almost anything to be sure they got a seat. It was a free-for-all! Finally we found seats, although not together. The train was clean, on time, and packed with passengers, as well as baggage of all kinds, including a lot of live farm produce.

Initially during the four and a half hour trip to Daegu, I felt conflicting emotions about speaking to anyone on the train. On the one hand, I love to talk with people when I travel. On the other hand, I was nervous about practicing my relatively untested Korean and afraid of looking foolish. Finally, my curiosity and natural garrulousness won out. I tried to strike up a conversation with the three older Korean women who shared the nearby seats—one next to me and two facing me. They were delightful, once they understood that I was not what, I am sure, they initially thought: some halfwit, demented foreigner intent on bombarding them with some strange gibberish for the entire trip.

After asking if I could practice my Korean with them, and getting what I took to be a tentative yes, I asked them all the questions that we had prepared for so long in language classes—about their destination, hometowns, family, marriage, children, and work, and they asked me what in the world I was doing on a train to Daegu and where I had learned to speak Korean.

As I recall, the conversation went something like this, with some eye-popping mistakes by me:

> Them: "Where are you from?"
> Me: "I was an American Peace Corps Volunteer."
> Them: "What? We don't understand."
> Me: "I teach English at Kyungpook National University in Daegu."
> Them: "What is he saying? I think he may be crazy."
> Me: "Where is your hometown?"

Them: "We are from Korea?"

Me: "Have you all eaten noodles?" (Trying to ask if they were all married—noodles being a traditional dish for festive occasions like weddings.)

Them: (Laughter) "Yes, we have eaten noodles. Are you married?"

Me: "I am not an egg."

I think that by the end of the trip, after I had repeated myself a dozen times and with some help from them, they understood that I was an English teacher, who was part of some strange, voluntary, service organization, and who expected to stay in Daegu for two years. None of them had met an American before. I was struck by their faces—heavily creased, sun-browned faces, with something in their eyes that I could not identify clearly at first. I later concluded that these middle-aged women had humor, resignation, and above all, determination in their eyes.

The conversation on this first train trip was my first opportunity in Korea for a sustained conversation with older Koreans. It was immediately apparent that the world of these three women was totally different from my world. Their experiences and outlook were wholly foreign to me. At the same time, I felt a close empathy with them. It was as though my genes were telling me that these were sisters—truly part of my own family's ancestral heritage. Sometime in the past we had shared a common ancestor, and my genes had recognized theirs.

I also recall my first impressions of the snowbound countryside south of Seoul. I was fascinated by the miles and miles of terraced rice paddies that flashed by the train, as well as by the small villages and cities we passed through, with their narrow, dirt roads, stone walls, and small mud houses—some with colorful tiled roofs and many more with straw-thatched roofs. Even in the snow I could see that every square foot of land that could possibly be farmed was being cultivated, right up to the edge of the stone walls, surrounding the farming villages, and right up the sides of the mountains—in most cases the bottom third of each mountainside was terraced into rice paddies.

At the railroad crossings there were no flashing lights or barriers to stop traffic. The whistle of the steam locomotive served as the only warning of the oncoming train. The whistle reminded me of childhood nights in Ontario, Canada, when I lay in a bunk in my parents' cabin on the northern shore of Lake Erie in the 1950s, listening to the distant, haunting whistle of freight trains approaching rural road crossings. Here, the lines of traffic at each crossing, waiting for the train to pass, included ox-drawn carts, rickety old trucks and buses, old motor scooters, and many bicycles, even in the packed snow and ice on the road surfaces. As soon as we left the Seoul environs, the military vehicles and the more modern trucks and buses—so prevalent in the big capital city—seemed to disappear.

As we traveled south, more and more mountains loomed on each side of the tracks. We crossed wide, shallow rivers encased in snow and ice. Some had groves of trees growing near them—trees that looked scraggly and ill-formed, as though they had been trimmed to death. But at least there were trees! If there were trees, there might be birds, I thought. In Seoul I had searched in vain for any birds, besides sparrows and pigeons. During training, we had been taught that Korean birds "cry," rather than "sing." With so few trees, and people desperate to eat anything that moved, I thought, it was understandable. This was not a bird-friendly country.

Again, rural Korea reminded me of Vermont with its snow-covered mountains, clouds spilling over the peaks into valleys, and small villages and farms. Only there was no skiing here. Well, if I could make it until spring, remembering New England's glorious springs, I might be able to enjoy the beautiful landscape all around me even more.

We arrived in Daegu around noon. The Peace Corps regional director, Mel Merkin, the assistant regional director, Lee Myung-hwa, and the Peace Corps secretary, Miss Chang Yun-hong, met us at the Daegu Railway Station. Mel had a cigar in his mouth. Miss Chang was very pretty and had laughing eyes. She and Mr. Lee spoke fluent English. Mr. Lee was a pleasant, round-faced man who told us to call him "Bright Flower," which was the English translation of his surname. When Miss Chang smiled, which she did often, several gold teeth flashed brightly. They ferried us in the Peace Corps' old Land Rover to the small Peace Corps office in Daegu, which was located on the second floor of the Korean Airlines building on the main downtown thoroughfare, about one half mile from the station.

Mel had the responsibility for administering the Peace Corps program in two provinces: North Gyeongsang Province and South Gyeongsang Province, which together filled the southeast quarter of Korea.

After lunch, we checked in to a nearby yogwan, and waited to meet the representatives from the respective colleges and universities, where we would be teaching. The yogwan initially caused me some concern. One of the major dangers we would face in Korea, we had been taught in training, was asphyxiation from carbon monoxide resulting from a faulty heating system. The heating system used by virtually every Korean home and yogwan is the ondol system. If not properly built, or if the home or yogwan had cracks in the floor, the carbon monoxide byproduct of the ondol system could leak into the room. Being heavier than the usual components of the air in a room, the carbon monoxide is most concentrated near the floor. Because Koreans sleep on the floor, any leakage of gas can be fatal.

Although no PCVs had yet died because of this problem, there were countless stories of close calls—PCVs stumbling outside from their mattresses on the floor in the middle of the night, with splitting headaches that had awakened them. We had been warned repeatedly to check any floor on which we were sleeping for signs of cracks or other problems. Peace Corps even provided each PCV with a kit for checking the integrity of an ondol floor. Essentially, the kit consisted of a miniature smoke bomb, which was triggered at the source of the ondol system's heat and sent purple smoke through the system. Theoretically, the smoke would leak through any flaws in the ondol system and be detectable, indicating a dangerous leak. The yogwan we had stayed at while in Seoul had been thoroughly checked by Peace Corps prior to our arrival. I eyed the old floor of my room at this aged yogwan with some trepidation, until Miss Chang assured me that she had checked out this yogwan thoroughly, and that it was safe.

The ingenuity of Koreans never failed to amaze me. One example was this ondol heating system. Ondol, literally meaning "warm stone," is comprised of three main components: a fireplace or stove, which is also used for cooking and located below floor level; a heated floor underlay by horizontal smoke passages; and a vertical chimney, located lower than the roofline, to provide a draft. A network of underground flues, just below the floor, and connected to the kitchen fireplace or stove, transports heat from the kitchen to each room. Thin, flat, wide stones, two or three inches thick, called *kudul,* cover these flues, which lay underneath the floor. Kudul, literally meaning "fired stone," are covered with earth, and the floor is leveled.

To top it off, several layers of yellow paper sheets are pasted on the floor. This process is efficient, since the heat and smoke generated during cooking are transported automatically to each room in the house. Usually the kitchen is built at a lower level (about three feet), and the heated rooms are in an elevated position to allow the flues to run underneath. Incredibly, with just one heating the floors retain their warmth for extended periods, ranging from more than half a day to weeks, depending on the design of the flue structure.

Miss Chang, whose family was from the northern part of Korea, explained that the traditional ondol rooms found in the north differed somewhat from those in the south. In the north the ondol-heated room and the kitchen are usually not separated by a wall. Heat from both the fireplace and the ondol floor keep the room warm. In the south, a wall normally separates the kitchen from the living room, preventing the smoke from disturbing people sitting there. This was the first of many explanations and insights into Korean history and culture provided by Miss Chang. Her welcome smile and good nature helped all of the PCVs who visited the Peace Corps office in Daegu survive many difficult times.

In future winter months, I tremendously appreciated the ondol rooms I visited in private homes and in more traditional restaurants and "wine houses." I learned that in a room heated by ondol, the floor at the far end of the room tended to be cool. Elders, such as grandparents or parents, as well as guests (even young Peace Corps Volunteers), are always invited to sit in the warmer area as an expression of respect. There was usually a polite argument every time I was invited to sit in an ondol room, as I tried to defer to the older people or women in the room by taking the cooler seat. Almost always, insistent Koreans persuaded me that I must take the warm place of respect (which sometimes turned out to literally be the hot seat—more than once I almost blistered my rear end on the heated floor).

Early in the afternoon, several distinguished-looking men from Kyungpook National University showed up to meet those of us assigned to Kyungpook. One of them was Professor Kim Young-hee, who was then the director of the Language Institute in the English department of the Liberal Arts College at Kyungpook. He greeted me warmly in near-perfect but rather slow and heavily accented English. We retreated to a tearoom to talk, while Moe Cain and Russ Feldmeier met another man—Professor Chae Joong-ki—from the Teachers College at Kyungpook, and Rachel and Peter Wenz met a professor from the Medical College.

Professor Kim was a truly remarkable man. He had studied in the United States, which accounted for his good English. He told me that he was very glad to have a native English speaker in the Language Institute and that I could be a tremendous asset for the university. He had waited for years, he said, for someone like me. There had been other English teachers at Kyungpook—missionary teachers and even a Peace Corps Volunteer in the previous year who had transferred from a middle-school assignment—he told me, but no one before qualified to be a full-time teacher in the institute. Professor Kim was also well connected, I discovered later. He had been a classmate in elementary school and middle school of Korea's President Park Chung-hee and so knew him personally. This connection to the president was extremely significant.

Professor Kim told me that he was still looking for a Korean family for me to live with, and he was hopeful that by my return in ten days he would have good news for me. He then asked me about my background, including my hometown and academic career. When I mentioned that I had graduated with a Bachelor's degree in English from Dartmouth College, he surprised me by saying that he knew about Dartmouth. (None of the Korean language teachers in our training program had heard of Dartmouth. Most educated Koreans knew about Yale, Harvard, Princeton, and Stanford, but not Dartmouth.) Then he told me that the first English teacher, and probably the most beloved of the first Americans to come to Korea, had graduated from Dartmouth. He couldn't remember the name of the teacher or when he had come to Korea, except that it was a long time ago in the nineteenth century. That was news to me.

(Much later, after I had left Korea, I discovered that the Dartmouth graduate to whom Professor Kim had referred was Homer B. Hulbert

(1863–1949), who graduated from Dartmouth in 1884. Hulbert played on Dartmouth's second and third football teams of 1882–83. He came to Korea first as an English teacher in 1886 and later as a Methodist missionary. His accomplishments included founding the Korean branch of the YMCA, writing several books about Korean history, culture, and the Korean alphabet, becoming a close friend of the Korean Emperor Kojong, acting as Emperor Kojong's personal and most trusted emissary to Washington in 1905 and to the Hague in 1906 in unsuccessful efforts to thwart Japanese imperialism, and remaining a steadfast ally of and articulate advocate for Korea—in Japanese imposed exile in the United States—over a period of more than four decades. After Korea was liberated from Japanese rule in 1945, Hulbert returned to Korea in 1949 and died there, at the age of eighty-six, after only one week on Korean soil. On a later visit to Korea I discovered his gravesite in the Foreigners' Cemetery in Seoul. This phrase—what he often told his friends during the forty-two years that he was forced to live far away from his beloved Korea—is inscribed on his tombstone in hangul: "I would rather be buried in Korea than in Westminster Abbey.")

Professor Kim then asked me if I would like to see Kyungpook National University. Of course I was eager to see the university, even though it would be deserted on a Saturday afternoon, during winter break. We took a taxi together to the northeast quadrant of Daegu, crossing the Shinchon River, which bisects Daegu on a north-south axis, and the railroad, which cut through the city on an east-west axis. The narrower streets were crowded with buses, trucks, motor scooters, and bicycles, as in Seoul, but the wide boulevards had much less traffic than Seoul and were lined with thousands of small trees—many of them gingkoes—which looked as though they had been planted in the last ten years. The sidewalks were not as crowded as those in Seoul, either. Daegu had a population of about one million people. Seoul's population was five and one half times bigger. It seemed to me, as we drove to Kyungpook University, that the pace of life was much slower in Daegu than in Seoul. That appealed to me a lot.

Two things particularly delighted me about Daegu on that brief trip to Kyungpook National University and back to our downtown yogwan. Mountains ringed the city. On that Saturday, all had snow on their peaks. The natural setting was truly beautiful. Second, this was a city with a low horizon; there were very few buildings of more than several floors. This was a city you could walk in, explore neighborhoods, and investigate nooks and crannies without feeling overwhelmed—a city you could wrap your arms around, a city you could hug.

The grounds of Kyungpook University also appealed to me. A high fence seemed to completely enclose the campus. The taxi sped us through a main gate, where the guards recognized Professor Kim and bowed. We drove through trees and expansive, open areas between various structures. Ponds were scattered about the campus, between groves of evergreens. There appeared to be about ten buildings of all different styles, ranging from drab concrete to red brick. The taxi stopped next to what seemed to be a large, frozen, circular pool with a sculpture in the middle, which was apparently the center of the campus.

To the left, an open area slanted up to a long series of wide steps that climbed up to an impressive, white building with six four-story-high pillars at the top of a stone staircase. The building itself had a round dome on the top and reminded me of the Buffalo Museum of Science in my hometown. To the right was a brick building, about four stories high, on the top of a hill, which was covered with stone sculptures, depicting Buddha and other exotic figures. Professor Kim pointed out this building as the university's museum, and told me that the Language Institute was located on the third floor. From the outside the building looked quite impressive.

We got out of the taxi, which was ordered to wait for us, and climbed the path up the hill to the museum. Once inside, we took the three flights of stairs to the Language Institute, and Professor Kim showed me the language laboratory where I would be teaching some of my classes, as well as the small rooms where the Language Institute staff had their offices. That day, the building was stone cold. No one was there. There was no interior heating except for small potbellied stoves in each office. The building itself was not really finished in the interior, as you could see the wiring for light switches and electrical outlets on the unpainted, interior concrete walls and ceiling. But the offices seemed snug and attractive nevertheless. Professor Kim said he hoped I would be happy at the Language Institute. I responded, truthfully, that I already felt at home.

After returning to the downtown area of Daegu, thanking Professor

Kim, and saying goodbye, I met Mel, Moe, and Russ. We compared notes. Russ and Moe seemed to be as satisfied as I was with what they had seen and found out about Kyungpook National University and their situation. Professor Chae, of the Kyungpook Teachers College, was extremely kind and spoke even better English than Professor Kim. We three felt quite lucky. None of us had a Korean family yet, but we were prepared to live in the yogwan for a while, if necessary.

We returned to Seoul on the Sunday afternoon train. For some reason I was exhausted and slept most of the train ride back. On the bus from Seoul Station to Shin Chon Rotary, I compared the crowded sidewalks and streets of Seoul to the quieter, smaller scale streets and buildings of Daegu. Seoul was a huge city and much more modern than Daegu. There was no question that I preferred the latter.

Our Korean language classes continued at KLI, and our English teaching at Myongi University entered its last week. On Wednesday we had a nice party with our students to thank them for their many kindnesses. I was very sad to be leaving the Myongi students and faculty, who had been so generous of their time and friendship. I never saw most of them again, as I rarely visited Seoul during the next two years.

A Korean reporter at the party spoke with several of our K-VIII group of volunteers. The next morning an article appeared in Korea's main English language newspaper—the *Korea Herald*—that was very interesting to us, at least as an indication of how we were viewed by a Korean journalist. It also demonstrated how a simple conversation with a newspaper reporter could result in some misquotes and misunderstandings despite the best intentions on the part of all participants in the interviews. For example, the concluding question attributed to me by the reporter was never asked:

### The *Korea Herald*
### Thursday, February 13, 1969
*To Teach English, Learn Korean*
*Peace Corpsmen Begin Missions*
By Kyoung-sun An

The popular notion of Peace Corps and its projects has been, in many cases, agricultural, technical, or health projects designed to help raise the standards of living in the underdeveloped countries. And a typical place that would benefit from these "help them help themselves programs" would be some remote village in Africa or somewhere near the jungle in Southeast Asia or South America, where the primitive way of life still lingers on and the populace is just coming into contact with a modern know-how of the American Peace Corps Volunteers.

Shattering all these stereotype images of the Peace Corps and the picture of a remote countryside are the recently arrived group of young men and women whose average age is in the mid-20s.

These volunteers are the seventh and eighth groups of the American Peace Corpsmen to come to Korea since 1966, and these men and women have, as a group, perhaps the highest educational background and sophistication gained through their extensive travel experiences as shown in their dossier.

All have minimum BA degrees, twenty out of eighty have master's degrees, and a few are doctors and lawyers. And many of them will return to further studies, probably in the East Asian area study, as confirmed by Eugene Severens, a graduate of Princeton with a degree in Oriental studies who is here with his wife, Cathy.

What, then, are these young intellectuals going to do in a big city like Seoul as Peace Corps Volunteers? Their project is a special one—that of teaching English to students at various colleges and universities in the country. In group seven, twenty-eight will be assigned to the Seoul area, and twelve to other provincial cities with colleges and universities.

This means that their major contact will be young college students and professors, not the simple farmers or the deprived of the slum area or the ignorant. Asked how they feel about their contact being limited to a certain degree to an elite class, one volunteer noted that, "It will be interesting to meet the young people of our own age with similar backgrounds." He thinks there will be some truly meaningful exchange of ideas and opinions as well as mutual benefit from such contact.

## Uniquely Qualified

They seem to be uniquely qualified for the present project. Like Cathy Severens, most of them have majored in English and have experience in teaching English. In addition, they have received special training at the Hilo (Hawaii) Peace Corps Training Center, in the technique and method of teaching English as a second language as it would apply to the Korean students.

Equally important was the three months' intensive language course and other related studies in Korean culture, history, or modern development, etc., which Charles Hobbie said gave them an "accurate" picture of the country. "But actually seeing Seoul is more exciting and the mountains surrounding the city are much more beautiful than I had imagined," said Pat Donegan.

Asked why they chose to come to Korea, William Ryan said because his best friend (at Hilo) was a Korean by the name of Sang-soo Sul. The majority, however, seemed to have chosen or been assigned to Korea because of their academic specialization or interest in the Asia area in general. Also, a former Peace Corpsman who served here before is said to be coming back to study, apparently as a result of his prior experience in this country.

As their training at Hilo had a dual purpose, so is their reason for being here, to learn Korean and to teach English. And there is a certain conflict. As English teachers, they know that they should speak only English to their students at all times and this will naturally lessen their opportunity to practice Korean. The solution, at this time, seems to be to hope for enough free time from their teaching duty so that they will meet Koreans from all walks of life and, above all, with whom they can speak Korean.

As any language student knows, it is such an elation to be understood by a native when you finally utter a phrase with all the hesitation, doubt and all the courage you can muster. And that is exactly what happened to Pat Donegan the other day on the street. "They UNDERSTOOD me," she said with a surprised look.

Finally, Charles Hobbie summed it all up: "We are here because we wanted to come, not because we were sent," hinting that their reason for coming and, consequently, their behavior would be different from those who live in "little America" or in the compound. Then he touched upon a delicate question of "what do you think of the Americans here who do not speak Korean?" Well, I told them, that is a question I often ask myself too, but a subject to be pondered on another occasion.

We were scheduled to depart for our sites to begin our service as English teachers on February 18. In the meantime, we had a last series of immunizations and health checks with the Peace Corps physician and then packed our suitcases.

The lunar new year arrived two days before our scheduled departure. On New Year's Eve I went to a favorite restaurant with half a dozen PCTs for a farewell dinner of bulgogi—the delicious beef barbecue. It was the last day of what was the longest Peace Corps training program in history, we were told. We talked of how much we had learned in the past four months of training, what we liked and disliked about Korea so far, and what we had experienced during our site visits.

It really was incredible how much our view of life and of the world had changed in such a relatively short time. I had not known where Korea was located in the world a mere seven months before, much less know about its amazing history, culture, language, and people. Now I probably knew more about Korea than about my home state of New York.

Perhaps the most remarkable result of my training was how I felt about Koreans as individuals. When I had arrived in Hawaii and first met the Korean training staff, they seemed so different in appearance and behavior that I felt it would be impossible to get to know or even recognize them. I did not even imagine then how close I would become to many of the Koreans in a period of four months.

As the Year of the Monkey came to an end, I remembered the Tet Offensive in February of the previous year and thought how much happier I was now, one year later, with a single exception—I missed Dariel so much I could hardly stand it.

Spring Plowing, North Gyeongsang Province, April 1969

Daegu, North Gyeongsang Province, Korea, March 1969

Taebaek Mountains, Korea, April 1969

Museum and Language Institute Building, Kyungpook National
University, Daegu, Korea, June 1969

# THE YEAR OF THE ROOSTER

# CHAPTER FIVE—LIFE BEGINS IN DAEGU

O ne of the finest things that happened during the nearly three weeks in Seoul was the opportunity to get to know the family of one of my best friends, Yim Chun-bin, among the Korean training staff. His older sister contacted me the first week I was in Seoul, and I spent several delightful evenings with her and Mr. Yim's family, exploring Seoul and visiting them at their lovely, traditional Korean home. On New Year's Day—the first day of the Year of the Rooster, February 17, 1969—I was invited to the Yims' home, where we ate traditional Korean holiday food, such as noodles and *duk* (a kind of rice cake), and played *yutnori* for several hours.

Yutnori is a traditional Korean board game much like Parcheesi, in which teams move pieces around a board trying to get all of the team's pieces over the finish line. The number of spaces a piece may be moved during each player's turn is determined by throwing four short sticks in the air. Each stick has one flat side and certain markings. Depending on how the sticks fall and then lie on the floor, the throwing player or team may move their pieces the number of spaces indicated by the pattern of the thrown sticks—forward or backward. In Parcheesi, the number displayed in the role of the dice determines the progress of pieces around the game board, so the sticks are like dice in their function. The game was very complicated but lots of fun and very noisy, as each time the sticks were thrown there were shouts of encouragement or despair from the players. At the Yims' home, all the family members took part in the game, sitting cross-legged around a blanket spread on the floor, onto which the sticks fell after being tossed high in the air. Each team had six or seven members.

After the game, the Yim family introduced me to the traditional New Year's Day ritual of paying respect to the elders of the family. Each of the members of the family, in turn, stepped in front of their grandparents and parents and then, in a smooth and graceful downward motion, knelt before them and touched their foreheads to the floor. Everyone was expected to do this bow, called *saebae,* so of course I also repeatedly performed the saebae, although it was difficult and my bow was pretty jerky and disjointed—the precise opposite of smooth and graceful—causing some amusement. The family elders gave all the children who offered saebae some money.

Mr. Yim's family seemed to consist mostly of sisters and female cousins. Girls and young women surrounded me during my entire visit. They treated me like a king—feeding me, refilling my glass with beer, massaging my legs when they began to get rubbery from too much cross-legged sitting, and singing beautifully. I had a wonderful time! It was a fine beginning to the new year, which was going to be a great year for me, they assured me, because I was born in the Year of the Rooster (1945), and this was my special year.

Mr. Yim's sister further explained that most people in Korea still used the Lunar calendar, although the Korean government had officially adopted the Gregorian, or Western, solar-based calendar, in 1895. Most Koreans celebrated the holidays of both calendars, so there was usually a holiday coming up in any given week! In the Lunar calendar, the fifteenth of each month is always the day of a full moon. Some months have twenty-eight days; others have twenty-nine or thirty days. Every three years an extra month, called *yuntal,* is added. Each year is named according to a combination of two sets of Chinese characters. One set has ten basic characters, and the other set has twelve. Every sixty years the combinations reset to start the cycle again. When a person reached his sixtieth birthday, or completed sixty years, he returns again, or has a *hwangap,* meaning he is starting a new cycle. This is perhaps the most important birthday.

If one knows the sequence of the names of the years, one can easily figure out how old someone is by asking in what animal year they were born. When asked how old I was—which is among the very first questions inquisitive Koreans asked me on most occasions—I was taught to respond either that I was a rooster or that I was born in the year of Korea's liberation from Japan. The questioner then quickly knew how old I was. Of course, the system also enabled me to find out how old a Korean was without seeming disrespectful, by asking what the name of the year of their birth was. Although the system of years seemed simple, the entire system is incredibly complicated, because time is also divided into two-hour spans, based upon the combination of the twelve heavenly characters and the ten earthly characters. The identity of a particular two-hour period is very important for determining the suitability of time for important occasions, such as weddings, births, and funerals, as well as for determining—based on the time, date, and year of birth—one's future fortune and the suitability of prospective husbands and wives.

The next day, our group of eight Daegu-bound volunteers boarded a train in the morning. This time we were experts in purchasing tickets and elbowing our way onto the train and to our seats. In the countryside between Seoul and Daegu, most of the snow we had seen only eight days before was gone from the mountainsides, valleys, and rivers, but the tops of the mountains were still white. As soon as we left the Seoul environs, I noticed that the air cleared as well. Above Seoul, almost obscuring the nearby mountains was a smoky haze from the charcoal fires heating every ondol and every bathhouse. The farther south we chugged behind the old steam locomotive, the clearer the air became.

On this trip, as we approached Daegu, I noticed, for the first time, the hundreds of apple orchards around the outskirts of the city, which seemed to compete with the rice paddies for dominance. Apples being my favorite fruit, I was glad to see that there would be apples to eat in Daegu. I soon learned that Daegu is famous for its apples, as well as for its beautiful women, whose luster and loveliness were attributed to the abundance of apples in their diet.

We settled into the yogwan, where we had stayed earlier in the month on our first visit to Daegu. Professor Kim visited me the next morning with the welcome news that he had found a family with whom I could live. The other volunteers were not so lucky, and most ended up staying in boarding houses that catered to students or teachers.

I met my Korean family and moved to their house on Friday

afternoon. Professor Kim had arranged for me to live with a kind Presbyterian minister, Reverend Na Chae-woon, his wife, and their three young children on the grounds of the Daegu Bible Institute, where he was a teacher. The Na family shared a house with another Korean family, right in the heart of Daegu, on a high hill that overlooked the western side of the city. Each family had one half of the small house. A locked door in the central hallway connected the two halves. I never was in the other half.

From the outside, the house looked like a miniature American house in many ways, with a straight roof and two floors. On the first floor, on our side of the house, there was a small, primitive kitchen with a dirt floor and a cooking stove, fueled by a round charcoal briquette. You entered the kitchen through a separate door from outside the house. The room next to the kitchen was the ondol room where the family slept, ate, and lived. Across the hall from the ondol room was a Western-style room with large windows, a polished wood floor, and a small potbellied stove for heat. So our half of the house consisted of two rooms for living—one ondol room and one wood-floored room—and the kitchen. It was a snug, comfortable house, which obviously had been built for a foreigner—probably a Presbyterian missionary years ago.

The toilet was an outside facility, housed in a small structure, accessible up a short path about ten yards from the house. It was the usual squat arrangement, but there was no flush. There also was no door, but the entrance was turned away from the house, facing downtown Daegu, so anyone using the facility could not be seen from the house or the path. I soon learned the "cough system" of determining whether or not the toilet was in use. You started coughing in a loud manner as you started up the path toward the toilet. If there were someone in the toilet, there would be an answering cough, prompting you to stop your journey. If not, you continued coughing as you entered the toilet and did your business, hoping that any visitors would not be deaf.

From the toilet there was a magnificent view of the city! Reverend Na was fond of pointing out that you could see about fifty churches from it. Daegu was definitely a city of churches—there were steeples everywhere. I replied gently that, if we could see fifty churches while we were doing our business in the toilet, then fifty churches could see us. I imagined congregations lining up with binoculars, perhaps as part of a stewardship campaign or another fund raising opportunity, to watch the strange foreigner do his business in the outhouse on the hill. One hundred won for a peek!

In the kitchen was a spigot for water. Mrs. Na kept a large kettle full of hot water over the stove. For shaving and washing my face in the morning I used a basin with hot water from the kettle, which I carried to the western-style room, which was to be my room. There was a small mirror there. It was a very nice room; it even had a western-style bed with a mattress, a bureau, and a kind of nightstand, in addition to the small stove. I was very comfortable there; in fact, I was too comfortable. I felt uneasy that I had a large room to myself while the rest of the family and a visiting helper—six people—had to share a much smaller room. Moreover, I felt quite embarrassed by the presence of the bed. It was kind of the Nas to think I would enjoy sleeping in a bed, but actually, I wanted to learn about Korean life, in part by doing what Koreans did—sleeping on the floor with a yo (mattress) and an ibul (comforter). I also was worried about what other PCVs would think ..." Hobbie has a bed! What's the matter with him?" I worried about this a great deal.

There was no bathroom in our half of the house. For my weekly bath, I found a bathhouse about two blocks away. The first several times I went to the bathhouse, I encountered a minor problem. Although the bathhouse's bathing areas were segregated by gender, I found that many Korean fathers brought their young daughters with them to bathe, so there were dozens of five- to eight-year-old girls in the men's bathing area. They had never seen a hairy American before (Caucasians have a lot of hair on their bodies compared to Asians). So I was the object of intense scrutiny.

In fact, I was usually surrounded by some of these young girls, who innocently giggled and pointed at my naked, hairy body while I tried to scrub up and soak in the heated pool. Their usual exclamation was: *"Igoo, tulli manta!"* (Wow, he has a lot of hair!) And they weren't talking about the hair on my head! It was hardly a relaxing situation for me. Several fathers tried to shoo the girls away to no avail. As soon as the fathers turned their backs to wash themselves, the girls were back.

After a couple of uncomfortable visits to the bathhouse in the afternoon, I decided to take my baths during slack periods of the day. I found that if I got to the bathhouse by about five o'clock in the morning, it was virtually deserted, and the water was cleaner than later in the day! Problem solved—once a week I got up very early and sneaked through the darkness to the bathhouse, hoping all the way that I wouldn't meet any fathers with their daughters there.

My first week at their home, the Na family presented me with a gorgeous pair of Korean dolls, dressed in the traditional clothes of Korean royalty, with crowns on their heads. It was a lovely, unexpected gift, which I still cherish, forty years later. The Na family struck me initially as a typical Korean middleclass family, except that I soon found that Reverend Na was extremely well educated—much better educated than a typical middleclass American. Before being a teacher at the Bible Institute, he had been an assistant pastor at the First Presbyterian Church, the largest in Daegu. I quickly discovered that the family was quite religious and that the parents were devout Presbyterians.

Being devout Presbyterians in Korea was a little different than being devout Presbyterians in the United States. My paternal grandparents in my childhood had been what I would consider devout American Presbyterians, but they drank an occasional glass of wine and enjoyed movies. In Korea, Presbyterians did not drink, smoke, or even go to movies. They went to church every day, if possible—the earlier in the morning the better, it seemed—and at least twice on Sunday. And of course they prayed before every meal and before going to bed at night. They *really* prayed, as if the length of the prayer would grab God's attention. I often wondered, to the contrary, if such lengthy prayers might have the opposite effect and put God to sleep.

Happily, as an Episcopalian, in the eyes of most Korean Presbyterians I was little better than a heathen. Episcopalians drank and smoked in Korea and did lots of other outrageous things, according to Reverend Na, which gave me a little latitude. I hoped that in their conversations with each other, Reverend Na and his wife might excuse my missteps and insensitivity, not only on the basis of my being a foreigner but also—much worse—on the basis of my being an Episcopalian.

The setup at Kyungpook University seemed very good as well. I would be teaching all levels—freshmen, sophomores, juniors, and seniors—and meeting four different classes twice a week, each class for one hour. That would be a total of eight hours of class each week. I thought this was a pretty modest schedule. If I wanted to accomplish some real progress in the English ability of my students, I would need to see them at least one more hour each week, and perhaps more, I thought. I decided to wait and see how things went before I tried to change anything. I was one of three English teachers in the Liberal Arts College. The other two teachers were Korean and spoke English quite well. Their classes were in Korean, however, and focused on English and American literature, at quite a sophisticated level, with no pretense of speaking English in the classroom.

With about three thousand students, Kyungpook was the third largest of the seven national universities in Korea, and the best university in the country located outside of Seoul. It ranked overall about eighth in the country, out of probably thirty or more. In the first several days I met all of the faculty of the Liberal Arts College and most of the administrators. Almost without exception, they asked me if I would have time to teach them English. I wondered what I could do to accommodate these requests and still have time to teach my classes.

Physically, the campus was beautiful, particularly in comparison to the relatively treeless surrounding city and mountains. It was well planted with mature trees, gardens, and shrubs, and strewn with ponds and secluded pathways. With the mountains as a backdrop, Kyungpook was quite lovely! Although the buildings were all rather newly constructed and appeared attractive from the outside, they lacked central heating and restrooms. The latter were in a separate small building, rather like the facilities in an American public park, except the toilets were the usual squat style. I hoped that the weather would warm up before my classes began on March 10.

To get to Kyungpook, I walked down the hill from our house to the maze of streets and boulevards below in the downtown part of Daegu and then about one mile to the main street, where I caught a city bus that dropped me off at Kyungpook University's main gate. The fare was about five cents. At the main gate, the uniformed guards greeted me every morning with deep bows, as I walked through the gate and to the museum building, where the Language Institute was located. Once classes began and students had arrived on campus, each student also bowed upon meeting me. I returned all these bows, of course. It took a while to walk from the main gate to my office, with the hundreds of bows in every direction.

Our neighborhood was in the part of Daegu called *Namsandong*, or South Mountain District. From our hill—known as *Dongsan* or East Mountain—to the bus stop was a fantastically interesting and fragrant walk, which took me through the heart of Daegu's famous *Yakryong*, or Chinese Medicine Market. On both sides of the streets were small shops selling herbal medicines of every possible type. The various herbs and other ingredients were set out in baskets in front of the shops to dry. The smell of herbs and other exotic concoctions permeated the brisk, February air. It was delightful!

During this initial period of settling in, I had a period of about three weeks before classes actually began. At the university I prepared some diagnostic tests to help me gauge the levels of my different classes and individual students, and I started preparation of the first month's lesson plans. I was able to type teaching materials and tests on an old typewriter in the Language Institute's main office on mimeograph master sheets. Miss Lee, our office assistant, then ran copies off for me. She was very helpful in my classroom preparations, as well as in keeping the stove fueled with *yantan* (charcoal briquettes). Ah, Miss Lee! Your cheerful greeting and smile illuminated my path through many gray days!

However, I had a lot of free time in the early evenings, after I returned home from Kyungpook University about five thirty each afternoon, and on the weekends. In these free periods, even in the dark of a winter evening, I liked nothing better than to walk the streets and alleys of Daegu, exploring the hidden nooks and dark crannies, where I might find a new tearoom or shop. On one of these walks I found a small food shop that sold Korean chocolate bars, similar to Hershey bars, but actually a little tastier. They were expensive, but thereafter I tried to keep at least one chocolate bar at all times in my room, a morsel of which would cheer me up considerably when I was depressed. On another such excursion, months later, I discovered a tiny restaurant that sold American-style fried chicken, as well as slices of potato, fried in oil, that approximated French fries.

Food was not the only objective of my explorations, although there were days when it was! I loved to find out what was being sold, besides food, in Korean shops. Very often, I discovered, shops of the same kind were grouped in one area. So, for example, all the bookstores were within one block of each other. Shops selling Korean dolls and souvenirs were all bunched together. Clothing stores or stores selling cloth of all kinds were in the same part of Daegu. Reverend Na told me that the shop owners took advantage of foreigners by overcharging them for merchandise, so he cautioned me to take either him or Mrs. Na with me when I wanted to buy something significant.

On the opposite side of the East Mountain, where our house was located, was Daegu's oldest and largest market—West Gate Market. It was perhaps a fifteen-minute walk to this incredible marketplace, where hundreds of vendors sold everything under the sun. It was one of the few places where I could buy *Time* magazine, *Newsweek* magazine, and the English language *Korea Herald* to keep up on the news of the outside world. You could buy literally anything there (except ice cream, hot dogs, hamburgers, and other Western food) if you knew whom to ask and where to look. I was even asked if I wanted to buy an American jeep. I loved that marketplace! It was always jammed with people, produce, and merchandise and was chock full of strange sights and interesting sounds and smells.

I liked the way that natural features in Daegu identified places, but I found it confusing. For example, the Na family and I lived in the South Mountain District, on the East Mountain, near the West Gate Market. South, East, and West—it was all quite confusing. We were living on the west side of Daegu, so at least the name of the market near our house made sense.

About three weeks after I had arrived in Daegu to begin my service at Kyungpook University, I had quite a surprise in the West Gate Market. One Saturday morning, in the midst of the tremendous crowd of market goers, I thought I saw an older Caucasian man ahead of me in the crush of pedestrians, walking through the market. I hadn't seen a Caucasian face—not even Moe and Russ at the university—for several weeks, so at first I wasn't sure whether I could believe my eyes. The man ahead of me looked like a professor of psychology whose class I had taken at Dartmouth my freshman year. I recognized him, not only because I had taken his class, but because I had seen him on hundreds of occasions, pedaling his bicycle around the Dartmouth campus and town of Hanover, New Hampshire, where Dartmouth was located. I then recalled that I had read in the *Dartmouth Alumni Magazine* almost a year before that the professor—Dr. Chauncey N. Allen—was going to the Far East as a missionary, with his wife, Margaret, after having taught at Dartmouth for more than forty years.

I overtook the man and introduced myself to him and to the young Korean man, Mr. Choi, accompanying him. The Caucasian man was Dr. Allen, or "Chince," as he was fondly known at Dartmouth, and at that moment a close friendship was born between us that lasted almost thirty years, until his death in 1997 (at the age of ninety-seven). Of course, Chince Allen did not remember me from Dartmouth. I had been an English major, and he had been the head of the psychology department. But he was delighted to meet me, especially when I mentioned that I was Dartmouth, class of 1967. We had coffee at a tearoom in the marketplace, and afterward I went with him and Mr. Choi to his house, which was in a missionary compound on the grounds of the Presbyterian Dongsan Hospital, only several hundred yards from my Korean family's house. It was a wonderful coincidence to meet another Dartmouth graduate (class of 1924) and someone I actually recognized from college days.

At Chince's house I met Margaret Allen, his warm and gracious wife, who had been a nurse at Massachusetts General Hospital before marrying Chince decades before, and was now offering her services as a nursing instructor and English teacher at the School of Nursing associated with the hospital. Margaret was the kind of woman who loved to "mother" Dartmouth students, and I appreciated the affection both Chince and Margaret showered on me for the next four months, until they returned home.

Chince told me stories about Dartmouth and about members of the Dartmouth faculty, whom we both knew. He was a close friend of Professor Richard Eberhart in the English department, former Poet Laureate Consultant in Poetry to the Library of Congress, whose book *Selected Poems 1930–1965* had won the Pulitzer Prize for Poetry in 1966, when I was a junior at Dartmouth, studying with him. I always considered Professor Eberhart a mentor and fondly remembered his poetry classes on winter evenings at his home, in front of the Eberhart fireplace, with cocoa and brownies served by his wife, Helen.

Chince was also a close friend of Professor Paul Zeller and his wife, Fran. Paul was the director of Dartmouth's Glee Club, under whom I had sung for four years, and whom I liked immensely. He had taught in the suburbs of my hometown of Buffalo, New York, before coming to Dartmouth's music department in 1946.

About the same time, Reverend Na introduced me to another American missionary who lived nearby—Reverend William Grubb. In turn, Reverend Grubb and his kind wife, Louise, introduced me to a tall surgeon from Dartmouth Medical School, Dr. John Sibley, and his wife, Jean, who were also Presbyterian missionaries. The Sibleys had been responsible for bringing the Allens from Dartmouth to Korea, and they too lived in the same Korean neighborhood as the Na family, at the bottom of our hill.

I admired the Grubbs and the Sibleys for their evident longstanding dedication to the cause of helping Koreans and for their facility in Korean. I particularly admired the Sibleys, who had lived in Korea for many years, providing medical expertise and other assistance to Korea, because both John and Jean spoke Korean pretty well (as did their four children), clearly loved Koreans and their culture, and lived in a Korean-style house in a Korean neighborhood—like the Grubbs—rather than on a compound, as most of the other missionaries did.

The same week that started with the chance meeting in West Gate Market, I was invited to dinner at both the Allen's house and at the Grubb's house. I accepted the invitations with some misgivings, unsure of what my relationship should be with American missionaries. After two fine evenings of conversation and laughter, I concluded that the missionary community was, in many ways, a group of extremely kind and generous people. And I enjoyed the company of Americans, as well as the American food.

The two dinner engagements gave me the opportunity to meet most of the Korean and American hospital administrators and staff, as well as most of the Korean Presbyterian Church hierarchy, in Daegu. There were perhaps twenty Americans associated with the hospital, church, and Presbyterian schools (including Keimyung College), and without exception they were welcoming and friendly to the newly arrived Peace Corps Volunteer. The dinners were delicious, and I thoroughly enjoyed both evenings.

Afterward, I determined that I would have to limit my contact with the missionary community because extensive contacts such as these would not be appropriate or further Peace Corps' three goals. I felt that I was not a Peace Corps Volunteer in Korea in order to associate with Americans—missionaries or military personnel. I had to be careful to not let personal comforts, such as speaking English and good old home cooking, distract me from what I really enjoyed most doing and was there to do—to teach English to Koreans, to learn about Koreans, their language, and their culture, and to help Koreans become acquainted with Americans who were neither missionaries nor military.

Having said that, on the other hand, besides being extremely nice people with the energy levels of people half their ages, the Allens had a Western-style bathroom, complete with a huge old tub and hot water! For the remainder of their year in Daegu, they graciously offered to let me use it whenever I wanted, which temporarily solved my problem at the bathhouse! In exchange, I was able to help Chince secretly procure several bottles of Chivas Regal (blended Scotch whiskey) from the thriving black market and smuggle them onto the strictly alcohol-free missionary compound without anyone finding out. We mutually agreed that some things in life absolutely demanded the compromising of a few principles.

Classes at Kyungpook National University began on Monday, March 10. At the Language Institute, besides Professor Kim, I worked with a delightful, kind, younger professor, Lee Woo-gun. Professor Lee and I became close friends. He was to be my *chitokyosu*, or mentor, and I was extremely fortunate to be able to work with him. His English was very good, although he had never been outside Korea, and I soon found that we had the same feelings about teaching, the same sympathetic attitude toward our students, and many of the same philosophical and political perspectives. We had to be careful where we discussed the latter, particularly because he was slightly deaf and prone to speak loudly, even when he was being critical of the university's administration or Korean government.

As I began to meet other professors at Kyungpook University, I had to overcome a major Korean language problem for me that started in Peace Corps training and continued to haunt me after I arrived in Korea. The honorific form of the word "teacher" in Korean was *sunsaengnim*—*sunsaeng* meaning "teacher" and *nim* connoting "respect" or "honor." In a combined form they were placed after the family name of the person you were addressing, so any time that you addressed another professor or teacher, for example, you addressed them as Kim sunsaengnim or Park sunsaengnim. My problem was that the Korean word for fish was *saengsun,* so a mere reversal of the first and second syllables of the word for teacher produced a different—and not very honorific—word, meaning "fish." For some reason I had a mental block about this problem and persisted with this mistake. I went around the campus my first day addressing everybody as honorable fish, to the amusement of all except me, until I discovered my error.

I was more than a little apprehensive about teaching my first classes. Although I had by this time taught perhaps fifty or more classes in the Peace Corps training program, both in Hawaii and in Seoul, these classes at Kyungpook were really *my* classes. Whether or not I taught well, and how the faculty and students responded to my efforts, would determine my happiness for the next two years, I suspected. So there was a lot at stake. I was as prepared as anyone could be and had my lesson plans ready for the next month, but nevertheless, I entered the classroom at Kyungpook for the first time with trepidation.

In Korean primary and secondary schools, students were required to wear uniforms, which usually identified the school and the name of the student. Sometimes the students wore hats as well. Uniforms were of many different colors and styles. I liked this custom, because I could immediately identify the age, school, and often the class year of any secondary school student I met in Korea. Boys were required to wear their hair in a brush cut. Girls usually cut their hair short, in a kind of bowl look (meaning that someone had put a bowl on their head and chopped off all the hair around the bowl), or wore it in pigtails.

At the university level, however, uniforms were abandoned. The boys in my classes wore dark pants and light-colored or white shirts. Their hair was cut a little longer than a brush cut, unless they were in the Korean equivalent of American ROTC, requiring the military brush cut, which many of them were. The girls wore knee length or longer skirts with plain blouses. Their hair was often quite long—shoulder length or longer. Meeting university students on the street, you couldn't be sure that they were students at first. After a while, I began to be able to identify students from non-students, lower-class Koreans from middleclass or upper-class Koreans, and rural Koreans from urban Koreans just by their clothes and hairstyles.

Most of my classes were smaller than I had anticipated. In training we had learned that the typical high-school class was between eighty and ninety students. Discipline had to be strictly enforced at the secondary school level, in order to keep such huge classes under control. I had worried that I would not be able to keep control of so many students. At Kyungpook, I didn't have to worry; my English classes had between twelve and fifteen students, which was a great class size, as it allowed much more personal contact between me and each one of my students. I was also pleasantly surprised by the English ability of most of my students. With a few exceptions—primarily in the freshmen class— their spoken English was already quite good. One girl spoke with a slow Mississippi drawl, which interested me—she had been taught by a Korean high-school teacher, whom I later taught in one of my teacher workshops, who had learned his English at "Ole Miss."

When I entered the classroom for the first time, the students immediately stood up and bowed. Since I had already experienced this custom at Myongi University in Seoul, I was prepared for that—it gave me a welcome feeling. I bowed in return, asked them to be seated, and launched into an introduction, in which I explained that in class we would speak only English, but that I hoped they would all help me learn the Korean language and about Korean culture outside of class. Then I asked them to introduce themselves to me, telling me their name, birthplace, interests, major, and why they wanted to learn English. I noticed a marked difference between the seniors and the freshmen in the way they handled this initial conversation with me. The former were confident and spoke quite eloquently. The latter were very nervous. The girls laughed and giggled and covered their mouths with their hands in embarrassment. All of the students, like those at Myongi University, seemed much younger in the way they acted than American university students.

My students impressed me greatly. They seemed eager to work hard and were very attentive in class. Since students' motivation is probably the single biggest problem facing any teacher, I was pleased with their initial earnestness and hoped that their determination would continue. That first day I met all four of my classes. When Professor Kim asked me how things had gone on my first day, I told him without reservation that I was quite happy with my classes.

Like the schools in Seoul, Kyungpook University had two terms a year. The first term ran from early March until mid-July, about eighteen weeks, and the second term ran from mid-September until mid-December, about fifteen weeks. The hottest and coldest months were avoided. In the unheated and un-cooled classrooms I was grateful for such planning, especially in Daegu, where the winters were colder, and the summers hotter, than in Seoul.

During the vacation periods, the members of our K-VII and K-VIII groups were expected to teach some teacher workshops. Our students would be English teachers in Korean middle schools and high schools. Peace Corps also expected us to have an independent project of some sort, approved in advance by Director O'Donnell, for the periods when workshops or other classes were not scheduled. The independent project could be anything from voluntary work with a non-profit Korean organization, such as an orphanage, to studying a Korean instrument or cultural activity, such as learning to play the kayageum (Korean zither or harp) or write Korean poetry. I was keeping my eyes open to find such a project, for when classes and summer workshops had ended.

I was also very happy with my Korean family. I soon learned from Reverend Na that he had graduated from the College of Law of Korea University in Seoul, which was probably the best university in Korea. He then continued studying at Divinity School in Seoul, where he met his wife. She was also a student there. They married after graduation, after he had been ordained in the Presbyterian Church. They were both in their thirties.

At the Daegu Bible Institute, Reverend Na taught Greek and German. At the same time he was studying for his master's degree in Korean Language and raising their three beautiful children. The oldest of the Na children, Kang-yup, was the son and was four years old. The middle child, Eun-shin, was a pretty girl of two, who was definitely going through what we called the "terrible twos" back home. The last was six-month-old Eun-jin, who was as cute as she could be.

We ate in the main room around a little rectangular table, at which we sat cross-legged on the ondol floor. At least I tried to sit cross-legged.

After about half an hour with my legs crossed, both legs would get numb, so I would have to stretch them out under the table until I could feel them again. The noise at the table from the three children was tremendous, although the children were generally well behaved. At the table, however, Eun-shin often would throw her bowl or spoon or food. It was always a lively dinner.

I soon taught some English to Kang-yup, who quickly learned to greet me correctly, depending on the time of day: "Good morning," "Good afternoon," "Good evening," and "Good night." He also quickly learned to say, "How are you?" while the middle girl, Eun-shin, despite my best efforts, persisted in saying "Good morning good night" very rapidly together whenever she saw me. I am sure she thought this was my name.

We all got along very well, using both Korean and English at first. Both Reverend and Mrs. Na spoke a little English, and with my broken Korean we managed to communicate, regarding many subjects. As I got to know him better, I realized that Reverend Na was a very accomplished man. He spoke Japanese fluently and was able to read German, Hebrew, Chinese, and Greek. He was familiar with the Western classics, as well as with a lot of English and American literature. His friends—mostly other ministers—indicated to me that they thought he was quite conservative in many ways. That may have been, but I found him open to all new ideas and very interesting to talk with.

It took Reverend Na several weeks to accept the fact that, although I considered myself a Christian, I liked to drink (as I have mentioned already, Presbyterians neither drink nor smoke in Korea) and did not wish to go to church four or five times a week. On Sunday I was happy, at first, to go to church. There were several services, each lasting about three hours. The Nas were very content to attend all of them and to spend most of Sunday at church. Although the First Church (and biggest church) in Daegu was quite impressive from the outside, inside you sat on the floor, cross-legged, and shivered in the cold—no central heating system. In the light of the facts that I understood almost nothing for the first few months, and that the sermons lasted for hours, it was not the best experience of my life. Nevertheless, I attended one service at the First Church every Sunday—when I was in Daegu—for almost a year with the family. After my first year in Daegu I attended on a sporadic basis, arranging to be out of town on Sundays if possible.

Reverend Na was initially quite concerned about my spiritual health. He often dropped hints about this or that church service or activity, and frequently sang hymns at home, after I told him how much I enjoyed the music at church. He and his wife had excellent voices, and I enjoyed hearing them sing. I think he also found it hard to understand that in my American family we had Episcopalians, Presbyterians, Catholics, and Mormons—all together. When I asked him why Korean Presbyterians didn't smoke or drink, he answered that he wasn't sure exactly, but he thought that the money and time wasted on these bad habits should be devoted, instead, to doing good deeds. I could understand this point of view, particularly in an impoverished country, where it was a struggle for most people to even survive. When he wasn't talking excessively about religion, Reverend Na had a great sense of humor and was a delight to be with!

Mrs. Na was an attractive woman who worked very hard. The amount of work that she accomplished in a day made me shudder! She was up at four thirty each morning preparing breakfast, and she didn't go to bed until about eleven at night. During the day she cooked, cleaned, washed clothes, cared for three children, studied, sewed, shopped for food, and otherwise was busy every minute. She always dressed very simply but with a touch of elegance. And she was often laughing, it seemed—either at something her husband said or did or at my Korean. I had the feeling that she went along with Reverend Na's religious zeal with her tongue in her cheek or a kind of secret amusement. Watching her and Reverend Na, I thought that it was people like this good-natured and highly intelligent couple, with their incredible energy and thirst for information, who were pushing Korea's amazing growth rate in just about everything.

Also living with our Korean family was a fifteen-year-old girl—Jung-aw—from the countryside near Daegu, who helped Mrs. Na with chores and with taking care of the children. She was a relative of Mrs. Na and seemed to be staying with us to be able to attend a better school in Daegu. She was a jolly, happy girl who found my appearance—my hairy arms especially—quite funny. Jung-aw slept in the family room with the Nas and ate her meals with us. So there were a total of six sharing the ten-by-ten foot ondol room. In my single room of the same size I felt very guilty with the luxury of space I enjoyed.

Until the first week in March, I had been lucky not to have had any health problems. As I was preparing for the first day of classes, I became deathly ill for a period of twenty-four hours, with non-stop vomiting and diarrhea, as a result of food poisoning from a Chinese restaurant downtown another PCV and I had visited. Mrs. Na was concerned that I was sick from her Korean food. I assured her that her cooking was delicious, which it was, and that my sickness came from the restaurant's food, pointing out that the other PCV had become very sick at the same time.

The day after my bout with food poisoning, the weather turned quite warm for several days, prompting the university to shut down all the small heating stoves in the faculty offices. So of course the weather immediately turned cold again, and I was freezing in our stone cold office and classrooms at Kyungpook. As a result, I caught a very bad cold, and after the first week of classes, I lost my voice and taught for several days with a whisper.

I soon recovered, and for a long while I had no further health problems. Of course I was careful not to drink water that had not been boiled or eat any fresh vegetables and fruits that had not been washed by either Mrs. Na or someone else I trusted. Since virtually all Korean crops were fertilized by "night soil" (recycled human or animal feces), we were trained to be extremely careful.

It took only one observation of the beginning of this recycling process to drive home for me how careful I had to be with food. In my first month with the Nas, we were visited by the "honey wagon," which was a small, open truck. Several men lowered buckets into our outhouse and carried out the buckets full of excrement, depositing them in the truck. The smell was horrific! This process went on for hours and was repeated throughout our neighborhood at other homes on a weekly basis. You could usually tell that a honey wagon was in the neighborhood from several blocks away. Later, small tank trucks with large suction hoses replaced the open trucks, which helped cut down on the smell, but the signature odor was always present. And the hoses could not reach our little palace on the hill.

Not only feces were recycled and put to good use. Koreans seem to recycle everything, from glass bottles and jugs to clothes and paper products of all kinds. It was not a formal system but an effective, unofficial operation driven by poverty. Men and women would comb through garbage containers for any item that could be reused and, presumably, sold for a small profit. In the market, there were booths that sold nothing but recycled bottles, cloth, or paper.

As soon as I arrived in Korea, I began to lose weight. Most of the men in groups VII and VIII also lost a lot of weight and began to look quite trim. The average weight loss in the first several months after our arrival was between thirty and forty pounds for the men. I lost about forty-two pounds, not because of sickness or poor food, but because I was eating healthy, non-calorie-laden food for the most part and was walking a lot.

With the women in our groups it was usually the opposite. Most began to gain weight. There was a lot of speculation as to why. The most popular theory was the prodigious amount of rice we were eating on a daily basis, which seemed to affect men and women differently. I also noticed, when I began to visit other PCVs at their Korean homes later in our first year in country, that the female PCVs seemed to have a lot of baked goods—cookies and cakes and pies, either sent from home or made by themselves—available for nibbling. The only chocolate chip cookies that I saw for more than two years were in the occasional box that I got from home or at the homes of the women in our group. Other theories were that the men were engaging in a lot more drinking than the female PCVs and were physically more active than the women, because in Korean culture, men socialized with a lot of alcohol, while women stayed at home.

Part of the reason for my weight loss was that, although the food was quite delicious, I was eating smaller portions, just because I was not used to the type of meals available at restaurants in Seoul, and later, which Mrs. Na prepared. In our family, breakfast was our largest meal, usually consisting of the omnipresent huge bowl of rice (twice the size of a cereal bowl); a fried egg; a large bowl of soup made with bean sprouts, noodles, onions, cabbage, and many other vegetables in a broth; a plate of *kim* (dried, salted, and sliced seaweed); a plate of very spicy cabbage kimchee, made with hot peppers, garlic, onions, and salt; a plate of sliced sausage, carrots, potato, and cabbage, all mixed together with a

131

mayonnaise-like sauce; and finally, a plate of slices of the delicious apples that Daegu was famous for.

Lunch, which I ate at the university, consisted of a boiled egg and an apple that I would take with me from home, or else I would eat a hot soup and noodle dish at the student restaurant—it was the only dish served there but was quite good. It warmed you on cold, winter noons and cooled you on hot, summer days, as the sweat, generated by the spicy soup, evaporated. I could also buy the Korean version of a carry-out lunch, called *dosirak*, consisting of a small amount of rice, kimchee, and assorted vegetables, such as fermented radish.

Dinner at home was almost the same as breakfast—only the portions were smaller. Sometimes Mrs. Na served fried rice or scrambled eggs or a kind of omelet with ketchup over rice. Occasionally, for variety, we had pieces of chopped chicken or a kind of porridge, which I liked a lot. Overall, the food was excellent. Variety, however, was not an outstanding virtue of Korean cooking. Three things in the realm of foods that I missed tremendously: orange juice in the morning, milk, and baked goods, such as breads, rolls, and cookies. At times, I felt like I would have gone to almost any length, short of murder, to have some fresh tropical fruit—such as the mangos, papayas, pineapples, bananas, and other fruits we enjoyed in such abundance in Hawaii.

For every meal at home, we all sat on the floor at the low table in the ondol room, each of us with our own small plate, soup bowl, and rice bowl, but otherwise eating communally from the dishes of food in the center of the table. Everything was sliced or chopped so that it could be easily eaten with chopsticks. A large soupspoon and a set of slippery, stainless steel chopsticks were my utensils (stainless steel chopsticks were much thinner and more difficult to use than wooden chopsticks). After the dinners—which I usually enjoyed very much, despite the noise and confusion of the children—we wiped down the table, folded it up, stored it in a closet, and then sat for a while sipping hot barley tea and discussing the day's events.

At the university, after my second week of classes and several consultations with my students and other faculty, I was able to increase the number of classes from eight to twelve per week, so that each of my four levels of students met for an additional hour each week. Every class also spent one hour per week in the language laboratory.

The lab equipment was about four years old when I arrived, but it was always breaking down, so among the first things I learned was how to fix the tape recorder at the master control in the front of the lab, as well as problems with individual student's headphones. It was set up so that each student could hear the tape recording and listen and repeat the recorded phrases. The teacher at the front of the room could listen to each student but not communicate with individual students. So if a student was making a serious error in pronunciation, the teacher had to leave the laboratory monitor's raised desk at the front of the laboratory and go to the student's seat to correct the student there. I could barely hear the students anyway, over the static in the system, but at least the lab hour provided me the opportunity to speak one-on-one with each student at his or her lab desk, without other students overhearing.

Another project I was asked to undertake was the recording of the university's various English language books. No native English speaker had ever recorded most of these books, so the pronunciation drills and other spoken English exercises in a whole series of books needed to be recorded. I started right away on these recordings. It was tedious work, but it was something that needed to be done as quickly as possible so that the English students at Kyungpook University—including those in the Teachers College and Medical College—would be able to learn correct pronunciation.

My major problem in undertaking these recordings—besides having to repair the tape recorder and splice broken tapes from time to time— was the background noise from the military aircraft that flew quite low over the university campus. Most of the aircraft were extremely noisy jets, and they came over at the rate of about a dozen per hour, or one every five minutes, all day long. You got used to hearing them and forgot about them, until you listened to the recordings and found that the jets' noise made it very difficult to hear the speaker at times. I tried to find the time of day when there were the fewest jets overflying, thinking that I would limit my recording times to these periods. I discovered, however, that from dawn until dusk there really was no good time to record—jet flights were regularly scheduled throughout the day. It didn't help that there was a Korean Air Force base located with the Daegu City Airport, as well as with an American base, known as K-2, not far from the university's campus.

After mentioning this problem to Professor Lee and Professor Kim, I came to work one morning to find that part of our office had been transformed into a small recording studio, lined with corkboard. Inside the little studio, which was about six feet by six feet by six feet, I could record in relative quiet, safe from the jet noise, for the most part. Of course there was no heat in the studio, and it was like recording in an icebox (and in the summer it was swelteringly hot, like a sauna). But I had to hand it to my colleagues. They solved the problem!

The jets' frequent presence in the skies over Korea was just one of many signs that Korea was still very much at war. In my first several weeks in Daegu, this fact was emphasized by a border incident. Six North Korean infiltrators crossed the border near Chumunjin, Gang Won Do, in northeastern South Korea and killed a South Korean policeman on guard duty. The infiltrators reportedly terrorized several Korean families before they fled back to North Korea.

The March infiltration was followed fewer than six months later in October 1968 by an incident in the same northern province, when one hundred and thirty North Korean commandos entered the Ulchin and Samcheok areas in Gang Won Province. Eventually one hundred and ten were killed, seven were captured, and thirteen escaped. There were many South Korean casualties during that time.

The South Korean government of President Park Chung-hee took advantage of every such incident to strengthen security and its control to the fullest, keeping the populace constantly aware of the threat from North Korea. Kim Il-sung, the "great leader" of North Korea, obligingly kept up a steady stream of provocations, which were then reasonably used by President Park as justification for the military curfew, military maneuvers, and omnipresent military—in other words, a tight political hold. President Park was nearing the end of his second term as South Korea's president, and the Korean constitution limited presidential terms to two. The whispered speculation among the academic community was that he was laying the foundation for a change in the Korean constitution to permit him to serve a third term. Kim Il-sung seemed to be trying to prolong President Park's presidential tenure.

Although I was careful not to discuss politics with anyone outside the Peace Corps community, it was clear to all of my PCV friends that if President Park tried to serve a third term, there would be a great deal of civil unrest and probably strong opposition. In spite of Korea's incredible economic progress, even to my relatively naive eyes the domestic situation seemed quite volatile. To the degree, however, that the average Korean perceived that there was a security threat, Koreans would support their government's harsh measures in dealing with antigovernment speech or actions—such as student demonstrations against the government— and overwhelming military and police presence, which enabled a tight governmental rein.

So the threats from the north fed the general acceptance of tight government control and of the military and police means to effectuate such control. The fact that North Korea *had* invaded only eighteen years before gave a certain credibility to the threat. In Daegu there were many army bases, including two American bases—Camp Henry and Camp Walker. Soldiers were everywhere. Armored vehicles patrolled the streets, and convoys of military vehicles were an everyday sight. Every police station was protected with sandbag fortifications in front. During the curfew—midnight to four o'clock—all kinds of military and police exercises were happening in the streets. Heavily armed police and military personnel tightly guarded public facilities, such as the airports, train stations, and bus stations, as well as municipal buildings. For someone like me, who was not used to such an intimidating police and military presence, it was quite depressing at first.

On the other hand, Korea's political and military situation taught me a few things. First, I appreciated the relative absence of heavy- handed, government intimidation back home in the United States— except for the occasional national guard actions on university campuses and civil rights violations by police. I also appreciated the United States' neighbors, Mexico and Canada, and the fact that neither was poised (as far as I was aware) to invade the United States or to send infiltrators to terrorize the population. Additionally, I was grateful for the rule of law at home and for the American constitutional provisions that safeguarded regular elections and stable transitions between outgoing and incoming presidents and members of Congress.

In a situation like Korea's, however, with a proven threat to national security a daily reality, and a society recovering from a recent devastating war, I began to understand that perhaps there was a need both for a stable government without wrenching transitions (i.e., a third term for

President Park) and for a strong military and internal police structure. It was difficult to strike the balance, under Korea's circumstances, between the rule of law and the need for firm, sustained leadership to counter North Korea's threat and to build the economy. Some of my strongest beliefs were beginning to be swayed, or at least I was beginning to see the world's issues in shades of gray, rather than in black and white.

My Kyungpook University Students, Professor Lee Woo-gun, and
Me; Daegu, Korea, June 1969

Language Laboratory, Kyungpook National University, Daegu, Korea,
June 1969

Professors in my English Conversation Class and Me; Kyungpook
National University, Daegu, Korea, July 1969

PCV Moe Cain Teaching at the Teachers College, Kyungpook
National University, Daegu, Korea, July 1969

# CHAPTER SIX—SPRING OF THE YEAR OF THE ROOSTER

As the vernal equinox approached, I began to see signs of spring. It was just in time—the chill wind from Siberia, the lingering snow on the mountaintops, and the bleakness of the city's streetscapes were beginning to get me down. On the grounds of the hospital and the Bible Institute, on the other side of the hill on which our house perched, forsythia began to bloom—ropes of bright yellow, snaking along the fences. The trees on Kyungpook University's campus took on the fuzzy, expectant look of tree buds ready to leaf out. Around the pool and fountain at the center of the campus, crocuses opened their tiny white, yellow, and purple blossoms.

The air was getting noticeably warmer. Spring's tantalizing, first hints in mid March were much earlier in Daegu than in Buffalo, Hanover, or Madison—my last three places of residence. Daegu's latitude was 35 degrees 55 minutes north—about the same as Raleigh, North Carolina. (Seoul's latitude was 37 degrees 30 minutes north—about the same as Richmond, Virginia, ninety miles south of Washington DC.) My thoughts turned to spring in Buffalo and Madison, and to Dariel.

The girl I left behind had been a faithful writer. Half a year had passed since I had seen her and touched her hand. Her letters, however, had grown increasingly distant, which I understood. And then one day I read that she was dating someone new. I guess, in retrospect, I snapped emotionally. I had been longing for her so very much and at times had felt so alone in Daegu. I wrote Dariel a letter, expressing my frustration and anger, that I regretted as soon as I mailed it.

Two weeks later it was returned to me in an envelope, without comment, but torn into little pieces. That was the last letter I ever got from Dariel. I didn't blame her, but she had torn my heart into tiny bits. As the world warmed around me, my emotional despair at losing her—which I had known would happen but never truly confronted or internalized in the excitement and stimulation of all that had happened since I joined Peace Corps—deepened to perhaps the lowest point in my life.

My depression over losing Dariel was even more acute, because I had no one to talk to about how I felt. I didn't feel close enough to my Korean family or friends yet to discuss such personal matters, and I seldom saw any other PCVs. For a few weeks I was in bad shape. The great thing about being in a new culture, however, is the incredible stimulation each day brings. Your mind and senses are bombarded every minute with novel sights and ideas. I found that the best antidote to my despair was to get out into the streets of Daegu, to be with my students or faculty colleagues, or to do something I hadn't done before.

At about the same time, I discovered a little attic in our house on the hill. A narrow staircase led up to a low-ceilinged room (five feet, six inches high) with a floor of straw mats. Koreans called such a floor, which was Japanese style, a *tatami*. The little room was about twelve feet by twelve feet and had windows on three sides. About a third of the room was used to store personal effects of the Na family.

I was still staying in the comfortable Western-style room, with a bed, and feeling embarrassed by the luxury of the space and Western-style furniture, at the time of my discovery. I asked the Nas if it would be all right with them if I moved upstairs, and they agreed. So I moved my little kerosene space heater upstairs and began my stay in the attic. It was perfect for me. The view from the windows was superb. I looked out over most of western Daegu, toward the central downtown part of the city. The space was small enough that the heater warmed it quite adequately in the cold months, and by opening the windows, which were screened, I got fine cross ventilation in the warm months.

The straw mat floor was comfortable for sitting and sleeping. With my ibul and yo I was snug and warm at night. There was also enough room in the attic to seat about seven or eight people on the floor, as I began to conduct informal English language classes there for anyone who wished to come. The Nas were very understanding of all the students and other people who visited their attic. Reverend Na was then able to use the Western-style room, which I had vacated, as a kind of study.

Shortly after my move upstairs, one of the American missionaries—Reverend Bill Grubb—invited me to go with him on the last Sunday in March to a small Presbyterian church in a village. We drove about thirty miles into the countryside in an old Land Rover, through miles and miles of orchards and rice paddies, on a rutted dirt road that looked and felt like the lane leading to the pastures on the New York State farm where I spent many childhood summers. It was a beautiful trip! At our destination—a small, rural village of thirty or so mud cottages with straw roofs—Dr. Grubb preached in the local Presbyterian church—a single room, mud-walled structure with a straw roof, like the rest of the village—while I sat cross-legged on the floor. There were no chairs or alter. A small table in front held a simple cross. I could understand very little of what was being said, but I enjoyed the lovely singing. Bill Grubb's Korean was very good. After the service, we were treated to a sumptuous lunch with all of the local village and church officials.

Everywhere we went in the village swarms of adults and children followed us. It was my first experience with rural Koreans, and their curiosity was amazing. In the cities where I had lived until now, Koreans were fairly used to seeing foreigners, so all that I merited were friendly stares and whispered exclamations of *Megook saram*, which means "American." Of course no one spoke any English. In this village, people had never before seen an American or any other foreigner. It was as though I was leading a parade everywhere I walked! Bill Grubb and I towered over everyone else in the village by at least a foot.

My nose seemed to be the focus of attention. The younger girls touched their noses, after a look at mine, and said to each other, "What a huge nose!" I could understand their Korean, because we had learned the phrase in Peace Corps training in anticipation of the issue. A couple of the braver children ran up and touched my arm, probably acting on a dare, before running away, screaming in excitement and feigned terror.

"I touched the foreigner!" King Kong had arrived with his tall, hairy body and big nose, although it was no longer the Year of the Monkey!

Surrounding the village, the rice paddies were either cloaked in light green—where young rice shoots were already poking up—or being plowed by hand with a wooden plow and oxen. Each paddy was separated from the next by a raised dike of mud about one foot high. Paddies were connected to each other by a channel and small gate that could be opened and closed to either let water in or out, and each paddy was at a different level from the others, so that water flowed naturally from one paddy to the next. The highest paddy was where, from a water source, such as a well or stream, water was introduced to the terraced fields, either by waterwheels, that were operated by a person walking on the wheel to turn it, so that its catch basins dipped into the stream and then dumped the water into the paddy, or by huge, hand-operated dippers, like giant ladles, hefted into the stream and then swiveled above the paddy and dumped.

All had been painstakingly constructed by hand. The amount of work it must have taken to build these paddies over acres and acres of land was phenomenal, particularly when the paddies were terraced up the sides of mountains! I thought of the European cathedrals that had taken a century or more to build, in such homes of my past as Montpellier, France, or Uppsala, Sweden. The rice paddies surrounding this one-room simple church had undoubtedly taken many more centuries and man hours to build and maintain than the loftiest cathedral.

I related to my students how much I had enjoyed visiting the village. As a result, they soon invited me to take a trip with them. During the first week in April, about a dozen of my students and I caught an old country bus to Gyeongju—ancient capital of the Silla Dynasty (57 BC–935 AD), which was one of the Three Kingdoms of Korea and one of the longest sustained dynasties in Asian history. It took about one and a half hours to go about thirty-five miles on a hard-packed dirt road, which wound through lovely mountains and hundreds of gorgeous apple orchards in full bloom. The bus stopped about every five minutes to pick up passengers along the road.

I learned on the bus trip that, at the height of its influence in the fifth century, Gyeongju was the fourth largest city in the world, behind Rome, Constantinople, and Chungking, with a population of more than one million. When we visited, it was a sleepy town of about forty thousand people. Left over from the Silla Dynasty, however, were many impressive royal tombs, looking like one-hundred-foot-high mounds, as well as historic temples, picturesquely scattered in the hills above the city. We visited several, including Pulguk Temple, which was one of the oldest and most famous in Korea.

These were the first Buddhist temples I had ever visited. I was extremely impressed by the beautiful structures—the graceful swoop of the tiled roofs; the incredibly huge wooden beams inside, supporting the roofs; the magnificent, painted murals; the carved stone, wood, and gold statues of Buddha and other exotic entities; and the ornate alters and other decorations. The gray-clad monks, who lived at and tended the temples, had planted gardens and nurtured the surrounding trees over thousands of years, so that the areas around the temples were oases of foliage and flowers in the otherwise treeless and barren mountains.

Temple chimes and bells tinkled in the wind, which rustled through the ancient trees and buildings. The smell of old wood and incense wafted on the air. Swallows twittered above the roofs and nested under the temples' eaves. The rhythmic tok-tok-tok of a *moktak* or woodblock-like hollow gong, sounded like a slow woodpecker's drumming on a tree. I resolved to make many visits to these peaceful, spiritual places, which were free of the crowds and clamor of Daegu. Many of my students were Buddhists and eager to share their knowledge of the religion with me. It was a fascinating trip!

Easter was on April 6, one week to the day before my birthday, and just after I returned with my students from Gyeongju. Reverend and Mrs. Na and I awakened early and headed for Keimyung College, where there was an Easter sunrise service on a hill overlooking the city. I think we got to the hill about five thirty, and there were already a thousand people waiting for the service to begin. A stiff breeze was blowing. It was quite cold. The music and fervor of the crowd were incredible, especially in view of the frostiness of the dawn. It was the first and only Easter sunrise service I have ever attended. I was impressed that the Nas, and so many other Daegu citizens, were devout enough to brave the cold and dark on that April morning. The enthusiasm and commitment of the members of the Presbyterian Church in Korea easily surpassed what I was familiar with in American churches.

The day after Easter Sunday, I received a note from a local printer informing me that my business cards, which I had ordered one week before, were ready to be picked up. This was very important. My university colleagues had business cards that identified their names and positions. When you met someone for the first time, after the initial greeting, it was customary to politely exchange business cards with them, always using your right hand to accept and give cards and touching your left hand to your right wrist (as though to hold back the sleeve of your shirt), as you did so. Of course it was important to read the business card that you were given and then immediately make some indication of your appreciation of the position and importance of the new acquaintance. Reverend Na had a nice way of sucking air through his lips, I noticed, to indicate appreciation of the status of people he met. When I first tried this, it sounded as though I was choking, but I soon learned that a small intake of air—a kind of hiss of pleased surprise—was adequate.

At the same time I received my *tojang,* or "seal," from the tojang shop. In Korea, instead of a signature on a letter or document, people used an ink stamp, applied by pressing on the paper a short piece of wood (traditionally made from a Boxwood shrub), the end of which has been carved with the name of the person using the seal. The wooden stamp is called a tojang, and with ink applied from an inkpad to the tojang, an impressive seal resulted. Some professors used Chinese characters on their tojangs. Others used the hangul version of their names. Mine had my Korean name, of course, in hangul. You carried your tojang with you wherever you went. When I first got mine, I stamped everything in sight. Now I was ready to officially sign the student records that had been piling up in my office at the university, awaiting my official seal.

Shortly after Easter Sunday, I was exploring a new part of Daegu one Saturday morning when I turned a corner and was unexpectedly confronted by an American flag snapping in the breeze. The flag flew from a pole in front of the office of the United States Information Service (USIS), whose existence was news to me. I was dumbfounded to see that flag—it was so totally unexpected, and it had been a month since I had last seen one. I stopped walking and stood there, watching it curl and flutter in the wind. Tears came to my eyes and a huge lump came to my throat. I was overcome with emotion. I stood there for about ten minutes, unable to move, transfixed by the flag and by my wholly unexpected, uncharacteristic, and incapacitating feelings of love for my country, for my Buffalo home, and for my family.

Venturing inside the USIS I met a young Korean man, who greeted me in English and asked if he could help me. His name was Lee Tae-shik, and he was the USIS assistant director in Daegu. I discovered that, among other programs designed to educate Koreans about the United States and American culture, USIS had weekly screenings of American movies. The next week *From Here To Eternity* would be showing. There was an extensive movie library, including several films that caught my eye, such as *Years of Lightning, Day of Drums* (a great film about the life and death of President John F. Kennedy) and (to my great joy) *My Dartmouth*.

The last was an amazing coincidence. There were no other movies about any other American college or university in the USIS' collection. It was almost as if some prescient, USIS administrator in the past had selected *My Dartmouth* for the Daegu USIS collection, out of all the films about American colleges and universities, knowing that someday a Dartmouth graduate would be there, whose heart would be warmed on a brisk spring day by memories of Dartmouth (or perhaps that administrator somehow knew in advance that four decades later Dr. Jim Yong Kim would be installed as the first Korean-American president of Dartmouth, and as the first president of Asian descent of an Ivy League institution).

Films could be checked out for educational purposes, so I made arrangements to borrow films in the future, thinking that they might be a means of jazzing up the English program at Kyungpook. Mr. Lee was helpful and anxious to do what he could to help PCV teachers. The USIS also had English language classes, usually taught by military personnel or missionaries, who volunteered their time as teachers. I told Mr. Lee I could be called as a substitute teacher in an emergency, but I had my hands full teaching English already at Kyungpook and at home.

Over the next two years I used a lot of materials from the USIS, weeding out the more blatantly propagandistic movies and tomes and borrowing many films that helped my students with their English comprehension, motivation to learn English, and understanding of

Western culture. And these films were not censored! You could actually see a kiss on the screen, unlike Korean movies, where kissing and touching were strictly censored. I guess I was engaging in a form of cultural imperialism, to be honest, but the movies were effective teaching tools, and my students seemed to love them.

The following weekend I brought a group of student with me to the USIS building to see *From Here To Eternity.* I had publicized the event in my classes. About fifty students showed up. We all met at the USIS building and trooped inside, astonishing Director Lee with our numbers. I hadn't before realized that the movie had been filmed on Oahu. Shots of the mountains and beaches brought back fond memories of the Peace Corps training there. And what an amazing cast (I even recognized TV's Superman—George Reeves—in the movie)! I think that the girls in my classes especially liked the movie, particularly the steamy scene on the beach with Deborah Kerr and Burt Lancaster. The boys liked the background of the Japanese attack on Pearl Harbor. I liked the movie, but I adored the crown jewel of the USIS building and operation: a men's restroom, tucked in a corner of the first-floor reading room, with an American classic, sit down, oh-so-comfortable toilet.

The next evening I had an excellent Sunday dinner with the American surgeon from New Hampshire, John Sibley and his wife, Jean, and their family, at their Korean home. The Sibleys had two boys and two girls. I showed my slides of Dartmouth to them, to the other missionaries, and to the Korean hospital staff members from Dong San Hospital who joined us for dinner, including Chince and Margaret Allen. At the dinner I met a young Korean psychiatrist, Dr. Shin Kyung-joon, and his exquisitely beautiful and kind wife, Ju-young. Over the next several years, the Shins and I became fast friends. They asked if I would teach English to their two small sons, Kum-ho and Chul-ho, because they were planning to emigrate to the United States in 1971. Of course I agreed, and the ensuing friendship was one of my fondest memories of Korea.

John and Jean Sibley were planning to leave Daegu soon to move to Geoje Island, off the south coast of Korea, where they planned to start a rural public health facility that would minister to the health needs of some of Korea's most isolated and poorest communities. Geoje Island had been the site of a large prisoner-of-war camp during the Korean conflict and was reputed to be one of the most beautiful spots in the Far East. I remembered reading about the island during Peace Corps training. They invited me to visit them once they got established on the island. I immediately thought that helping them might be a meaningful project for the university vacation periods, when volunteers, who were teaching, were expected to do something worthwhile. Also, from the Sibleys' description of Geoje Island, it seemed a place of beauty and need. I could perhaps see another side of Korean life and make a small contribution.

The Sibleys and I felt comfortable with each other from the beginning. It certainly helped that John had taught and practiced at the Mary Hitchcock Hospital and Dartmouth Medical School in Hanover, so we shared a common background in the Hanover area. Both Jean and John spoke Korean very well, and their two daughters, Anne and Meg, were fluent. The Sibley boys, Don and Norman, were less fluent than their sisters but shared the family's appreciation for Koreans and Korean culture. The Sibleys also knew the Peace Corps director's family, as the Sibley children had attended the same school in Seoul as the O'Donnell children.

That evening, I met again the young Korean man, Choi Hwa-wook, whom I had first met with Dr. Allen in the West Gate Market. Mr. Choi told me that he had once been a driver and assistant for the Peace Corps physician in North Gyeongsang Province. He now was helping the Sibleys and planned to assist with the project on Geoje Island. Hwa-wook was an amazing man. He had been raised in an orphanage during and after the Korean War and then had associated with a lot of American soldiers over a long period of time, in various capacities, learning English and American ways. He was tough talking and had a rough demeanor, but his heart was gold.

Other Koreans told me that Hwa-wook's accent indicated he was probably originally from North Korea, although he had no idea how he had come to be raised in the orphanage in Daegu. I think that he decided at some point to take me under his wing. We became drinking partners and close friends in a short time. His favorite name for me was "candy ass," which was a term he picked up from his American military friends. I would have been offended if anyone else had called me that, but from him I understood the term was used with ironic affection.

Hwa-wook introduced me to his "sister" after we had known each other for a month or so. The girl he called his younger sister was named Shin Young-ei, and they had spent many years together in the orphanage, where he had befriended her. Through him, Miss Shin had met several of the missionary families, including the Sibleys. I liked her immediately. She was beautiful and had a smile that lit up the room, but she was quiet and demure. Hwa-wook told me she was studying to become a nurse, and unlike him, had been fortunate enough to have been able to find her real family in recent years. During the spring, when I visited the Allens on Wednesday evenings to take my weekly bath in their Western bathroom, the lovely Miss Shin was often visiting with Margaret Allen, practicing her English.

For about an hour each evening after dinner, Reverend Na and I had long philosophical and religious discussions, in mixed Korean and English—which kept the content down to my level in these areas! I never before realized how little I knew about Christianity and the *Bible*! I am afraid that I shocked him quite a bit with my accounts of American life, growing up in Buffalo, New York, and college life at Dartmouth. But I was careful not to mention my escapades in France, or the student clubs in Uppsala, Sweden, when I was in college, as I felt that might go beyond his limits of understanding and tolerance. I didn't want to be thrown out of his home! The hour-long chat gave him an opportunity to practice his English and me a chance to practice Korean, so it worked out well for both of us, while it also helped us better understand each other and each other's culture.

One evening in early April I took Reverend and Mrs. Na to see the movie *Sayonara*, staring Marlon Brando and one of my favorite actors, James Garner. A downtown theater was showing it in a heavily censored form—in fact, so heavily censored that you could barely follow the story line. The movie was in English with Korean subtitles. Going to the movies was quite a loose thing for a Korean minister to undertake, and in telling one of his friends later about the movie, I overheard Reverend Na justify his presence there by my invitation, which it would have been rude to decline.

To my surprise, however, the next week he invited me, along with an elder, or lay officer, from his church, to see a "girly revue" from Seoul, which came to Daegu for two nights and played to packed houses. I took my binoculars. I think Reverend Na and the church elder thoroughly enjoyed the show, which was a combination of singers, comedians, and dancing girls in tights and skimpy costumes. Although they clucked their tongues continuously and voiced their disapproval of the female dancers, they borrowed my binoculars a lot.

On the day after my birthday, the Na family hosted a wonderful birthday party and ceremony in my honor. They invited several American missionaries, including Bill and Louise Grubb, and another missionary woman, named Mary, and Korean friends—Reverend and Mrs. Kiel— to our house to celebrate. It was really a big deal, complete with the singing of the American and Korean national anthems! From my Peace Corps training, I knew Koreans love ceremonies and at the drop of a hat are ready with elaborate ceremonial procedures, songs, programs, and prayers. It was the largest and best birthday celebration I had experienced in many years! Reverend Na had hand-printed programs in English, which set forth the order of events, as follows:

Congratulatory Program For Chuck Hobbie's Birthday
'69.4.14 PM 6:30
1. Entrance: Hobbie (Handclapping)
2. Congratulation Hymn [400]—together
3. Prayer—Na
4. Congratulation Speech—Grubb
5. Presentation—Na & Mrs. Kiel
6. Birthday Song—together
7. Greeting—Hobbie
8. Meal: Prayer—Mary Thanks.

The "presentation" in the program was a fine gift from the Nas: a Korean *Bible*. After a sumptuous Korean meal, there was even a delicious cake, baked by Mrs. Na, complete with birthday candles. I tremendously appreciated the elaborate celebration and the thoughtful and kind preparations that had gone into the entire affair.

The day after the Daegu birthday party, about two hundred miles to the northeast of our house on the hill, North Korean MiG jet fighters shot down an unarmed US EC-121 reconnaissance plane over the Sea of Japan, about ninety miles off the North Korean coast, resulting in the loss of thirty-one American lives. Immediately, all of the armed forces and police went on full alert. A ten o'clock curfew was imposed for all military personnel. I was stopped several times by Korean police and American military police in the following weeks on Daegu's streets, after the curfew had begun, demanding rather gruffly why I was not back at the American base—Camp Henry. Luckily, I was able to flash my showy new government identification, which I had just received from the Korean government, and which quickly corrected my problems with the police.

As a result of the attack, my Korean colleagues and students at the university all wanted the United States to declare war on North Korea immediately, regardless of the consequences for South Korea. They were really angry at North Korea and itching to fight. In a few weeks, fortunately, the full military alert was lifted and the incident was replaced in all of our minds by the beauty of the awakening Earth all around us.

My students at Kyungpook University continued to be a delight! I already felt close to most of them. Several of my best female students invited me out with them for dinner on my birthday, and my freshman students presented me with a fine three-record set of recordings of Korean lyric poetry, set to music and sung by Korea's leading artists. Three faculty members, as well, invited me out to celebrate.

Even people I met on the streets of Daegu, who engaged me in English conversation, were inviting me out to have dinner. Koreans were all too kind! I was eating out so much that the Na family was getting a little miffed at me. It was really delightful to meet so many people and to visit so many homes (many more than I ever saw in either Sweden or France). I was aware that the many invitations often had the ulterior motive for the issuers of learning English or forming a connection with an American, with possible future benefits. This was natural and perfectly acceptable to me. I also had an ulterior motive in accepting the invitations: pure enjoyment and realization of Peace Corps' second goal (helping promote a better understanding of Americans on the part of the peoples served).

Very typically, after having dinner out, the men in the dinner party would retire to a so-called wine house, beer hall, or some other drinking establishment. These came in a variety of sizes, décor, and expense, but all featured alcoholic beverages of some kind, attractive hostesses, lots of singing, and inebriated men. In April, I began an infatuation with the Korean—and perhaps universal—custom of sharing laughter and songs with friends over glasses of whatever alcoholic concoction is available. I consumed more of such beverages in Korea in my two years there than in my total life before, or since, even counting my four years at Dartmouth, where I was not known to refrain from over-drinking.

The senior male students were the first to introduce me to a *makoli chip*, or *makoli* house, in an old part of downtown Daegu, just off the main street. There were perhaps fifty such establishments, located in a maze of narrow alleys. As you walked through this charming area, the women at the doors of the makoli houses, who were usually dressed in beautiful, traditional Korean dresses, called out to you and tried to pull you into their establishments. "We have the sweetest makoli and the prettiest girls inside!"

At the front door, you removed your shoes and stepped up onto the raised *maru* floor, which served as a kind of veranda. You then entered a hallway with a wood floor, off which were located individual rooms separated from the hallway and from each other by opaque screens, made of thin rice paper, which slid open or shut to permit entry and exit and ensure privacy. The screens at the ends or sides of each room could be slid open to create a larger room, or a smaller room, depending on the size of the party, or on the level of intimacy desired. The rooms were ondol rooms, with a low table in the middle of each and beautifully embroidered cushions surrounding each table. Often, exquisite decorative screens—featuring lovely painted or silk embroidered images—were placed around the room, giving the entire setting a feeling of warmth and luxury.

The hostesses welcomed you effusively, picking up your shoes and storing them carefully (on at least two occasions I lost my shoes at makoli houses, when drunken customers mistakenly took my shoes, leaving their own much smaller shoes for me to ponder). You were then escorted into one of the rooms, helped out of your coat, and guided to a comfortable cushion around the table where often you would be seated between two gorgeous women. Sometimes, the first thing the women did was relieve you of your tie, or on hot nights, your shirt—sometimes even your pants.

When all members of the party were comfortably seated, the *anju*, or snacks, such as peanuts, dried strips of octopus or squid, fruit, vegetable pancakes called *pajeon* or *bindaetteok*, or small dishes of other food were served, followed immediately by bowls or kettles of *makoli*. Makoli is a traditional alcoholic beverage, native to Korea. It is made from rice, which gives it a milky, off-white color, and sweetness, by fermenting a mixture of boiled rice and water, and is about 6.5–7 percent alcohol by volume. My students sometimes called it *nongju*, meaning "farmer liquor." It was refreshing, had a small alcoholic kick, and was very cheap, so for students it was the preferred alcoholic drink.

The women seated on both sides of you fed you, kept your cup filled with drink, and entertained you with singing, games, compliments, and jokes the entire evening. One dubious compliment that I always received (after a woman had rubbed my arms or sometimes my legs) was that I had a lot of hair. "*Igoo, tullimaniyo,*" they would say, seemingly impressed, while I thought to myself that their unvoiced impression was probably that I looked like a monkey with my hairy limbs. Depending on the nature of the drinking party and the composition of the participants, the women would be either sisterly or extremely coquettish.

With my students, the parties involved a lot of singing and wild banging of our chopsticks on the rice bowls and plates. The women were on their best behavior, as was I. After all, I didn't want to scandalize the university with any kind of drunken or wild goings-on, particularly with my undergraduate students. With some of the younger professors or with the graduate students, things sometimes got quite wild, with all participants at these parties—including the lovely hostesses—behaving with risqué abandon.

At my first makoli house I was able to put some of the cultural lessons learned during Peace Corps training to good use. First, in this regard, was the seating at the table. The oldest man in the party typically was honored by being seated at the end of the table closest to the source of heat for the ondol pang. Very often this seat was positioned in the room so that the person so honored faced the entrance to the room. Everyone waited to be seated until the honored person was settled on his cushion. Then in order of age or rank the other men took their seats. With my students, usually I was given the place of honor, even though some were older than I was. If I was with university faculty, they would try to give me—as an honored guest—the special seat, but I was able to defer to the senior faculty member present on most occasions.

When the drinking began, there was a great deal of ritual. The honored person's cup or bowl was filled first with makoli, and then the other bowls, again in order of age or rank. A person drank his bowl completely and then, after ritualistically emptying the bowl of any remaining drops by shaking it upside down, offered his empty bowl to the next person in rank, pouring makoli to the brim. You always used your right hand to extend a bowl to a drinking partner. The recipient, in turn, drank, emptied, and offered the bowl back to the original giver.

As with an exchange of business cards, when receiving the bowl, again always with your right hand, it was important to stand up, bow slightly (making protesting sounds regarding the honor that was being bestowed), and lightly touch your left hand to the right wrist (as though touching a long sleeve to prevent it from interfering with the process) as you received the bowl. The same rules governed giving your bowl to someone else: drain, empty drops, stand, bow, touch right wrist, give bowl, and pour. One never poured one's own drink or poured with your left hand.

By the end of the evening you should have honored everyone in the room with this ritualistic bowl offering, being careful to complete your offerings to all the men before you started to give attention to the women. As an honored guest, I was often in the position of having bowl after bowl of makoli offered to me, every one of which had to be quickly consumed and returned to the giver. Fortunately, being physically bigger than most Koreans (and having had some practice in my college days in the art of chugging alcoholic beverages), I found that I could hold my own without too much trouble. These drinking rituals, although quite unsanitary, were cherished parts of Korean culture for me.

The parties at these makoli houses went on for hours. Unfailingly, however, at about a quarter past eleven the parties would end. Everybody had to be off the streets by the time the curfew siren wailed at midnight. Stories abounded of people who had been arrested or even shot by police on the streets after curfew. I was never tempted to test how far I might get walking home after the curfew began. Of course, the transportation system—all buses and taxis—stopped running by eleven thirty. It was prudent to be well on your way home by that time.

Although at first I found the curfew irritating, it later occurred to me that it was very convenient to have a set time to end social events, guaranteeing that you could get a good night's sleep. The most insistent hosts immediately understood if you asked to be excused so as to get home well before midnight. Also, it was quite beguiling to hear the constant, relatively loud sounds of the city—industrial noises, vehicles, voices, and all of the usual night noises—suddenly still as midnight approached. It was like the birds in a wood quieting after the sun has set. As soon as the last strains of the curfew siren died away into the night air, you could hear a pin drop—the city was so quiet.

As my drinking bouts with students and faculty grew more frequent, the Nas seem to become resigned to the fact that I was an Episcopalian and thus clearly corrupted already, at least insofar as drinking was involved. I had one problem. Most urban Korean homes and any surrounding yards were enclosed by high walls, often topped with barbed wire or broken glass, and accessible only through one gate or door, which was always locked. If you returned home late at night, someone had to get up and let you in. Many of my students, faculty friends, and other PCVs avoided this problem by staying at a nearby yogwan after drinking parties, so as not to disturb their families by arriving home late at night—particularly if they were inebriated—as well as to avoid awkward questions about the night's drunken activities.

On only one occasion I tried staying at a yogwan after an evening of drinking, when one of my graduate students and I had become quite drunk and realized too late that the curfew was upon us. The next morning, when I returned home, Reverend Na knew already that I had spent the night at a yogwan, as well as which yogwan and which makoli house I had been drinking at. News travels fast in Daegu, especially if you are an American staying with a Presbyterian minister who knows virtually all of the one million people in Daegu. On future occasions, when I was tempted to stay the night with a comely hostess at a yogwan in Daegu, I remembered the glass bowl in which I was living.

The Nas' home was on the grounds of the Bible Institute, which had a wall encasing the entire grounds, and two access gates, which were usually manned by daytime guards. The gates were closed and locked by eleven o'clock in the evening, and there was no one around to open them. Happily, I discovered a way to climb over the wall—with the assistance of a little apple tree—avoiding the broken glass cemented into the top of the wall to discourage thieves. The Nas gave me a key to their house (it was unusual to have a door with a key in a home). So after scaling the eight-foot wall and then silently dropping to the ground, I could tiptoe up the path to the house and quietly remove my shoes, enter, slink up the attic stairs, and fall asleep on my yo without disturbing anyone.

Several professors did not drink at all. One day in early spring, an older professor of English, Kim Sung-hyok from the Teachers College, approached me. Professor Kim was a short, balding man who had the best command of English of any Korean I had met. Reverend Na knew professor Kim as a personal friend because the professor was a respected elder in his own Presbyterian church and well known in Presbyterian circles in Daegu. Professor Kim asked me if I would be willing to help him by explaining English idioms and other references to Americana that he found in his English teaching materials. He taught an English writing course, which was more like an incredibly well-informed reading course. His course materials were *Time, Newsweek, Reader's Digest,* and the English version of the *Korea Herald.* He had an insatiable thirst to know about everything mentioned in these publications, and when his dictionary was no help, he came to me.

For example, in one of our first meetings he asked me about "triple plays" in baseball and how it was possible to have a triple play, when no fielder touched the ball. That explanation took a lot of consultation with other PCVs before I came up with one possible answer. (There are runners on first and second with no outs. The batter hits a fair fly ball that can be fielded by one of the infielders. He is out by the infield fly rule, even if no one touches the ball. The runner on first passes the runner on second, so the runner on first is out. Two outs. The runner at second is then struck by the batted fly ball as it lands; there are three outs, and no fielder has touched the ball.) Professor Kim was very familiar with baseball and immediately understood.

On other occasions, in somewhat less familiar subject areas for him, he asked me to explain "French kiss," "hat tricks" in hockey, and "blow jobs," to mention just a few of his more memorable questions. I probably spent several hours each week with Professor Kim, and I came to respect him as a well-educated, kind, and dedicated teacher. Moe, Russ, and I called him Professor *Time.*

After several weeks of our English consultations, Professor Kim invited me to his home for dinner with his family. That evening was one of the most pleasant I had spent in Korea. His entire family spoke excellent English and was well-informed about world affairs and Korean politics. For whatever reason, the discussion was lively and uninhibited by the usual fear of official retaliation, due to some government informer or secret police. I particularly remember his daughter, who was one year younger than I was, was quite outspoken and critical of the repression in Korean society and was absolutely charming and gorgeous in every way.

Several days later I asked Professor Kim about his daughter during one of our English consultations. He seemed very pleased at my interest, asking me what I liked about her, and I thought that perhaps I could get to know his daughter better. At the end of our session, he thanked me for my compliments to his daughter and invited me to her wedding in three months! I thanked him and accepted, a bit disappointed, but pleased to be invited to see another important aspect of Korean life.

My former language teacher and good friend, Kim Hae-shik, contacted me at the end of April. He had returned for a brief visit to Daegu and was concerned about my well-being in his hometown. We had a fine dinner together, and I was able to pour my heart out to a friend. The next night, to cheer me up, he arranged for us to go to a beauty contest—the Miss Gyeongbuk Pageant. Hae-shik had worked as a newspaper reporter in Daegu before joining the Peace Corps training staff, and he knew everyone and every place in Daegu. We had front-row seats. The contestants were something else—talented, beautiful, and shapely, although the bathing suits they wore were extremely conservative and looked like suits from the 1930s at home. The evening improved my feelings and outlook on life considerably. The winner turned out to be a lovely bank teller I had admired from a distance, whenever I went to the local bank to obtain my monthly living allowance, which the Peace Corps regularly sent there.

Later that same evening, Hae-shik introduced me to his charming mother. Without telling his mother (who disapproved of beer halls), before he left Daegu for the States, we spent several evenings together at beer halls, enhancing my cross-cultural understanding and language skills with the short-skirted hostesses. Hae-shik was a fine friend.

By the end of my first full month of teaching, my weekly routine had become fairly well established. I usually worked from nine o'clock in the morning until five o'clock in the afternoon, recording English language tapes and preparing lesson plans and tests when I was not otherwise occupied. I had agreed to write articles for the university's English language newspaper, which was published monthly, as well as to proofread each issue. Several hours each week were devoted to these journalistic obligations. I was also the faculty mentor for the student English club, which met once each month.

Besides the weekly twelve hours of classroom teaching and four hours in the language laboratory, I had English conversation classes with a group of about a dozen professors in my office, for one hour each Tuesday and Thursday afternoon, right after lunch and before my afternoon classes began. On Mondays, Wednesdays, and Fridays I had an open conversation hour in my office with any undergraduate or graduate students who wanted to come.

With the professors, I usually chose a *Reader's Digest* article to discuss each week. The students liked more freewheeling discussions. We talked about everything, except Korean politics and the Vietnam War (Korea had two divisions of soldiers fighting in Vietnam with the United States, and many of my male students had served in Vietnam). I requested that these two subjects not be discussed, because my feelings were strong on both subjects, and I was afraid I might cross the line of propriety as a guest in Korea.

Additionally, on Monday and Wednesday evenings I held a one-hour conversation class in my attic room at the Nas' home. Typically, six to fourteen male and female students—mostly from other colleges and universities, or from the nearby Dongsan Nursing College—as well as some adults attended these home sessions. These conversation classes were my response to the hundreds of requests I had received to teach English to individuals. Rather than saying I was already too busy—which was an unacceptable reply to a request for a favor—I invariably invited the requestor to come to my house on either Monday or Wednesday, or both, for an hour or more of English conversation. In this way I tried to accommodate all requests and could screen out those who were really not well motivated—who came once or twice and then stopped coming. I was pretty busy. Although I tried to keep the remainder of my evenings free of commitments, I was often invited to go to the movies or to a concert downtown with my students.

There were several dozen Korean movie theaters in Daegu. Each had huge signs mounted in front over the entrance, depicting the name of the movie and a scene indicative of the nature of the movie. You could tell at a glance which one of the four typical movie types was playing inside: a pure Korean movie, which was usually either historically based, telling the story of some Korean historical figure or legend or a modern Korean romance, featuring a story of unrequited love with lots of tears, in which one or the other of the main characters left for the United States; a war movie that was usually either American or European with subtitles; a Chinese movie, which was usually a romance or historical epic, with subtitles; or another genre of American movie, with subtitles, which was usually a cowboy movie, such as *Bonanza: The Movie*, with Lorne Greene, or a well-known movie such as *A Thousand Clowns* with Jason Robards or *The Sound of Music* with Julie Andrews.

As I mentioned before, Korean movies almost always featured the same theme and showed no kissing or touching between the sexes, even in the romances. It also intrigued me that many of the Korean films were apparently filmed in unheated sets during winter, so that the frosty breathing of the actors was clearly visible, even when they were supposed to be on the beach in summer or in a warm climate. The foreign movies were heavily censored for sexual and political content. Sometimes the censorship was so pervasive, you couldn't follow the plot. I remember seeing, for example, *Dr. Zhivago* for the first time in Korea and wondering why anyone would consider it a great movie—all of the romantic scenes had been cut, together with any reference to communism, leaving very little left.

My favorite movies were the Korean or Chinese historical movies, which were really quite interesting. Either type gave me a chance to practice my listening comprehension skills, when the dialogue was in Korean, or my reading skills, when there were Korean subtitles. My students seemed to like any kind of movie. After seeing a show, we would head for a tearoom or for the only place in Daegu where you could buy ice cream: the Crown Bakery. My students learned quickly that one of my favorite foods was ice cream, and the Crown Bakery version was not half bad!

Although the movie experience in Daegu left something to be desired, I was pleasantly surprised at the excellent quality of the Daegu Symphony. In April and May, several students invited me to a series of three concerts at the concert hall near the Daegu Station downtown. I was particularly impressed by a concert featuring Brahms's *First Symphony*. On another occasion the symphony performed Handel's *Messiah* with combined choruses from the Daegu area universities, colleges, and churches, and several fantastic soloists. I loved those concerts and went to several dozen in my two years in Daegu, always accompanied by some of my favorite students. As I have previously mentioned, Koreans were excellent musicians!

In the first week in May, all thirty Peace Corps Volunteers in the Daegu area, including secondary school English teachers and health workers in the tuberculosis control program, got together with the Peace Corps staff at Keimyung College for a jam session regarding the campus crisis in the United States. No Koreans were present in the small auditorium where we met. We had all heard news reports and read sketchy articles about students rioting and being shot at on American campuses. Many of us were quite concerned with the information we were receiving. We had a very intense, four-hour-long verbal battle, often pitting the newly arrived PCVs against those who had been in Korea for a year or more.

It was interesting to me that a lot of the so-called senior volunteers, who had left home almost two years before, considered themselves leftist "radicals" of sorts when they left home, but now their views hardly qualified as being left of center on the political spectrum. There had been a tremendous shift to the left in the past two years among American students, and the newly arrived PCVs, like me, reflected that shift. The more recently arrived volunteers were quite antigovernment and extremely antiwar.

I had been closely following the events at Cornell, Dartmouth, and Wisconsin via the army's newspaper *Stars and Stripes*, as well as *Newsweek* and *Time*—all increasingly available in some of Daegu's markets. The news was two weeks old and sometimes heavily censored by Korean authorities. It seemed as though the censors used paintbrushes to apply black ink to offending passages or pages. What I was able to read was all quite confusing to me. From what I could understand, American students on these campuses were so poorly organized that their objectives became lost in the chaos of their violent actions. I remembered that while I was at Wisconsin—with the single exception of the crosses on the lawn of Bascom Hall—never once had there been a definite plan in evidence or a clear objective on the part of the student demonstrators beyond the disruption of classes and the usual demands for amnesty. In my opinion, a majority of the faculty at the institutions I was familiar with was even more radicalized than the students. The faculty and the students seemed like natural allies. The students would have been far more effective in influencing public opinion and, ultimately, government policy if they had worked with the faculty against the more conservative administration and alumni.

In any event, the long meeting served to permit the release of a lot of frustration regarding the Vietnam War, in private, among the Daegu area PCVs. Although much of the PCV anger was directed at our own government, the Korean government received its share as well. After the meeting, we headed for Mel Mirkin's house, where we partied until just before curfew. It was very good to have met, as we did, for many reasons, including the chance to vent, as well as the opportunity to meet other PCVs and to get to know Mel Merkin, the regional director, better.

I liked Mel. He was an attorney, and who liked to smoke cigars and talk in his office with his feet up on his desk. I sometimes wondered, however, where he had come from and what qualified him to be a regional director. The important thing was that he seemed to have our best interests at heart.

Several weeks after the meeting, Moe, Russ, and I were summoned to Mel's office. He told us that he was concerned about reports he had received about us, but he wouldn't be specific. We asked him what exactly had been reported. He was vague and just said that we had better correct our behavior. Then he dismissed us.

None of us understood what Mel was talking about. We knew we had undoubtedly made mistakes and had probably committed many cultural faux pas. We three discussed this meeting afterward at great length, trying to comprehend what we had done wrong over three months that might have been "reported." We were very upset. We never did reach any conclusion, and to this day I don't know what Mel was talking about. When I mentioned this experience with Mel to other PCVs, who had been in Daegu for a year or more already, they mentioned that they had had similar meetings with Mel, equally confusing.

May 11 was Mother's Day in Korea. Virtually everyone wore a red carnation in honor of his or her mother. Many of my female students wore traditional Korean clothes to classes that day as well, because they were either meeting their mothers to celebrate the day with them after classes or just because they wished to honor them by dressing up. I continued to be entranced by Korean women's traditional costumes—the very high-waisted, colorful, graceful long dresses that rustled as they walked. Most of the older women, and most married young women, as well as most women engaged in the entertainment industry—such as tearoom hostesses and makoli house waitresses—wore these exquisite clothes with lovely accessories, such as hair ornaments, silk pouches, fans, bows, and jewelry. Many of these traditional accessories featured interesting, attractive knots of intricate designs in the silken cords supporting neck pendants, attaching fans, or securing pouches. I learned that everything that was part of a traditional ensemble was steeped in symbolism, from the design of a hairpiece to the knot in a silken cord.

With their Korean dresses, the women wore elaborately embroidered silk slippers. Other shoes were made out of various materials, such as leather, rubber, or cloth, depending on the occasion. Men and women often wore white, rubber, slipper-like, canoe-shaped shoes called *gomooshin*, or literally "rubber shoe," on virtually any occasion. Even farmers wore gomooshin working in the rice fields. I found them very comfortable and wore them at home or in the office at the university when I wasn't teaching or meeting with faculty or students.

When Korean men and women were dressing in Western-style clothes, they usually wore leather, Western-style shoes—always well shined. I noticed that, as with almost everything in Korean society, Western-style shoes were beginning to replace the more traditional shoe ware. There was a shoeshine boy on every corner, it seemed. Western-style purses were also beginning to be popular and were rapidly replacing the traditional, fancy pouches that women carried, when dressed in hanbok.

One of my students, Cho Sun-doh, dressed in hanbok on Mother's Day and was the only girl in my senior class of students. Her English was quite good when I first started teaching her, and she usually came to the extra English conversation classes. I remember her well, because she introduced me in mid-May to what became my favorite tabang in Daegu—the *Pyunghwa* Tabang or "Peace Tearoom." The Pyunghwa had a peaceful interior and played Western classical music. The hostesses were friendly, older women who were quite well versed in Western classical music, so you could ask them for a particular composition and they would play it for you on the tabang's sound system. I think that after a while they got pretty tired of playing my favorite works— Tchaikovsky's *Violin Concerto in D, Opus 35*, Dvorak's *Cello Concerto in B minor, Opus 104*, and Brahms's *Double Concerto for Violin and Cello*. The Pyunghwa became my refuge and my listening studio. Nowhere else could I find on a daily basis the music I needed to calm troubled thoughts and lighten my spirits. I went there at least several times a month for the next two years. Miss Cho, whose father (Dr. Cho Ja-yong, otherwise known as Dr. Zozayong) had founded the Emilie Museum in Seoul the previous year—a wonderful museum, featuring traditional Korean folk art primarily—gave me a beautiful 1969 calendar depicting paintings of tigers from the museum, which I treasure to this day.

Toward the end of May, my parents sent me a clipping from the *Buffalo Evening News*—my hometown newspaper. It mentioned that I was teaching English in Korea on a two-year program. It never once mentioned the Peace Corps. I guessed that either the Peace Corps or the university's public affairs department had sent news of my teaching assignment to Buffalo. In checking with other PCVs, I discovered that they had had similar experiences. We were not supposed to broadcast the fact they we were in the Peace Corps in Korea, for our own safety, so we all surmised that it was for safety concerns that the Peace Corps was not mentioned.

The North Korean government seemed to know all about us anyway, for hardly a week went by without a broadcast from North Korea condemning our subversive service in South Korea, and listing our names. The first such broadcast occurred on the day we first arrived in Seoul, listing our names and condemning us at American spies. Some of the nasty things that these broadcasts claimed about us were truly amazing!

The last week in May, two of the freshmen girls in my class invited me to go to a temple near Daegu with them. Miss Pak and Miss Rhee were excellent students and spoke very good English. I was surprised when they invited me, but their descriptions of the ancient temple quickly persuaded me to accept their invitation. We visited Dong Hwa Temple.

To the north of Daegu stretches a great ridge of high summits and deep valleys known as the Palgong Ridge. The highest peak is called Palgong Mountain, or the "mountain of the eight generals," in honor of eight ancient warriors who died defending its slopes. On the lower slopes of the ridge a temple was established in the middle of the fifth century. It was replaced in 1832 by the lovely temple there today, which is named for the beautiful, purple-blossomed Paulownia trees found in the surrounding forests. In May, these trees were just coming into full bloom and looked like huge wisteria bushes, with their hanging purple cones of blossoms.

The monks at the temple were preparing for the celebration of Buddha's birthday, which fell on Friday, May 30. There were both male and female monks. All were wrapped in gray robes and had been shorn of hair. The temple complex of more than a dozen buildings had just been renovated, and the walls of each building had been stained a lovely dark red. Flowers were everywhere. The grounds had been carefully raked. A gentle breeze from Mount Palgong rustled through the pines. My students painstakingly explained to me what the temple signs, murals, and statues meant. Both Miss Pak and Miss Rhee were Buddhists and seemed to delight in explaining Buddhism to me.

After touring the various buildings that comprised the temple complex, my two students and I hiked several miles along a stream, further up the mountain. The fragrance of the pine trees, gurgling waters of the stream, and magnificent views of neighboring mountains reminded me of New Hampshire's White Mountains. We spent a delightful day together at Dong Hwa Temple, which from that day on became my favorite temple of the thirty or so temples, which I later visited in Korea.

On Buddha's birthday, after classes were finished, many of my students rushed to their homes to get ready to visit the dozens of temples in the mountains around Daegu. Having just visited Dong Hwa Temple, I turned down several invitations to hike into the mountains that evening with them. From our house on the hill, however, I watched the torch-lit procession of people in the streets of Daegu below, streaming out of the city into the mountains to visit the temples, where elaborate, celebratory rituals would soon take place. Everyone carried lanterns or candles in these processions. As darkness fell, I saw the streams of light, climbing into the mountains, and then, several hours later, returning to the city.

The weather in Daegu on June 1 was very pleasant—warm, but not yet hot, with clear, sunny skies. The spring of 1969 had been lovely up to this point. Although flowers and trees in Daegu were few and far between, in several parks I saw beds of tulips in April and then iris and petunias in May. An occasional magnolia or cherry tree peaked over the high walls surrounding homes in the early spring, suggesting that hidden inside the walls was a garden of spring delights. Trees had been planted along several of the main boulevards in the city in the past ten or twelve years, but these were still small and struggling. Every day, however, I saw freshly planted street trees downtown—eventually Daegu would become a beautiful city of trees, I thought, if its citizens kept up the planting.

After several months in Daegu I felt that two of the most physically attractive places in the city were the Kyungpook University campus and the grounds of the Bible Institute and neighboring Dongsan Hospital, where the Nas' home was located. Both had mature trees of all kinds, as well as gardens of flowers, so I was fortunate to work in one oasis of green and then to be able to go home in the evening to another.

Brightly colored parasols blossomed everywhere in June, with the late spring clothes of the women. Korean women, including college-age girls, apparently did not like the sun. Mrs. Na told me that it was a longstanding custom for women to aspire to lighter skin, since a darker complexion was an indication of an outside laborer, such as a farmer, and thus an indication of lower status. Almost every woman carried a parasol, even relatively young girls. The female PCVs in my group, who had started to develop nice tans from the June sun, told me how horrified their classes were at this development and how they had been cautioned to use parasols at all times in the open air to protect their skin.

With the dazzling parasols on the streets came the shouts of children, as schools—from the kindergartens to the universities—held weekly parades, athletic games, and picnics, so the streets were filled with marching students and student bands. At Kyungpook University, the combined English departments of the Liberal Arts College and the Teachers College decided to have a softball game—faculty against students. We played on one of the grassless athletic fields. Professor Kim Hong-gun, an expert in Shakespeare, pitched the faculty to a close victory over the undergraduate males (none of the female students or faculty felt it was appropriate for them to participate).

Of course Moe, Russ, and I played on the faculty team. The students were well ahead of us in the later innings of the game, when miraculously, the faculty started to catch up and then finally passed the student team, winning by one run in the ninth inning. I suspected that the outcome of the game was predetermined. There was no way the faculty could be allowed to lose to the students. But the engineering of the faculty victory by the students was so deftly and subtly accomplished with strategic errors that it was a thing of beauty. I remember that game with a great deal of fondness. It was the first and last student-faculty game like it that we had while I was at Kyungpook, because political issues soon thereafter adversely affected the relationships between faculty and students, and even between faculty members themselves.

The fine weather also brought out the smaller neighborhood children, who escaped in June from the confines of their walled homes and often played games, such as the Korean equivalents of Patty-cake, Hopscotch, and Skip Rope in the alleys outside their front doors. I liked to sit on the steps leading up the hill to our house and listen to their songs and cries. In so doing, I often heard mothers calling for their children and realized that a significant number of them seemed to have the same names; at least, when mothers or fathers called for their children to come inside, they seemed to be using the same name.

When I asked Reverend Na about this, he thought a minute and then explained that there are many terms used to express family relationships. As in other aspects of the Korean language, there are many "levels" of speech, reflecting the stratification of interpersonal relations in Korean society, depending, among other things, on the status of the speaker, the status of the person spoken to, and the status of the person spoken about.

For example, the word a man uses to refer to his wife will depend upon the man's relative position to the person with whom he speaking. When speaking to a higher-ranking person, one's wife is referred to as *chaw*. To an equal, one's wife is *chipsaram* ("house person") or *ansaram* ("inside person"). To a very close friend, a wife is *anae*, while to a person of lower status, she is *agiomoni* (his "child's mother"). To me, Reverend Na referred to Mrs. Na as *chipsaram*, while she referred to him as *moksa* ("minister") and to me as *sunsaengnim* ("honorable teacher"). I usually addressed Reverend Na as Na *moksanim* ("honorable Minister Na"), although sometimes I mixed up the word for carpenter, which is *moksu*, with *moksa*, calling him "honorable carpenter," which always set Mrs. Na off into gales of laughter. I called her *samonim*, which is a polite form of addressing a friend's wife.

In the case of the neighborhood children, what I was hearing was the commonly used term in Daegu to refer publicly (in the context of shouting for a child to come home) to a young son as *gaedong* ("dog poop") and to a young daughter (in the same context) as *cokchee* ("apple stem"). These terms were used, I was told, rather than the given names of the children (which usually connote some lovely or noble meaning), so that evil spirits, hearing a mother call for dog poop or apple stem, will not be tempted to take a child away. Infant mortality was still high in Korea.

As the weather warmed, the herbal and spice fragrances along the route I walked every morning, through the *Yakryong* Market to the bus stop, grew in strength to the point that my senses reeled in pleasure as I passed the shops. From the Nas' house to the main street in Daegu, called *Tongilro*, where I caught a city bus every morning to Kyungpook University, I walked through the heart of the herbal medicine market on the street known as the street of the Chinese drugstores. Both sides of the narrow street were lined with medicine shops selling herbs, snakes, ginseng, spices, and all sorts of weird concoctions. Like most Korean shops, they opened onto the street, and the grinding, milling, and mixing of the herbs and other ingredients were all done in the front of the shops, right next to or in the street. In the afternoon, as a result, when the sun hit the baskets and piles of ground bark and roots on the curbs of the street, warming them, there was the most delicious aroma permeating every corner of the district. It was a mélange of cedar, pine, and other exotic, spicy smells.

One shop in particular, called the *Kwangshin* Chinese Medicine Shop, with its array of baskets and pots of shredded barks, chopped herbs, and other delightfully smelling ingredients right next to the street, lit up your olfactory senses as soon as you came within sight. I loved those smells! At another store—the *Cheil* Chinese Medicine Shop—a wide variety of ginseng roots, in all shapes and sizes, were displayed in the front window in glass containers. Ginseng smelled and tasted like the dirt pies I made as a child, I found, when I was invited to sample some (to enhance my male potency) at this shop one afternoon on my way home.

Other PCVs, when they visited me, often commented how appealing the walk down that street was! When I mentioned this to my students—many of whom walked the same route from downtown to get to the classes at my home—they were incredulous that Americans *liked* these odors, because for them the smells were medicinal and evoked unpleasant feelings, as the smell of disinfectants and rubbing alcohol did for me.

Early in June I received a letter from the Peace Corps office in Seoul advising me that I had been designated as the representative of the PCVs in North Gyeongsang Province to attend a Peace Corps conference in Seoul, scheduled for the next weekend. The letter had been mailed in Seoul two weeks earlier. It had taken more than twice as long to reach me as letters from home, which normally took about five days. This was the first of five trips I took to Seoul over the next two years. It had been more than three months since I had left Seoul for Daegu. I was quite apprehensive about going back to the capital city! The Nas cautioned me repeatedly about the dangers of Seoul, although I knew that, like all Korean cities, it was one of the safest cities in the world, with almost no violent crime at all.

I took a train north to Seoul on my brother's birthday—June 5. By train the trip took about four hours, which was a little faster than previously, as several new express trains had recently been added to the main train line between Seoul and Busan, and I was able to catch one of these faster trains from Daegu.

After three months in Daegu, coming back to Seoul was quite a shock! Seoul and Daegu were like two different worlds! The conference was held at Kyunghee University—a magnificent, lavishly ornate university with a lovely campus, complete with hundreds of statues of naked women. The newspapers were reporting that the administration of Kyunghee University was under investigation by the Ministry of Education for misuse of funds. If the campus was any indication of how funds were spent at Kyunghee, perhaps the investigation was justified.

It was great to see so many friends from the K-VII and K-VIII groups in Seoul, many of whom I hadn't seen for four months. They all looked just as lean as I was, which made me feel better about my more-than-forty-pound weight loss. We learned that so far—more than four months since our arrival—no one had terminated from our groups after arriving in Korea. That had never happened in the previous six Peace Corps groups, in which some PCVs had left for home almost as soon as they had arrived. I was not surprised. Our training had been very thorough, our assignments were well structured and in academic environments we were already somewhat familiar with (having just come from American campuses), and Koreans had been extremely kind and determined to make us feel at home.

Ed Klein—my former Peace Corps training staff member—invited me to stay with him in his apartment in Seoul for the three nights I was there. Ed had been hired as a troubleshooter for the university TESOL program, because his Korean was excellent, he was very familiar with the English teaching program, and he had been one of our trainers in Hawaii, so he knew us. Peace Corps couldn't have picked a better person for the job. Another good friend from training—Brian Copp—was representing PCVs in North Jeolla Province at the conference. Ed, Brian, and I spent three great nights on the town in Seoul, with several of the Korean professors and other Peace Corps staff visiting various drinking establishments.

Ed seemed to know all the best places for imbibing liquor in Seoul. We visited several of his favorite makoli houses the first night. On the second night we moved on to a higher level of drinking establishment, where *soju* was served. It is a kind of extremely potent, clear liquor distilled from starches, such as rice, barley, or potatoes. On the last evening together we visited several maekju chips or beer halls. Korean beer was excellent—especially OB Beer—and reminded me of my favorite European beers, such as Tuborg or Heineken. Of course, the purpose of the Seoul visit was not to explore Seoul's drinking establishments, but adjourning to such places to share drinks each evening with other conference participants assured that all attendees knew each other well and felt comfortable in candid discussions with each other.

The conference began on June 6 and lasted two days. Essentially, it was a frank, open dialogue among about ten PCVs, representing all of the college- and university-level English teachers and a dozen or so Korean university faculty members, as well as several Peace Corps staff, including Director O'Donnell and a new Korean staff member named Song Yun-ki.

Mr. Song had joined the staff the previous year as an assistant regional director. I liked him immensely. He was fifteen years older than I was but had been a pharmacist before he had joined the Peace Corps/Korea staff and was delighted when I told him that my father was also a pharmacist. He was a particularly effective mediator between the Korean participants and the PCVs during the days of discussions. Years later we became close friends.

For two days, Koreans and Americans aired complaints back and forth in the most delicate and face-saving words imaginable. The biggest complaint by the Koreans about us was that some PCVs were leaving the schools in the afternoon, when their classes were finished for the day, well before five o'clock. Their excuses were often that they were taking lessons in some aspect of Korean culture—such as a traditional musical instrument, poetry, calligraphy, singing, or taekwondo—or Korean language lessons. The professors wanted more time devoted to English teaching and preparation of teaching materials, and felt that, since Korean faculty members were required to stay at schools until five o'clock, PCVs should follow the same schedule. They had a good point.

The PCVs' major issues were housing and money. Many of the K-VIIs and K-VIIIs were still living in yogwans and eating at restaurants, for the most part. Their schools had not been able to find housing for them with a Korean family. Especially in the smaller cities—outside of Seoul, Daegu, and Busan—it was difficult to persuade a Korean family to bring an American into its home. When I described my living arrangements with the Na family, I felt fortunate indeed!

The other primary problem for the PCVs was the relatively low living allowance provided by Peace Corps, which was based upon faculty salaries at our respective schools but did not reflect the additional outside income that all faculty members received from various sources. When we first arrived in Korea, Director O'Donnell had explained that living allowances for PCVs were different for each PCV, depending on each individual's circumstances. Living allowances were supposed to be set at a level that permitted you to live like your Korean colleagues in your workplace—no better and no worse.

So, for example, a PCV who was working as a tuberculosis control health worker in a small rural village would receive a relatively modest monthly stipend, so as to enable the PCV to live and spend at a level equivalent to a Korean coworker in the same village. A PCV health worker doing the same work, but living in the relatively more expensive city, would receive a higher monthly living allowance, to compensate for the higher cost of urban living.

Similarly, a PCV teacher in a rural high school would receive a lower monthly stipend than a PCV teacher in an urban high school. Living costs also varied with your local climate. It was more expensive to live in a colder climate, due to the cost of the expensive kerosene necessary to fuel a small space heater, than it was to live in the milder climate zones of Korea—along the south coast or on Jeju Island, for example—where space heaters were not necessary.

All of us had received a settling in allowance when we first arrived at our sites, in addition to the monthly living allowance. This initial lump sum was to enable purchases of such necessities and small luxuries as ibuls and yos, space heaters, electric fans, bicycles, winter boots and jackets, and even clothes. Again, PCVs were expected to be frugal, to live simply, to avoid luxury purchases, and to make due without supplemental income from any source (with the possible exception of occasional birthday or holiday gifts from home). Above all, since we were *volunteers*, we could not accept money for any outside work or other activities.

As our combined programs were the first college- and university-level teachers to come to Korea, there was some initial uncertainty as to what the level of our living allowance should be. Peace Corps/Korea had had no prior experience at the higher economic levels of society, where we worked. Korean college and university teachers were comparatively well paid relative to teachers at elementary and secondary schools, and most supplemented their salaries tremendously with fees from their private tutoring of students, which more than doubled their incomes.

From the beginning of the Peace Corps programs in Korea in 1966, Director O'Donnell had wisely decided to trust PCVs with setting their own living allowances, depending upon their circumstances, in consultation with Peace Corps' fantastic and charming finance officer, Mrs. Shim Jai-ok. If you wished to raise—or lower—your monthly allowance, you had to write to or visit Mrs. Shim to present your reasons. Peace Corps was generous in paying for cross-cultural activities and Korean language tutoring. The system worked pretty well.

For the college- and university-level teachers, the money issue raised at the June meeting in Seoul was whether the cost of reciprocating for Koreans' many kindnesses—such as the dinners and drinking parties to which our faculty colleagues and students were constantly inviting us—should be reflected in higher living allowances. One fancy dinner for twelve people, for example, with tips and an evening of drinking could cost about forty dollars—more than an entire month's living allowance. Should the cost of the dinner be a one-time increase in a PCV's living allowance, or should the costs of reciprocity be budgeted on a monthly basis with justification presented to Mrs. Shim?

In the end, the PCV representatives took this issue back to the PCVs in the provinces we represented to find out how best to handle the problem. Ultimately it was left to each PCV, as usual, to work with Mrs. Shim to determine an appropriate monthly living allowance that would reflect each PCV's circumstances. In my more than two years of service in Korea, I found I raised my living allowance several times a year—a consequence of my becoming more familiar with Korean etiquette and thus incurring more reciprocity costs, of the rising room and board monthly fee that I paid to the Nas, and of the increased travel I undertook around Korea.

The conference lasted all day Friday and Saturday. On Saturday night I saw three of my Korean friends off for the United States. They were going to American graduate schools.

On Sunday afternoon, I was invited to a breathtaking dress rehearsal at the National Academy of Fine Arts. Miss Yim Hyo-bin—the sister of my Korean language instructor, Yim Cho-bin, whose family I had visited on New Year's Day (the lunar new year)—was starring in a dance-drama performance of the Korean story *Choon Hyang Jun*, which was the Korean equivalent of Shakespeare's *Romeo and Juliet*.

*Choon Hyang Jun* is one of the most famous, classic stories of Korea, based on a supposedly true story of the Yi Dynasty. According to the legend, Yi Do-ryung, a son of a magistrate, falls in love with Choon Hyang, who is not of noble blood. Yi Do-ryung's father gets a new government assignment in Han Yang (Seoul). Yi Do-ryung promises Choon Hyang that he will return for her. The new magistrate, who replaces Yi Do-ryung's father, wants Choon Hyang as his mistress, and tries to force her compliance. She refuses to give in to his harsh demands, despite torture and imprisonment. In a dramatic conclusion, Yi Do-ryung returns as a special magistrate, discovers his lover's predicament, saves her, and marries her. Choon Hyang's chastity and faithfulness in the face of great adversity are vindicated.

Her virtues are revered even now in Korea. Hyo-bin and I later discussed this story, and she indicated her dismay that the virtues of chastity and faithfulness in Korea were regarded as exclusively *feminine* virtues. She had been the victim of an arranged marriage at the age of sixteen, and her former husband had not had Choon Hyang's virtues and would not have been expected to in Korean society—quite the opposite.

Hyo-bin was extremely talented and beautiful in the role of Choon Hyang. Many in the audience told me she was an artistic genius. The dancing and music were superb! I was totally entranced during the entire performance, and I think of her whenever I see one of the film versions of *Choon Hyang Jun* or encounter the legend in other artistic forms.

While I was in Seoul, Deputy Director Wayne Olson approached me with a proposition. He said that he had heard that I took a lot of pictures and wondered if I would be willing to be an official Peace Corps/Korea photographer. Peace Corps would pay for film and developing; it would make duplicates of any pictures that I took for use in training and other programs. I agreed, of course. Over the next year and a half I took about four hundred 35-millimeter slides.

I also heard news at the Peace Corps office about other Peace Corps friends. Four former language teachers—Ahn Hee-ja, Song Sook-ja, Choi Seung-deuk, and Kim Chang-whan—were working for Peace Corps again as language teachers at the current Peace Corps training program at Fairleigh Dickinson College in Madison, New Jersey. My good friend Chang Hae-ung had extended his visit in Toronto and probably would not be returning to Korea. I also heard that a conference participant—Professor Chae Joong-ki, who was a Teachers College professor at Kyungpook University, who had been very helpful to Moe, Russ, and me—was going to Indiana University on a Fulbright grant in the autumn.

I was glad to return to the more familiar environs of Daegu early on Monday morning. The train rides to Seoul and back provided lovely, panoramic views on both sides of the train of the Korean countryside in late spring, with its hundreds of shades of light green in the rice and barley fields, blue sky, and purple mountains. Everywhere there were crouching people, working in the paddies or washing clothes in the occasional river that we crossed. I reflected that I felt at home in Korea now, after almost five months, and it was a good feeling.

June 1969 was a month of presents and *putaks*, which may be loosely translated as "favors." Koreans had a wonderful custom of doing something for you before they asked you for a favor, or conversely, reciprocating for a favor you have performed by giving you a present or doing something nice for you. Reciprocity could be called a lynchpin of Korean culture. Often, engaging in this tradition was formally announced at the outset, as in "I would like to invite you to dinner, as I am about to ask you for a favor." I liked this tradition, although sometimes I had to emphasize that I could not accept monetary payment for any favors I performed.

This last rule sometimes created a serious problem for my Korean students, friends, and colleagues. On more than one occasion, Professor Lee Woo-gun came to me and said that someone had asked him to ask me, since I wouldn't accept money, what I would accept as a reciprocal gesture for a putak, or favor, that I had performed. Well, my honest answer would have been either a hamburger and French fries with a milkshake or a date with some hot Korean girl who yearned to sleep with a horny American guy—probably in that order. These both being impossible, of course, I didn't mention them to Professor Lee. My usual response was as culturally correct as I could make it. I often replied that something small, but typically Korean, that would remind me of my good life in Korea would be much appreciated.

So in June, the professors in my weekly conversation classes presented me with an expensive new summer suit (I think they had noticed the threadbare condition of the two wool suits I had brought to Korea and worn for the past five months). It was a lovely present, and I was overwhelmed by their generosity. Several days later the graduate students who had joined my weekly conversation classes in my office and who I permitted to sit in on any of my other classes gave me a lovely, traditional Korean painting on a silk scroll. As the term drew to a close, other faculty members and several students invited me out for dinners and drinking parties. One week I was out six straight nights—all this at a very busy time at the end of the term, when exams had to be prepared, administered, and graded.

In mid-June, Reverend Grubb asked me if I would accompany six American boy scouts on an overnight weekend hike. He and his wife had been very kind to me. I thought that this trip might reciprocate for some of their gracious acts (they spoke English already, so offering to teach them English—one of the few reciprocal gestures I could afford—would not be appropriate). I had just concluded the exam period and finished several tedious days of grading exams, so I was ready for a change anyway. A hike seemed just the thing!

We climbed *Apsan*, which translates as "Front Mountain," right next to Daegu's southern border. It was the first of dozens of my climbs of this thirty-four-hundred-foot mountain, which was conveniently close, provided spectacular views of the city to the north and of other mountains and valleys to the south, and had a well-trodden trail leading from a city bus stop.

We walked from the bus stop on that first trip along the edge of several rice paddies and then up a ridge on a dirt trail, through mostly barren terrain strewn with rocks and boulders. The trip to the summit took about three hours. There was no one else anywhere on the mountain, as far as we could tell. We camped on the ridge on a perfectly clear and calm night, with the city lights twinkling below and the stars above. After the boys had fallen asleep, I sat and watched the lights wink off in the city below until well past the curfew. It was incredibly peaceful.

Although I carried a two-quart container of water, which we all shared, none of the scouts had remembered to bring water, and there was no water available on the mountain. So after my water was depleted, we ran out. I kicked myself for having forgotten to check this important detail before we set out. The weather was so cool, however, that we managed quite well without water on the second day. We hiked more than five miles along the ridge trails on the south side of Apsan, which overlooked valleys of deep woods and provided lovely views of a large wilderness area.

Late on Sunday afternoon, after a vigorous hike and repeated complaints from the boys about how thirsty they were, we retraced our steps down to the bus stop, where we bought bottles of the popular Korean carbonated drink called Chilsung Cider—much like Seven-Up or Sprite and not at all like American cider—and quenched our thirsts.

I was puzzled on the way down that on the north side of the mountain there were virtually no trees, while the south side was green, heavily wooded, and looked like New Hampshire's White Mountains. I surmised that sixteen years before, during the Korean War, the north side had been denuded, either by military action or by frantic people, desperate for fuel. As far as I could tell, there was no effort to plant trees on Apsan or to take advantage of the proximity of this fine mountain to Daegu to make it more accessible to people. I hoped that in the future, trees could be planted on the denuded mountainsides, but I also hoped, selfishly, that not too many Koreans would discover how wonderful the mountain's views and peacefulness were, for I appreciated tremendously the solitude of the trails on which we had hiked.

Spring wound down in Daegu in a burst of glory on the grounds of Kyungpook University and on the Bible Institute and Dongsan Hospital grounds at our little hill, where rose bushes of all varieties were blooming in mid-June. I only knew of two public parks in the entire city of Daegu, and they were poorly maintained, except for a handful of flowerbeds. There were a few rose bushes in these parks, but their isolated brilliance only underscored the almost total lack of flowers in public places elsewhere. The climbing roses, spilling over the stone and concrete walls that surrounded most of the residences in the city, testified to Koreans' love of flowers. The occasional peek I got at private gardens behind those walls, such as at the home of Dr. Shin Kyung-joon, where I went one evening each week to teach his boys English—convinced me that Koreans were excellent gardeners. I guessed that scarce resources for public works required that public urban beautification be a low priority.

As the end of the first term approached at Kyungpook University, the faculty grew increasingly nervous about the undercurrent of student unrest, which in June had subtly insinuated itself into classes and student events with increasing strength. Exams were scheduled for early July, but the rumor floating around was that exams would be postponed until autumn, after the summer vacation break. For the teachers who wanted to wrap up their courses, this was an unhappy prospect.

I was confident that all of my students would pass my examinations, whether they took them in July or September. I just hoped that none would get into political trouble and be forced out of the university. While worrying about that possibility I ended my first term of teaching, generally pleased that classes seemed to have gone well. I had many friends among the faculty, graduate students, and undergraduate students. My Korean family, as well, was all anyone could ask for. I felt extremely lucky to be in a Peace Corps program that was so well structured and fulfilling in many ways. Most of all, I felt fortunate to be in a country like Korea, with natural beauty, an amazing history, an ethic of hard work and academic excellence, and tremendously hospitable people. I remembered my initial negative information and fears about Korea, gleaned from encyclopedias and general American sources, and realized how poorly informed Americans were about this amazing country and its incredible people.

Street in Daegu, Korea, July 1970

My Junior Students at Kyungpook National University, Daegu,
Korea, July 1969

Sophomore Students' Class with Me, Kyungpook National
University, Daegu, Korea, July 1969

Freshmen Students (Miss Pak with Hairpin and Miss Rhee Touching
her Lip), Kyungpook National University, Daegu, Korea, July 1969

# Chapter Seven—Summer of the Year of the Rooster

n Daegu, the weather was getting hot and humid on the summer solstice. I bought an electric fan with some of my living allowance and had it on most of the time I was in the little attic, as the daytime temperatures soared into the mid-nineties. Usually at night a breeze sprang up from the mountains, and the temperature dropped into the fifties or sixties, so I could turn off the fan and still get a pleasant breeze through the attic's open windows.

Reverend and Mrs. Grubb had generously loaned me their stereo tape recorder, as well as about two dozen tapes of classical music, before they left in June on a one-year sabbatical back to the States. Because I had my own source of classical music right at home now, my trips to the Pyunghwa Tearoom grew less frequent. I also had a small but powerful radio on which I could easily pick up AFKN (Armed Forces Korea Network). AFKN played 90 percent Country and Western music. Classical music was not popular with the army, apparently, as only about two hours of classical music was programmed weekly. Additionally, I clearly received Radio Moscow, Radio Peking (now Beijing), and both the South and North Korean government stations. Radio Pyongyang (North Korea) was broadcast at several different frequencies, which changed daily. Although it broadcast in Korean, it was easily distinguished from the South Korean stations by the harsh, strident announcements and strange music.

Another wonderful source of excellent classical music, as I have mentioned already, was the Daegu Symphony, which performed twice each month. I went to as many concerts as I could. Admission was less than one dollar. I soon concluded that the Daegu Symphony was about on par with the Dartmouth Symphony, which I knew well from having sung many concerts with it when I was in the Dartmouth Glee Club. Small but good, the Daegu Symphony had several very excellent musicians, and others who were not so good. The string section was quite excellent. The woodwinds needed help! A typical program, which was performed the last week in June, featured Sibelius's *Finlandia*, Beethoven's *Piano Concerto No. 1 in C Major, Opus 15*, and Beethoven's *Symphony No. 4.*

All the soloists I had heard to this point were under the age of sixteen. They were, without exception, really terrific! The pianist on June 24 was a fifteen-year-old girl named Mi Hyun-moon, who played magnificently! The thought occurred to me that there were probably very few older musicians, because Korea had only been free of the harsh Japanese occupation since 1945, and the Korean War had shortly afterward devastated the country—including its music education. The war had ended only fifteen years earlier. It was remarkable that in such a short time, high-quality musicians had emerged.

In June the Seoul Symphony played an awesome concert in Daegu. I felt it was comparable to the Buffalo Philharmonic Orchestra, which is one of the better ensembles in the United States. I was pleased to have been invited to the concert by several students. Generalizing from the two Korean orchestras that I had heard by the start of the summer, I ranked the quality of Korean musicians and orchestras as very high. The string players, in particular, were of the highest caliber, as were the piano soloists.

When I stopped to think about it, I realized that in Korea I could often hear Western classical music wherever I happened to be. I have already mentioned that many tearooms played classical music. At middle schools and high schools, I often heard classical music being broadcast outside by loudspeakers. Sometimes on city buses, classical music was featured (although the usual fare was Korean popular music, with its characteristic beat of "ja-ja-jung-ja"), and on trains, classical music was omnipresent.

Most amazing to me were the piano practice rooms, scattered

throughout Daegu, where for a small fee you could rent an upright piano for an hour. Music students practiced in these establishments, for no one had a piano at home. Typically, ten to twenty pianos were squeezed like sardines into these rooms, back to back. The students practiced in the midst of a tremendous cacophony of music, with other pianos playing on all sides. The din was overpowering! I wondered whether these abysmal practice conditions were the reason the Korean piano soloists I heard were all so excellent.

I had my first blind date in Korea on the last weekend in June. Miss Chung was an attractive graduate student of nursing from Youngnam University who was a friend of one of my graduate students at Kyungpook University. We double-dated with another Korean couple from Youngnam and enjoyed an evening of mixed Western ballet, classical Korean dance, and traditional farmers' dances, performed by students at Youngnam. It was incredible! I saw for the first time the amazing Korean drum dances that I had heard so much about, as well as a dance performed by a single drummer, moving quickly between two rows of eight suspended, gong-like drums and beating so many drums at the same time that it made my head spin. In the farmers' dance, streamers tied to hats on the dancers' bobbing heads were swirled around the dancers, who danced over and under the flowing ribbons of color while beating drums and cymbals. The faster dances had heart-stopping rhythms, pounded out by every kind of drum imaginable. All of the dancers were dressed in either traditional Korean hanbok or in farmers' clothes—white, baggy shirts and pants with bandanas around their heads. I was totally entranced by the performance.

On July 1, the trouble began as Daegu began to live up to its reputation as Korea's dustiest and hottest city in summer. Students at Kyungpook National University clashed violently with the local police, and then with Korean troops, in a huge student riot, euphemistically referred to as a "demonstration" by Koreans, outside the main gate of the university. The riots lasted three days. From my office window I could hear the popping of small-arms fire and smell the tear gas.

I could clearly see what was going with my binoculars and was dismayed to see that many of the police vehicles, shields, and other riot paraphernalia were plainly marked with the clasped hands of friendship and/or the American flag—obviously indicating that they had come from the United States. Just great! How could my country be so stupid? I anticipated the questions from my students as to why the United States was helping to silence free speech rights in Korea. Reportedly, similar clashes at universities in Seoul had earlier closed three prominent schools—Yonsei University, Seoul National University, and Korea University—before the end of their terms. Kyungpook University closed on July 3, about one and a half weeks ahead of the scheduled end of the term.

Students had a time-honored tradition of political "demonstrations" in Korea, dating back to student actions in 1919 against the Japanese during the occupation of Korea. My students informed me that they were taking action to prevent President Park Chung-hee from amending the Korean constitution to allow him to serve a third term as president. President Park was in the last year of his second term. Time was running out for him. Since 1945, past Korean leaders had established a precedent of ignoring constitutional restraints.

The university students I knew liked President Park—particularly his refusal to personally benefit financially from his position. He was known to be a stickler for avoiding personal gain and for prohibiting his family from taking advantage of his position for their personal betterment. His wife was also well liked. But the students, nevertheless, were determined to force him to abide by the current constitution and his prior promises to eschew the constitutional meddling of the previous administration.

The so-called April Revolution in 1960, which resulted in the resignation of then President Rhee Syng-man, was based to a large degree on student dissatisfaction with Rhee's indifference to legal restraints on his power. Park benefitted from the students' actions in 1960 and 1961 and rode them to power. He owed the students a lot, and he probably was afraid of what their actions could trigger. So the Park government was doing everything it could to cool the volatile situation—closing schools early, forbidding any broadcasting of the news of the students' demonstrations, and heavily censoring news from outside Korea about the unrest in Korea. Both *Time* and *Newsweek*, for example, had about half their pages snipped out or blackened with ink. Although I was outwardly neutral, of course, about what was going on, my sympathy lay with the students. I was especially upset with the government censorship.

I felt sure that the issue would come to a head in the fall. The schools could not be closed forever, and when President Park made his move to establish a legal basis for his third term, I was afraid that there would be real trouble. How it would play out I had no idea.

As I watched the rioting outside the main gate at Kyungpook University, I was struck by the seemingly reluctant attitude of the police, and then of the military, to intervene forcefully. Most of the "police," I then realized, were conscripted soldiers who had themselves recently been students at Kyungpook or similar universities and probably shared the students' viewpoint. They went through the motions of trying to stop the riot, but their hearts were not in it.

The soldiers were also very young and had probably recently been in a college or university themselves. Military service was mandatory for two years. The soldiers were not about to harm the students that they had probably gone to high school or college with, prior to military service. Moreover, student political activism was a time-honored tradition in Korea. The students who had challenged the Japanese during Japan's occupation of Korea, and the students who had tumbled the post-war regime of President Rhee Syng-man, were considered heroes by most Koreans, including the soldiers who were now supposed to suppress the demonstrations.

The faculty's reaction was also interesting, since many of the younger faculty had themselves been leaders in the student revolution nine years earlier, fighting police on the streets for the same reasons. They dared not speak out or do anything publicly that could be construed as antigovernment, because their positions at a national (government) university would be in danger. It was a difficult situation for all involved, and my heart ached for the participants and the emotional and physical conflicts they were experiencing. For someone like me, who had previously experienced only the much less intense and smaller-scale student riots at Wisconsin, it was a heart-wrenching but fascinating time to be observing this power struggle in Korea.

The student demonstrations in Daegu were confined to Kyungpook National University. The other institutions where PCVs were teaching— Keimyung College, Hyosung College, and Youngnam University—

were quiet and unaffected by the riots elsewhere. Mary Frantz—the K-VII group member who was teaching in Daegu at Hyosung Women's College—told me that her students were totally apolitical.

I liked Mary a lot. She had been in many of my language classes during Peace Corps training and was an attractive, smart, and genuinely nice person. Of the fifteen or so single women in the combined groups K-VII and K-VIII who had survived training and been assigned as English teachers, she was the only one assigned to a school outside of Seoul. That assignment reflected the high opinion of and confidence in Mary that the training staff and other PCTs had, due to her self-assured, friendly demeanor, good humor, and common sense. In the spring I introduced Mary to the Sibley family, and she decided to join me, Moe Cain, Jon Moody, and Brian Copp to work on the Geoje Island Rural Public Health Project, at the Sibleys' invitation.

While I was fretting over the student violence and preparing to leave for Geoje Island, I received an invitation to attend July Fourth festivities at the United States Information Service (USIS). Most of the American missionaries in Daegu, as well as prominent Koreans in Daegu, attended this fine event at the USIS building, featuring Korean and American food and an open bar.

Every PCV within one hundred miles was there as well. I saw for the first time the legendary phenomenon known as the "Peace Corps Volunteer frenzy," which is manifested by uncontrollable, frantic ingesting of food and alcoholic beverages in prodigious quantities by PCVs. It is a rare phenomenon, only seen in developing countries of the Third World, and best viewed at events hosted by the American government, such as embassy parties or, in this case, a USIS party. Viewing can be dangerous. Observers should be cautioned not to stand between a PCV and the buffet table or open bar. Happily, despite the "frenzy," the evening was a success, the approximately twenty PCVs there departed with extended stomachs, and there were no casualties.

On Saturday, July 12, early in the morning I left Daegu's oppressive summer heat and humidity and headed for Geoje Island with Brian Copp and Moe Cain. Brian had come to Daegu the previous night by train from Iri City, where he was a teacher at Iri College in North Jeolla Province, which is now called Chunbuk National University. The monsoon season had just begun. Every day we had afternoon showers of great intensity, and we hoped our trip would have good weather.

The trip to Geoje Island came just in time. I was tired of the dust, heat, and humidity in Daegu. My shirt collar had a ring of dirt by the end of each day. Air conditioning was virtually nonexistent, except in a few of the upper-class tabangs and at the Peace Corps office. The excitement of living in Daegu was beginning to wear off for me, together with the novelty of the new American at Kyungpook University for my students and colleagues. Invitations, as a result, began to decline. Boredom began to rise. There was no escape from Daegu's depressing summer doldrums. I began to wonder if the summer would ever end, and the hottest month—August—hadn't even begun! The promise of ocean air and sea breezes was tantalizing.

On the first leg of our journey, we took a train to Busan—a trip of about one and a half hours. None of us had visited this busy port city before. I was impressed by the lovely mountains on three sides of the city and the sparkling waters of the harbor on the fourth side. Our destination was the famous fish market called Jagalchi Market, located right at the water's edge in the harbor area.

In the market we bought tickets for the ferry to Geoje Island. While we waited for the boarding call, we explored the market, which was jammed with vendors selling anything you could possibly want. Of course it specialized in fish and produce from the sea. The market had more kinds of fish, eels, turtles, sea cucumbers, and other seafood than you can imagine! It was a fascinating place.

In one vendor's stall I spotted a case of Coca-Cola. The bottles had Korean writing, so these were not black market American goods, which I had seen before in Korea, but honest-to-goodness, bottled-in-Korea Coca-Cola! Wow! What a shock! Needless to say, our joy was only slightly tempered by the cost of one bottle—three hundred won (about one dollar)—which was a small fortune. Three of us shared one delicious, mouth-watering bottle. It was an auspicious sign of good things to come, I hoped.

The ferryboat turned out to be a small steamer-like ship that was probably an old fishing boat originally. It was named *Young Bok*, which was undoubtedly the name of some sweetheart. There was a sign inside that stated the ship's capacity was fifty people. I think that there were at least one hundred passengers, plus a crew of about six. We were packed inside and on the outside decks so tightly that you could hardly move. Two cows and countless crates of chickens were on the stern deck. There were no lifeboats or life vests that I could see. Fortunately, the weather was clear and the seas were calm when we chugged out of Busan harbor and headed west along the southern coast of Korea—the start of a three-hour voyage into one of the most beautiful areas of the world I have ever seen.

The ship had two decks and a little cabin at the bow on the second deck, from which the captain and several crew members operated the vessel. We headed for the top deck, above the cows and chickens, where we found a spot along the small rail behind the cabin from which to view the coast and then the spectacular islands off the coast, just south of the small port cities of Masan and Jinhae. For the first two hours, we seemed to be on the open seas with the coast barely visible to the north, off the starboard side. Boats and ships of every size and style were all around us, including chugging fishing boats and full-sail Chinese junks. The small islands we passed were heavily wooded and quite mountainous, for the most part. Tiny fishing villages, with terraced paddies climbing the mountainsides behind, clung to the coast above rocky beaches. Occasionally, a boat would approach our ferry from one of these villages and either add or take off cargo or passengers.

The passengers seemed quite poor. For the most part they were older men and women whose weathered faces testified to countless years in the fields, on the beaches, and in fishing boats. There were a few students in high school uniforms and several men in army fatigues. Otherwise, we were the only passengers dressed in Western-style clothes. We attracted a lot of attention, and as soon as our fellow passengers realized we spoke Korean, the questions came hard and fast. Why were we going to Geoje Island? Did we know that there was no electricity there, no hotels, few vehicles, and no large towns? The people were very friendly and concerned for our welfare.

Finally, one of the passengers pointed out two islands ahead. On the port side was Geoje Island, and on the starboard side was Chilcheon Island. We headed for a narrow passage between the two islands and threaded a route with picturesque villages of stone walls, mud houses, and thatched roofs on both sides, beneath exquisite rugged mountains forested with pine and spruce. At last we reached a small fishing village called Changmok, where the ferry docked at a short pier. On that day the boat would not stop as usual at the Chilcheon Island pier—which was the stop after Changmok and closer to our destination—because of a very low tide, we were told.

Upon disembarking, we spied Mary Frantz waiting for us. Mary had arrived one week before. From Changmok to the site of the building project was about two miles, she explained, so we hoisted our sleeping bags and packs on our backs and started hiking south along a narrow dirt road.

The road wound around several small mountains and through a tiny village called Shilchon. We passed countless rustic houses and precisely built stone walls, beyond which rice paddies, filled with undulating grain, marched up the mountainsides. There was a constant breeze, so although the weather was quite warm, we were comfortable with our loads. We shared the otherwise deserted road with an occasional woman from the villages we passed, invariably balancing a pot or a box on her head and carrying a small child on her back, tightly bound to her by a small blanket. After about half an hour, we turned onto a smaller road leading toward the coast, climbed a small hill, and descended onto a peninsula with a narrow path leading from the road to the tip and the beach beyond.

This peninsula was to be the site of the rural health clinic. It was strategically located close to a main, well-traveled waterway and at the point from which a small boat, powered by single oars at the stern and at the bow, ferried passengers every hour or so back and forth from Geoje Island to the much smaller neighboring Chilcheon Island. At the end of the peninsula was a small stone pier that served as the ferryboat landing.

The camp's location was indescribably beautiful! To the west was the narrow passage between the two islands that I have already described. This broadened into a huge bay just to our south, with a couple of small islands visible in the bay several miles from us. To the north was a smaller bay that ended at the fishing village we had walked through to get to the peninsula. Chilcheon Island lay between us and the Korean mainland, obscuring what would have been a distant view of Masan City. Above us, at the top of the peninsula lay several mountains.

The overall effect of the water, islands, and mountains made it seem as though we were on a large lake, surrounded by distant land and mountains, with rocky beaches on three sides of the peninsula. All of the islands were quite mountainous, sparsely settled, and very lightly farmed. Most were covered with a lush forest. It was so wonderful to see trees en masse!

The constant sound of the wind rustling through the grass, bushes, and sparse trees on the peninsula was punctuated by the chug-chug-chug of an occasional ancient fishing boat, plying the waters around our camp. Dozens of women from the nearest town—Hachung, about two miles farther south along the road we had walked from Changmok—squatted from sunup to sundown along the beaches with trowels and other digging implements, combing the rocks for crabs, shells, and whatever else they could find to eat or sell. It was peaceful and about as different from the bustle and noise of Daegu and Busan as you could get.

There were twenty or so of us at the camp. The number varied from day to day as people arrived and departed without notice. Besides the six members of the Sibley family, there were two Korean project engineers, a Korean nurse, a Korean medical secretary, several local Korean women who cooked for us all, four Korean construction workers, and the four PCVs. We ate at first in shifts, by gender, using a small mud and stone Korean farmhouse nearby as a kitchen and dining area. The women slept in the farmhouse, which was located right on the water, next to the ferryboat landing, and had a tall stone wall enclosing it and a tiny front yard. At high tide, the water lapped at the base of the high stone wall encircling the old farmhouse and its small yard.

The men slept in canvas tents located higher up on the peninsula. When we arrived, the concrete frames and roofs were already up for two small buildings, each about forty-five feet by eighteen feet by twelve feet, which housed construction materials and equipment. These unfinished buildings also provided shelter and a place to eat, work, and relax out of the hot sun.

It was still monsoon season, so we had periodic brief, violent squalls of high wind and rain sweep across our campsite on the peninsula every day. When there was more than a brief deluge of rain, construction work became impossible at the exposed worksite. At such times, we turned our energy to transplanting pine trees from the lower slopes of the nearby mountains to the periphery of the project and to hauling rocks for the base of a new road, planned to run from the pier to the top of the peninsula. The old road tracked right through the middle of the future cluster of clinic buildings, so Dr. Sibley planned another narrow road, just above the beach to the south of the project, to skirt the clinic site.

In our tents we slept as best as we could on muddy ground plagued by mosquitoes, unless the wind was blowing. Our third day on Geoje Island, we managed to erect a huge army squad tent, which provided room for about twenty people to sleep comfortably. The first night that we had moved from our pup tents to the squad tent the poles collapsed around two o'clock in the morning, in the midst of a thunderstorm, burying us all in sodden canvas. We would have been terribly upset, except that it was so funny! From then on, we slept in the small tents, using the large one for our meals and relaxing during the day. With the flaps open, it provided a relatively cool spot in which to write or nap.

Our construction work was essentially making foundations, supporting pillars and beams, and bricks. The foundations, pillars, and beams were made out of a cement mixture, while the bricks were fashioned out of mud and cement—all for the later construction of the dozen or so small buildings planned for the health clinic. Dr. Sibley had detailed plans and was tremendously well organized. The idea was to build the clinic buildings in such a way—using cheap materials found locally and a simple, construction design—that the clinic could be duplicated anywhere for minimum cost.

Moe, Brian, and I worked with several Korean men from the town of Hachung, mixing cement with water, sand, and a rock aggregate scoured from nearby beaches, and pouring the cement mixture into pillar-like forms, with reinforcing metal rods. These hardened to form concrete supporting pillars and beams. We also made wooden forms and placed them in rectangular trenches, into which we poured the cement mixture to form the concrete foundations of each new building.

The brick-making process was the most difficult, I felt, mainly because we had to make so many—literally thousands—and the work involved an infernal device, which reminded me of a huge garlic press, that compressed the clay, water, sand, and cement mixture into twelve-by-six-inch bricks. It took the strength of three men, working together, to apply enough pressure to the arm of the compression machine to properly shape the bricks. Three other men dug and hauled the clay from a nearby pit and gravel from the beaches. These materials were shoveled into a kind of sturdy, basket-like carrying device that was mounted on an A-frame and carried on one's back. Called a *chigeh*, this device was omnipresent on the backs of Korean laborers of all kinds. Clay and gravel are very heavy! Before the materials could be compressed into bricks, they had to be mixed and sifted. All in all, it was backbreaking work. After making several hundred bricks in a day, you were exhausted.

Although there was generally a pleasant breeze blowing across the peninsula from the ocean, there was little shade, and the temperature was in the high eighties at midday. The construction work was extremely hot and tiring, especially for the three of us who were used to the relatively soft life of university teaching, where the major exercise of the day was squatting over a Korean toilet. I marveled at the strength, endurance, and good humor of the Korean men we worked with. They generally worked with no complaining and few rest periods for eight hours per day in the hot sun, with a one-hour break for lunch. They told us about their lives in the villages nearby, about their families, and about their hopes and aspirations. In the evenings, our conversations were periodically continued over bowls of makoli in their villages. To a man they were optimistic about the future, hopeful that the clinic would significantly improve health care on Geoje Island, and happy to be working on the project, which paid them three or four times what they could earn either fishing or farming, they said.

When we weren't drinking with the workmen before going to bed, we often sat on the pier at the end of the peninsula until well after dark. We had kerosene lanterns for light. With no electric lights on the islands, the blackness of the night was total, and the millions of stars seemed so close you could touch them. I have never seen more beautiful night skies! The northern hemisphere constellations were familiar to us and reassuring.

At night, in the waters around the peninsula and on all sides of the pier, blooms of luminescent dinoflagellates, or algal blooms, flashed when disturbed, sending ripples of light across the water into the darkness.

I had never before seen anything like this. When we went swimming, our bodies were seemingly outlined in phosphorescence in the water. Stones we skipped across the water's surface created moving patterns of light, as each point of contact with the water prompted rippling circles of light to move on the surface away from the impact point. Schools of flying fish, passing by the peninsula, left glowing circular footprints across the black water. With the magnificent night sky overhead, and the water glowing eerily beneath, the nighttime beauty of Geoje Island surpassed even the spectacle of Hawaii's erupting Kilauea.

During that first week on Geoje Island, I couldn't help thinking each night, while watching the glowing water, that the ripples of light emanating from any spot where I touched the water reflected my experiences so far in Korea. What had been an unknown sea of dark water for me, illuminated only by faint points of distant starlight prior to Peace Corps, was aglow in the quiet Korean night wherever I touched it. The water's light was neither brilliant nor all revealing. Rather, each contact gave off just enough illumination to be intriguing in its brevity, incomparably beautiful in its patterns, and spellbinding in its ageless mystery.

On July 20, the other PCVs and I took the ferry back to Busan and caught a flight to Seoul, where a Peace Corps conference was scheduled to begin the next morning. Ordinarily we would have traveled by train, but we had been told to be in Seoul by late afternoon, and a combined three-hour ferry trip and six-hour train trip would have taken about nine hours and brought us to Seoul too late in the day, given the single daily ferry leaving Geoje Island late each morning. So the Peace Corps office sent us airline tickets, to our surprise. We arrived in Seoul's Kimpo Airport in time to watch Neil Armstrong's historic moon landing, late that evening on a friend's television.

The conference was held at a hotel and conference center called the Academy House on the outskirts of Seoul, situated in the beautiful mountains. The Academy House was one of the very few luxury hotels in Seoul with sit-down toilets and Western food. It was tremendously fun to see the other members of our combined Korea VII and VIII groups, and I felt wickedly indulgent the entire three days of the conference whenever I sat down on a toilet or visited the dining room for a Western meal.

The purpose of the conference was to brush up our Korean-language and English-teaching skills. We also had lengthy discussions about our Peace Corps training and its effectiveness in preparing us for what we encountered in Korea. At one point we were all asked to write down our thoughts about our training program, what aspects of Korea we had not expected, and what could be improved for the training of the next group of PCVs in the university TESOL program, which was scheduled to start in the autumn. These comments were collected and combined in a lengthy handout provided to us at the end of the conference.

Some of the comments of the PCVs, regarding unanticipated aspects of Korea, were interesting and for me quite surprising in light of my own generally positive experience. The following comments were fairly representative of those from the eighty PCVs regarding what they had encountered that was unexpected:

The friendliness of Koreans—training was so damn negative!

The housing shortage for married couples and the Koreans' insistence that we cook for ourselves. The utter black despair resulting from being stared at continually in the street and at the market.

I really didn't expect Korea to be as dirty and run-down as it is. Also, I didn't expect the hostility toward Americans that I have found here. I also didn't realize that there would be so much staring.

I was not prepared for the attacks by Korean *gangpei* [thugs], public urination, and in general being hated by most people.

People insisting you sleep at their house and being hurt if you don't. Adults giving you shit on the streets, drunk or upset people telling you that they will never be your friend anymore if you don't do what they want you to do. Being suspected as CIA.

Korean grandmothers telling their grandchildren to yell "hello" at us.

The hard-sell by some Koreans to "be my friend."

How poor the universities are, how few if any of the staff

give a damn, or that most of the students are not particularly eager to learn English.

Constant hostility on the part of Koreans, the fierceness of the putak [reciprocal favors] system, Korean inability to understand prior commitments, the extreme rigidity of the class society and the antagonism between the classes, constant cheating by merchants.

Korea is a much more interesting and pleasant country than I had been led to believe.

Friendly Koreans who don't want to learn English.

The complete lack of privacy in a family situation, the restraints put on a girl PCV by the family (lack of freedom to come and go as I please).

The lack of creativity in school, and resentment of teachers toward foreigners, especially foreign language teachers; the absolute rigidity of social standards and assumptions; the relative ineffectiveness of the PCV in Korea.

There is such a magnificent cultural background to be developed by the PCV in Korea. I never dreamed I would have so many opportunities to attend operas, concerts, plays, dance programs, art festivals, etc. Seoul has so much to offer!

Popular dancing and students drinking makoli at a school picnic. Sleeping and having to dress in the same room with the whole family and having to use a small communal pot for urinating.

Friendly people, sympathy for our problems, a thoroughly enjoyable situation.

The emotional and intellectual unhappiness or frustration of most of my colleagues and students at the university took me by surprise. The heavy drinking and strained husband/wife relationships I was warned about, but I never anticipated or understood the reality in training.

Having the time and opportunity to do various activities at night away from home, such extreme poverty, such hard-working people, schools to be so poor physically, Koreans accepting me as well as they have, Korea to be so dirty, so many television sets in Korean homes, to meet so many Koreans who can speak some English, and to find the rising of the status of women.

The conference lasted from Wednesday until Saturday morning. On the last evening we had a fine, wild party—eighty PCVs releasing the pent-up frustrations of the first six months in Korea. After leaving the Academy House, several of us went to see the 1968 American movie *Romeo and Juliet* starring Olivia Hussey, playing in Seoul to packed houses. I tremendously enjoyed the movie on Saturday night. Coincidentally, sitting next to me in the theater with her boyfriend was a tabang girl—Kim Ok-jung—with whom I had become quite friendly four months earlier, when I had first arrived in Korea. She was surprised that I had survived so far in Daegu and that my Korean had become pretty good since last winter. Considering that the population of Seoul was about five and a half million people, I was pleasantly amazed to find Miss Kim next to me at the theater—and I admit the thought crossed my mind that she might have been shadowing me, as a government agent. Perhaps all the stares from Koreans were making me a bit paranoid.

On Sunday morning I took a train to Daegu, visited my Korean family, and picked up my mail at the university. My friend Choi Hwa-wook was heading back to Geoje Island the next morning, and we decided to go together. That evening we went out to a rather low-class *soju chip*, where we drank prodigious amounts of soju—the strong, Korean rice liquor I had been introduced to on several previous occasions in Seoul. As we drank together, Hwa-wook told me all about his life, including the hardships he had endured as an orphan during and right after the Korean War. He had lived on the brink of starvation for several years, surviving by every possible kind of employment. Hwa-wook had then served in the Korean army as a KATUSA (Korean Augmentation To the United States Army), after studying judo in Seoul. His English was excellent as a result of his KATUSA service, when he had known many American soldiers. At some point he had come to know the Sibley family in Daegu.

Before he started working for the Sibley family and then for the Geoje Island project as a construction director, the Peace Corps physician in Daegu had once hired him for a short period as a driver and assistant. Another young man he knew, who had been the driver for the physician, had died tragically of carbon monoxide poisoning one night while sleeping in a faulty ondol pang, so Hwa-wook had succeeded him briefly to that position. Hwa-wook told me how happy he was in his current job, helping to build the rural health clinic, as he felt that he was really making a contribution to improve the life of Korea's poorest citizens.

Earlier that day I had been thinking of the negative comments made by some of the PCVs at our conference the previous week, about their lives in Korea. Up to that time, although I had certainly been the object of stares and children's yells, such as "hello, hello," or *Meguk saram* (American), I had not experienced any hostility or rudeness on the part of adult Koreans, and I had certainly not experienced any hassling from Korean gangpei (hoodlums). I wondered what the other PCVs had been experiencing that was so foreign to my own experience. That night I had my first taste, ironically enough, within a week of my having doubted the negative experiences of other PCVs in the K-VII and K-VIII groups.

When Hwa-wook and I had entered the soju chip, a group of young, tough-looking Korean men was seated by the door. They had been drinking and singing for quite a while, it seemed. We went to a table in the back of the bar and were there for more than an hour. At some point, several of the men at the table near the door started to make comments about me. They called me *geseki* ("son of a bitch") and *sang nom* ("low-class person"), along with other names that I didn't understand. Hwa-wook and I ignored them.

Then I got up and went outside to the restroom through a back door. When I returned, the four men were gone, and it looked as though there had been a major fight in my two-minute absence, as several chairs were overturned and the bar girls were arguing with Hwa-wook. We left quickly, and I saw the four men on the ground outside, nursing their wounds. Hwa-wook had taken matters into his own hands to stop the insults as soon as I had left the bar. He had apparently disposed of the four men with no difficulty, for he seemed calm, unruffled, and cool. I asked him what had happened. He laughingly said that the men had decided to leave in a hurry because they were so embarrassed by what they had called me.

The next day, as we headed together for the Jagalchi Market in Busan to buy ferry tickets, Hwa-wook suggested I consider buying the ferry captain a present, such as a bottle of Scotch. When I presented the bottle to the captain upon embarking, he was extremely pleased and invited Hwa-wook and me to join him on the bridge. The gift was the first of several bottles for the captain over the next year and a half. For the duration of that trip, and on every one of the dozens of future trips to Geoje Island on the ferry, I shared Captain Yi's quarters and traded drinks, stories, and information with him for hours. He was a delightful person, full of stories of sea life on the Korea Strait.

After returning to the health project, we helped put the finishing touches on a well, which several of the workmen had been digging for the past several weeks. It was now providing cool, clean water for the project. At about forty feet down we had hit water, to everyone's great surprise, despite repeated admonitions from the local Koreans that there was no water where we were digging. "A gift of God," and a "miracle," the villagers said. The well may, indeed, have been such a gift, but the few Christians in the nearby village were so avid and insistent in their proclamations that the rest of us at the project—Koreans and Americans alike—resented their zeal. We spent several evenings debating with the local Christians about the merits of any claim that the well was a miracle.

On his return to Geoje Island, Hwa-wook brought about a dozen rattraps, at John Sibley's request. Soon after our return, John Sibley asked me to help him get rid of the rats, which infested the old mud Korean farmhouse at the end of the peninsula, where we all had our meals and where the women slept at night. We baited the traps with peanut butter—a precious, black market treasure—and put them out in the courtyard and in the stone wall surrounding the house. Within minutes the traps began to spring, as the peanut butter worked its magic. In thirty minutes or so we killed two dozen rats. By the end of the evening we had doubled that number. The local Christians were amazed and wanted to borrow the traps. The local Buddhists were appalled.

The rainy season drew to a close in mid-August. As the clouds lifted and the weather cleared, we were able to appreciate even more than before just how gorgeous the worksite was. During the day, the blue waters surrounding the peninsula sparkled in the sunshine under puffy clouds. At night, the flying fish, water bugs, and other unseen, agitating forces stirred up the eerie, phosphorescent glow of the dark sea, or an occasional evening rainsquall unleashed ribbons of advancing light as the approaching sheets of water struck the sea's surface.

On the lower slopes of the mountains, visible from our campsite, terraced paddies of rice and barley alternated with small fields of corn, peppers, watermelons, beans, tomatoes, and potatoes. The paddies and fields were light green under the mid-August sun, in contrast to the dark green of the pine forests that touched the farms at their higher edges. Where the wind caressed the maturing grain, ripples of alternating light and dark green swept across the slopes in a sinuous, lovely dance. Above the entire scene were the purple outlines of Geoje Island's mountains.

Despite the amazing geographic beauty of the area, even more impressive to me were the stone walls that were everywhere. My first thought upon seeing them was that labor must be very cheap, for the work that had gone into building the walls must have been phenomenal. In our vicinity, Geoje Island was completely ringed with a tall stone wall. The tides were quite pronounced, so at high tide the sea lapped at the base of this peripheral wall, while at low tide perhaps fifty feet or more of rocky beach below the wall was bared. A similar stone wall at the edge of the shore was visible on Chilcheon Island, just across the narrow strait at the foot of the peninsula. Other islands nearby were also similarly ringed by stone walls. These monumental stone testimonies to centuries of hard work at the water's edge seemed designed to hold the soil from eroding into the sea.

As you moved from the shoreline to the villages and farmlands, stone walls were omnipresent, encircling every home, sustaining the soil on the perimeters of every rice paddy, protecting every orchard. Hundreds of stone walls and thousands of huge rocks were everywhere. As on the mainland, the terraced rice and barley paddies were part of an intricate irrigation system, with ditches and stone waterways leading from the head of each valley and connecting to each terraced paddy to assure ample water for the entire growing season—from April through October.

In the midst of the natural beauty of the project's site, work continued between the periodic rains. Morale was very high on the peninsula despite the dampness, high humidity, mosquitoes, scorpions, and hard work. The Sibley family was amazing. While John Sibley deftly managed the project's construction work and provided health care to the nearby villages—together with several volunteer Korean doctors and nurses from Daegu—Jean Sibley balanced the demands of raising her children with managing the support staff of local cooks, laundresses, and other workers and with assuring that the spiritual and religious components of the project were implemented. (The project was being supported in substantial part by the World Council of Churches.) John and Jean were good-natured, wise, even-tempered, and careful to be sensitive to the culture of Korea and of Geoje Island in particular. They made a good husband-wife team, and everyone—Koreans and Americans alike—felt welcome and valued.

In mid-August one of the men with whom we were working invited Brian and me to spend the weekend with him at his home on the mainland in a tiny village about ten miles north of Masan. The worker, Park Yong-dok, was from this small village originally, and his wife and baby daughter were living there temporarily with relatives while he headed community development efforts at the health clinic project and surrounding villages, as a representative of the Seoul-based Cooperative Education Institute. After taking the ferry to Masan, we caught an old bus from Masan harbor to Mr. Park's hometown of Haman. The trip took about five hours.

We stayed with Mr. Park's family in a small mud house with a thatched straw roof. There were three rooms in the house, each about ten feet by ten feet. The toilet, of course, was outside in back of the house—an open pit. Chickens ran in and out of the house. There was no electricity and lots of mosquitoes and rats. I lay on my back at night on the yo, which Mrs. Park kindly lent us, listening to the rats scurry back and forth in the ceiling above and occasionally seeing a small, rat foot poke through a hole in the paper that covered the rafters. Brian and I, sharing one of the rooms, hoped no rat would come falling out of the ceiling and land on us. Before we went to bed, we were royally wined and dined at a huge outdoor dinner attended by virtually everyone in the village, and featuring an abundance of beer, strawberry wine, delicious grapes, and luscious watermelons.

During the dinner, we were told that during the Korean War, on the mountain which jutted up right next to Mr. Park's barnyard behind his house, more than two thousand American troops lost their lives in an assault on the summit, then held by North Korean and Chinese soldiers. Now the town and the mountain were so peaceful and idyllic, with no sign whatsoever of any past conflict, it was hard to imagine what it must have been like only about seventeen years before. I thought about the Vietnam War, when I heard about the battle in Haman, and hoped that in the not-too-distant future, villages in Vietnam would be as peaceful, welcoming, and dreamy as Haman was that weekend.

Upon our return to Geoje Island on Sunday evening, we were advised that a typhoon was heading directly for the island, with winds of up to ninety mph. We spent hours digging trenches around the tents, tightening the tent ropes, covering the construction equipment and materials, and otherwise preparing for the worst. The storm hit on Monday night, and for several hours I thought we would be blown away. Fortunately, there was more wind than rain, and the brunt of the storm swerved to the east of Geoje Island. We escaped relatively unscathed.

That storm was the last major storm of the summer. The monsoon season on Geoje Island up until then had been one of the rainiest and most destructive in a long time, causing tremendous property damage and the loss of a dozen lives. We had experienced repeated storms. One in particular, in early August, had dropped several inches of rain in several hours. As a consequence, not far from our camp a dam had burst, causing a flash flood that wiped out more than a dozen farms and even damaged some of our equipment, which had been stored close by. Inspecting the damage was one of the saddest experiences of my life. The work of several generations of Korean farmers in an entire valley had been wiped out in a few hours. You could see the pain in the faces of the members of the affected families. No one would starve because of that flood, but some sons would have to cancel marriage plans, some daughters would forever be working instead of marrying and raising a family or going to school, and many belts would have to be tightened for years to come.

As the end of August approached, we made plans to return to our colleges and universities for the start of the new academic year. Classes were scheduled to begin September 1, and at least one week of preparation would be necessary before then.

In the course of the six weeks we had spent there, we had accomplished—as part of the mostly Korean work crews—a lot less than we had hoped to accomplish, for the rainy season, delays in the arrival of equipment and materials, and other interruptions had slowed the progress of the project. We had helped get the frames made and erected for three buildings, roofs finished for those buildings, and the foundations dug for two more. Additionally, more than one hundred pines had been transplanted and about five thousand mud bricks made. Truthfully, the Koreans could take most of the credit for what had been accomplished. All of us were as brown as berries from the outside work. I had gained weight, lost some hair, and built up muscles in places that had never before seen such manifestations. I couldn't remember when I had had as much fun before, roughing it and working outside.

Boarding the ferry for the return trip to Busan, I reflected how extremely fortunate I was to have met the Sibleys and to have been able to spend the summer vacation helping them with the Geoje Island project. I hoped I would be able to return on subsequent vacations and participate in the completion of the rural health project, for several reasons. First, the great Koreans and Americans with whom I had worked and formed close friendships on Geoje Island; second, the awesome natural beauty of the water, mountains, and forests surrounding the project; and third, the accomplishment of something visible and tangible, such as the building of the clinic or the transplanting of trees. Although I loved teaching English, it was difficult to see much progress or any other tangible achievement resulting from my teaching. On Geoje Island, however slow the project's progress may seem, at least you could see the end product of your hard work.

When I mentioned this to Captain Yi on the trip to Busan that day, he disagreed with my feelings. He cautioned that young people, like me, were too anxious to quickly obtain a result. He thought that a student's English ability, or the actual provision of health care to a rural area, or the planting of trees, were short-term achievements and very small steps on the road to achieving bigger goals overall, he said. The importance of the work that John Sibley or the Peace Corps was doing, he felt, lay in the new ideas and world perspective for Koreans that resulted. Why, he said, he had never before met an American before he had met the Sibleys, and he had never talked at length with young American men and women before he had met the PCVs going to and from Geoje Island. Already he was thinking about how our ideas could affect his ferry's future and his children's lives. He said that he was going to get his crew to study English, because they needed to communicate with the foreigners who had started to travel on his boat, and although his family lived in Busan and had decent health care, for the first time he understood the need to get health care out to the most remote parts of Korea, like Geoje Island.

Reverend Na echoed Captain Yi's sentiments, to my great surprise, upon my return to Daegu, when we resumed our evening discussions. A close friend of his, another minister by the name of Kil, had decided to go to the United States to study, and Reverend Na was starting to think about that possibility himself—an option he had never before even remotely considered.

Classes did not resume on September 1 as they were supposed to have. Instead, the opening of the university was postponed indefinitely. We were told that it would be mid-September, at least, before classes started again. The Language Institute and the Teachers College seized the opportunity to conduct a workshop again with middle-school and high-school English teachers from the Daegu area schools.

Moe Cain, Russ Feldmeier, and I quickly put together a weeklong workshop. The word went out to the schools in the area. Because the middle schools and high schools had resumed their classes on schedule, our workshop classes had to be held at odd hours late in the afternoon or in the evening so as to permit teachers to participate after their own classes were finished. Attendance was poor compared to our previous workshops, but we managed to train about one hundred teachers for several hours each day during the first week of the month.

After the completion of the workshop, I took Reverend Na to Geoje Island with me for a brief visit, during the second week in September. I wanted to show him what we had been doing during the summer as well as a part of Korea he had never before seen. He seemed suitably impressed and was happy to meet Captain Yi, my friend Hwa-wook, the Sibley family, Mr. Park (from Haman), and the other Koreans with whom I had worked for six weeks. We had a lot of fun together.

As soon as we returned together to Daegu, I wrote an article for the next issue of the Peace Corps/Korea newsletter *Yobosayo*, describing the Geoje Island health project. It appeared in the September–October 1969 issue:

### Six Weeks
By Chuck Hobbie (K-VIII)

Those of us in the university English teaching program are especially fortunate to have two long vacations each year, when university activity is at a minimum, during which to indulge our own individual urges and interests with regards to experiencing different aspects of Korean life, seeing Korea, and involving ourselves in projects other than teaching, if we feel so inclined. Frankly, at the end of last term I was quite tired of teaching and longed to experience life in Korea outside of the big city and the academic environment, especially during the long, hot Daegu summer. I'm sure such feelings were shared by many other PCVs. In the middle of July, three of us from Daegu—Mary Frantz, Moe Cain, and I—and the lonely soul in Iri, Brian Copp—joined the Geojedo Community Health and Development Project to lend our meager muscle in the construction and other work now underway as the project unfolds. We found both an experience in the "other Korea" and a job that was a refreshing change from teaching.

Geoje, the second largest island in Korea, lies off the southeast coast about three hours by boat from Busan. A population of 119,000 is scattered across an island twenty-three miles wide (E-W) and fifteen miles long (N-S), and of course, approximately three quarters of the island people are agrarian dependent, for there is little industry, no electricity, and few roads. The average annual per capita expenditure of 72 percent of the populace is less than seventy-two dollars—an eloquent indication of the economic level of most of this area.

Early in 1968, Dr. John Sibley, then a surgeon at the Dong San Presbyterian Hospital in Daegu, began to organize support for a project, which he envisioned as a new approach to medical care in Korea. As Dr. Sibley noted, in both rural and urban areas of Korea there are large segments of the population that cannot afford the expensive medical care offered by most hospitals. Church institutions cannot meet this need because the cost of high standard medicine leaves too few funds for charity. Obviously, the Korean government is not able to meet this need fully either at the present time, due to the shortage of necessary resources and interested, qualified personnel. And so Dr. Sibley proposed the Geojedo Community Health and Development Project, designed as a "pilot project" to test the feasibility of providing high quality medical care at the local level in such a way so as to make this medical care available to a rural populace at reasonable cost—with maximum involvement on the part of the community in the efforts to provide the same.

A site on the northern coast of Geojedo, near Shil Cheon Ri and in Ha Chung Myun, was selected finally as being a rural area in which the government health officials and the local community recognized the need for further implementation of the government's health programs, as well as being a location readily accessible to the surrounding islands and south coast. This part of Geojedo, consisting of three northern townships with a total population of thirty thousand became the immediate or primary target area of the project. In July construction began on simple medical buildings and living facilities (each building approximately forty-five feet by eighteen feet by twelve feet), centrally located at the project site, from which medical coverage of the area will be gradually expanded by phases, largely through the use of mobile units radiating out from the central site to simple dispensaries set up in the surrounding villages. When completed next year, the central facility will provide X-ray and surgical services, as well as treating patients too ill to be treated in their homes or at the dispensaries.

Although designed primarily with a medical objective, the project has other equally important goals, which in the long run may prove more significant. Paralleling the medical program will be both a broad community-centered health program, consisting of family planning, public health, and scientifically controlled, sub-maximal curative medicine, and a community development effort to encourage the local residents to organize and participate in cooperatives and other self-help projects. These programs will be carried out in close cooperation with and along the lines of the Korean government's plans, with a major effort made to adapt the scope of the programs to the potential resources of the community, thus making self-support a feasible objective. At the village, the church congregations, it is hoped, will be a concerned, organized, and motivating force in the communities, providing both support and leadership in the programs, as well as a means of contact with the local people. And finally, one of the project's primary concerns is that costs be kept to a minimum and that major capital investments be avoided which cannot be recovered or easily incorporated into other programs. Although support is being provided by the medical commission of the World Council of Churches, the cost factor is one that will be important in determining the feasibility of inexpensively duplicating this pilot project elsewhere.

To assist with the implementation of the project, early this year Dr. Kit Johnson from Johns Hopkins University, a pediatrician with advanced degrees in public health, joined Dr. Sibley on Geojedo. Together they will form the nucleus of a medical team, which will eventually include a Korean doctor and a staff trained to meet the demands of the unique situation on Geojedo. A representative of the Cooperative Education Institute in Seoul, Mr. Park Yong-dok, will be heading community development efforts aimed, for example, at developing the economic potentials of the local communities, by such programs as medical insurance, so as to be able to avoid dependence in the future on outside financial help.

Approaching Geojedo on the small steamer from Busan, one sees first a distant line of low mountains marking the island and its rugged neighbors. The coast in this part of Korea has been compared to the Irish Coast—pine-covered mountains and green valleys dropping into the sea. To reach the project's camp we disembarked at Chil Cheon Island and were rowed across a narrow channel to the small peninsula on Geojedo that is the construction site. When we arrived in July, we found only five tents housing the Sibley family and a small permanent staff, a nearly completed well, and an old Korean house that was originally on the land. Barley and potato fields were being cultivated on the cleared areas of the otherwise pine- and bamboo-forested hills. Cows and goats grazed in the pastures. To the south lay a small village, and Hachung, somewhat larger, was several miles to the southwest. Fishing boats chugged the bays on either side of the peninsula.

As part of the cost-cutting goals of the project, most of the building materials—bricks, blocks, and concrete forms—are made at the construction site. Only the reinforcing steel, cement, wood beams, and slate roofing come from Busan. For our first week on Geojedo, as a result of almost continuous rain, we occupied ourselves transplanting pines and sitting in our tents, slapping mosquitoes. When it rains on Geojedo, all work at the project comes to a standstill, for the bricks, blocks, and forms must be kept dry, and any digging is nearly impossible in the red clay that overlays Geoje's granite. Most of the rest of the summer we joined teams of local workers making bricks, loading and unloading supplies from the freighters that brought them from Busan, digging foundations, carrying cement, and doing whatever else could be done between rain showers. We soon found that it was impossible to keep pace with the Korean workers, for months of teaching and years of comparatively easy living had left us softer than we cared to admit. Blisters, infected hair follicles, and fatigue took their toll, as did the mosquitoes, ants, and centipedes.

Although our contribution was slight, when we left Geojedo at the end of the summer there was tremendous satisfaction in seeing, amidst the potato fields, the outside shells of two buildings well on their way to completion. Now, a month later, having recovered from my blisters and settled into university life again in Daegu, Geojedo seems like another country, worlds away, where the peace and beauty seemed impossible, only a steamer-ride distant from Busan. O'Donnell willing, I'm looking forward to returning to Geojedo next winter to try again.

After returning to Daegu on September 11, I initially found myself a little bored. Kyungpook University's gates were heavily guarded and closed to all undergraduate students. The Korean government had provided the university with a brand new faculty bus, which picked up faculty members on Daegu's main streets and carried us safely through the university gate. The bus's windows were covered with strong screening so to prevent the occasional thrown rock from shattering a window. Although I went to the Language Institute every day, there was no one else around.

Fortunately, the graduate schools opened right after I got back from Geoje Island with Reverend Na. Since I taught four hours each week in the graduate school of the Teachers College, I had something to do. Of course I was also recording English language tapes for the language laboratory—my never-ending project. And Professor Kim had several months' accumulation of *Reader's Digest* and *Time* magazine questions to ask me. I had also agreed to become the assistant editor of the Peace Corps/Korea magazine in Korea, called *Yobosayo* (which generally means "hello," as in when you answer a telephone or try to get a waitress's attention), effective September 1, so I was pretty busy writing articles and editing other PCVs' articles for the magazine. I was burning up that old typewriter in our office at Kyungpook University.

On Saturday, September 13, the Korean National Assembly met to consider the constitutional amendment that would allow President Park to serve a third term, and even a fourth term, if he so desired. The amendment was actually passed at two o'clock on Sunday morning, according to reports, in a secret session of the assembly, with only members of President Park's party present. As a result, the university students, as well as most of the faculty, were quietly seething. I thought that the secret session was a stupid move, because President Park's amendment had enough votes to pass anyway in a regular assembly session. Early in October, a referendum was to be held to vote nationwide on the issue, and unfortunately, I shared the students' doubts that the vote would be fairly and openly conducted, in view of the secret assembly vote. I was also beginning to doubt that we would have any regular undergraduate classes at all during the entire term, for it seemed a certainty that the students would erupt in even more violent demonstrations than had previously occurred.

The action of the national assembly occurred in the middle of the heaviest rains in Korea in more than sixty years. About three hundred people lost their lives in flash floods, there was a tremendous amount of property damage, according to newspaper reports, and the main railroad lines were out of commission for several days because of the extensive flooding. The storms may have had something to do with the timing of the action of the national assembly, I suspected, for the tragic consequences across the country helped deflect media coverage of the Constitutional amendment. It poured for five days. On September 17 the sun finally reemerged, and Daegu began to return to normal. Except for being cooped up for almost a week and pretty bored, I stayed cheerful, dry, and comfortable in the Nas' attic and at the Language Institute.

The following week five more new PCVs arrived to begin teaching at Kyungpook University—members of the K-IX group (known as the "dogs" or "canines"). They were to teach laboratory techniques in the science departments of the Teachers College. Now there were seven PCVs teaching at the Teachers College and one (me) at the Liberal Arts College, for a total of eight PCVs at Kyungpook National University— the most of any university in Korea. There would have been ten, but Rachel and Peter Wenz, members of the K-VII group, who had been teaching in the Kyungpook Medical College, had terminated early in June, after five months in Korea.

In late September I received a letter from a Korean student, Kang Young-ae, who had been one of my first English students in Korea. She had left Korea to study in the United States midsummer, she wrote, had visited my sister, Cecilia, and her husband, John Pehle, in Sandusky, Ohio, and was now staying with her sister in Madison, Wisconsin, before beginning graduate school next February at Washington State University in Pullman, Washington. Although she sounded lonely and in culture shock, she wrote how grateful she was to have been able to visit my sister's family, to have been able to see a typical American family's lifestyle, and to have experienced the concern for her and welcome of my sister's family. Several of my Korean students and other Korean friends wrote similar letters over the course of my years in Korea, after visiting my sister, brother, parents, and cousins. I was grateful that my family at home was so supportive of them.

As the long hot summer drew to a close, the weather began to get cooler, and the humidity disappeared. The rice was high in the paddies in the countryside, the apples were ripening fast in the hillside orchards surrounding Daegu, and the crepe myrtle—referred to as *paekilhong,* or "hundred day red," with its lush crimson, white, and purple flowers, began to look exhausted. Vendors in the streets were now selling their autumn fare from their pushcarts: peanuts, chestnuts, corn, and apples. As the Korean Thanksgiving, or *Choosuk*, approached, I started discretely dating several of the graduate students at Kyungpook University.

I had waited more than half a year before deciding I knew enough Korean language and was sufficiently culturally aware to be able to approach several Korean women and try to develop a relationship beyond that of a teacher to a student. Several PCVs from earlier groups in Seoul were living with lovely Korean graduate students and clearly had satisfying intellectual, emotional, and sexual relationships. I was envious. Several PCVs from groups K-I through K-VI had already married outstanding Korean women. At the same time, the tragic heroine of my favorite opera—*Madama Butterfly*—was always on my mind. I knew I was not ready for marriage at the age of twenty-four, and I was not about to become a "Pinkerton," deserting a Cio-Cio San ("Butterfly") when it was time to return to the United States. During training with our Korean instructors, we heard repeated observations to the effect that American soldiers were considered sexual predators by many Koreans.

That said, I began to enjoy the company, at least, of several attractive students, who spoke little English but seemed to be happy to meet me secretly at tearooms, go to a movie, and end the evening talking quietly in a bakery over ice cream or listening to music in a tearoom until curfew. These students were extraordinarily brave to be seen dating an American. In the streets, while we walked together, Korean men sometimes spat at them or called them prostitutes for going out with Americans.

One of these students, who was studying French, had a secret second career as a hostess in a tearoom, which I discovered by accident when I stumbled into her tearoom on the far side of Daegu one evening, to her great embarrassment. The other was a medical student, who surprised me by passionately kissing me goodnight on our first date, in a manner that could only have been learned from an American movie. I remember that kiss, because it was the first kiss of passion—if you could call it that—that I had experienced since I joined the Peace Corps eleven months before.

The Na Family (My Korean Family),
Daegu, Korea, August 1969

Graduate Students' English Conversation Class with Me, Kyungpook
National University, Daegu, Korea, July 1969

View of Daegu from my Room in the Attic, Daegu, Korea, July 1969

Professor Chae Joong-ki, Teachers College, Kyungpook National
University, Daegu, Korea, September 1969

# CHAPTER EIGHT—AUTUMN OF THE YEAR OF THE ROOSTER

After the autumnal equinox, for several weeks I was busier than I had been yet in Korea, despite having very few classes. It seemed as though autumn was the time of year for Korean celebrations. The university remained closed. I was teaching only four hours each week, holding my English conversation classes with faculty and spending about twenty hours per week recording language tapes for the Language Institute.

Right after the official beginning of autumn by the solar (Western) calendar, Koreans celebrated their Thanksgiving Day, which was on September 26 in 1969. As mentioned, it is called Choosuk, or the Harvest Moon Festival, which is held on the fifteenth day of the Eighth Moon, according to the lunar calendar. That is usually in September or October and is marked by the rising of a full harvest moon. We had learned in Peace Corps training that this popular Korean festival occurs near the end of the harvest season and combines elements of thanksgiving and remembering family and ancestors. Families visit their ancestral homes to be with grandparents and to celebrate together with feasts and games. Offerings are made of newly harvested foods. Several friends presented me with small gift boxes of *songpyon*, a crescent-shaped rice cake, stuffed with sesame seeds, chestnut paste, or beans, which is the traditional food favored on Choosuk.

The night before Choosuk, Mary Frantz invited me to an event at Hyosung Women's College. Mary's students performed a lovely dance, consisting of a circle of about twenty girls in traditional hanbok, who sang a lilting melody, while holding hands and dancing in a kind of circle dance, in which the line of girls wove in and out, tracing dance patterns to the haunting song. Traditionally, the dance and song, both of which are called *Kang Kang Su Wol Lae*, are performed in the light of the full moon either on or during the eve of Choosuk. I subsequently saw this dance performed many times in Korea by professional dancers, but I never saw a more beautiful or moving performance than that first performance at Hyosung College on the eve of my first Choosuk.

My Korean family invited me to go with them to the home of Reverend Na's elderly parents, not far from Daegu, to celebrate Choosuk. All of Reverend Na's family members were there. After the usual introductions, Reverend Na held a memorial service in a part of the house where pictures of his grandparents were prominently displayed. Offerings of food and soju were made to the ancestral spirits, and all of the members of the family performed the saebae as a gesture of respect. Many of my students had told me of their plans to visit the actual gravesites of their ancestors on Choosuk, to make the offerings of food and perform there the bowing ceremony as a kind of memorial service, with their families.

I was especially interested to see devout Christians, such as the Na family, fusing the ancient tradition of ancestor worship in Korea with the Christian prayers that were offered as part of the ritual. Reverend Na explained that most Korean families still keep and maintain their ancestral shrines, which often include four generations of ancestors among those ritually memorialized. The rituals themselves are of several types: the *esangjung* ritual, which only takes place during the period of mourning, right after death; the *ki* ritual, which is a memorial service held on the anniversary of the ancestor's death; the *wcharye*, which is the ritual performed on Choosuk, or New Year's Day; and the *ymyosa* ritual, conducted in memory of old ancestors, which is performed at the tomb site in the lunar month of October.

As part of the ritual at the Na's home, offerings to the spirits of the deceased were placed in front of the pictures of the ancestors. Several ritual greetings, called *kangshin*, followed. The first entailed an offering of rice wine; Reverend Na then recited a written prayer. At the conclusion of the first ritual offering, Reverend Na paid his respects by performing a ritual bow twice.

Another son then performed the second offering of wine. Following this offering of wine, another offering was carried out by other men of the family. I was asked to make an offering, and of course I did. When the offerings of wine to the deceased spirits were concluded, a sequence of rituals that symbolized the spirits' arrival and acceptance of the food and wine was undertaken. These rituals were carried out to assist the spirits in accepting the offerings, according to Reverend Na. For example, the rice bowl was uncovered and a spoon placed next to it on the table to assist the spirits. Similarly, a pair of chopsticks was placed on the barbecued meat, while all the family members stood in respectful silence for the few minutes it would take the spirits to savor the food and the wine.

After all of the ritual offerings were completed, the family members at the ceremony bowed twice, and the spirits were joyously sent off until the next year. The table with the food and wine offerings was then cleared, and the written prayer, recited by Reverend Na earlier in the ceremony, was burned. Once all of these steps were completed, the feasting of the food and wine (or *cumbok*) by the family members followed. Consuming the ritual food and wine was considered an integral part of the ceremony, as it symbolized the receiving of the blessings bestowed upon the family. The rituals and the luncheon took about four hours. I was so interested by what I was observing, however, that the time flew by.

On September 29, 1969, the third of my articles was published in the *Kyungpook University Press*, the university's English language newspaper. One of my responsibilities in the English department was to proofread this monthly newspaper and to periodically contribute articles. In this article I accurately summarized my feelings to date about Peace Corps service in Korea:

### After Seven Months
Charles A. Hobbie

Recently, five new Peace Corps Volunteers arrived at Kyungpook University to work as laboratory assistants to professors and instructors of science in the Teachers College. They are members of the ninth group of volunteers to come to Korea, and they join Mr. Feldmeier, Mr. Cain, and me of the eighth group, already teaching at Kyungpook. The arrival of these new men inevitably brings to my mind memories of my own arrival in Daegu last February, and at the same time, I am spurred to an assessment of exactly how the realities of Korea and of my situation here compare with my expectations more than seven months ago.

Just before I arrived in Korea, I learned that I would be teaching in Daegu, so naturally I asked people who had been here for their impressions of the city and of Kyungpook. I was told that Daegu is famous for apples and for pretty women, that Daegu is extremely hot and dusty during the summer and bitterly cold in winter, that I would alternately freeze and roast while teaching at Kyungpook, and that Daegu is conveniently close to many interesting places, which would provide an escape from the city. I was also told that teaching would be difficult, because professors and students alike would resent any strange manners or new ideas.

Now of course, most of the people who provided me with these expectations were trying to prepare me for the unpleasant aspects of life that I might encounter during my years in Korea, so they tended to emphasize the harsher realities of Korea and downplay the delights. In any case, I arrived in Daegu and began teaching at Kyungpook with, quite frankly, low expectations of happiness in Korea, as well as with a "defensive attitude" that was alert to recognize and buffer all the offensiveness I expected to experience.

After more than seven months in Korea and one term at Kyungpook University, I must admit that Daegu apples are delicious and Daegu women are beautiful, that Daegu is extremely hot and dusty during the summer (I was glad to be able to work during the summer on Geoje Island, where it was comparatively cool), but not so cold in winter relative to the New England cold I am accustomed to, that I have sometimes been uncomfortable teaching—both cold and hot, and that this part of Korea is really fascinating, although I have yet to find a great urge to escape from Daegu, which is quite a pleasant city by any standards. Finally, teaching at Kyungpook has been a pleasure so far, for both students and faculty have been overwhelmingly friendly, helpful, and cooperative. I could not ask for better friends than those I have made here.

There are unpleasant realities in Korea, many similar to equally harsh realities at home, which the majority of Americans fail to see—poverty, starvation, racial prejudice, hazardous health conditions, and ignorance, to name just a few. In Korea I meet and see every day what is hidden but still exists in the United States. This is unpleasant, but such seeing and meeting is terribly important for someone who has not seen and met before. So many other elements of Korean life have provided endless pleasure—traditional music, art, and dancing; Korean temples and history; "tabangs," "beer halls," and "makoli houses"; Korean dress; and much more.

Looking back at the apprehensive and slightly bewildered Mr. Hobbie who came to Daegu last February, I would say now that his fears were unjustified and his defensive attitude very regrettable—it took him a long time to relax in Korea. Of course, the real test will come after two years when all of the volunteers, as they leave Korea, are asked: "Would you do it again?" Now I can say quite honestly and unreservedly, "Yes." I hope that the new volunteers at Kyungpook may meet with experiences and friendship in their first seven months here that will allow them to say the same.

Professor Kim Sung-hyok, who was one of the people responsible for the thoughts expressed in the above article, prompted me to experience another traditional Korean celebration that took place soon after Choosuk. During the first week in October, Professor Kim's lovely daughter was married. I was entranced months before by her beauty and charm. There were two ceremonies—Western-style and Korean-style. I had already attended almost one dozen Western-style marriages in Korea in nine months, including several marriages of PCVs to Korean women, but I had never attended a traditional Korean-style wedding. It was fascinating.

Professor Kim's daughter was simply beautiful, although also frowning, in a white Western-style wedding dress at the Western-style ceremony in a local Presbyterian church. Many of the Korean Presbyterian ministers, whom I had met previously in Daegu, were in attendance, as well as many of the Kyungpook University faculty members. I was the sole Westerner. The major difference between it and the usual American wedding ceremony was that the bride was very solemn, looking as though she was going to her death. In Korea it is considered very bad luck for the bride to smile on her wedding day. If the bride smiles on her wedding day, she will give birth to only daughters.

In the male-dominated Confucian society that still prevailed in Korea, it was perfectly understandable that the Korean bride would take no chances, scowling the entire ceremony, as a reflection of the importance to her of bearing the sons who would assure her place in her husband's family, as the mother of the males, carrying on the family lineage. In the future, if she had a son, red peppers would be strung up over the door of the home in celebration of the son's birth. If she had a daughter, pieces of coal would be strung above the door, and she will be blamed for being unfruitful.

After the ceremony at the church, the bride and groom changed into traditional Korean wedding clothes—the groom in silk, baggy pants, with an elaborately embroidered blouse, and the bride in an exquisite red and green Korean bridal dress, with her hair tightly pulled into a bun. At Professor Kim's Korean-style house, against the backdrop of the lovely gardens surrounding the house, the bride and the groom each performed the saebae in front of their parents and other older relatives of each family, who then gave them envelopes containing money. I particularly liked the bowing part of the ceremony, as it conveyed the new couple's respect and appreciation for their respective families.

Throughout the evening, while the guests ate a magnificent meal and toasted the wedding couple with grape juice, the bride sat demurely next to her new husband, eyes downcast and unsmiling. I remembered the evening, months earlier, when I had talked at length with her and found her to be so charming, outgoing, and seemingly not very traditional in her thoughts and demeanor. On her wedding day, she was evidently careful to follow time-honored customs. As the guests departed, they received the traditional Korean gift for wedding guests of a small cake, much like an American pound cake, as well as a small hand towel.

On October 6 I had another wonderful experience. I went with my favorite freshman student, Rhee Sook-hee, to Haein Temple, which was located in the mountains about forty miles from Daegu. It was the first trip I had taken with only one of my students. Up until that time I had always been careful to travel in groups of students. Miss Rhee had invited me repeatedly to go with her. She was persistent, but also very intelligent, charming, and lovely, at the age of eighteen. (If she had been five or six years older, I thought, I might have wished to marry her.) Despite some misgivings about traveling alone with a student, I accepted her invitation. It turned out to be one of the best weekends I had in Korea.

The scenery en route was incredibly lovely. After leaving the Daegu environs, our old bus passed mile after mile of apple orchards and then hundreds of paddies of partially harvested golden rice, rippling in the autumn wind, as farmers and their families stooped to bring in the grain. In the mountains, as we entered South Gyeongsang Province, the trees were a welcome sight, with their leaves beginning to turn red, yellow, and orange. The bus wound along a narrow dirt road that climbed precariously ever upward, skirting high cliffs and offering spectacular views on both sides. The trip took several hours. At last we arrived at the temple complex, which is one of the most famous in Korea.

Miss Rhee explained, as we arrived, that *Haeinsa*, or Haein Temple, is one of Korea's so-called "Three Jewel Temples." The jewel that Haein Temple is famous for is the *Tripitaka Koreana*, which is a complete composition of Buddhist scriptures (*Dharma*) that have been hand-carved onto wooden printing blocks—among the oldest in the world. There are no known errors on the characters of the wooden blocks, and they are the most ancient, intact, and complete collection of Buddhist treatises, laws, and scriptures, written in Chinese characters, in existence. The wooden building in which this unique collection reposes is called the *Jangkyung Panjeon*.

We went directly to see the Tripitaka Koreana. The enormity of what I was seeing at Haein Temple took a while to sink in. Completed in 1251 by an estimated thirty monks, working for more than sixteen years, the scripture was carved onto 81,340 wooden printing blocks. The 52,382,960 characters, which are organized in more than 1,496 titles and 6,568 volumes, are flawless. Each wood block measures about twenty-seven and a half inches in width and about nine and a half inches in length. The thickness of the blocks ranged from about one inch to one and a half inches, and each weighed about six to eight pounds. I was totally amazed, wondering how it was humanly possible to create a treatise of more than 81,000 printed pages—without an error—much less to carve each page's characters into a wood block.

After viewing the Tripitaka Koreana, Miss Rhee and I spent several perfect days in the mountains, exploring the twelve or so temple complexes that make up Haein Temple. We picnicked at the temple located at the highest elevation and then hiked down to each of the other temple buildings, along well-worn paths that meandered under fragrant cedars and along bubbling brooks.

Miss Rhee had spent the summer at one of these lovely old temple buildings, meditating with the monks. That evening we had a delicious dinner with the monks she knew, sitting cross-legged on the floor of a six hundred-year-old structure, with the wind gently pushing the wind chimes into song and gray-robed men and women with shaven heads talking with us of world harmony and inner peace. I had to pinch myself—as I often had to in Korea—to believe I was actually at this place and at this time, experiencing what I was experiencing.

According to the eldest of the monks at our table, I was one of only a handful of foreigners who had dined with the monks at Haein Temple in the centuries of its existence. The monks were fascinated to hear about the Peace Corps and about my family in Buffalo. When I mentioned that my parents' wedding anniversary was approaching on October 14, they invited me to come back to Haein Temple with my parents anytime for a meal to celebrate. I particularly remember the incredibly delicious soup and stew-like dish that tasted like delectable, marinated meat of some sort but which, I was assured, was entirely vegetable in contents—primarily ferns and bean curd.

We spent several days at Haein Temple. There were dormitories, segregated by gender, with ibuls and yos for visitors, and a dining room where we ate most of our meals with a handful of other Korean visitors. The weather was perfect—a blue, cloudless sky with temperatures in the fifties. The autumn colors, the sounds of the wind, birds, and rushing water, the fragrance of incense, the smell of the pines and cedars that were mixed with the hardwoods in the surrounding forest, and the overall relaxed ambiance of the temple and its grounds were totally bewitching. We hiked and picnicked every day to our hearts' content. Above us rose the rugged, protective forty-two hundred foot-high peaks of Mts. Sangwang-bong and Chulbul-bong, which had safeguarded the Tripitaka from invading Japanese armies over the past seven centuries. I could have stayed at Haein Temple with Miss Rhee and the friendly monks for the rest of my Peace Corps service!

On the next weekend, the annual farmers' dancing competition was held in the Daegu stadium, with thousands of people watching and hundreds of teams participating in wonderfully flamboyant and colorful costumes. Reverend Na and I went together, and after milling around in the crowd outside the stadium gates for more than an hour, we finally sneaked in at the tail end of a group of American military VIPs and were escorted to the best seats in the house. Farmers' dances are extremely lively and feature tremendous drumming, clashing of cymbals, and banging of gongs. My favorite dances involved dancers who wore hats with long ribbons attached to a swivel on the top. By moving their heads in a constant swiveling motion, the dancers caused the ribbons to gracefully sweep back and forth among the dancers, who danced over and under the long ribbons while beating their instruments in an amazingly beautiful, rhythmic, and graceful dance.

Reverend Na told me that the Farmer's Dance, or *nongak*, is one of the oldest dance forms in Korea. It originated about two thousand years ago and was traditionally performed during planting, harvesting, and other agricultural events, representing Korean farmers working to the beat of percussion instruments. Until recently, the dance was performed in the rural areas, in particular during the planting and harvesting, to give encouragement to the farmers and to provide them with a beat to work by. It was also often performed as a part of shamanistic rituals to protect houses from thieves and fire, to purify the village, and to give thanks to the river or mountain spirits, according to Reverend Na.

There was also a unique team competition, featuring a kind of boat-shaped vessel made of thick ropes wrapped around and around each other and carried on the shoulders of perhaps fifty men on each team. In the "vessel" were perhaps a dozen men, holding poles tipped by cushions. The teams rushed at each other, the vessels clashed over the shoulders of the respective team's members, and the men with the poles tried to knock the other team's members out of the vessel. It was very dramatic, and the cheering was deafening. The drumming and dancing reminded me very much of American Indian dances I had witnessed at home.

My close friend, PCV Brian Copp, from Iri City, visited me several times in October. Several other PCVs came for brief visits as well. Most of the members of our combined groups—K-VII and K-VIII—were in the same situation as I was, with very little to do because the universities were still closed. Due to the uncertainty regarding when classes would resume, teacher workshops—which required considerable advance planning—were not possible. Moreover, October was a month of Korean holidays. It seemed as though there was one each week: Armed Forces Day on October 1; National Foundation Day on October 3 in honor of Korea's founder, *Tangun*; Hangul Day on October 9 in honor of the Korean phonetic alphabet; and October 24, United Nations Day. Any attempt at serious work was interrupted each week by festivals and parades on each of the holidays.

Autumn was a terrific season in Korea. The skies were clear and bright blue, the air was refreshingly cool, and people in general seemed to be in a good mood. We were taught a Korean proverb in Peace Corps training—*Chungomabi*—which loosely translated means "the sky is high and my horse is fat," as an apt expression of this delightful season. I thought this was a very appropriate description of a Korean October and never missed an opportunity to drop this into a conversation with Korean friends in autumn, who were usually impressed that I would know this proverb. In truth, I remembered it so well because it sounded almost exactly like the name of one of the members of Group VIII: John Kumabe.

My parents' thirty-sixth wedding anniversary was close at hand. Before I left for Peace Corps training, we had discussed the possibility of their visiting Korea in October to celebrate this occasion with me during

Korea's most spectacular season. Despite my urging, however, Mom and Dad advised me in early September that a trip to Korea was financially beyond them and that they would not be coming. I was disappointed but understood how difficult such a trip would have been.

With the crisp, invigorating weather, October was a time to take advantage of the respite from teaching and to travel, to visit other PCVs, and to engage Korean culture and language in new and different ways, if possible. In talking with these other PCV visitors to Daegu—most of whom were extremely envious of the wonderful teaching situation I had at Kyungpook National University and of my delightful Korean family—I thought again and again how very fortunate I was to be in Daegu, teaching at Kyungpook University, and living with the Na family!

During his October visit, Brian and I walked around downtown Daegu in the brisk, clear air. I showed him the Chinese Medicine Market, the West Gate Market, and Kyungpook University's superb campus—my three favorite places in Daegu. Then we climbed Mt. Ap, which was swarming with October hikers. I had had an MMVSP flag made at a local shop, and we planted it on the top of the mountain.

In the evening I took Brian out to Daegu's nightlife. Not the least of the attractions I frequented in Daegu were the numerous mekju houses, or beer halls. I have already mentioned in detail the makoli houses. Beer halls were a step up in quality and had the advantage for me of being able to sit at tables on chairs, rather than having to sit cross-legged on the floor. My legs preferred beer halls to makoli houses.

When I craved some excitement, either graduate students or faculty colleagues were happy to accompany me and always seemed to know when I was in the mood for an evening of imbibing. In the autumn of the Year of the Rooster, my Korean language skills were just beginning to get to the point that I could go by myself to a beer hall and have a perfectly good time. It was customary, however, for men to go in pairs or groups to these establishments, and it was much more fun to go with my Korean friends, or with another PCV, anyway. At the typical beer hall, an evening could cost about five dollars per person, including tips to the girls, so an evening could be very expensive for the one person who picked up the tab. I always came prepared to pay for my friends' evening and argued vociferously that it was my turn to pay. Usually, however, my efforts were in vain, which was a good thing, for I would have exhausted my monthly living allowance in one week. I was lucky to have had friends who could afford an evening in a beer hall even once a month.

At the typical beer hall, you entered a lavishly decorated club and were seated with hostesses at a booth, which was screened off from the rest of the club. Bottled beer, or draft beer—*saeng mekju*—was available and was served with peanuts, strips of dried octopus, or raw fish with a red pepper paste. You sat with your friends and with the hostesses talking, singing, and complimenting the hostesses, who were always young (eighteen to twenty-five years old), pretty girls dressed in short skirts—very short skirts. Since the lights were very dim and the music was always conducive to romance, my Korean friends usually "fell in love" with the hostesses, with resulting kissing and "pawing," especially after a few beers. I never felt comfortable enough to engage in this kind of activity, remembering what my Korean instructors had said in training about American sexual predators. I preferred to flirt with the hostesses but not to try to engage them sexually in any way. You could say that I was overly concerned about what my Korean friends would think if I did.

I was also careful, whenever I went drinking, not to get drunk. To be honest, I certainly did not want there to be any chance that my Korean family might see me inebriated, but I also did not trust my American predatory instincts, particularly in the presence of the very beautiful and sexy women who were available in most of the places where social events occurred.

Brian and I went together to several of my favorite beer halls, where I introduced him to some of the hostesses who knew me. We had a fine time, chatting with the girls and getting each other caught up on the news of the volunteers in groups VII and VIII. During the course of the evening we discussed the fact that volunteers had to be careful when they went out together socializing, as we were not to engage in culturally insensitive behavior. Most volunteers were extremely considerate of Korean cultural norms when they were by themselves or with Koreans. Observing the volunteers in groups of exclusively volunteers, however, we had both seen that their behavior was often quite different. There was a tendency to tell war stories to each other about what strange things they had encountered or about the negative aspects of life for Americans in Korea. It was probably a means of blowing off steam—venting the frustrations they were experiencing—but they usually did so together with loud voices and laughter—oblivious to who was overhearing them. The "ugly American" behavior was always more of a possibility when two or more volunteers got together. Brian was one of the volunteers who was sensitive to this problem. I appreciated that in him.

In talking with the girls, we discovered that most were surprisingly sweet and innocent. Some of the girls were students, earning their way through college by working evenings in the beer halls. Others were helping put brothers through school. A few would sleep with you for money—seven dollars was the going rate—but the vast majority would not. It was common to hear that the oldest brother had to be helped to succeed so he could care for his parents. When asked if they minded the kissing and groping that seemed to be part of their work, most said they understood how frustrated Korean men were with their lives. Men worked hard and earned enough to support their families in most cases but had little chance of any real improvement in their lives. The girls seemed to understand this and were willing to be sympathetic listeners—and more, on occasion.

A beer hall that featured dancing was slightly more expensive. I liked to dance with the girls, who were usually terrific dancers. Some halls played American pop songs and jazz. Others played exclusively Korean pop songs, which I was not particularly fond of. Korean pop music reminded me of the worst of the "big band" sounds of my earliest childhood memories. Imagine a fundamentally decent folk song, like "Old Black Joe," or "Home on the Range," or "Danny Boy," played with a big band sound, and you have an idea of what Korean pop songs were like. Brian and I visited both types of beer halls that night and then retired to the Nas' attic just before the curfew siren sounded.

As October drew to a close, several of my students and two faculty members invited me to go with them to climb Mt. Chiri in South Gyeongsang Province. Mt. Chiri is located in the Sobaek Mountains, which is the longest mountain range in Korea, stretching more than two hundred miles in a southwesterly direction from Gang Won Province in northeastern South Korea to near Yeosu City on Korea's south coast. The highest peaks of the Sobaek Range are more than five thousand feet in elevation. Mt. Chiri (6,283 ft) rises skyward from its southwestern branch, about sixty miles from Daegu, but is difficult to access.

We took a bus, starting before dawn, to a small town near Mt. Chiri named Sancheong, changing twice. The trip took six hours on mostly narrow dirt and gravel roads, on which our bus created a small dust storm as it careened through the mountains. The scenery was gorgeous, although many of the leaves had already fallen from the trees. The day was clear and crisp.

After visiting a lovely temple—Hwaeom Temple—on the first day, early on the second day we climbed the main peak, taking a trail that had been in use for a thousand years or more. At the top of the mountain, where there were dozens of hikers, I planted the MMVSP flag, explaining to the hiking team what it was and why it was important to me. Closing my eyes on the summit, I heard the sound of the wind, which whispered the same songs that New Hampshire's winds sang in the White Mountains. The view that greeted us was of dozens of purple-blue mountain ranges, stretching as far as we could see. I marveled at how similar the Sobaek Range seemed to the Northern Appalachians at home. The beauty was overwhelming! No wonder the founders of Korea's many inspiring temples were moved to build their shrines in such stunning locations, as well as for perhaps the more fundamental reason that isolation in the mountains meant security. We returned, exhausted, to our small country yogwan just after dark had fallen.

On the third day of our trip we returned to Daegu, taking a bus about two hours to Chinju, where we changed to a train from there to Busan. The train ride from Busan to Daegu was the last leg of our trip home. On the five-hour train ride, I began to prepare to resume teaching.

Autumn was just about over. The colorful leaves of the few trees in Daegu had vanished, all the rice paddies and orchards were bare, and the wind was whipping dust around once again. Temperatures began to drop below freezing at night, although during the day it was a comfortable forty-five to fifty degrees. I was quite warm and cozy in my attic room with my kerosene heater. At Kyungpook University the potbellied charcoal burning stoves were installed in the offices of the Language Institute around November 1, in quick response to our complaints that we were freezing to death in our north-facing office on the third floor of the museum building.

Weeks of arguing between the Korean ministry of education and Kyungpook University's leadership finally were resolved by an agreement that classes would start on November 5 and end on December 24. The fall term would be only eight weeks, and final exams would be postponed until the start of school again in February so as to avoid holding classes during the coldest time of the year in Daegu. My class load was doubled to accommodate this plan. I would be teaching twenty-two hours per week, plus my language laboratory instruction and conversation classes—all together averaging about seven hours per day. But the term would be short. Everyone would receive full credit for the term, despite its abbreviated length, so the students and faculty were happy.

In the midst of my satisfaction that the semester would resume, albeit on a shortened basis, I heard that North Korean soldiers had recently killed four American soldiers on the south side of the Korean Demilitarized Zone, about one hundred and eighty miles north of Daegu. Once again, the Korean government conducted military exercises in response and denounced the constant provocations from the north. The Republic of Korea military went on full alert for a week. Thanks to Kim Il Sung (North Korea's president), any interest in renewed student demonstrations against President Park's government was considerably dampened by this attack.

President Park won his referendum with a greater majority than most of us anticipated, although the outcome was never in doubt. I was interested in the coverage by American reporters, as set forth in *Time*, who commented that the election was scrupulously democratic. "Democratic" depends upon one's definition and context, of course, and I suppose that by Korean standards the referendum was conducted fairly—probably very little ballot stuffing or false counts, according to my Korean reporter friends. However, the opposition party was prohibited from holding any public demonstrations or meetings, and the opposition was barred from radio, television, or newsreel (theater) coverage.

Some newspapers, to their credit, defied the government ban on press coverage of the student demonstrations and opposition rallies, and there were editorials supporting the opposition—all carefully worded and weak, according to Reverend Na. In addition, home-improvement programs, sponsored by government funding, which had been idle ever since I arrived in Korea, suddenly zipped to life about two weeks before the election, and my students told me that the rural areas received traditional payoffs of wine and rice before the voting. The list was endless. Korean politics were just like American politics, only more obvious! Despite my abhorrence of the tactics of his party, I felt that the outcome and Park's inevitable third term were probably best for Korea.

Professor Lee Woo-gun and I often discussed President Park and shared the same feelings about him. Professor Lee and I had become very close friends. I could not have had a finer *chitukyosu* ("mentor"). He was a delightful, kind, and generous man with a lovely wife and two children, to whom he was devoted. At least twice a month we would spend an evening together, either at his home or at the New York Grill in downtown Daegu, which featured passable Western food—especially a delicious pork cutlet. He insisted on treating me to such food, although by this time I was happier, most of the time, eating Korean food. I was concerned for his health, for I suspected that he was diabetic, and the after-dinner drinking that he undertook could not have been good for him.

Professor Lee and I always went to the same makoli house for our evenings together. We got to know the girls there quite well over time. Several of them gave me little presents, such as cufflinks and a tiepin, and they delighted in teaching me Korean. On an evening in the late fall they surprised me by teaching me the Korean names of all the body parts. One woman, Miss Jung, amid much laughter and cheering, insisted on disrobing and literally showing us all of her body parts as a part of the language lesson. It was a totally unexpected striptease. For the first time I learned the names of the undergarments worn by women under their beautiful Korean dresses, as well as the names of their sexual parts. I suspected that Professor Lee, for whom I had the highest respect and affection, had put the women up to this language lesson, but he stoutly denied it.

On other evenings Professor Lee and I spent hours at tearooms, discussing world affairs, politics, and other faculty at the university.

Several members of the faculty of the English department were being dismissed by Kyungpook University because of their outspoken criticism of President Park's government. One of these men—an expert on Shakespeare and a passable pitcher—was a good friend of ours. Both of us were devastated by his firing and agreed that the government's retaliation was a travesty. Professor Lee and I made a point of inviting him to go out with us whenever we could, although for Professor Lee this might have been damaging to his career at a national university. Professor Lee's deep concern for a colleague and disregard of potentially damaging consequences for himself were typical of him. I found him to be very open, smart, and insightful, and one of the most understanding friends I ever had in Korea. I will always be grateful to him and his family for their friendship and assistance.

My first class of the fall term was on November 5. All of my former students were back. I was pleased that several new students had also joined my classes. My friends on the faculty seemed happy to resume our English conversation classes. Life was returning to normal, it seemed.

I continued to use movies, borrowed from the USIS, as teaching aids. I would pass out a short synopsis of the movie's plot, list perhaps thirty questions about such things as unusual vocabulary or the geographical setting of the movie, show the movie, and lead a discussion in English about the questioned topics. On other occasions we read short plays in English or engaged in role-playing. Of course, the more traditional substitution drills, pronunciation drills, and question-answer drills constituted the bulk of the classroom work, but I tried to have as much variety as possible in class and keep my teaching lively.

Occasionally there were embarrassing moments. Once, when I was vexed about several students who persisted in whispering to each other at the back of the class. I deliberately used a low form of Korean speech in admonishing them. There was a stunned silence in the class, and I could tell from my students' shocked faces that I had overreacted and used improper speech. Of course I immediately apologized.

On another occasion, when I asked my students what I could do to make my classes more interesting, a comely, shy freshman girl replied that she would like to have more "oral intercourse" with me. (She had the same Korean-English dictionary, with its archaic translations, apparently, that Peace Corps trainees were provided in our training program, as I have mentioned.) My red face indicated that she had said something terribly wrong, and I had a tough time explaining her misuse of a seemingly straightforward phrase.

In early November I received a letter from the Peace Corps director, Kevin O'Donnell, reminding me that I was approaching the halfway point of my volunteer service and exhorting the members of groups K-VII and K-VIII to continue our good work. It seemed impossible that thirteen and a half months had passed already! I was shocked when I realized that in the near future I would be reentering life in the United States. My initial reaction to the letter was disbelief. Then I became anxious. What in the world was I going to do after Peace Corps service? Reflecting on this issue, I realized I was a very different person now from the individual who had sipped champagne on the flight from Los Angeles to Hilo, Hawaii, in October 1968. I wondered how the changes in my perspective on life would affect my future at home.

Peace Corps headquarters in Washington had a special department specifically charged with helping former PCVs with employment and educational opportunities following the completion of volunteer service. Each month I received a booklet from this department, listing all the job opportunities in the United States—government, teaching, social services, diplomatic, and the like—particularly suited for returned volunteers. Up until this time, I had discarded these booklets without reading them. Suddenly, with the end of my service looming on the distant horizon, I started reading this information and thinking seriously about my future.

One very welcome piece of information from Peace Corps headquarters was that our teacher training and two years' experience as English teachers satisfied most states' requirements for certification as a teacher. If I wished to pursue a career in education at the primary or secondary levels, I could do so immediately when I returned. I certainly loved teaching and felt that I was a good teacher. Most of the teachers I knew were very happy people and made tremendous contributions to society. A career in teaching was an attractive prospect.

Another valuable piece of information was that former Peace Corps Volunteers could join the federal civil service—become federal government employees—on a non-competitive basis for one year after the completion of their volunteer service. It took me a while to understand what this meant, but I finally figured out that as a returned Peace Corps Volunteer, I could be hired by a federal agency as an employee without having to take the civil service examination or formally competing against other persons for a position. It was not until much later that I realized how beneficial this non-competitive advantage could be.

Shortly after receiving the letter from Director O'Donnell, we had an African-American visitor from the headquarters of Peace Corps in Washington DC. Joe Kennedy, who was the director of the East Asia/Pacific region of the Peace Corps, visited Daegu and met with about a dozen PCVs in the Peace Corps office in Daegu. I liked Joe a lot. He brought news of events from home and expressed great interest and appreciation for our service in Daegu. When he returned to Washington, Joe wrote to my parents, telling them of his meeting in Daegu and conversations with me. They were very pleased that a high level Peace Corps official would go to the trouble to contact a PCV's family.

In late November, a group of PCVs in the Daegu area got together at the Daegu Peace Corps office for a pre-Thanksgiving party. The weather turned suddenly cold that week, prompting thoughts of holiday celebrations back home. Everyone was a little bit glum as a result. The party was an attempt to cheer everyone up. One of the women, in a stroke of genius, had brought a dozen or so books by Theodore Geisel—a.k.a. Dr. Seuss—that she had obtained from the USIS library. We started to read the books out loud, one at a time, marveling at the amazing poetry, consistent meter, philosophical message, and evocative images in such books as *And to Think That I Saw It on Mulberry Street, Green Eggs and Ham, Horton Hears a Who, The Sneetches and Other Stories, How the Grinch Stole Christmas*, and *The Cat in the Hat*. What fun we had! We read each book several times, recounting how each book had affected us as children. Then several PCVs wrote their own verses in the anapestic tetrameter used by Geisel. I retold, as well, several anecdotes from Chince Allen about Ted Geisel, who had been a friend of Chince's at Dartmouth in the class of 1925, one year after Chince's own class. At the end of several hours of contemplating Dr. Seuss's insightful absurdities, we all felt much better.

Our "Dr. Seuss party" at the Peace Corps office prompted me to introduce one of his books—*Horton Hears a Who*—to my senior class and then to my English conversation class of professors. After struggling for a week and bewildering all of my students and faculty colleagues (except for Professor Kim Sung-hyok, who was already familiar with Dr. Seuss), I soon realized that the delight of Seuss did not translate well to Koreans, because of both insurmountable language and cultural differences.

As soon as classes began, my students again invited me to attend several concerts with them to hear the new conductor of the Daegu Symphony Orchestra, who had come from Seoul. He was an excellent conductor, and I recall three or four wonderful concerts in the autumn of 1969. The orchestra seemed to improve dramatically each month.

Six of my junior students—four males and two females—accompanied me to Busan in mid-November to visit Beomeo Temple, the largest temple in Korea. The temple is located on Kumjong Mountain, next to Busan. We took an early morning train to Busan and then a bus about one hour from the center of the city to a small town not far from the temple. Around midmorning we hiked for almost an hour up to the series of ancient buildings that constituted the temple. I was told that the temple's water has magic powers, and we all drank copiously from the well, before exploring the lovely complex. Once again, I was very moved by the serenity and physical beauty of the temple and its mountain site. The company of my students was great fun, as each of them was quite different from the others, with different perspectives on life. Two were Presbyterians, one was a Catholic, two were Buddhists, and one professed to be an atheist. This mix was not unusual in Korean society, which tolerated a wide variety of religious and other beliefs.

After visiting the temple and returning to Busan in the early evening, I had planned to take the boat the next morning from the city to Geoje Island to visit the Sibleys at the rural public health project for the weekend. Vendors at the Jagalchi Market, however, who by now recognized me as one of the crazy Americans who periodically headed to Geoje Island, told me that the ferryboat to the islands was not running during the stormy season in November. So I returned to Daegu with my students, disappointed not to have been able to visit one of my favorite places in Korea. Before leaving for Daegu, my students introduced me to the New York Bakery in Busan, which had the best ice cream—in three flavors—that I ever had in Korea! In the following year I would visit this bakery so often that I wore a rut in the street from the Busan Station to it.

About this time I noticed that I had a kind of skin condition on my back. It was in a difficult-to-see location, right in the middle of my back, and I had no idea how long it had been there. I suspected it was a kind of fungal condition of little consequence, but I scheduled a medical consultation in Seoul with the Peace Corps physician, just in case. In the back of my mind I was worried that something initially benign might develop into a medical problem of some magnitude, as so often seemed to happen to PCVs in Korea. I wrote to my parents, jokingly, that the fungus was eating away at my skin and bones and threatening my brain! Having said that, I knew my parents would never forgive me, and I would be ticked off at myself if my statement actually turned out to be true and I had done nothing about it.

In response to a summons from the Peace Corps office in Seoul, I hurried to Seoul on November 15, on a cold, blustery day with light snow in the air. Scott Duncan, who was the director of our Peace Corps training program in Hawaii, was in Korea for a two-week visit and wanted to interview members of the Korea VII and Korea VIII groups about our experiences in Korea and evaluations of the training in the light of these experiences. I again stayed with Ed Klein at his apartment in Itaewondong. Scott, Ed, and I, together with three of my former Myongi University students, went out for dinner and then watched a marvelous performance of Korean music, singing, and dancing at the Korea House—a touristy, cultural center that featured an evening program in a traditional setting. We all thoroughly enjoyed the performance. It was great to see Scott again! How far from cold and windy Daegu, it seemed, were the waterfalls and tropical heat of Hilo, where I had said goodbye to Scott eleven months earlier.

I took the occasion of being in Seoul to ask the Peace Corps doctor to look at my flaky back. He diagnosed it as a benign fungal infection, which would disappear if I would shower at least twice a day with lots of hot water. We both laughed at that prescription, and I accepted the probability that my fungus might be with me until I left Korea.

While I was nursing my deformed back, I decided to visit the American embassy in Seoul to be sure my passport was in order and that I would be permitted to travel to the six foreign countries I hoped to visit on my upcoming vacation early in the new year. The embassy was located fairly close to the Peace Corps office in the busiest part of downtown Seoul, on the road leading from the Kwanghwamun Rotary to Gyeongbok Palace. I could easily walk to it. I considered myself pretty much a country bumpkin with respect to Seoul, and my mastery of the bus system was minimal. My knowledge of the huge city was limited to the area around the Peace Corps office near Kwanghwamun Rotary, a part of the city called Insadong, which had wonderful antique and art stores, and the two-mile corridor from Kwanghwamun, leading past Duksoo Palace and Namdaemun (South Great Gate) to Seoul Station. On the way to the embassy I decided to explore some back alleys, leading in the general direction I wanted to go, and encountered the first and only criminal I ever met in Korea.

A young man furtively approached me as I was walking along a side street. He was wearing the uniform and cap of one of Korea's top universities. I thought he was going to ask me if I could teach him English, as hundreds of students like him had asked me in the past ten months. Instead, he asked, in almost perfect English, if I was an American teacher. When I responded affirmatively, he held up an American ten-dollar bill and stated that he had just come back from a visit to the United States, had brought back some American money, and was trying to exchange it for Korean currency without paying the high exchange rate at a Korean bank (which was the only place where you could legally change American money into Korean won or vice versa). Then he asked if I could I help him out by exchanging Korean won for a ten-dollar bill and handed me the bill.

I paused and briefly reflected. I had enough Korean money in my pocket to do him a favor. He was obviously a student. On the other hand, I knew it was illegal to change money without going to a Korean bank. Korea needed American dollars and controlled such exchanges tightly. In the end, I inspected the ten-dollar bill and handed it back to him while I counted out the several thousand won to exchange with him. He handed the bill back to me, folded in half, and I handed him the Korean money. Of course when I looked down to put the ten-dollar bill away, I realized he had switched the real bill with a fake, hand-drawn bill, which I was now holding, and that he had vanished in a twinkle of an eye.

I felt stupid, betrayed, angry, and violated—all at the same time. I couldn't do anything because I had also broken the rules. I was too embarrassed to tell anyone at the Peace Corps, and I never did. In retrospect, I had to admire the execution of the perfect scam—just like the old switcheroo scam that opens the movie *The Sting* (which would come out four years later). But at the time I felt as though someone had kicked me in the stomach. I learned a good lesson. It cost me one week's living allowance. I survived by really cutting back on expenses.

As soon as I returned from Seoul, I plunged into preparations for mid-semester exams. In the shortened autumn term these were scheduled for late November. At the same time I decided to prepare the rest of the term's lessons plans through December 24. The autumn term's classes would end on the day before Christmas. Final exams had been postponed until February 1970.

In the meantime, the fourth, fifth, and sixth groups of volunteers to come to Korea (groups IV, V, and VI) had just completed their volunteer service and were about to leave for the United States. They would be home for Thanksgiving. At the Daegu Peace Corps office we had a huge sendoff party for the PCVs departing from Daegu. The remaining PCV members of K-VII and K-VIII in Daegu, who had arrived with me, also marked the official halfway point in our service. We were now the senior volunteers in Korea and entitled to the respect and obedience from the other PCVs that Korean culture demanded for the wise and aged.

While I waited in vain for the aforementioned entitlements of respect and obedience to materialize, I accepted two invitations for Thanksgiving, which occurred rather late in the month—on November 27. Dorothy Compton, an American missionary working at Dongsan Hospital, kindly invited several PCVs to her home for a noontime Thanksgiving dinner. Mrs. Compton lived on the missionary compound near the hospital and taught nursing. I had already visited the compound often in the past to see Chince and Margaret Allen, who had returned to New Hampshire at the end of the summer after completing their missionary service in Daegu. Seven PCVs attended Mrs. Compton's lovely dinner and enjoyed her hospitality, and the company of her teenage daughter, as well as turkey and apple pie!

On Thanksgiving evening we were all invited to another dinner at Camp Henry, one of the US Army bases in or near Daegu. It was my first visit to Camp Henry. During my year in Daegu, I had religiously avoided any contact with American military and restrained myself from being tempted by the sinful delights the base offered, such as hamburgers, French fries, and American ice cream. Except in the vicinity of the military bases, you seldom saw any American military personnel. Occasionally a convoy of army vehicles with American soldiers would pass through the streets of Daegu, and the American fighter jets flew overhead everyday, but other than that, the American military presence was not very visible. When you did see GIs off duty in civilian clothes, they were always in groups of four or six, as though they were fearful of some unidentified danger—in probably the safest country in the world. Since most Americans are about a foot taller and twice as big physically than Koreans, a group of Americans stands out and frightens, by its very size, anybody nearby. The few times I met American soldiers on a street in Seoul or Daegu, I was friendly to them but felt intimidated myself!

I also had limited contacts with American missionaries, except on Geoje Island, where the rural health project was a joint Korean-American undertaking based on virtually equal involvement by Koreans and Americans. When I received the dual Thanksgiving invitations, I struggled to resist. It was not that I personally didn't want to meet fellow countrymen or associate with Americans on the base or on the missionary compound. Rather, I thought that going to the base or missionary compound—where most Koreans were not permitted to enter because of surrounding walls and fences and guarded gates—might hinder effectuating Peace Corps' second official goal: helping promote a better understanding of Americans on the part of the peoples served.

In the end, the attraction of American food on Thanksgiving Day proved irresistible. With several other PCVs I had a fine time at both events and returned to the Nas' home late at night stuffed with turkey. The Compton family was very kind, and the military personnel I met at Camp Henry were all extremely hospitable and fascinated by encountering PCVs who were living with Korean families.

After visiting Camp Henry and meeting several GIs there, I realized how misinformed American soldiers were about Korea and Koreans. Most told me that the army discouraged any kind of fraternization with Koreans and even advised them that it was not safe to go out into

235

Korean culture. Those who did went in groups because they were told to do so. I began to think that perhaps there was a limited possibility that I could further Peace Corps' third goal while I was still in Korea, in a way besides the copious letters I wrote to family and friends at home about Korea. The third goal was helping promote a better understanding of other peoples on the part of Americans. Perhaps I could bridge some chasms between American soldiers in Korea and Koreans.

Toward this end, over the next year I occasionally invited some of the American Army officers to join my classes at Kyungpook University, where my students were happy to engage different Americans with different English accents, in question-and-answer sessions and casual conversation. I think the officers were quite surprised and happy at their experiences, which gave them a perspective of Koreans and Korean life that they otherwise might have missed. Several made arrangements to meet students at the USIS building for tutoring, and I was gratified to sometimes see them thereafter, usually by themselves, venturing into downtown Daegu's markets and tearooms.

On the weekend after Thanksgiving, I finally made it to Geoje Island. The boat trip was through the roughest seas I have ever experienced, with twenty-foot waves. It was very cold and windy, with slow progress. Most of the passengers were seasick and vomiting over the rail. Captain Yi invited me to the bridge, as usual, where I was dry and could avoid the smell of vomit. He told me stories of past storms and close calls and pointed out the area where the Korean Admiral Yi Sun-shin, who is perhaps Korea's greatest hero, battled the invading Japanese fleets repeatedly in the sixteenth century.

Captain Yi was a wonderful raconteur. He regaled me for hours with stories about Admiral Yi, with whom he seemed to feel an affinity—both being captains named Yi. We had studied about Admiral Yi during Peace Corps training and marveled at the odds he had repeatedly overcome to prevail in every one of his battles. What I had not understood before was that many of Admiral Yi's historic battles had taken place in the waters we were slowly churning through on that wintry afternoon.

Of Admiral Yi's twenty-three sea battles, perhaps the most significant was the Battle of Hansan, which took place within sight of Geoje Island, just to its southwest. In the Battle of Hansan, considered among the greatest naval engagements in history, Yi, by means of his famous Crane

Wing formation, achieved a great victory by sinking and capturing fifty-nine of the seventy-three Japanese ships that opposed him, thereby frustrating the Japanese ruler Toyotomi Hideyoshi's plan of advancing along the coast and invading Korea.

In another naval battle—the Battle of Myongnyang—he defeated one hundred thirty enemy ships with only thirteen ships of his own. Part of his success was his design of so-called turtle ships, which were small ships with great maneuverability, covered with planking from which iron spikes protruded, to protect the oarsmen and gun crews from enemy fire. The bulk of his incredible success seems to have resulted from his strategic brilliance. Over seven years of war, he lost only two ships in winning twenty-three engagements, without a loss, against a far superior enemy navy. Lord Nelson, read and weep!

Hearing Captain Yi tell stories of Admiral Yi during that stormy crossing made the time pass quickly. Nevertheless, I was really happy to arrive safely at Geoje Island and thaw out. Living conditions at the project had improved considerably since the previous summer. There were no more tents. Several buildings had been completed to the point of allowing them to be used as sleeping quarters, as well as a small dining area, so visitors and workers were now relatively comfortable. The wind did not penetrate the clay brick walls, and ondol rooms kept us all cozy, despite the howling November wind buffeting the peninsula.

Jean Sibley had been extremely sick for three months with typhoid fever, and now had an as yet undiagnosed lingering fever. They would be forced to return to the States, and temporarily abandon the project, if Jean's condition did not improve soon. We spent all of my first evening discussing this unfortunate prospect.

My second night on Geoje Island, the Koreans with whom I had worked the previous summer invited me to a makoli party. We spent most of the evening telling stories about the last summer and singing Korean songs. One of carpenters at the project, Mr. Lee, told me about a ghost he had met several weeks before on the road between the project and Hachung, the closest large village.

Mr. Lee had been returning alone after midnight from drinking in Hachung on a moonlit night (there was no curfew on the islands) when he met the shadowy figure of an old women, who indicated that he should follow her. With some trepidation he slowly followed the apparition several hundred yards off the road and up a mountainside, where the women pointed to a grave mound and vanished. Mr. Lee passed out on the grave, awakened the next morning, and made his way back to camp, deeply frightened.

Inquiries among the villagers as to the identity of the person buried in the grave mound were fruitless. The villagers remembered when the grave had first appeared—many years before, in the year that Mr. Lee's mother had disappeared from Daegu during the Korean War—but told him that it must be the grave of an outsider, since no one on that part of the island had been buried there. Mr. Lee, as a result, was convinced that the grave was his mother's and that her ghost had led him to her grave. From then on, he made offerings of food and rice wine every week at the gravesite. The next morning he showed me the grave mound, and together we bowed repeatedly before it. He was very happy to have found his mother's grave.

I remember Mr. Lee's story well because almost every Korean of his generation had lost family members during the Korean War. His story was typical. Many families had been separated from loved ones: parents from children and siblings from siblings. Some had been killed; others had been caught north of the DMZ and had been unable to return south at the time of the armistice; others had simply vanished. Newspapers and television programs were filled with stories of miraculous reunions, or more often, sadly, of frustrated hopes over many years of searching. After the guns had fallen silent on the Korean peninsula in 1953, this legacy—unfamiliar to most twentieth-century Americans—continued to terribly scar Koreans more than fifteen years later.

After the weekend, I returned to Daegu to find that Ed Klein, who had recently replaced Mel Merkin as the Peace Corps regional director for the two Gyeongsang provinces, was dealing with a crisis. Members of the newest group of PCVs—K-IX—who had arrived in September and were supposed to be teaching laboratory techniques in the science departments of Daegu's colleges and universities were having major problems. One PCV had already terminated and returned home. Most of the others were requesting to be transferred to schools in Seoul.

I was surprised. They had all seemed far better adjusted to Peace Corps service in Korea than I had been, and most had reportedly been placed with good families. The problem was that their work

238

situation had deteriorated steadily, ever since it had become obvious that their students and colleagues in their science departments were far more interested in learning English from them than in learning the laboratory techniques and skills, which the PCVs had been trained to teach. The result was unhappiness, frustration, and boredom. Similar results were reported throughout Korea. Ultimately, many of the PCVs were reassigned to teach English at other schools, and this particular programmatic initiative was discontinued.

I almost felt guilty, thinking about the K-IXs at Kyungpook University who were so unhappy, that so far my volunteer service had gone pretty well. There had been moments of extreme depression and periods of near despair, caused invariably by thoughts of home, of Dariel, and of family, all of whom I missed tremendously. But these had been short-lived. I was usually able to come out of these depressive episodes by thinking about something positive that would be happening soon, such as a change of seasons, a scheduled visit with my students to a temple, a planned hike with faculty or other PCVs, or in the first week of December—as I thought forlornly about spending another Christmas away from home and about the looming Daegu winter—an upcoming vacation trip.

The trip I was looking forward to would take place in January, only one month away. Brian Copp and I planned to visit six countries in Southeast Asia during our universities' vacations and during the worst part of Korea's winter. Peace Corps had planned for every group to have a vacation at or around the midpoint in a volunteer's twenty-seven months of service. For the groups K-VII and K-VIII, the midpoint vacation was happily during the winter. Travel in Korea was extremely difficult during the winter, so volunteers were encouraged to go outside of Korea for their vacations.

Visiting Japan was out of the question. In fact, Peace Corps/Korea's policies forbade travel to Japan, as a consequence of the Koreans' strong anti-Japanese feelings (how could one explain to Korean friends that a pleasure trip was planned to the hated Land of the Rising Sun?). Because of Korea's location, the only proximate countries—besides Japan—were North Korea, China, and the Soviet Union, which were all off limits to Peace Corps Volunteers. As a result, volunteers were forced to go south to Southeast Asia to vacation, as unpleasant as the prospect of sunny beaches and warm temperatures in January might be!

Peace Corps provided a sufficient vacation allowance to permit volunteers to take a three-week vacation, including airfare, with minimum hardship if you planned carefully and stayed in cheap lodgings. Fortunately, many of the previous groups of PCVs in Korea had already made the vacation trip to Southeast Asia, scouting out the best airline fares, restaurants, and places to stay, and bringing the information back to Korea for successive groups. Group fares were available on some airlines, government rates applied (we had government passports), and several of the countries we were visiting (Thailand, Malaysia, and the Philippines) had Peace Corps Volunteers who were delighted to take in PCV visitors from other countries.

Brian and I had planned our trip carefully for months, saying very little about it to our Korean families, colleagues, friends, and students. It was awkward that we could leave for almost a month on such a fine trip while they could not leave Korea under the tight travel restrictions then in place, even if they could afford it—which most could not. So the less said about our trip the better, we felt. We planned to visit Taipei, Hong Kong, Bangkok, Phnom Penh, Kuala Lumpur, Singapore, and Manila between January 7 and January 29, before returning to Seoul.

The first several weeks in December were a blur of frantic activity as I wrapped up my courses and finalized my vacation plans. Once again, I could not afford to send out Christmas cards or send presents home on my meager living allowance. Very few Christmas decorations could be seen in Daegu. The USIS building and the Peace Corps office had strings of colored lights in their front windows, but generally Christmas decorations were few and far between. Except for the cold weather, there was little to indicate—outside of church—that Christmas was approaching. At church, at least, the advent season before Christmas was celebrated, as at home, with the wonderful Christmas story of the New Testament and the singing of many Christmas carols, all of which brought back fond memories of my childhood in Buffalo. The Nas and I attended church often and joyously together in December, when I was in Daegu.

Several weeks before Christmas, I was pleased that Miss Shin Young-ei invited me to a holiday tea party at the Dongsan Hospital. The tea party was being held at the Dongsan Nursing College, where she was a student. It was held on the Saturday before Christmas. Before accepting the kind invitation, I checked with my friend Hwa-wook—her close childhood friend—who explained what I should expect. Hwa-wook said that it would be a very formal affair, with no alcoholic beverages and no dancing, since it was being sponsored by a Presbyterian hospital. He was right.

The nursing college had carefully set up the parameters of the evening's activities. I picked Young-ei up at seven o'clock at the dormitory, under the watchful eyes of the nursing school staff, and we walked together to the party in a building several hundred yards away. We were both dressed quite formally. At the tea party, there were a lot of introductions and surprisingly good food. We sang songs and talked. Young-ei told me about her childhood suffering during the Korean War, as well as about the difficult working conditions endured by the nursing students.

John and Jean Sibley were there, as were my friends the Shins, whose sons I was teaching English to. Joon Shin was a psychiatrist on the hospital staff, and Ju-young was a nursing professor. Overall, it was a very pleasant party, but I felt as if I was in a Jane Austen novel, or back at an American elementary-school party, as a result of the strict protocol of the evening. Young-ei had to be back at her dorm by ten o'clock sharp.

After that evening in December, Young-ei became a good friend, whom I often saw with Hwa-wook at various hospital social functions, or on Geoje Island at the rural health clinic. Her gentle demeanor, profound insights, and demure beauty charmed me from the first time I met her. She was like Korea personified. It would take me several years to realize how much I had come to admire her and how very much I would miss her when I was away from her.

On December 11, 1969, a Korean Air Lines passenger plane en route from Gangnung to Kimpo Airport at Seoul was hijacked by a North Korean agent and flown to North Korea. All four crew members and forty-six passengers were held hostage by North Korea. The hijacking caused a sensation in Daegu. The military forces of the Republic of Korea and of the United Nations command went on full alert for several days, which meant that the customary checkpoints at every highway

241

and railroad bridge, at every major public facility, and at all bus and railway stations were redoubled. Passengers on planes, buses, and trains were subjected to searches at these checkpoints and had to produce identification papers. Although most of the passengers and the airplane crew were released by North Korea several months later, seven were not, causing speculation that they had somehow resisted the hijacker and were being punished by the North or that they may have been espionage agents themselves, returning to the North. Reverend Na and I talked about this for days afterward.

No significant snow had yet fallen in Daegu, although the surrounding mountains had dustings of snow on their summits, as the autumn of the Year of the Rooster drew to a close. The shortest day of the year was just before Christmas on December 23. I was sorry to see Korea's most beautiful season come to a close, but I looked forward to the promise of new adventures in and outside of Korea during the upcoming winter months.

PCV Russ Feldmeier Teaching at the Teachers College, Kyungpook
National University, Daegu, Korea, September 1969

English Teachers' Workshop with Russ, Moe, and Me, Kyungpook
National University, Daegu, Korea, October 1969

Girls in Daegu, Korea ("You have a big nose!"), October 1969

West Gate Market, Daegu, Korea, October 1969

# Chapter Nine—Winter of the Year of the Rooster

O n the winter solstice, Russ Feldmeier and I received notices from the post office that packages were waiting there to be picked up. We went together to claim them. Receiving packages by mail was horribly complicated, particularly if the packages came from overseas. At the central post office, Russ and I spent three hours in various lines, cutting through the red tape and obtaining the necessary stamps from various officials. While in line, we marveled at the ingenuity and foresight of the government officials who had designated *one* post office, and *one* window at that post office, for foreign parcel deliveries, in a city of *one million* people. Finally we made it to the front of the line and claimed our prizes.

Russ's two packages had been broken into and the baked goods consumed by rats. Several crumbs testified to the delicious contents the rats had enjoyed. Miraculously, my package arrived unscathed—filled with wonderful chocolate chip cookies, which Russ and I almost completely consumed before I remembered to save some for the Na family. It was a nice way to start the Christmas season, enjoying one of my favorite foods!

The next day was Christmas Eve. Brian Copp arrived from Iri City in time to go out with me and two Korean friends on the traditional round of drinking downtown until early on Christmas morning—Christmas Eve and New Year's Eve are the only two nights of the year without curfews in Korea. Most Koreans, as a result, are up until the early morning hours, walking and partying downtown. We had a fine time at several beer halls, and it seemed as though we met most of the Kyungpook University faculty and many, many of my students downtown, in a kind of street festival enjoying the night without a curfew as much as we were.

On Christmas morning, the Na children found the stockings I had prepared filled with candy, fruit, and small toys. This was a new experience for the children, and they seemed to be delighted and surprised. The cards and lovely gifts I received from the Nas and from other Korean friends equally surprised me. After breakfast, the Nas and I went to the First Presbyterian Church for a fine, three-hour Christmas service, overflowing with marvelous music, while Brian slept in.

We were invited, with several other PCVs, to Dorothy Compton's home on Christmas afternoon, where we had a fine holiday turkey dinner with Mrs. Compton and her daughter—my second and last lovely holiday with the Comptons. In the evening we attended the Christmas party sponsored by the English students and the English Club at Kyungpook University. The party featured singing, games, and folk dancing. Virtually all of my students were there. It was really quite a wild party, and we had lots of fun together! For the first and only time in Korea I got to dance with my female students, when popular dance music was played toward the end of the party—a rare treat in Korea, which I tremendously enjoyed. Brian couldn't get over how beautiful the female Kyungpook students were!

Because of stormy seas, our attempt to visit Geoje Island on the day after Christmas was thwarted. After returning from Busan, Brian and I decided to head for Seoul several days earlier than we planned, so that we could finalize travel plans there before our Peace Corps mid-service conference and medical examinations began at the end of the month.

We were very busy in Seoul, consulting our travel service, obtaining last minute visas, and undergoing all kinds of medical tests, including several trips to a local dentist for cleaning and the filling of one small cavity. We stayed at Ed Klein's former apartment in Itaewondong, which still was leased by Peace Corps and served as a haven for the poor, out-of-town PCVs like us, who had no other place to stay.

During this visit, I was introduced to the clubs in Itaewondong, where Korean women—many of whom were prostitutes—went to pick up foreign men. The clubs featured Western food and more recent American and British music than you could find anywhere else in Korea. Lots of English, German, and Scandinavian men were there, as well as American military officers. We spent an enjoyable evening in several clubs, talking and dancing with the pretty Korean girls and wondering what it would be like to sleep with them.

On New Year's Eve our four-day Peace Corps conference began, once again at the comfortable Academy House resort hotel in the mountains near Seoul. The first night, of course, we celebrated the New Year with a magnificent party, hosted by Director Kevin O'Donnell and his lovely wife, Ellen. We even had eggnog to welcome 1970! I was stiff and sore the entire conference, a consequence of the eleven immunizations I had received just before the conference started. The medical examination found that I was perfectly fine except for the fungus on my back, and that I was one of the few PCVs who was free of worms. This was very unusual for someone eating Korean food every day. (Mrs. Na was a careful and excellent cook.)

The entire conference was a relaxed and informal affair. We had some refresher language instruction each day, talked in groups about how the TESOL program was progressing, discussed our good feelings and bad feelings about service in Korea, and generally had a fun time. The weather was bitterly cold in Seoul for the duration of the conference—the coldest January in twenty-eight years, we were told. Temperatures were just above zero Fahrenheit. We didn't stick our noses outside once but played cards, danced, and talked, interrupted only by an occasional discussion about teaching methodology or language class. I delighted in several things: sit-down toilets, orange juice and bacon for breakfast, hamburgers and French fries for lunch on occasion, and such Western dinners as turkey with stuffing, mashed potatoes, gravy, and cranberry sauce.

Jon Moody decided to join Brian and me on our trip to Southeast Asia. Jon had joined me in being a coeditor of the Peace Corps/Korea newsletter *Yobosayo*. Fifty-one PCVs from groups VII and VIII were flying south on three different days. Most of us were traveling in small groups of three or four. Right after the conference ended, I discovered that the travel service had somehow messed up my flight arrangements, and I had forgotten to get a visa for Cambodia, so I hurried around

Seoul for two days, making sure that my travel plans were complete. The American embassy cautioned me that Cambodia might soon be closed to foreigners because it was becoming increasingly involved in the war. We purchased a kind of flight pass that was good for thirty days and allowed us to fly among six destinations in virtually any order, if seating was available on a given flight. This "pass" gave us a lot of flexibility planning our trip.

Our last night in Seoul before the departure, Jon, Brian, and I took three Korean professors to the Scandinavian Club for dinner. This club had the best buffet of Western food in Korea—truly a sumptuous feast, as well as an atmosphere of relaxation, soothing music, and quiet conversation. It was frequented largely by members of the Scandinavian and German communities in Seoul, or by Korean diplomats who had spent time in a Scandinavian country, and it was probably my favorite Western establishment in Seoul. When I first was referred to it by another PCV several months before and managed to find it, I felt like I was back in Uppsala, Sweden, where I had spent several delightful summers in college. Moreover, the price of drinks and the buffet—although high for a PCV's budget—was much more reasonable than at the Bando Hotel or at the soon-to-be-opened luxurious Chosun Hotel (neither of which I could afford a meal in as a PCV).

Our flight left on January 7. Other groups left on the fifth and the ninth. Considering that more than four dozen PCVs from our groups (Jon and Brian were in the K-VII group) were all traveling on roughly identical itineraries in the same three-week period, it was surprising that, except on the flights themselves, we seldom saw anyone else we knew at our various destinations across Southeast Asia.

During most of our trip, we flew on Thai International Airlines, which had the best service, most delicious food, and most active bar I have ever seen while flying. In Malaysia we flew on Singapore-Malaysia Airlines, which was almost as good as Thai International. The other airlines we flew on—Air France, United Burma, and Japan Airlines—were mediocre at best, but to us every second of each flight was incredibly luxurious, given the food, drinks, comfortable seats, and beautiful flight attendants! Even the cramped aircraft toilets were a luxury for me!

Our first stop was Taipei. Chilly, overcast, and blustery weather there limited us somewhat, but we managed to see several museums of impressive Chinese art and history and to explore the downtown part of the city. Not knowing Chinese was a definite handicap there. Taipei was the only city that we visited where English or French would not see us through. It was fortunate that Taipei was our first stop, or I would have been disappointed in its general lack of obvious and inexpensive amusement. It was quite an uninteresting city, by Korean standards, with virtually no nightlife we could find. In comparison to Seoul, however, we found its cleanliness, its parks and gardens, and its strolling, hand-holding couples—not usually found in Korea—very refreshing.

When we checked into our quite nice hotel, Brian and I encountered in our room a charming, rather young-looking Chinese chambermaid who was as pretty as she could be and was trying to orient us to the bathroom and other hotel facilities, although she didn't speak English and neither of us spoke Chinese. We were trying to figure out how old she was—she looked so young! As she busied herself turning down our beds and freshening up the room, we attempted to engage her in conversation. I asked her how old she was by indicating with my hands and fingers—in my best TESOL teacher manner—that I was twenty-four years old and that Brian was twenty-three, and then asking her age. I tried this repeatedly. Finally, I resorted to pen and paper, writing down "24" and "23" over stick figures representing me and Brian and then a question mark over the stick figure of a girl. After some deliberation on my artwork, she indicated with a giggle and a smile that she would be right back and disappeared.

Moments later she returned with another young, beautiful girl, who looked about fourteen, and indicated, by pretending to count out money into her hands and counting on her fingers, that she would cost only twelve (presumably dollars) and the other girl ten. She then made quite clear that she was talking about sleeping with us. Brian and I looked at each other in astonishment and then started to laugh. This was definitely an unexpected development! We respectfully declined, tried to explain the mix-up to her and her friend, and tipped her well when we left two days later.

From Taipei we flew to Hong Kong, which was definitely the most impressive city we saw on our trip. It was incredibly crowded, noisy, and vertical, with skyscrapers reaching to the sky, it seemed (for someone used to Daegu's rather low and flat horizon). I loved the mingling of the Chinese and British influences, as well as the food, bargains, uncut movies, ease of getting around in English, and the cosmopolitan ambiance of it all! We went up the Peak Tram to a mountain summit overlooking Hong Kong and Kowloon, peered into Mainland China, and marveled at the spectacular view of the cities and New Territories.

After eating lunch at a small restaurant at the summit, we took the tram railway back down the mountain, toured the Botanic Garden with its fantastic aviary, strolled along the waterfront, and visited the Red Chinese Department Store, which featured a lot of rather cheap, touristy goods, manufactured in China, but also had some beautiful vases, paintings, and other artworks for sale. There I recognized Senator Hugh Scott, one of the United States senators from Pennsylvania and the leader of the Republicans in the Senate, who was also shopping, and told him about our Peace Corps service and how much we were enjoying Korea and the Korean people. I exchanged business cards with him in the best Korean tradition. (He later wrote me a very cordial handwritten note, directed to Kyungpook University, expressing his thanks for the conversation during our encounter.)

Throughout our trip, we stayed at inexpensive hotels and ate at cheap restaurants. Most of these had been investigated previously by PCVs from Korea on past trips, who passed on the information in a series of informational sheets, describing the best places to visit, where to stay, what to eat and where, and how to survive. We all had copies of these guides and were grateful to the past generation of PCVs who had preceded us on this trip.

When we arrived in Bangkok, however, we found that the hotels recommended by previous PCV travelers were all completely full—with American soldiers on "R & R" from Vietnam service. A part of the information provided for us was the location of the Peace Corps' offices in Thailand and Malaysia, so in Bangkok we headed for the Peace Corps' office to ask advice regarding accommodations.

I unexpectedly found my Dartmouth classmate, fellow English major, and Tri-Kap fraternity brother Dave Davenport at the office, working on staff, following his Peace Corps service as a volunteer in Thailand. Dave and his girlfriend took us out to dinner, Thai style, and set us up in a cheap but comfortable nearby hotel before helping us find our way around Bangkok and suggesting things to see. The weather was really hot in Thailand. We headed for the hotel's swimming pool, after we returned from visiting some of Bangkok's nightlife, to find a petite, beautiful Thai woman, performing mouth-to-mouth resuscitation on a beefy American Special Forces officer, whom she had dragged from the water after he had hit his head on the edge of the pool. He came around as we entered the pool area and fully recovered in a few minutes, to everyone's relief. Thai women were remarkable in more ways than life saving.

We enjoyed Bangkok tremendously! The city reminded me of Los Angeles—modern, flat, smoggy, hot, and far-flung, with poor public transportation. The magnificent royal palace and surrounding parks, the national zoological gardens, incredible museums, and several lovely temples all made Bangkok one of our more interesting stops. Dave also showed us the Patpong area of the city, with its infamous bars of naked women and sex shows. I was quite shocked, and without passing judgment on the propriety of such places, was secretly glad that in Korea such things were carefully hidden, for the most part, behind sliding opaque paper screen doors in alleys.

From Thailand, we headed for Cambodia. During our three days in Bangkok, we constantly heard rumors that Cambodia was either closed, or about to be closed, to foreign travelers, and to Americans in particular. Nevertheless, we proceeded to Phnom Penh, Cambodia's largest and capital city, hoping our trip would not be affected by the growing military actions in Cambodia. After spending our first night in a small hotel, and enjoying a tour of the city, with its modern buildings, wide boulevards (all named with political correctness: Kennedy, Mao, and Khrushchev Boulevards, side-by-side), bougainvillea, hibiscus, and other flowering shrubs and trees, early on our second day we took a taxi to Siem Reap—a six-hour ride through idyllic pastoral scenes of rice paddies and small farming villages. Incomparable peacefulness! And the ride cost us three dollars each, including tip!

We stayed in Siem Reap at an old French hotel with a wide, front veranda and overhead fans, slowly pawing the humid air—the Hotel de la Paix (Peace Hotel), one of the few hotels in a sleepy, dusty, quiet, faintly French-looking town. I didn't realize at the time how ironic the hotel's name was in the light of future events in Cambodia. My French came back quickly, after my brain finally realized I wanted to speak French, not Korean, so we were able to get around quite nicely. Siem Reap was a delightful old town with only a few streets, whose purpose for existing seemed to be its proximity to Ankor Wat, which was the object of our visit. There was one other American at the hotel, who turned out to be a girl I knew from Buffalo—Linda Vogel—whom we met the next day, when we visited the indescribably magnificent temple complex of Ankor Wat. It was an incredible surprise and coincidence to see Linda in the remote heartland of Cambodia!

At the hotel we rented bicycles and peddled out into the countryside nearby, along a dusty road, which soon turned into a path once we hit the jungle. By bicycle it took about half an hour to cover the roughly three miles to the main and most imposing temple, known as Ankor Wat, for which the entire temple complex is named. You could see the Ankor temple complex from quite a distance. It was easy to see immediately why many consider Ankor Wat one of man's most spectacular and inspiring architectural achievements. The temple's spires and walls rose from the plain like a tremendous fortress ahead of us.

Brian and I were both overwhelmed by the beauty and immensity of Ankor Wat and its surrounding temples. There were more than one hundred temple complexes stretching over a vast area of jungle, waterways, and stone courtyards, and each featuring spires shaped like lotus buds and ornate bas reliefs. We bought more than a dozen of the rubbings of these bas reliefs from the local people in Siem Reap and at stalls near Ankor Wat.

The temples of Angkor were built by the Khmer civilization between 802 and 1220. From Angkor, the Khmer kings ruled over a vast domain that reached from Vietnam to China to the Bay of Bengal. The structures we saw at Angkor were the surviving remains of a grand religious, social, and administrative metropolis whose other buildings—palaces, public buildings, and houses—were built of wood and had long since decayed and vanished. Most of the temples were hidden in the jungle still, overgrown with vines and other tropical forest flora. We met almost no one, except an occasional monkey, and Linda, in the two days we visited the temples. My strongest lingering impression of the entire complex was of the stillness, naturalness, and grandeur of the deserted temple complexes.

On our last evening, we watched the Cambodian Royal Dancers perform traditional Cambodian dances on a sort of stage, in front of Ankor Wat. A full moon rose behind the dancers, as a soft breeze cooled the day's heat. It was a magnificent moment in my life. We left Ankor and Siem Reap the next morning, each feeling that the visit was one of the most memorable events of our lives. As it turned out, other Korea PCVs, scheduled to arrive several days later, were not allowed into Cambodia. We were indeed fortunate to have experienced Cambodia and Ankor when we did, as among the last Westerners into Cambodia before its decades of internal strife began.

Malaysia was our next stop—Penang and Kuala Lumpur. The former reminded me very much of Hawaii. We spent several delightfully lazy days at the beach at Penang, where our hotel was right on the beach, sipping tropical drinks and feeling incredibly guilty. Having forgotten what it was like to luxuriate on a beach under an equatorial sun, we burned to a crisp.

Kuala Lumpur was one of the most beautiful cities we visited. Again, we visited countless art museums and a lovely botanic garden. We also discovered an A&W Root Beer restaurant, where we gorged ourselves on hamburgers, milk shakes, and ice cream sundaes!

In Singapore, we spent the morning of our first day helping a PCV from group K-VII find a local physician to treat his gonorrhea, picked up in a careless moment in Bangkok. One quick dose of penicillin seemed to be all that he needed. He was very scared until reassured by that physician. My resolve to be extremely careful, and to always use a condom in sexual encounters, as we had been repeatedly admonished to do in Peace Corps training, had not yet been tested as a PCV. My colleague's plight served as a potent reminder for the future, should the occasion arise, to always be prepared.

The botanic gardens and parks that we visited in Singapore were among the loveliest I have ever seen. We each bought a bag of peanuts to eat as we strolled through the gardens, being very careful to pick up each and every shell. In Singapore, we were told, you could be arrested for dropping even one shell on the ground, or walking on the manicured grass. At one point, as we passed a grove of trees in the gardens, a group of monkeys came bounding out and chased Jon Moody for several hundred yards before he realized they were after his peanuts. We kept yelling, "Drop the bag! Drop the bag!" As soon as Jon abandoned the bag, the monkeys stopped chasing him. Brian and I laughed until we cried. The monkeys were also careful to pick up each shell.

We visited the historic Raffles Hotel in Singapore and tried for several hours to comprehend a cricket match that was taking place next door. The match had been underway for several days, we understood, and after three hours of watching (and almost falling asleep), we gave up.

As our trip drew to a close, the heat was beginning to be oppressive for us, so we decided to skip going to Manila and to return to Hong Kong for several days of shopping and further sightseeing there. Hong Kong was cool and breezy. Its tall, mountain-hugging apartment complexes and commercial skyscrapers, together with the amazing neon signs that lit the downtown nightlife, were about as far from the generally flat cityscapes of Daegu, and even Seoul, as you could get. I felt that someday both Korean cities would inevitably look like Hong Kong, for better or for worse.

In Hong Kong I purchased a 135 mm telephoto lens for my old East German camera, and Brian bought a pair of binoculars and a camera. The prices were unbeatable! The new lens would enable me to take pictures in Korea from a distance that I had been reluctant to take previously, for fear that I would offend the Korean subjects. Older Koreans especially seemed to dislike having their pictures taken. I was always careful to ask permission before I took a picture of a Korean adult, and most of the time my politeness was rewarded with permission. My only problem was in getting adult Koreans to smile. Unless I really worked hard at creating laughter as I snapped a picture, Koreans tended to scowl at the camera at worst, or at best, to freeze their faces into an expressionless deadpan. It seemed as though it was bad luck to be captured on film looking happy.

Although we were in the middle group of PCVs to leave on our vacation trip, we were the first ones to return to Seoul, arriving at Kimpo Airport on January 30. We found the weather in Korea to be mild and sunny. I was very happy to be back in the land of the morning calm. The vacation in Southeast Asia had recharged my batteries. While away from Korea, I had enjoyed the relatively modern and developed cities that we had visited, and the absence of Korean stares, shouted "hellos," and government security anywhere. On the other hand, even with my limited Korean language skills, I could communicate and understand the culture better in Korea. I relaxed in a way that I had not during my vacation. To my surprise, I felt like I was home.

Brian, Jon, and I stayed in Seoul for the lunar new year, which was on February 6. For the half-week prior to the new moon we rested, visited the magnificent Gyeongbok Palace and Duksoo Palace, and roamed Seoul's beer halls and makoli houses. Jon Moody and I worked at the Peace Corps office on the next edition of *Yobosayo*, which was to be published in the spring. Being in Seoul provided an opportunity to get caught up on the news of the outside world and on the rumors and concerns circulating among PCVs serving in Seoul.

I was fascinated by the discussions among the PCVs in Seoul, regarding what Korea represented to each of us, the significance of the events and culture that swirled around us, and where Korea would be half a century from now. For me, as the Year of the Rooster quietly wound down, I knew it had been a spellbinding and confusing year for me in a myriad of ways. I was filled with hope for Korea's future. Koreans inspired me. Looking at the Korea we had come to know, and comparing it to the countries of Southeast Asia we had just visited, I was reminded of the image that concludes Thornton Wilder's *The Eighth Day*, which I had read just before leaving for Hawaii and Peace Corps training. In his book, Wilder presents the image of a homemade rug, like so many of Korea's woven fabrics:

> It had been woven long ago, but a complex mazelike design in brown and black could still be distinguished.... No figure could be traced on the reverse. It presented a mass of knots and of frayed and dangling threads.... Those are the threads and knots of human life. You cannot see the design....
>
> History is *one* tapestry. No eye can venture to compass more than a hand's breadth....
>
> There is much talk of a design in the arras. Some are certain that they see it. Some see what they have been told to see. Some remember that they saw it once but have lost it. Some

are strengthened by seeing a pattern wherein the oppressed and exploited of the earth are gradually emerging from their bondage. Some find strength in their conviction that there is nothing to see. Some... . —Thornton Wilder, *The Eighth Day.* New York, NY: Harper and Row, 1967, 428–35.

Some Koreans and Americans, unsure of any design, with a wild leap of faith, have tied a small knot or two and become thereby forever a part of the fabric.

Movie Theater with Advertising for the Movie *Is Paris Burning?*,
Daegu, Korea, October 1969

Ferryboat from Busan to Geoje Island, Korea, June 1969

PCV Brian Copp at the Geoje Island Rural Health Project, Korea,
July 1969

Shin Young-ei, Geoje Island, Korea, July 1969

Me on Ferryboat near Geoje Island, Korea, June 1970

First Building under Construction at Rural Health Project, Geoje
Island, Korea, July 1969

# The Year of the Dog

# Chapter Ten—Winter of
## the Year of the Dog

The first full moon of the Year of the Dog was on February 20 of the Western calendar. On Geoje Island the villagers placed straw dolls at the crossroads of each of the small dirt roads that led from the peninsula to the nearby villages to ward off any evil spirits that might be abroad. From the rural health project I could see people gathered on the shores on all sides of the peninsula to sing and dance around bonfires. Koreans called the day *Taeporum*, or "day of the great new moon." Traditionally on this auspicious night, girls prayed to the moon for an early wedding, and married women prayed to the moon for sons. At the project, two local women who were employed as cooks prepared the five kinds of traditional vegetables for the Taeporum evening meal: millet, red beans, Indian millet, large beans, and glutinous rice. We also drank some rice wine, in accordance with the custom for this day, to prevent deafness. The Koreans at the rural health project took these rituals very seriously, for most of them were as superstitious as I was.

I went to Geoje Island early in February during the university's winter vacation to work for several weeks on the rural health project. Jean Sibley had recovered from her bout with typhoid fever, and the project had progressed impressively since my last visit months ago. Eight buildings were now up. Six more had to be built before the summer. The clinic was scheduled to open sometime in April, and other parts of the health project, such as the community health education and development programs, were supposed to begin in March. John and Jean Sibley repeatedly voiced their frustration at the slow pace of the project, which was then many months behind schedule. For someone like me, who visited the project several times a year, the progress seemed impressive! Now there was a dormitory for men and one for women, as well as a dining hall, kitchen, several clinic buildings, and several small houses for the Sibleys and Korean staff. The transformation from the previous summer's field of tents was amazing!

Two days after I arrived, the four nurses at the project, together with John Sibley and other medical staff, interviewed more than fifty high-school girls from Geoje Island to select ten for training as nurses' aides. It was my job to lead the girls to the interviews in the right order and to keep them amused while they waited—which I accomplished with relish! It was a lot of fun talking with the girls and finding out about their families, hopes, and reasons for wanting to be a part of the clinic's staff. The interviews took more than five days.

On the afternoon before Taeporum we were witnesses to a rather fantastic sight. Early in the evening, one of the Korean navy's three destroyers bombarded a target not far from us with its huge guns. We could barely see the ship, which was about four miles from us. The flashes and thunder of the guns were spectacular, and each round produced a noise like a sonic boom that shook the buildings. I had never before seen naval guns in action, except in movies. It was an impressive sight that left me somewhat shaken. I wondered what Admiral Yi would have thought had he heard those guns in this place, where he battled the Japanese fleet centuries before. I hoped that this display of war machinery in the first month of the Year of the Dog was not a harbinger of future events in Korea.

Geoje Island is far enough south to show signs of spring in late February, while the rest of Korea was still in the grips of cold temperatures and occasional snowstorms. We heard the weather reports from Daegu and Seoul daily. Both still had below-freezing temperatures and snow. On the island, however, it was quite warm during the day, with temperatures climbing into the sixties, and comfortably cool at night, with temperatures in the high thirties. In the rice paddies surrounding us on every hillside the green shoots of young rice plants were appearing, and the village folk were out again in the fields, from sunup to sundown, stooping over their emerging crops.

On the Korean mainland, except for the blizzard that welcomed me to Korea in January 1969 and an occasional snowstorm since, my winters in Korea had been relatively mild, at least compared to what I was used to in Buffalo, Hanover, and Madison. In Daegu, however, I encountered a damp cold, and the wind from Siberia seemed to blow constantly and with a ferocity made all the more unnerving by the absence of trees to challenge its assault. As mentioned, Korean homes and buildings were quite cold during the winter because of the lack of Western-style central heating. All in all, and perhaps as a result of having spent most of the past January one thousand miles to the south, and most of February on Geoje Island, I felt the two winters I had experienced in Korea were not bad.

Besides the relatively milder climate on the island, what I liked best about Geoje Island was the friendliness of the people. Rural Koreans were unfailingly friendly, kind, and polite on the island, even to strangers. Inevitably, I measured the more sophisticated Koreans I had encountered in Seoul or Daegu as a stranger against the people of Geoje Island. In both places—the island and urban centers—Koreans who knew you were friendly and courteous. If some sort of relationship existed between you and a Korean, no matter how tenuous, you were always treated with respect and kindness—with very few exceptions. It was in the public arena—in the circumstance where you met Koreans who didn't know you—that PCVs sometimes had a problem on the mainland.

I have already described the incident in the soju chip in Daegu with my friend Hwa-wook, when we encountered several rude young men, whom Hwa-wook felt it necessary to chastise physically. Many PCVs reported having similar insults shouted at them on streets. All foreigners seemed to be subjected to this treatment. Missionaries and most other foreigners, not understanding Korean epithets, shrugged them off. (Indeed, the insults are probably not intended to be understood, since they are in Korean and most foreigners do not understand Korean.) PCVs, being inquisitive about new Korean words, quickly learned the meaning of all the Korean obscenities and other insults, and knowing the meaning, were less able to shrug them off. My students were appalled when I asked them to explain the meaning of some of the words shouted at me from time to time on Daegu's streets.

In new neighborhoods or unfamiliar cities, where PCVs were strangers, it was not uncommon to have small boys throw stones in their direction or to have older males spit in their direction. For female PCVs the problem was most acute, as the women, understandably, seemed to feel more vulnerable in the face of menacing gestures and insults. Even a friendly "hello, hello" begins to have a taunting feel to it the millionth time you hear it.

On Geoje Island, I never experienced anything but kindness. In reflecting why there was this difference between mainland, urban Koreans and the people on the island, I realized that foreigners were a relatively unknown phenomenon in those urban centers of Korea outside of Seoul. The sixty thousand United Nations troops (mostly American) stuck pretty closely to their bases, and missionaries were few and far between. My guess was that, for the masses of relatively uneducated and poor urban inhabitants, the usual warm hospitality that Koreans offered to Korean strangers hadn't yet caught up to the new situation of meeting foreigners. In this reality, Koreans were no different from Americans. The difference between urban and rural people seemed similar in both countries as well, in that the latter are almost always open to welcoming a stranger—even a hairy, ape-like person like me.

One evening on the island I walked by myself from the health project to the nearest large village—Hachung—and back, just to get exercise and enjoy the evening air. The round trip was about four miles. The village was a mix of farmers and fishermen. Their houses were all constructed of mud and stone with straw-thatched roofs. Stone walls lined the several streets and separated each home from its neighbors. I heard the quack-quack-quack of a drake mallard herding his brood of hens toward nighttime roosts on a nearby rice paddy. As darkness fell, a soft, diffuse light from oil lamps spilled from each home. Except for the wind, the duck, and the distant murmur of the waves on the beaches, there were no sounds.

I encountered an older man with a cane making his way home. He wore a battered straw hat and the white linen clothes of a village elder. His name was Mr. Oh, he told me, as we introduced ourselves to each other. He had retired from being a blacksmith. As I walked with him, he asked me who I was and what I was doing in Hachung. We talked for a while, until we came to his home, where he had lived for more than sixty years. He invited me to come in for a cup of tea. As it was late and almost dark, I politely declined and told him I had to get back to the project. No English words passed between us.

In subsequent months I met Mr. Oh on several occasions, and he turned out to be the uncle of one of the young girls selected to be a nurse's aide at the health project. His niece told me that her uncle had described to her in detail his twilight encounter with me on the road, remarking to her that he had never before realized how well he could communicate *in English*!

It was a simple encounter on a dark, dirt road—one of the hundreds of instances of Koreans' kindness and hospitality that I experienced. As I walked back to the health project, I felt as though I might be in fourteenth-century England, perhaps on a road to Canterbury, walking past fields, woods, and small houses lit by candles and oil lamps, as they had been for centuries. I felt fortunate to be on a kind of pilgrimage myself at this time and in this beautiful place, so unchanged for so very long. I was also very lucky, I felt, to be able to communicate with the people in their own language, probably better than I could have communicated with Chaucer himself or with his Canterbury pilgrims in England.

Kyungpook University's graduation was on February 26, so I returned briefly from Geoje Island to Daegu to see my senior students graduate and then returned to the island the next day, accompanied by Ed Klein. At the graduation exercises I was pleased that one of my favorite students—my only female senior student, Cho Sun-doh—won the prestigious President Park Prize for graduating with the highest overall average in the entire university. This was the first time a woman had won the prize. I took this as a significant sign that the historical, repressed role of women in Korea was slowly beginning to change.

Another senior girl, who was not one of my students, was known to be a brilliant student and quite an independent person, especially for a Korean young lady. She came to me one day and explained that she wanted to marry last year's valedictorian, and then they wanted to study in the United States for graduate degrees. However, her father, who was the chairman of one of the science departments at Kyungpook

University and one of Korea's most famous scientists, wanted her to marry someone else and settle down in Daegu as a housewife. She asked me to help them.

I was in an awkward position. If I followed my heart and helped them, I would be opposing the wishes of a colleague and friend, who was one of my faculty English conversation group. If I didn't help them, I would feel overwhelming guilt. I decided to help them, at least by arranging for them secretly to take the tests of English competence that they both had to pass in order to be eligible for American scholarships. (Although I lost track of them not long afterward, I was happy to hear they both passed the English examination, received scholarships, and persuaded reluctant parents eventually to let them go abroad.)

Ed Klein and I had a fine week on Geoje Island. I delighted in introducing Ed to Captain Yi on the ferry from Busan to the island, and then to the Sibleys and to the Korean staff at the rural health project. We had pleasant, warm weather. Hwa-wook and his friend Han Jae-chul drove us to several of the neighboring villages to show Ed what *very* rural Korea was like. Mr. Han had been a close friend of Hwa-wook for many years and was also like an older brother to the exquisite nursing student, Shin Young-ei, I had met in Daegu. He was working as a project manager for the health clinic, handling operations from Seoul. I had not gotten to know him before this visit, but he would become a very close, valued, brother-like friend in the future.

While I had been in Southeast Asia in January, Ed had been appointed as the Gyeongsang regional director for Peace Corps based in the Daegu Peace Corps office. Ours was the largest of Peace Corps/ Korea's regions, both geographically and in terms of the number of PCVs in the region—more than one hundred. Ed was very busy. The charming Miss Chang had left her position as the Peace Corps secretary in Daegu. The former assistant regional director, Lee Myung-hwa, had moved to Seoul to prepare to visit the United States. Ed brought with him from Seoul a new regional secretary, Alice Lenarz, who was one of the two PCV secretaries working for Peace Corps/Korea. Ed had also hired a new assistant, Mr. Kwon Hwa-soon. I liked Alice and Mr. Kwon immensely.

Alice was petite, pretty, and quiet. She was always ready to assist the other PCVs in any way possible. Mr. Kwon had just returned from a tour in the Korean army in Vietnam. At first I thought that he was a tough military type because the Korean divisions assigned to Vietnam had a reputation for being ruthless. Hwa-soon turned out to be an extremely sensitive, kind, and generous person. As the assistant regional director, he was a tremendous help to all the PCVs in Daegu, and I remember him as a good friend.

After returning from the island with Ed, I was busy preparing for the start of classes. During the first week in March I conducted an English workshop at Kyungpook University for about three dozen high-school English teachers from Daegu's high schools. Like previous workshops, this one focused on the methodology of teaching English, including how to prepare lesson plans, what drills were most effective, how to engage students in role playing and other teaching devices to encourage speaking in English, and similar teaching techniques.

We conducted the workshops in English, and some of the teachers spoke English surprisingly well. One in particular was quite fluent but had a heavy Mississippi drawl as a result of having studied at the University of Mississippi for two years. He had taught one of my Kyungpook students, who had the same southern accent. I worked hard to try to change that drawl. Moe Cain and Russ Feldmeier—the other two PCV teachers in the Teachers College from K-VII—were conducting identical workshops at the same time.

Just after I resumed my English conversation classes, my exceptional friend Shin Young-ei graduated in March from nursing school. During one of the English conversation classes she occasionally attended, she told me she had just received her diploma and would be leaving the following week for Inchon. She had accepted a nursing position at a hospital there and would begin in late March. Young-ei was a charming friend and, as my friend Hwa-wook's "sister," she was a special person whom I would miss a great deal. Of the Korean women with whom I had become close friends, she was my favorite, for her smile and news of her life always cheered me up. It was one of my deepest regrets that I met her again only on a couple of occasions in my remaining ten months in Korea.

The university opened for classes on March 16. My weekly schedule again had sixteen hours of classroom instruction, four hours with my classes in the language laboratory, several hours in the laboratory with students from other departments, two hours of teaching students in the engineering department, and four hours of informal English conversation classes with graduate students and faculty. The recording of the English texts continued—I estimated that I had already recorded more than four hundred hours of text and had perhaps another one hundred to go.

In the first term of 1970 I had fifteen new freshmen students—ten boys and five girls. They all looked petrified in our first class together. After the first week with me, they began to relax. The rest of my classes remained pretty much intact, except for several male students who had been called to military service. Miss Rhee and Miss Pak were now sophomores and among the best English students in the Liberal Arts College. On the first day with each of my classes I told them sincerely what a privilege and honor it was for me to be able to teach them at Kyungpook University. I also told them how grateful I was that it was always my Korean colleagues, friends, and students who cheered me up whenever I was homesick or lonely. Somehow my students and colleagues were extremely sensitive to my mood and determined to help me cope.

As winter entered its final weeks, the weather was unseasonably cold, with bitter winds, temperatures in the teens on most days, and snowstorms every week. Daegu was lovely beneath almost one foot of snow as classes began, in contrast to March of the previous year, which had been quite spring-like. A new group of PCVs had just arrived after four months of training in Hawaii, and they were really suffering in the cold. Among the new PCVs was a classmate from Dartmouth, Frank Lagay.

As the new PCVs settled in, I heard from the Peace Corps office in Seoul that several more PCVs from groups VII and VIII had terminated their service early in the month and a half after returning from vacations. Twelve had left recently, making a total of twenty-five early terminations or about thirty-one percent of the eighty who had arrived in Seoul a year ago. Our combined groups had done so well through the first year of service, I was upset and disappointed upon hearing of these terminations. In particular, the remaining PCVs were surprised at the timing of the departures, coming as they did so soon after our one-month vacations in Southeast Asia, when all of us had experienced such a wonderful time. As far as I was concerned, the remainder of my service should be comparatively easy, with warmer weather coming and the end of service rapidly approaching in December.

Morale was very low in Korea among the foreign communities—military personnel, missionaries, and PCVs alike, according to reports from my acquaintances. It had recently plunged to new depths for reasons unique to each group.

The American military was disappointed in the Korean military, as a result of the February 20 penetration of the Korean air defense network by five North Korean jets. There had been no resistance from the Republic of Korea Air Force. The US Air Force watched until they could bear it no longer and then scrambled fighter jets to chase them off.

The missionaries were worried about the astonishing rise in disease in Korea in the past six months. Outbreaks of cholera and typhoid had occurred in very strange and suspicious patterns and in places where these diseases had previously not been a problem. The missionary and public health communities suspected that North Korea was experimenting with germ warfare.

PCVs were becoming increasingly disenchanted with their work, believing Peace Corps service to be an instrument of American foreign policy in a country where the government was still tyrannical—especially since we were actually working for the Korean government. Besides this disenchantment, PCVs were feeling politically fettered, as PCVs all over the world must, for we could not express our opinions as freely as we would have liked to in Korea, particularly regarding the war in Vietnam, where Korean troops were on the ground with American forces.

I had many friends in Peace Corps service in other countries write to me regularly. They were equally frustrated and angry about the Vietnam War. They were also very critical about Peace Corps' programs in their countries of service. In comparison, I felt much better about Peace Corps in Korea as an organization than they did about the Peace Corps in their countries.

In Korea, the American ambassador, William J. Porter, was seemingly quite liberal about allowing PCVs to protest in certain ways, such as in direct "confrontations" with him (a more apt term would be

271

"discussions"). Additionally, Peace Corps Director Kevin O'Donnell was very accommodating, allowing any expression of opinion or protest that "does not interfere with our job effectiveness" (which was more liberal than it may sound). PCVs had been discussing in informal meetings all over Korea what, if anything, we could do to express our dissatisfaction with American foreign policy in Southeast Asia. In groups VII and VIII, although we realized that having spent several weeks recently in that part of the world did not make us experts on Southeast Asia at all, the vacationers had experienced several democratic societies and been exposed to freedom of public opinion in Malaysia, Thailand, Singapore, and Hong Kong. These experiences, together with the increasingly discouraging news from abroad as to the progress of the war, primed us to take some action, if only symbolic.

At the same time, a letter concerning the Vietnam War from Peace Corps Volunteers in Panama fueled our collective desire to express our opposition to American foreign policy in Southeast Asia. The letter had been sent to all Peace Corps programs worldwide. I never saw the letter, but it was circulated widely among PCVs in Korea, and I heard about its fervent message. Its call to take action to express forcefully our antiwar feelings resonated strongly with all volunteers. The question was how to do this without compromising our effectiveness in Korea as Peace Corps Volunteers—that is, without alienating Koreans.

On the vernal equinox, I decided spring had forsaken Daegu. We still had snow on the ground and fairly cold weather. The Siberian wind was still howling across the Korean peninsula and seemed particularly intent on keeping winter firmly entrenched in the Daegu valley. The good news was that the university had installed more charcoal stoves to keep the classrooms and offices tolerably warm. In my small attic room I was comfortable as I resumed my English conversation classes there on Monday and Wednesday evenings. Despite the cold spring, I was happy in anticipation of warmer weather, blossoms, and a couple of planned mountain-climbing expeditions to the tops of several of mainland Korea's spectacular peaks.

Construction at the Geoje Island Rural Health Project,
Korea, June 1969

Women on the Beach, Geoje Island, Korea, July 1969

Land of the Morning Calm, Geoje Island, Korea, October 1969

Dr. John and Jean Sibley, Geoje Island, Korea, June 1969

# Chapter Eleven—Spring of the Year of the Dog

I went to the barber on the first day of spring. Young Korean men wore their hair quite short. Long hair on other than old men was frowned upon, and facial hair was reserved for the elderly and men deserving respect. I had shaved off my mustache before I started Peace Corps training in accordance with the instructions I had received from the Peace Corps/Korea Country Desk Officer John Middleton in Washington. My symbols of defiance were my sideburns, which I was careful to keep trimmed, along with my hair. To keep my hair relatively short, I went to the barbershop once each month.

On this particular visit to the barbershop down the street from the Nas' house, I decided to get rid of my sideburns and indulge myself with a shave. I had never had a shave at a barbershop in my entire life. During Peace Corps training, visits to Korean barbershops had been carefully rehearsed and all the necessary vocabulary drummed into our heads. It was one of the situations in Korea where I felt most comfortable, conversing with the barber and the girls who trimmed your nails and massaged your neck and back. Until that day, however, I had never asked for a shave, preferring to use the basin in my attic room, my little mirror, and hot water from the kettle in Mrs. Na's kitchen to accomplish this daily task.

The barbershop was quite similar to an American barbershop. The barber wore a white apron; the adjustable chairs, although very old, swiveled and adjusted to different heights by means of a pedal (just like at home), and the barber made a great show of sharpening the straight razor before lathering my face with a foamy soap. He then carefully shaved my face, including my sideburns, as I had requested. Before and after the shave, hot cloths covered my face for several minutes. I left the barbershop free of my sideburns. The barbershop girls told me how handsome I looked without my sideburns. My face tingled with a fresh clean feeling.

The next morning my face and neck were covered with red pimples that itched terribly. Every place touched by the barber's razor was inflamed. Mrs. Na gave me some ointment to sooth the burning sensation. I speculated that the razor had been contaminated with some bacteria and that perhaps the facial infection would link up with the fungal infection on my back, permanently disfiguring me. My lost sideburns were taking revenge for their removal. I missed two days of classes—half of the total "sick days" I took while teaching at Kyungpook University. After the third day the pimples disappeared, and I was fine. I never had a shave at a barbershop in Korea again.

Shortly after my face healed, on a cold evening late in March I found myself in an unfamiliar part of Daegu. I was alone in a small ondol room with sliding, paper-covered screen doors on two sides and a soft light emanating from the single low wattage bulb on the ceiling. The room was one of many traditional Korean-style rooms in a row, facing a courtyard, in a long, low, old-fashioned Korean structure with a tiled roof gracefully sweeping down to the edge of the structure. There was a tiny bathing tub in one corner and a chamber pot in another, next to a short stool. On the floor were several ornately decorated cushions, a large ibul, and a yo. An embroidered, six-panel screen, or *pyungpoong*, depicting country scenes and mountains, stood against the wall facing the sliding doors on the courtyard side. The room was warm despite the cold wind outside that rattled the sliding doors and whistled through holes in their papered screens. It was as though I was in a Korean room of long, long ago. I was on a centuries' old mission. I waited quietly, wondering what to expect.

A blast of cold air from outside slipped through the door as it slid open. The wind rustled her white, slip-like wrap as the woman turned to slide the doors shut and turned toward me carrying a kettle of hot water. Her name was Miss Kim, like one third of all the women in

Korea, and I had just met her moments before in another room, filled with twenty or so attractive women in their twenties and thirties. She had been knitting quietly in a corner, which is why I picked her. She asked me to undress and sit on the stool. After bathing my feet in the tub, she slipped off her wrap, and we lay down. I was the first foreign man she had ever slept with, she told me. She was a few years older than I was and had worked part-time here during the past year to earn extra money for herself and two children.

I was a first-time visitor to *Jagalmadang*—one of Korea's oldest and most notorious red-light districts. Jagalmadang means the "place of gravel." In that district, roads and paths were covered with small rocks or gravel that crunched as you walked on them, to make it difficult for people to enter or leave the area undetected. I never went there again, although I found the experience fascinating, as well as exciting. According to the two graduate students who had brought me to this place that dark, early spring evening, most young Korean males frequented places like Jagalmadang for sex, because women who were potential wives almost never engaged in premarital sex. Korean society forbade such conduct on the surface.

The two Kyungpook University graduate students with me were both several years older than I was and were preparing to take the TOEFL (Test of English as a Foreign Language), a major hurdle to overcome for Korean students who hoped to study in the United States. In helping them in my free evenings, I had become quite good friends with Mr. Cha and Mr. Kwon, both of whom loved poetry as much as I did. Among the many questions they asked during the course of our classes were several about American women and sexual practices in the United States. Well, I was perhaps the least qualified expert in such matters they could possibly have asked. But I shared with them my social experiences in college and graduate school, as well as my memories of the Swedish female friends with whom I had had relationships in Uppsala.

They shared their feelings about women and explained the social restraints in Korean society. Although Korean women were now much freer to engage the outside world than they had been a mere generation ago—when many marriageable women were confined to compounds and glimpsed the outside world only when swinging sufficiently high on swings to see over the compound's walls—there were still many societal constraints.

They also told me about Jagalmadang. When they proposed that I should see this side of Korean life, I made the mistake of protesting that the experience would be too expensive for me, given my relatively tight living allowance. I had heard that the cost of a visit to such places was about five American dollars, which was a lot of money for me then. The proposed visit did not particularly appeal to me. If a young man was looking for a sexual encounter, the bar girls and hostesses in the various drinking establishments were available, and these were women with whom a relationship could be established, however brief, before sleeping with them. I had not yet gone that far with a Korean woman. My students argued that I was missing a part of Korean culture. Although prostitution was not something I favored for many reasons—including the exploitive and degrading aspects of the profession—I didn't wish to tell them that, for it was a significant part of Korean culture for most men and many women.

On the other hand, I had never before been to a brothel anywhere, although I didn't want to admit this to my male students. The experience—moral considerations aside—might be interesting and valuable. Of course my protest had the unintended consequence of their becoming more insistent and then arranging, and paying in advance, for the evening, despite my protests, to thank me, they said, for helping them.

The next morning I visited the Central Market in downtown Daegu to buy kerosene for my small space heater. After making my purchase, I was threading my way through the hundreds of shoppers when I accidentally bumped into a well-dressed Korean woman. We were both startled. It was the knitter from the previous night. Our eyes met briefly, and with the slightest flicker of recognition she disappeared into the crowd. Somehow I had not anticipated ever meeting "Miss Kim" again among the million people in Daegu. After my surprise, I fully expected that she would turn up next in Reverend Na's church on Sunday morning.

As the weather slowly warmed to a full-fledged spring, the newspapers reported that three North Korean infiltrators had been shot to death at Kumchon, Gyeonggi Province, just south of the DMZ. Five South

Korean soldiers were wounded during the incursion from the north. Again, the Korean and United Nations military forces went on full alert in Korea.

It suddenly dawned on me, as my birthday approached, that this would be my last spring in Korea. From now on, each day, hour, and minute of each season, month, and week would not be repeated for me next year in this place. I would never see again the forsythia that had recently burst into full bloom, snaking around the hospital grounds and staff homes on our hill in ribbons of brilliant yellow, the crocuses and daffodils creating splotches of purple, white, and yellow on the grounds of Kyungpook University and in Daegu's parks, and the occasional flash of delicate, crimson blossoms from the japonica hidden behind residential walls. Time was fleeting. My Korean family, Kyungpook students and faculty, and my Korean friends would soon merely be fond memories—their vibrancy and the compelling details of living in Korea fading into the background of my thoughts and recollections. This was a very sad reflection. I determined to make the most of my remaining months as a Peace Corps Volunteer and to experience every aspect of Korean culture as fully as possible, before I returned home.

One of the best things about my status as a Peace Corps Volunteer was the ease with which I could move between levels of Korean society, among classes of different people, and from place to place—all without the constraints that a young Korean would face. In fact, my access to different classes of Koreans was much better than such access to lower and higher levels of society was at home. I was fortunate to be in Daegu. Many of the top Korean government officials, like President Park Chung-hee, were from Daegu and its environs. Most had attended schools in Daegu.

Alumni of Kyungpook University invited me to visit them. Many were people at the highest level of Korean society. I received invitations from and visited the ministers of education and defense, as well as a Supreme Court justice—all living in Seoul and gracious in extending dinner invitations to a young American from the Peace Corps. Where else in the world would I have been able to meet and dine, at the age of twenty-five, with the political and social leaders of a country?

In early April I received a surprise invitation to visit in Seoul a member of the Korean Congress, Representative Koh Heung Moon, who was the secretary general of the New Democratic Party—the party opposed to President Park Chung-hee's administration. The special invitation was a result of the secretary general's recent visit to the United States, where he visited Niagara Falls, New York, and stayed with my Aunt Betty and Uncle Bob Craig in nearby Lewiston. My visit was an especially unusual and exciting occasion for me in Korea in permitting a lengthy candid conversation with a Korean government official who was not a supporter of President Park and was not reticent in speaking against the government.

Just after I returned from Seoul, the faculty and students of Kyungpook University celebrated *Singmokil*, or Arbor Day, on April 5. Every faculty member and student were bused to the nearby barren slopes of the mountains around Daegu for a day of planting trees. It was a beautiful day to be in the mountains. Digging holes with my students and planting the thousands of small pines that were furnished by the Korean government were among the most gratifying things I have ever done in my life. We were joined by hundreds of elementary-school, middle-school, and high-school students, working in groups and singing mostly Korean folk songs. I knew some of the songs from Peace Corps training and sang lustily, to the surprise of my students. I thought that, if what I was experiencing in the Daegu environs was happening throughout Korea, in twenty years or so Korea would be bursting with pine forests. Planted areas were later marked with signs forbidding anyone from entering the pine nurseries for any reason.

The week after Arbor Day, the Na family surprised me on my birthday with a fine cake. We went to church in the morning at the *Cheil* (First) Presbyterian Church, where Reverend Na was still the assistant minister, and within an hour my legs were totally numb, as usual, from sitting with them crossed. After three hours I staggered from the church, glad I had communicated with God, especially on my quarter-century anniversary, but barely able to stand. Pain and numbness focus the mind.

Upon returning home for lunch, there was a lovely cake from a local bakery. This celebration was a rather quiet family celebration, which I appreciated, compared to the elaborate birthday ceremony of last year, which I have mentioned. Koreans seldom celebrate birthdays, except the one-hundredth day and sixtieth year, which are both very special. I was honored that the Nas remembered. Late in the afternoon, eight of my students took me out to dinner at the local bulgogi (barbecued beef) restaurant to celebrate. The restaurant, known as the *Dangchip* ("Earth house"), was one of my favorite restaurants and was located only one block from the Nas' home. We had a wonderful time there.

On April 18 my good friend Bruce Cochran, K-VII, married a lovely Korean girl named Sun in Seoul. With many other members of the K-VII and K-VIII PCV groups, I went to Seoul for the fine ceremony and accompanying party—one of more than a dozen such events that I attended during my two years in Korea.

The next morning I took an early train back to Daegu to celebrate with my students the holiday called *sailgoouinal*, or April 19 Day, which in 1970 was the tenth anniversary of the student revolution in 1960 that overthrew the government of former President Rhee Syng-man, leading to President Park ultimately seizing power. The killing of a student by riot police in Masan and the discovery of the government's cover-up of the death at that time sparked the revolution. In the university's stadium, hundreds of students participated in games and synchronized exercises in honor of the anniversary, complete with tremendous pictures of President Park formed by flash cards held in the stands.

Shortly after this huge celebration, the Korean government announced the launching of the *Saemauel Undong*, or "New Village Movement." Flyers describing this initiative in Korean and English were distributed everywhere at the university, and my students discussed it at great length. The announced objective of the program was to modernize the rural South Korean economy, to rectify the growing disparity of the standard of living between Korea's urban centers—like Seoul, Busan, and Daegu, which were rapidly industrializing—and the small villages, like Hachung on Geoje Island, which continued to be mired in agrarian poverty.

The most visible early fruits of the program were new wells, paved roads, and orange-colored tile roofs (replacing the straw-thatched roofs that were so picturesque). Many of my students were extremely skeptical of the Saemauel program, calling it political propaganda. Others— particularly those students who were themselves from small villages— praised the program and reported that there were improvements in their families' lives in the villages. I gave the government credit for trying, at least.

Toward the end of April, the apple orchards in the countryside around Daegu burst into their annual incredible display of lovely pinkish blossoms. Among many other of my experiences in Korea, Daegu's delicious apples, the beauty of Daegu women (undoubtedly a result of eating so many apples), and, most of all, the spring eruption of apple blossoms transforming hillsides into magical hills of puffy color are especially treasured memories.

In the midst of spring's glory I received a letter from my dear old draft board No. 65 in Buffalo, dated April 13, 1970, which renewed my occupational deferment indefinitely and granted me (unsolicited) permission to remain absent from the United States until mid April, 1971. I wondered about that letter. The letter had issued on my twenty-fifth birthday. My twenty-sixth birthday would be on April 13, 1971, and if I was going to be drafted into military service, it would have to be before I turned twenty-six. The letter reminded me that the draft board had not forgotten about me and was perhaps patiently waiting for me to complete my Peace Corps service before it pounced.

As the weather warmed, a group of us planned our first hiking trip of the year. Our goal was to climb Mt. Sorak in northeastern Korea—Korea's third highest peak at 5,603 feet. Mt. Sorak is the highest mountain in the Taebaek mountain range in Gang Won Province in eastern Korea. It is located in a gorgeous part of Korea near the city of Sokcho. The Taebaek mountain chain is often considered the backbone of the Korean peninsula, snaking along the eastern coast with its knife-edge ridges and jagged peaks. I had not yet climbed in the Taebaek Range. In contrast to my earlier expeditions, this one would be only Americans: Ed Klein, and PCVs Alice Lenarz, Sally Hardenburg, Jim Higgins, and me.

The train trip to the vicinity of Mt. Sorak took eleven hours. We took several trains to get to the city of Kangnung and then a bus up the east coast to the small city of Sokcho, near the new park at the foot of Mt. Sorak. The weather was wonderfully clear but still quite cool. The yogwans were all full by the time we arrived late in the afternoon. Since we all had sleeping bags, we decided to hike into the mountains and camp in the woods. Just as we were walking out of town, we were told by a policeman that North Korean infiltrators had been seen in the area—we were then north of the thirty-eighth parallel—and that it was not safe to be in the woods at night. We discussed this new information but decided to continue with our camping plans, since there really was no alternative place to sleep available in town.

After making our campsite, eating the food that we had carried into the woods, and telling stories around our small campfire, we turned in for the night beneath a star-filled sky. I awoke about two o'clock in the morning. Our fire had died, and the night was pitch black. Above us in the sky was a magnificent comet—the so-called Bennett Comet, I later discovered. Its tail stretched across half the sky. I had never seen a comet before. It was a spectacular and totally unexpected sight, and at first I was very happy that I had been awakened by something and could see it. Then I heard low, masculine voices in the woods not far from us, and the snapping of branches and twigs, as a group of men moved around in the dark woods nearby—sounds that had woken me.

My first thought was that the furtive noises I heard were from North Koreans who had crossed the nearby DMZ—the infiltrators we had been warned about. I became quite scared. The sounds were so close that I didn't even want to chance waking any of the other four because I was afraid that even low whispers, or muffled cries, might give our presence away. One of our group was snoring softly, with barely audible wheezes and snorts. To me, these soft sounds seemed like beating drums, or perhaps that was my racing heart. I was sure we would be discovered and immediately butchered in our sleeping bags.

The voices and sounds of boots came closer and closer, until our campsite seemed to be in the middle of the men as the sounds came from all sides. At this point I thought that the men might be soldiers or policemen searching for infiltrators. If they stumbled on our camp, I was sure they would shoot first and ask questions later in the dark. So whether the noises were from North Koreans or South Koreans, we were doomed. I was sweating and trying to breathe as quietly as possible.

After what seemed like an eternity, the sounds began to fade away into the darkness and then vanished. I fell asleep. When I woke at dawn, I thought I had dreamed the comet and the intruders, but Ed Klein confirmed that he had also awakened, seen the comet, and lay in frightened silence as the men circled our camp. We were happy to start on our way up Mt. Sorak early in the morning, shortly after sunrise.

Our hike to the summit and then down was a nightmare. It rained the entire hike. The wind blew fiercely, the temperature was just above freezing, and clouds engulfed the mountain. Visibility was about thirty feet. Within an hour or so we were all soaked and becoming chilled in the strong gale. After about six hours of hiking, we made it to what we thought was the summit—at least there was a huge cairn, and it seemed like the top. Jim Higgins took a picture of me with the MMVSP flag in the swirling clouds and rain. There was apparently no one else on Mt. Sorak that day.

I realized we had to get down into a sheltered area as quickly as possible, as we were all beginning to shake with the cold, and Ed Klein looked like he was turning blue. Several of our party wanted to stop and rest, but I felt that resting would be dangerous under the conditions we were experiencing, so we pressed on until we came to a tiny stone shelter about halfway down. We made a small fire at the shelter and warmed ourselves, eating the remainder of our candy bars and rice cakes. After several hours, we were in good enough condition to continue.

We were all relieved to make it to the base of the mountain and eventually find a room at one of the yogwans, as the rain finally stopped and darkness fell. The entire trip was about fourteen miles and took twelve hours, including our recovery period at the shelter. I have seldom in my life been more exhausted. The climb was easier than climbing Mt. Washington in New Hampshire, but not by much. Happily, the yogwan we stayed in was probably the finest I ever saw in Korea.

On Sunday morning we took an early bus to Kangnung but missed by minutes the daily train south. So we were forced to go from Kangnung to Pohang, in North Gyeongsang Province, by bus. The bus trip was a fourteen-hour ride down a rugged coastline above huge cliffs on a dirt road that hugged the cliff edges and had more bumps and dips than a roller coaster! Nevertheless, it was a beautiful and fascinating trip. Most of the North Korean incursions have historically taken place along this coast, so the entire area was bristling with troops, checkpoints, barbed-wire fences, bunkers, and minefields. The beaches had wooden barriers in the water to deter landing crafts and other boats.

We arrived in Pohang too late in the evening to get to Daegu before the curfew, so we stayed another night at a yogwan, finally taking a bus at four thirty the next morning and arriving in Daegu just in time to get to my classes on Monday morning. My students told me I looked like I had been through an ordeal, but I truthfully reported to them that the trip had been a real adventure and one of the most fun trips I had ever been on.

Soon after the Mt. Sorak expedition, I heard that President Richard Nixon had recently ordered US forces to cross into neutral Cambodia, threatening to widen the Vietnam War. The news of nationwide riots at home, sparked by the American invasion of Cambodia, swept through the Peace Corps community like wildfire. Then I heard about the killing of four students at Kent State University in Ohio and the wounding of nine others. The Ohio National Guard had opened fire on unarmed students during a student antiwar demonstration on May 4. The students were specifically protesting the United States' incursion into Cambodia. Phone calls went out from the Seoul PCVs to PCVs throughout Korea. We felt as though we had to do something.

Then in rapid succession we heard that one hundred thousand people had demonstrated in Washington DC against the war on May 9, and that during the second day of violent demonstrations at Jackson State University in Jackson, Mississippi, May 14, state law-enforcement officers had fired into the demonstrators, killing two and injuring twelve people. All PCVs were thunderstruck. What was happening at home? It seemed as though the world we knew at home had gone completely crazy. The Korean student demonstrations and the police response in Korea seemed tame compared to the lethal violence attending anti war protests in the United States.

PCVs were determined to voice our concerns and take action to show our support for the student demonstrators at home and our strong opposition to the war. We contacted Director O'Donnell, who was confronted with our plans to publically demonstrate in Seoul, perhaps in front of the American embassy. After much discussion, a compromise was worked out. Director O'Donnell approved a plan to send one PCV from Korea to Washington to meet with the president to state our feelings. The cost of the trip would be shared by all PCVs, who agreed to take a reduction in living allowances until the trip expenses were paid.

Hugh Rogers was selected to represent PCVs in Korea on this mission. Hugh was a smart, articulate PCV who had a law degree. While Hugh prepared to depart, in mid-May I heard that several more volunteers from groups VII and VIII had terminated early. Since the first day of training in Hilo, our combined groups had lost about sixty-four members, or well more than half. I was quite upset by the news of these terminations and couldn't comprehend why, with the fine spring weather and only seven months left in our service as PCVs, my colleagues felt they had to leave at this time. After much thought I finally penned a rather intemperate article for the forthcoming edition of *Yobosayo*, which other volunteers later heavily criticized me for.

The article, which appeared in the June 1970 issue, asked why PCVs were so quick to criticize Peace Corps staff and Peace Corps training for perceived inadequacies but never challenged their own motives for leaving Korea before their two years of service had been completed. I had heard many PCVs complaining within the volunteer community about boring assignments, about how Peace Corps had interrupted their career plans, or about how our December 1970 end-of-service date was inconvenient for travel plans or for starting graduate school classes at home. Some PCVs also complained that our Peace Corps training program had not warned them of the isolation, material deprivation, hostility toward Americans by some Koreans, lack of privacy, unsanitary conditions, and other issues.

Other PCVs had almost directly opposite views of the training we experienced, feeling that it had been an excellent training program. Usually these PCVs also had positive feelings about Korea, Koreans, and their teaching assignments. Such differences of opinion were to be expected and did not bother me. What upset me was the lack of consideration by the early departing PCVs of the impact their leaving had on the classes and students whom they were supposed to be teaching. I felt that in exchange for the commitment made by Peace Corps and by the Korean government to us—in selecting, training, transporting, housing, and supporting us—PCVs should be honoring their obligation to perform their assignments for the entire period of their service, at least unless and until exceptional circumstances, such as illness, pregnancy, marriage, or severe emotional issues justified leaving early. Too many PCVs, in my opinion, were deciding to leave prematurely for ill-considered reasons or for purely selfish motives. I guess I should have kept quiet.

At Kyungpook University the spring term was such a busy one for me that I had no time or inclination to think about leaving Korea. There were no student demonstrations to worry about, and with my students I enjoyed several trips to nearby cities and temples, a couple of one-day hiking expeditions, and lots of socializing at makoli houses. May was a pleasant month. I felt as though I was recharging batteries that had been exhausted by worrying about the Vietnam War, about my family at home, and about my future during the past year. In the beauty of my last Korean spring and in my efforts to live every moment to the fullest in Korea during my last months there, any lingering feelings of isolation or loneliness were melting away.

Two weeks after I returned from climbing Mt. Sorak, Reverend Na had an emergency appendectomy. I spent the weekend babysitting the Na children while Mrs. Na was at the hospital caring for him. I discovered that in Korean hospitals, although the medical staff was of a high caliber, a member of the patient's family is always in attendance to feed and otherwise care for the patient.

So until a cousin arrived to help out with the Na children, I was their sitter. I learned a lot that weekend. For example, when Americans want children to be quiet, we say "shhhhhh." Koreans use the same sound to encourage children to urinate ... I had a half dozen puddles to clean up before several nursing students from my English conversation class came by to help out and laughingly explained the reason for the messes.

On the third weekend in May, I went to Geoje Island to prepare for the summer work at the health project by eight Peace Corps Volunteers, whom the Sibleys had invited to assist. An older American couple, living in Seoul—close friends of the Sibleys—asked me to accompany them to the island, and I agreed. It turned out that the man had been a high-ranking naval officer before his retirement from military service. We took a train together to Jinhae, South Gyeongsang Province, where there was an American naval base on Korea's south coast. After an amazing feast on the base at the officers' club and a luxurious night at the officers' quarters in Western accommodations, the next day we churned across the Korea Strait in a small American naval vessel to the island at about three times the speed of the ferry I was used to taking, I was reminded of how different American life was from my life of the past one and a half years. As we sped across the water, I realized that on this trip, despite the enjoyable companionship of the American sailors and the couple, I missed the banter with the captain and crew of the ferry and the chance to savor the scenery and people of the Korean archipelago.

I also thought about the wisdom of the Peace Corps/Korea policy that forbade Peace Corps Volunteers from owning or driving vehicles, including motor scooters, motorcycles, and cars. I guessed the policy probably applied to motorboats too. Most Koreans still did not have motorized vehicles, although streets and roads were increasingly becoming congested with them. None of my colleagues at Kyungpook University or my Korean friends possessed a motor vehicle. Relying on public transportation was not only safer and cheaper, it required that Peace Corps Volunteers experience the same lifestyle—including inconvenient and slow travel at times—as the Korean people. Additionally, it provided opportunities to talk with people and experience adventures, while traveling on rickety buses and old trains, that we would never experience traveling in a car or on our own scooter or motorcycle.

The high-speed boat I was traveling in to Geoje Island whisked me by places and people so fast I hardly had time to enjoy them, and it effectively isolated me from Korean culture. It was the antithesis of a Peace Corps Volunteer's normal experience. I thought of the American soldiers, who moved through the Korean countryside and cities in military vehicles, and of the majority of the foreign missionaries in Korea (except for the young Mormon missionaries, who rode bicycles everywhere), who traveled by private vehicles or taxis. What they missed!

At the health project I met Dr. Joan Adams—an English doctor, formerly with Save the Children in Egypt—who had joined the medical staff at the health project. I found her delightful and tremendously enjoyed her company. Her frail appearance and English accent reminded me of my maternal grandmother Margaret Eyres Schultz, who was also English.

Another doctor, Kit Johnson from Yonsei University's Medical College in Seoul and its Department of Preventive Medicine and Public

Health, was visiting to prepare for a study of illness, health-care needs, and treatment patterns among the villages of Geoje Island that would take place later in 1970. Dr. Johnson, like Dr. Adams and Dr. Sibley, was very kind and dedicated to improving the health care of rural Koreans on this isolated island.

During my brief visit to the health project, I was busy arranging the accommodations for the Peace Corps Volunteers who would be working there during the summer. We would be doing our own cooking and would sleep in tents. Before everyone arrived in about one month, I had to make sure we had five tents ready and could use the project's kitchen area, with its charcoal fire, for food preparation. After completing the necessary arrangements, I was able to relax for a day before returning to Daegu. As always, it was extremely agreeable to be at the project with the kind Sibley family, engaging medical and support staff, friendly villagers, gorgeous scenery, and refreshing ocean air.

As May drew to a close, I met a young American Air Force captain in a downtown tearoom one afternoon. He was from Georgia, and we hit it off immediately. Captain David McCann and I talked for several hours. With him were several Korean air force officers—Captain Jung and Lieutenant Pak—who were also extremely personable. As they left, they invited me to visit them at their base on the top of nearby Mt. Palgong the following weekend. I was interested in seeing what there was to see on Mt. Palgong, for I had heard it was the headquarters of all military air operations in Korea.

Early on Saturday morning, I took a local bus to the base of Mt. Palgong and climbed up to Dongwa Temple, where I had visited many times with my students. From the temple, I had been told, it was an easy hike up to the top of the mountain. I started off alone in clear, cool weather, hiking through pine and hardwood forests just beginning to green up with tiny spring leaves. It was a delightful hike, except that the trail was very poorly marked and eventually disappeared altogether. I got quite lost. I finally managed to scale a steep and jagged peak on a shoulder of Mt. Palgong, from which I could see the air force base on the summit about two miles away and the easiest route to it from my vantage point.

It took me several more hours to struggle through the rocks and chasms until I thought I must be getting close. There was no trail, so I was bushwhacking and relying on my sense of direction. After a horrendous struggle, during which I repeatedly cursed myself for violating the cardinal hiking rule—"Thou Shall not Bushwhack" (try to cut through mountain areas that are off marked trails)—I emerged at the summit in a level clearing on the other side of which was a barbed-wire fence at the base perimeter.

I startled a Korean soldier with a guard dog, who was inside the fence, and who immediately yelled at me in Korean not to move. He was very agitated, pointed to signs in the clearing, and called for assistance on his radio. Within minutes several American soldiers arrived, told me I was in a minefield, and then instructed me to carefully back up to the woods from which I had emerged. Following their directions, I finally made my way to a heavily guarded gate where I was let in after giving the names of my American and Korean friends.

After that auspicious and dangerous arrival, I had an amazing time on the weekend. The air force base was largely underground. I was most interested in the snack bar, where they served hamburgers, French fries, and milkshakes, but I enjoyed seeing the bowling alley, movie theater, and operations room. In the latter, several dozen military personnel were hunched over radar screens in a darkened room with a huge map of the Far East on one wall, where winking lights traced what I presumed to be air traffic in that area. Captains Jung and McCann, Lieutenant Pak, and I had several beers in the evening as we discussed our respective lives in Korea. It seemed like boredom was the biggest problem they faced.

In the morning, after a tremendous breakfast of bacon and eggs, Captain McCann ordered a jeep to take me down the mountain to Daegu. It was a much faster and safer trip than my trip up had been the previous day. The jeep went through no minefields. Later that week I met all three men again in downtown Daegu and took them to one of my favorite beer halls, where we laughed about my foolish close call the prior weekend.

The last week of May we celebrated Kyungpook University's eighteenth anniversary. The students participated in mass games of all kinds, marching, and dancing, most of which took place in the university stadium. There was a very impressive taekwondo demonstration, in which the male students, who were training to be military officers (like American ROTC members), crippled themselves, it seemed, by smashing bricks, boards, and roof tiles with their bare hands, feet, elbows, and heads. It was really quite a spectacular display! Classes were cancelled during the anniversary week, but when my students returned the following week, many were wearing bandages from their athletic and taekwondo exertions.

Boxes of books began arriving from home in early June. I had asked family and friends to ship me whatever used books they had, because Kyungpook University had so few books in English. My family went at this task with a vengeance. Altogether about forty boxes of books eventually arrived—books of all kinds, including scientific textbooks and children's books. At first the Language Institute staff insisted on keeping all the books on shelves at the institute. Soon, however, there were far too many books to accommodate there, so we moved the books to the university library, where they were a welcome addition to the English language section.

The arrival of books from home compelled me to start thinking about my future. For months I had been combing literature from Peace Corps, as well as graduate school brochures from the USIS, for guidance regarding what studies, if any, I wished to pursue in the future. I seriously considered teaching. Many of the people I most respected were teachers. Combining my interest in Korea with an academic career was appealing. I knew that more than a dozen of the K-VII and K-VIII members were planning to pursue Korean studies.

In mid-June a law professor from Harvard University's law school visited the Peace Corps office in Daegu. Several days later another visiting professor from the University of Washington came to Daegu. PCVs were invited to meet with them. The former urged me to try law school, perhaps with a focus on international law and the Far East. The latter suggested that with my knowledge of Korea and Korean, I should apply to graduate school in a combined law and Far Eastern studies program that was offered at Washington.

After meeting with these recruiters, I decided to go to law school and study international law. One of the hurdles to overcome toward this objective was the Law School Admissions Test (LSAT). The LSAT would be given in Seoul later in the year at the American embassy. Since I had had very limited exposure to American life and periodicals over the past eighteen months, and had quite forgotten how to take tests like the LSAT, I started to worry. I was afraid I had forgotten a lot of my English as well. Happily, the USIS had an LSAT preparation book, so I began to spend some evenings there, preparing for the test.

The PCVs in Daegu felt the tug of American baseball as spring careened toward its end. A group of us challenged the English students at Kyungpook University to a softball game, which took place among much fanfare during the second week of June. The game pitted PCVs versus English students from the Liberal Arts College and the Teachers College. We insisted that it be a coed game, which was a first at Kyungpook. After the game, which became a comedy of errors because each side was trying to let the other side win, we all went on a hike up Ap Mountain, overlooking Daegu, which was an easy and favorite climb. That day was one of my favorite days with my students. All had a fine time and talked about it for weeks afterward. Some of the male students mentioned to me that they had not realized before how much fun it was to play a game, like baseball, with members of the opposite sex.

The coed baseball game—with women finally participating after all these years—prompted me to reflect on how much change had occurred in the brief period I had lived in Korea. The express highway connecting Seoul with Daegu and Busan had opened in the past few months—just like an American interstate highway, except that the Korean expressway had lovely beds of flowers on all sides—miles and miles of beautiful Cosmos dancing on the breezes. You could take a luxurious bus now to Seoul and back. Some of the buses were reconditioned Greyhound buses, with reclining seats and movies.

In the past year alone Korean construction workers, laboring day and night, had built hundreds of new buildings and paved thousands of streets and roads virtually overnight, it seemed, in Daegu. New cars and buses appeared everywhere. The volume of vehicular traffic on the streets and road had more than doubled in eighteen months. The entire train system had been revamped, with new track, engines, and passenger cars appearing every day. Zip codes had arrived. Straw roofs in the rural area were being replaced with tile roofs. Incredibly rapid change was the only constant.

One thing did not change. On June 5, 1970, North Korean patrol boats seized a South Korean broadcast vessel with twenty crewmembers on board off the west coast near the military demarcation line. The vessel was standing on guard for South Korean fishing boats, according to the newspaper reports. Again, United Nations and South Korean military forces went on full alert for several days. The Korean crew was never heard from again.

The next day was *Hyunchoongil*, or Memorial Day, in Korea. With thoughts of North Korea's aggression the day before and of the not-too-distant war in which hundreds of thousands lost their lives, my students and neighbors held emotional memorial services to honor the fallen men of the armed forces. Flags were flown at half-mast.

The good news in the spring was that my kind friend and former language teacher Kim Hae-shik was accepted for graduate school at the University of Illinois. I would miss him, but I was very pleased that his dream of studying in the United States looked as though it would be fulfilled. He was very excited. After he told me about the acceptance, we celebrated at our favorite beer hall until very close to the curfew and then ran for our respective homes.

I also heard in June that PCV Hugh Rogers had just returned from his trip to Washington, where he had met with the Peace Corps Director Joe Blatchford. Hugh had not gotten an audience with President Nixon but had been able to voice the concern of the PCVs in Korea about the ongoing Vietnam War and the violence on American campuses to Director Blatchford, as well as to members of Congress. We all felt that his trip had been worthwhile.

My last spring in Korea ended on the summer solstice. Koreans called the day "*Ha Ji*," which was the longest day, or midsummer. The rice paddies were brilliant green. The wind, caressing the ground, caused ripples of light and shade to move across the fragile plants, as shadows from clouds played in counterpoint on the surrounding mountain slopes. Although the monsoon season had not yet begun, the rivers and streams were full enough to tie the scene together in garlands of gurgling whitewater. I have never forgotten the beauty of the Korean countryside in June on Ha Ji with its whirling, gentle life and soft peacefulness.

Women Hunting for Clams and Crabs, Geoje Island,
Korea, August 1969

Women Building a Road, Geoje Island, Korea, July 1970

My Good Friend Kim Hae-shik, and Mr. Chae, near Gyeongju, Korea, September 1969

Dr. Chauncey (Chince) Allen and Margaret Allen, Daegu, Korea, April 1969

## CHAPTER TWELVE—SUMMER OF THE YEAR OF THE DOG

I have never liked summer very much, except when I happened to be on a beach or in the mountains. Even in my hometown of Buffalo, with its strong, cooling breezes off Lake Erie and relatively comfortable humidity, summer made me feel tired, bored, and restless. In Daegu, the warm weather was just beginning, and I was already suffering from the summer doldrums. I especially missed air conditioning, cold drinks, cold food, and ice cream. In Peace Corps training we were taught that the highest rate of disease for PCVs occurs during the summer. I always felt that the summer doldrums' effect contributed to poor mental health and resulting physical illness. On the other hand, despite feeling a bit listless, I felt fine otherwise at the beginning of summer. As the humidity and daytime temperatures climbed in Daegu, something happened that was totally inexplicable—something I don't understand to this day.

When I was ten, I became an acolyte, or altar boy, at St. John's Episcopal Church in Buffalo, New York, where I grew up. I was an acolyte for eight years, and I loved being part of the church service. Lighting and snuffing the candles, carrying the cross and flags into church as a part of the procession entering and leaving the church, and distributing and collecting the collection plates were cherished rituals. I went to church faithfully until I went to college.

In college, except when the Dartmouth College Glee Club sang at a Dartmouth chapel service, I seldom went to church. During graduate school at Wisconsin, I never attended. I was not what I would characterize as a dedicated Christian by any means. In fact, the silence of most of the mainstream American churches, regarding the American war efforts in Vietnam and elsewhere in the 1960s, had confirmed for me that American Christians were generally hypocrites, preaching love and peace on Earth but supporting by their silent acquiescence the killing of innocent people and the destruction of communities and cultures abroad.

Living with a devout Presbyterian family in Korea provided an opportunity to see how Christianity could have a positive impact. For many Koreans, the work of missionaries and the fledgling churches— Presbyterian or any of the countless other Christian sects—provided real hope and promoted many good works, such as schools, hospitals, and orphanages. I visited these Christian enterprises almost weekly during my Peace Corps service and saw firsthand the positive impact on peoples' lives. I noted, as well, that many Korean churches seemed obsessed with money and prestige, just like their American counterparts, but on the whole Christianity seemed to have a positive impact on Korea. If I needed further proof of Christian good works in Korea, I was very familiar with the Geoje Island health project, which was a tremendously worthwhile Christian endeavor supported primarily by the World Council of Churches, as I have mentioned.

All of which is to say that in late June of the Year of the Dog, I was a lukewarm Christian from a Christian background, somewhat disenchanted with the hypocrisy of Christianity overall, who occasionally attended church and sometimes thought about religion in my conversations with Reverend Na. I occasionally thought about God when I was emotionally upset or exhilarated, but I did not think of myself as a true believer or fervent Christian advocate. Despite my relative indifference to religion, and despite the absence of any event or emotion (or drug) that might prompt an unusual response, on a warm night in Daegu I had a compelling experience that I have thought about almost daily ever since.

It was a simple dream. In it I was an acolyte again in my youth, sitting in the chancel near the altar at St. John's Episcopal Church in Buffalo. As the sounds of worship droned on around me, and my eyes swept back and forth in boredom across the windows, ceiling, organ, and other features of the beautiful church, I noticed the simple chalice that was on the near end of the altar, just below the candelabra. I had handled that chalice many times in assisting the minister to serve wine from it during communion. It was silver and heavy. Its design was ordinary, without adornment. It had probably been given to the church as a memorial gift. Nothing about it was special.

Without warning, the chalice began to glow. I couldn't take my eyes from it. The glow gradually intensified over what seemed like a long time and became a blinding light to the point where the outline of the chalice was no longer visible in the brightness. The altar and the church's interior features were subsumed by the overwhelming radiance. Such brilliance should have caused my eyes to close or avert for protection, but I couldn't close them or glance away.

At the same time I felt all-consuming warmth, as though a blanket had been wrapped around me. I wondered what was happening but felt no alarm or discomfort. On the contrary, I felt so at peace and alive and full of soothing, calming sensations that I didn't want the experience to end. It seemed as though the chalice glowed for several minutes, before the brilliant light slowly faded. The chalice resumed its normal appearance. The warmth left me. No words or sounds had accompanied the experience. There was no message. No one else in the church seemed to have seen what I saw. And then I woke up and realized I had been dreaming.

I had never before experienced anything like what I had just felt in that dream. Words are inadequate to convey my feelings and the sense of well-being that enveloped me during the dream and for weeks afterward. I got up in the morning and went to the university to teach as usual, but for the next month or so I felt an inner glow and peacefulness that are beyond description. In the months that followed, for years afterward, and even now I remember that dream and am reassured by the contentedness and comfort it engendered.

Reverend Na and I discussed it when I finally decided to share the dream with someone else. I guess what I dreamed has probably happened to many people, who may have expressed their experience to others as a revelation or other religious message. Perhaps the dream was a long-hidden memory of my birth. Perhaps it was something else. For me, the dream merely represented reassurance. It came at a time when I was happy with my life and enjoying Korea. Notwithstanding Daegu's oppressive heat, early summer was a pleasant part of the year. I was dealing with no crises or problems at the time. There was no reason for me to seek reassurance, consciously or subconsciously, as far as I was aware.

The dream was an unsolicited gift. Its long-term effect on me, I realize now, is to calm me in the face of almost any challenge or potential adversity, as I remember that feeling. It is probably the closest I have ever come to an intense communication with God and the single event of my life—surpassing even the occasionally overwhelming beauty of music or the breathtaking loveliness of nature at times—that most persuades me of God's existence.

Another transformational experience of a different but more familiar nature occurred shortly after my dream. The Fourth of July was windy and rainy in Daegu. The annual USIS celebration added several pounds to my thin frame. A huge party on Saturday night brought most of the Americans present in Daegu together for one evening of relaxation, Western food, and an open bar. People representing USAID (United States Agency for International Development), United Nations Forces, US Army, US Air Force, Peace Corps, and missionaries were all there, together with ROK officers, Daegu officials, prominent businessmen, and officers and faculty from the area's universities and colleges.

Peace Corps Volunteers, as usual, ringed the buffet and bar area. There were more volunteers at this event than I could remember ever seeing before, probably because members of the K-X, K-XI, and K-XII groups were now living in Daegu, as well as the K-XIII group that had recently arrived. The Peace Corps frenzy around the buffet and bar was all the more terrifying because of the two dozen or more PCVs in attendance.

At Kyungpook University I completed my grading of final examinations and started a weeklong TESOL workshop with about three dozen middle-school and high-school teachers from schools in the Daegu area. It was my sixth such workshop. Moe Cain and Russ Feldmeier had identical workshops underway, and we sometimes switched classes to expose our students to different teaching styles and English accents. These workshops were always fun. The English ability of the teachers in the workshop varied tremendously. Some spoke little or no English. Others had a very good grasp of English structure, grammar, and vocabulary but abysmal pronunciation. A very few spoke relatively good English.

The best English speakers were almost always the few women in the workshop. If a male teacher was pretty competent, it was usually as a result of military service as a KATUSA (Korean Augmentation Troops to the US Army), where they had had an extended opportunity to work and converse with Americans on a daily basis. A few of the teachers had attended one or more of my previous workshops. It was gratifying to realize that the repeat participants almost always had significantly improved their teaching techniques and English ability since the last workshop and were relatively superior to the first-time teacher participants. Even my former workshop participant with the strong Mississippi drawl had lost much of the accent he had picked up at Ole Miss.

While the workshop was underway, I was eagerly anticipating the arrival of a Swedish friend, with whom I had worked during several summers at the University of Uppsala and in Lapland at Abisko, Sweden, earlier in the decade. My good friend Staffan Holmgren had written that he would be traveling in the Far East in 1970 and hoped to visit me in Daegu in July. Staffan was a limnologist (someone who studies bodies of freshwater, such as lakes and ponds) who had worked with my brother, John, in Sweden and Alaska, and despite being several years older than I was, he had become my very close friend. Through him, I had gained entrance to student life at one of Europe's oldest and most prestigious universities, met dozens of Swedish students, and learned a great deal about Swedish life and women.

At the same time, all PCVs were lamenting the departure of Kevin O'Donnell, the Korea country director who was leaving to assume a position on the Peace Corps headquarters staff in Washington. Kevin had been the director in Korea since the beginning of the program in 1966. We all knew him as a skilled, no-nonsense but compassionate and friendly administrator of the highest caliber. The great success of the Peace Corps/Korea program to date, under very difficult conditions, was largely due to his leadership. He and his delightful wife, Ellen, would be sorely missed. (Kevin later became Peace Corps' fourth director in Washington.) Deputy Director Wayne Olson was staying, to the great relief of all PCVs. He and his wife, Yvonne, with Kevin and Ellen, had been bulwarks of support for groups K-VII and K-VIII since we had arrived.

On July 18, five other PCVs—Mary Clare and Jim Eros, Howie and Eileen Tarnower, and Jon Moody—and I left the mainland's blistering heat for Geoje Island. I lingered as long as I could in Daegu, waiting to see if Staffan would arrive. Finally we could no longer bear the humidity and temperatures near one hundred degrees in the city, so we headed south for the coast. On the boat it was a wonderful relief to feel the ocean wind on our faces and to see the pine-covered mountains of the islands. As always, talking with Captain Yi and passengers on the ferry was a true joy. It was a smooth, pleasant crossing to Geoje Island.

After arriving and introducing the new PCVs to the project staff, I made sure that we pitched our tents and dug trenches around them immediately, expecting the monsoon season to begin at any time in July and to threaten to wash our tents into the ocean, as we had experienced the previous summer. Consequently, beautiful weather ensued for our first two weeks there. Not a drop of rain fell.

We settled into a daily routine of work. For us the major summer tasks included helping build the small road along the top of the beach on the south side of the peninsula, so as to bypass the small dirt road that historically led from the pier at the end of the peninsula right up the middle of the peninsula. The eight nearly finished clinic buildings and other staff structures now sat squarely on the old road, and diverting traffic slightly around these new buildings, via a new bypass, would facilitate the work of the health project and passage around the project of the many villagers who commuted from Chilcheon Island to schools and work on Geoje Island.

Construction of the road entailed first building a walled-in base of rocks, collected from the surrounding beaches and mountains, sufficiently high to withstand high tide, and then filling in the area between the stone wall and the edge of the top of the beach with enough gravel and dirt to provide a sustainable road surface of about ten feet in width. It was backbreaking work, hauling stones on our backs in the Korean chigehs—the basket-like carrying devices mounted on A-frames.

The local villagers turned out in force to build the road. Everyone

301

helped. Dozens of men, grandmothers, mothers with babies secured on their backs by wraparound blankets, teenagers, and young children all pitched in. I was particularly impressed by how the women carried large rocks on their heads, balanced in little plastic washbasins. It took about six weeks to complete several hundred yards of the bypass.

The other major PCV work was transplanting small pine trees from the forests on the mountain above the peninsula to the project area, which from the beginning had been cleared farmland with few trees. Pines helped stabilize the soil, prevent erosion, and provide much-needed shade. These were also transported in the chigehs on our backs and placed in holes hacked from the clay of the peninsula. We managed to transplant approximately eighty pines during the summer. With the hundred or so pines transplanted the previous summer, the new pines already enhanced the beauty of the peninsula.

The female PCVs agreed to take on an additional chore. They worked with the men during the day, or otherwise assisted in the clinics, but took the time they needed to shop for essential groceries in the nearby villages and prepare meals for all of the PCVs. Part of the plan for PCVs' involvement in the Geoje Island health project was that we would not be a burden at all, or cost the project any additional resources, as a consequence of our living and working at the project for the six weeks of summer vacation. So our Peace Corps living allowances were pooled and furnished the means, through the good graces of the female PCVs, by which we paid for food and other necessities, including the cost of the fuel for the fires over which our meals were cooked in the Geoje Project's crew kitchen.

In the second week of our work Jean Sibley and several of the male PCVs took the project's Landrover to pick up medical supplies and construction materials in Changmok, a village several miles from the peninsula. Because the PCVs were not allowed to operate motor vehicles, pursuant to Peace Corps/Korea's policy, Jean drove. Shortly after we left the peninsula, she stopped the car to offer a ride to a local village woman walking along the road in the same direction we were heading, who was carrying a huge squash balanced on her head. Although the project's Landrover had given rides to hundreds of the villagers over the past year, this woman was reluctant at first to ride in the car, protesting that she had never before ridden in a vehicle of any kind. With our help the woman and her load were soon settled in the back seat. She was very grateful for the lift to the village, which was a distance of several miles. We were all pleased to be able to assist her in getting her produce to the market.

When we arrived in the village and she started to climb out of the car, she asked us where her shoes were. We searched the vehicle. No shoes. Where in the world had they gone? We finally realized that none of us had noticed that when she had first climbed into the Landrover, she had respectfully removed her shoes, leaving them sitting in the middle of the road.

Back we went to the spot where we had picked her up. Sure enough, her shoes were still sitting neatly and patiently in the road. We retrieved them, and the woman happily rode back with us to the destination village's market, marveling at the speed with which we had covered the distance of several miles each way that would have taken her more than an hour. On subsequent trips we often picked up the same lady, who laughed with us every time at her lost shoes on her first ride with us.

Staffan arrived on Geoje Island with PCV John Justice. He had arrived in Daegu the day after we had left for the island, but the Peace Corps office had arranged for him to travel with John, who was also a day late in his departure. I had a delightful time with Staffan on Geoje Island for several days, introducing him to the project staff and local people and showing him the neighboring villages with their straw-roofed mud houses, stone walls, and narrow dirt roads; nearby picturesque fields of vegetables and rice paddies; mountains that dropped onto rocky beaches; the soft glow of candles and lanterns in homes at night; and the exquisite night artistry of the dinoflagellates—all the things I loved about rural Korea and the archipelago. He agreed that Geoje Island was like Europe must have been two or three hundred years or more ago.

After several days together on Geoje Island, we returned to Daegu on July 23 so Staffan could meet the Na family, some of my Kyungpook University colleagues and students, and the Peace Corps staff at the regional office. The next day we took a bus to Gyeongju, as I had the previous year, but the difference between this trip to the ancient Silla Dynasty capital with Staffan and my earlier trip was incredible. I had told Staffan that bus travel in Korea was rather arduous and to be prepared for some discomfort. Instead, our expedition was just the

303

opposite. Whereas a year ago the trip had taken about one and a half hours on an old, hot dusty bus on a hard-packed winding dirt road, this trip was on a relatively new, air conditioned, extremely comfortable bus—a reconditioned American Greyhound bus—on a newly paved, straightened two-lane highway that whisked us to Gyeongju in just under an hour. It was an amazing improvement in comfort and speed, although I missed the fun of bouncing around in an old bus on a dusty winding road through the mountains.

I told Staffan about the Silla Dynasty and about the Three Kingdoms of Korea. He could not believe that Gyeongju had been the capital of one of the longest sustained dynasties in Asian history and once was one of the biggest cities in the world. After we visited the ancient tombs of the kings there and Pulguk Temple with its magnificent stone art and paintings, we hiked up to the *Seokguram* Grotto—roughly translated as the "Stone Cave Hermitage." It was my first visit to Seokguram, and I was overwhelmed by the beauty and history of this eighth-century Buddhist cave temple, carved high in the mountains above Gyeongju and above Bulguk Temple. Besides being amazingly serene and graceful, the huge stone Buddha inside the grotto is the only structure surviving fully intact from the Silla era.

We were told that Seokguram was abandoned for many centuries until it was rediscovered by accident in 1909. According to local lore, a rural postman was caught in a rainstorm and sought shelter in the nearest cave he could find. Once inside, he lit a candle in the dark and found a gigantic stone Buddha looking back at him! Korea was under Japanese occupation at the time of the discovery. The Japanese authorities in Seoul ordered that the cave be dismantled and sent to the capital city. Fortunately, in the face of local recalcitrance the plan was eventually dropped.

Both of us were in awe of the carved Buddha, which was about eleven feet in height and radiated peacefulness. The view from the entrance on the crystal clear day we visited was wonderful. We could clearly see the East Sea, across several ranges of intervening mountains, and I vowed to come back to see the sunrise from this vantage point someday, as one of the monks at the temple urged.

On the following day we went by bus to the foot of Mt. Palgong and hiked up to enjoy a picnic at Donghwa Temple, which was my favorite temple close to Daegu. Several of my students went with us, including my favorite student—Miss Rhee—and were able to educate Staffan, as they had me previously, about Buddhism and the great significance of the temple for Buddhism in Korea. As always, the beauty of the surrounding mountains and cascading streams added to the total enchantment of the temple site. I recalled my earlier adventure near the summit of Mt. Palgong, at the air force base, as we hiked up to the temple along the path I had taken part way in the spring. This time, happily, we stumbled upon no minefields.

That evening we all went to my favorite Korean restaurant in Daegu, Dangchip. Staffan was very impressed with Korean food, especially bulgogi, and seemed to also like kimchhee and the other Korean dishes served. By now I was a regular customer at the restaurant, and the staff treated us royally.

After my students left for their homes, I took Staffan to a makoli chip, where we drank for several hours with a couple of beautiful Korean hostesses in traditional Korean dress. Just before curfew, it began to rain heavily. The monsoon season had been delayed for several weeks. That night it seemed as though the rains were trying to make up for lost time. As we left the wine house with the girls, the water in the street was already several inches deep. No taxis were anywhere to be found, so we laughingly hoisted the girls on our backs and ran the several blocks to the nearest yogwan. The women obligingly continued our party with us there and spent the night with us, as the storm raged around us until noon on Saturday. I don't think either of us will ever forget that night.

Early on Sunday morning we took a train to Seoul, arriving in time to visit the Korea House restaurant, where guests were entertained by traditional Korean music and lovely Korean dances performed by talented young women. I had been there several times before, as the guest of Korean government officials, and once with Ed Klein and Scott Duncan. It was always delightful.

Staffan departed for Kimpo Airport late in the afternoon, exhausted by his one-week visit to the Hermit Kingdom, where he had visited Korea's three major cities (Seoul, Busan, and Daegu), one of its most beautiful rural and undeveloped areas (Geoje Island), and three of its most famous Buddhist sites (Bulguk Temple, Seokguram, and Donghwa

Temple). For my part, his visit had been a welcome interlude and a chance to repay him for his great friendship and kindness in Sweden during my three summers there. As Staffan departed, I wished that my brother and sister and their families could someday visit Korea and, like Staffan, enjoy some of the incredible experiences I had relished.

As soon as Staffan left Korea, I returned to Geoje Island, taking the express train to Busan, where I stayed that night at a yogwan and took the next morning's ferryboat from the Jagalchi market to the island. In my absence, work on the road had slowed with the beginning of the monsoon season, but the five PCVs had continued to transplant pine trees, teach English to local project staff, and otherwise assist with various chores at the health project.

One project we all worked on during our off hours in the evenings was the building of a small raft, floating on several empty kerosene barrels that we scavenged from a nearby village. The raft was intended to provide a recreational outlet for staff who wished to swim or otherwise enjoy the warm waters of the archipelago. We finished it in several evenings, towed it out about one hundred feet from shore, and enjoyed it for several weeks before a storm destroyed it (just as the local Koreans had predicted).

In the evenings we joined Korean staff members on the pier at the end of the peninsula to talk or to sing together under the stars. Several times each week we had a small bonfire, around which we sat and told stories or sang. One volunteer couple, Mary Clare and Jim Eros, kept our spirits high, eliciting constant laughter with their regaling accounts each evening of the day's humorous and not-so-humorous exploits in trying to cope with the primitive living environment on the island.

Besides fighting an overwhelming urge to drink a non-existent cold Coke, Mary Clare was trying to get pregnant. Signs were posted on the critical days so that she and Jim would not be disturbed in their tent, which was not the most comfortable or romantic place to engage in this endeavor, in the heat, humidity, monsoon rains, and bugs (including scorpions) of a Geoje Island summer. We all cheered their daily progress and tried to ignore the sounds within, and shaking of, their tent. (Mary Clare finally announced that she was pregnant at summer's end.)

The weeks at the health project went by quickly. John and Jean Sibley, the various Korean and foreign members of the medical staff who shuttled back and forth from the mainland, and the Korean support staff and workers were friendly, interesting, dedicated, and fun people to work with. There were a few awkward moments.

One day, for example, I met a local medicine man from a nearby village whom I had overheard the project staff discuss on many occasions. Dr. Sibley wished to involve the indigenous practitioners of the healing arts as much as possible in the work of the health project, believing that the project and the local "healers," even witch doctors, could mutually benefit, educating each other. I finally met the individual the project nurses had repeatedly referred to in conversations with me as *tolpari ouisa*. I knew that the word *ouisa* meant "doctor."

When I met this man, I mustered my best Korean language skills in introducing myself and telling him how happy I was to meet him at last, referring in the honorific form to him as tolpari ouisanim. His reaction, and the faces of the nurses and doctors who heard me, indicated that I had misspoke. I later learned that tolpari translates roughly as stone-armed, heavy-handed, or in a medical context "quack doctor." So I had addressed him as honorable quack doctor. Mistakes like this continued to plague me throughout my Peace Corps Volunteer service in Korea. Happily, most Koreans were very forgiving.

As the summer vacation drew to a close, I tried to explore on weekends as much of the area around the health project as possible, visiting Hachung, Changmok, Youncho, and Changsungpo villages. The villages were all quite similar in appearance, but there were always new people to talk with and intriguing stories to hear. On one of these day trips I spoke with a middle-aged man named Jun Han-il, who had been a soldier stationed at the prisoner of war camp on Geoje Island during the war. I had read about the camp in Peace Corps training. It was located not far from the health project, farther south along the west coast of Geoje Island.

Home to 170,000 North Korean and Chinese prisoners of war during the Korean War, the sprawling Geoje camp was the scene of a notorious prisoner uprising in early May of 1952. An American brigadier general had been seized and held as a hostage by rioting prisoners for more than three days, until United Nations troops regained control, after bloody fighting, and freed hostages. Mr. Jun remembered the so-called "Geoje Island Mutiny" well. He told me that the prisoners had been treated very poorly, housed in appalling conditions, and guarded by a woefully small contingent of South Korean and United Nations soldiers. It was a disaster waiting to happen. A series of escalating prisoner riots in the previous months had been largely ignored, according to Mr. Jun, and the military leadership in control of the prison camp was ill prepared to deal with the well-organized prisoners and their Communist leaders. Mr. Jun's sympathies seemed to lie with the North Korean prisoner "brothers" inside the camp, who constituted the majority of POWs, although he was careful not to express this sentiment to me directly.

When I asked other Korean and American friends, who were familiar with the Geoje Island uprising, exactly what had happened there almost twenty years earlier, the absence of reliable information from them surprised me. I concluded that the prisoner of war camp and the prisoner riot had been a stain on the reputations of both the United Nations Command and the American Armed Forces. No one seemed to know very much, and military acquaintances did not want to talk about the incident. I decided not to visit the site, feeling that too close of an encounter with the harsh realities of the Korean War and with the atrocities surely committed there by both sides, only miles from our snug peninsula, might spoil my enchantment with Geoje Island.

On another day I took the small ferryboat from the pier at the foot of the peninsula on which the health project was located across the narrow passage of water between Geoje Island and Chilcheon Island to explore the several farming and fishing villages on that tiny island. Two oars powered the small ferryboat—one in the front of the boat and one in the back. It traversed the narrow passage infrequently, and its main passengers were students and other inhabitants of Chilcheon Island going to schools or markets on Geoje Island. The ferryman was an older man with strong arms. He charged a small fee for his exertions—the equivalent of about ten cents. He usually handled the large oar in the stern of the boat, while another passenger rowed with the aft oar.

In talking with him and his passengers, I discovered that the student passengers walked more than four miles daily to get to school—usually early in the morning—and then walked four miles home each evening. I marveled at the dedication to education demonstrated by their eight-mile daily trip, rain or shine. Most lugged backpacks filled with heavy books. The ferryboat crossing was a crucial part of their trip. In strong winds or heavy seas, when the boat was not crossing, they couldn't get to school.

Watching the boat come and go, I thought it was a kind of metaphor for the transformative process visible in every aspect of Korean life. Koreans were utilizing every tool available—even an old, wooden hand-rowed ferry boat with an aging oarsman (or the minimal contributions of inexperienced PCV English teachers)—to fight and claw their way from a centuries-old, agrarian, impoverished lifestyle into the late-twentieth century. They knew that education was the key and would walk hours every day to obtain it. I admired their determination.

In August, the PCVs sadly left Geoje Island to return to their teaching responsibilities. On my return to Daegu, I wondered if I would ever see a beautiful Geoje summer again, with the quiet villages, sturdy people, mountains, ocean waters, and rocky shores that I had come to love so much. The hot and dusty city that awaited me was now familiar enough to me that it was like meeting an old friend again, with stories and memories of past, shared adventures on every corner and in every nook.

But before I arrived, Reverend Na had begun commuting to Seoul to teach at the Seoul Presbyterian Seminary, Mrs. Na had left for several weeks with the young girls to meditate at a temple, my good friend Ed Klein had left for the States at the conclusion of his tenure as Peace Corps Regional Director in Daegu, and my steadfast Korean friend and language teacher Kim Hae-shik had departed for Seoul en route to graduate school at the University of Illinois. Nurse Shin had left earlier in the year to work in Inchon, taking her beautiful smile from Daegu.

Additionally, my wonderful colleague and mentor at the university, Professor Lee Woo-gun, had become quite ill with diabetes and had taken a leave of absence. So many of my friends in Daegu had vanished while I was away, and one was very ill. With the pleasure of returning to the familiar alleys and old neighborhoods of the physical city, I also felt sadness, concern, and a bit of loneliness at the disappearance of many of the people who constituted the spirit of Daegu for me.

Ed's replacement as regional director was another PCV from the K-I group, Tim O'Brien, who was married to a lovely and warm Korean woman named Hyon. I liked them both immensely. It was reassuring to have another fine Peace Corps administrator in Daegu, who would be there for the remainder of my service as a volunteer.

As I busied myself with preparations for the start of classes, Vice President Spiro Agnew visited Korea, causing quite a stir. The Korea press was very critical of him, commenting that Agnew confused the Korean government and misunderstood President Park's feelings regarding the upcoming American withdrawal of several thousand troops from Korea that had been recently announced. Koreans were generally reluctant to see any downsizing of the American military presence in Korea, feeling that their security was threatened by a smaller American commitment. As a result, for political reasons the Park government wanted to appear as though it was opposing the US downsizing. Vice President Agnew, however, publicly and repeatedly stated that President Park was in complete agreement with the US plans, which wasn't at all what President Park had said. Through his ineptness and perceived naïveté, Agnew created a political crisis and confirmed to Koreans, I suspected, that Americans are morons when it comes to knowledge of Korea and its politics.

Classes began in early September. All of my students were back and enthusiastic enough about learning English to lift my spirits and reanimate my passion for teaching. I felt that I was so lucky to be a teacher at Kyungpook University. However, there was one problem I had difficulty handling.

My colleague, a professor I will call Professor Ha, who had replaced my dear friend Professor Lee at the Language Institute, approached me early in September with a plan he wished me to help him with. He wanted me to write a new English textbook with him and asked me not only to do much of the writing but to record all of the exercises in the proposed book. He offered to share all the profits with me.

At first I was interested in helping, despite the fact that I had just proofread a new English textbook, prepared in the past several years by the English department of the Teachers College, which was about to be introduced to the freshmen. It was of dubious quality and could certainly be improved upon. When he mentioned profits, however, I suspected that he was interested in becoming rich through his idea and turned him down, explaining that as a Peace Corps Volunteer I could not participate in a money-making scheme. I certainly could not personally accept any money for helping him and felt it would be improper to support a for-profit enterprise.

In retrospect, I was probably unfair in questioning his motivation and refusing to help him. English professors did not make much money. Most supplemented their incomes by tutoring or other projects outside their formal teaching responsibilities. Professor Ha was merely trying to earn more money in a time-honored Korean manner. I think I was offended by the way in which he presented his idea and by his emphasis on profits. No other Korean had approached me like that.

On the other hand, many Koreans had asked to practice English with me or to have me teach them. They were motivated by the prospect that greater fluency in English would help their future and possibly increase income. I was motivated in joining the Peace Corps partly by quite selfish reasons. We were all alike and all human in seeking to better our own situations. After several months of reflecting on the problem, I regretted my abrupt dismissal of Professor Ha's overture and felt that I should have offered to help him in some way that would not be objectionable. He clearly felt that I had offended him and barely spoke to me again in my last months in Korea.

The second weekend in September I attended a meeting in Seoul for all PCVs to meet new Peace Corps Director Don Hess and his gracious and attractive wife, Nancy. The Korean Thanksgiving Day, or Choosuk, fell on Tuesday during the meeting, and since almost everyone returns home for this important holiday, Kyungpook University and most offices closed down for five days, giving all PCVs a chance to come to Seoul for the meeting and several holiday parties. Don and Nancy were kind and hospitable. We became attached to them immediately and welcomed them to the Peace Corps/Korea community while we all enjoyed Western food, the companionship of other PCVs, and sharing stories of our adventures.

I had spent a fascinating Choosuk in 1969 with my Korean family. This year I spent the holiday in Seoul, glad to avoid the crush of people in Daegu and to be able to have a quiet evening with several PCV friends and their Korean wives, sipping wine, munching crackers and cheese, and enjoying Western foods that I still couldn't find outside of Seoul.

A great many American foods and other Western products, which were not here when I arrived in 1969, appeared in Seoul. Ford and German cars and trucks, assembled in Korea, were visible everywhere. Pepsi Cola and Coca-Cola were now in most stores and markets in Seoul. Real cheese, butter, ice cream, and other dairy products—previously unknown except in military and missionary commissaries—were available for purchase everywhere, although quite expensive for most Koreans and PCVs. Made-in-Korea copies of Bufferin, Contact, and other medicines were in local drugstores, and even Western chocolate candy, cookies, and cakes were on stores' shelves.

So many other signs of fantastically rapid modernization were everywhere—new hotels in Seoul, the new superhighway between Seoul and Busan, and new elevated highways in Seoul along with parks, plazas, and shopping centers. Even the hippy look had arrived. Men and women's hair was getting longer. Korean women in Seoul were wearing shorter skirts and were more smartly dressed than Japanese or Western women.

Changes happened so fast that the Korean police had difficulty coping. While I was in Seoul, I heard of the arrests of several mini-skirted students whose outfits were too revealing, as well as of longhaired male students whose hairstyles offended. Skirts were stripped off the women and burned; longhaired men were shorn of their shaggy tresses. Two male PCVs of Asian extraction, as well as several male Japanese tourists, were jailed briefly because of their long hair, causing quite a furor. President Park personally intervened with the police, reportedly because elections were approaching and government crackdowns in the past had been political dynamite. (I found it ironic that, during the Japanese occupation, the Japanese forbade Korean men to have long hair. Violators of this rule had their hair forcibly cut, which prompted Korean uprisings. Now it was the Korean policemen who were cutting hair.)

On the return trip to Daegu, I noticed new and more comfortable cars on the train. In the fields near the railroad tracks I saw small tractors and other farm equipment that had replaced ox-drawn plows and carts. Korea was changing so rapidly, right before my eyes, that it was sometimes painful.

One thing was a constant in September, as the autumnal equinox came and went: the advent of Korea's blue skies, cooling temperatures, and gorgeous autumn weather. Chungomabi. As my last summer in Korea drew to a close and I tried to imprint in my memory the swirling, humming life of a Korean summer, I regretted its ephemeralness but rejoiced at the thought of the coming new, beautiful season.

Pulguk Temple, Gyeongju, Korea, October 1969

Mr. Park, and my Special Friends Shin Young-ei and Choi Hwa-
wook, Daegu, Korea, April 1969

Me on Top of Mt. Sorak, Korea, with Flag of the Mount Madison
Volunteer Ski Patrol (MMVSP), April 1970

Spring Plowing, North Gyeongsang Province, Korea, April 1970

# CHAPTER THIRTEEN—AUTUMN OF THE YEAR OF THE DOG

ctober was a month of holidays and weddings. In rapid succession we celebrated three official holidays and an unofficial one. You can tell a lot about a country by what it chooses to celebrate. On October 1 there was a flag-raising ceremony in the middle of the campus at Kyungpook University to commemorate the unofficial holiday called *Kookgoonuinal*, or Armed Forces Day, which marked the date the South Korean military broke across the thirty-eighth parallel in 1950 in its counterattack on North Korea. This year there was an emotional twentieth-anniversary celebration honoring the military heroes of the recent Korean War, as well as past heroes. Many of my students—male and female alike—were in tears as the Korean flag was raised. Several, who had lost fathers or brothers during the war, cried all day. I found myself crying too.

As the Korean flag was raised that day, there was enough of a stiff breeze that the flag was fully extended, so you could see all of the unique colors and symbols. Like almost everything about Korea, I found the flag—called *Taegukki*—fascinating. Reverend Na had explained to me that it stood for much of his country's thought, philosophy, and mysticism. For example, centered on the flag is a circle divided equally and in perfect balance. The upper half of the circle is red, representing the *Yang*, and the lower half is blue, representing the *Um*, which is an ancient symbol of the universe. The two opposites—Yang and Um— express the dualism of the cosmos: fire and water, day and night, dark and light, masculine and feminine, heat and cold, plus and minus, creation and destruction, and so on.

My students further explained that the central thought in the Taegukki reflects the philosophy that, while there is constant movement within the sphere of infinity, there is also balance and harmony. Good is counterpoised with evil. An act of creation also involves destruction by its nature. The three black bars at each corner of the flag also emphasize the idea of opposition and balance. The three unbroken lines stand for heaven. The opposite three broken lines denote the Earth. In the lower left hand corner of the flag the two lines with a broken line between signify fire. In the opposite corner the bars represent water.

Two days later we celebrated *Gaecheonjeol*, or National Foundation Day, in honor of the founder of Korea, called *Dangun*. The day celebrates the creation of *Gojoseon*, the first state of the Korean nation. According to historical records, Dangun founded Gojoseon on the third day of the tenth lunar month, 2333 BC, which is set on October 3 for the sake of convenience. Gaecheonjeol means Heaven-Opened Day. Kyungpook University was closed. It was birthday number 4,303 for Korea. In six years the United States would celebrate number two hundred.

One of my favorite Korean official holidays was Hangul Day—also called Hangul Proclamation Day or Korean Alphabet Day—which marked the invention and the proclamation of hangul, the native alphabet of the Korean language, by King Sejong the Great. I have already described this remarkable creation and the genius of this purely phonetic alphabet, promulgated in 1446. I really liked the idea of celebrating the written means by which people communicate. What could be more important?

The final official October holiday in Korea was United Nations Day on October 24. Koreans had the highest respect for the United Nations. Most of my students credited the United Nations, together with the United States, for saving Korea at the time of the North Korean invasion in 1950. Once each year, on the internationally celebrated United Nations Day, Koreans evince their respect and thanks with ceremonies, dancing, and drumming. The university was closed, but there was a student performance of traditional Korean dances at Hyosung College, which I enjoyed. I agreed with the Koreans that the United Nations deserved its own holiday.

I attended six weddings in October—two PCVs married Korean women from Daegu and four of my students got married. Each was a delightful, festive occasion. It is a modern tradition to give each wedding guest a small pound cake. The mice in my attic room and I feasted for weeks on those little cakes. I began to think that at the age of twenty-five I should start thinking seriously about matrimony. At the same time, I wondered about the PCVs who married in Korea. My emotions and mental stability were so volatile during my Peace Corps service that I doubted I could make that kind of serious decision until I had returned to familiar circumstances at home and completed a period of readjustment. When I inquired, the Peace Corps office in Seoul told me that one tenth of the male PCVs in the first sixteen groups of PCVs had married Korean women so far. Two female PCVs had married Korean men.

On October 7 the seven remaining PCVs in Daegu from groups VII and VIII had a fine dinner at a downtown restaurant with new Peace Corps Director Don Hess to celebrate the second anniversary of our joining Peace Corps. Time had surely flown fast. Three of the ten PCVs assigned from our groups to Daegu colleges and universities had terminated early. Don told us that this percentage—30 percent—was average for our two groups throughout Korea. Although this number seemed very high to me, according to Don our groups had had the lowest percentage of PCVs terminating early in Korea than any groups to date. I speculated that our relative success was probably due to our comparatively well-structured, familiar, and fulfilling assignments—teaching at colleges and universities. I knew I would have had a much more difficult time in Korea if I had been assigned to work in tuberculosis control or Hansen's disease control at rural public health clinics, as many PCVs had.

The monsoon season, which had started unusually late in the summer and dragged on well into September, was finally over. The days were much cooler, and the nights were beginning to get so cold that I closed my windows, which had been open since May. In mid-October I took out my winter ibul and put away the lighter summer ibul—sad that I would probably never again use the latter.

I was beginning to have the feeling, as I always do when I am preparing mentally to leave some place I have come to love, that I must dash around to see all the things I had missed seeing until now and to have one last visit with those places and things I had known. In response to this urge, one afternoon I went to watch my male students at military training in Kyungpook University's stadium. The noise from the target practice was deafening, and my students looked very intimidating, firing their M-1 rifles and machine guns and marching back and forth across the stadium grounds. It was easy to forget that Korea was still at war, as I devoted myself to teaching, getting to know Koreans and their culture, and enjoying the life around me. Seeing my students engaging in the arts of war was a harsh reminder that a mere armistice prevented the terror of war from descending on my Korean family and friends' lives at any moment.

Another new and lighter experience that I undertook was a visit to the US Eighth Army's base Camp Henry, located in downtown Daegu. One of the American soldiers I had invited several times to join my classes at Kyungpook University called me one day and invited me to see a new movie at the base, which had had good reviews stateside. It was called *M.A.S.H.*, which I thought was a very strange name for a movie. The movie was supposed to be about the Korean War, which interested me. MASH was the abbreviation of Mobile Army Surgical Hospital. The movie was about a group of army medical personnel stationed in Korea during the Korean War. It was supposed to be a comedy. Off I went, expecting little except some good old American popcorn. It turned out to be an incredible experience.

I had never seen a movie before that mocked the military so directly and was generally so irreverent about the values of Americans. Neither had the five hundred men in the base theater that night. You could tell by their whistles, hoots, and yells during the movie that they loved it! The movie's dialogue was barely audible above the GIs' screams of appreciation and laughter. The show was probably the most raucous I have ever attended. After the first showing, I decided to stay for the second show and moved my seat down to the first row, where I could hear what was being said in the movie and enjoy to the fullest the comments and din behind me in the theater.

Although I would never usually watch the same movie again immediately, to see *M.A.S.H.* in Korea with hundreds of soldiers in an army theater was a once in a lifetime opportunity. It was one of the best cinematic experiences of my life. There was even a reference in the movie to Dartmouth (Trapper John had been the Dartmouth quarterback). I was both surprised and pleased that such an irreverent movie could be made and receive such good reviews while the Vietnam War was raging in another Asian war theater.

Shortly after the movie at Camp Henry, several PCVs and I, accompanied by a dozen or more students of both genders and a Liberal Arts College professor from Kyungpook, set out to climb Mt. Songni. We took a late afternoon train on Friday from Daegu north to Kimcheon where the train turned northeastward toward the town of Sangju, which lies on the border between North Gyeongsang Province and North Chungcheong Province—a trip of several hours. Our destination was the only landlocked province in South Korea and the only curfew-free part of Korea. The trip through the Sobaek Mountains was gorgeous. The autumn colors were at their peak. The reds, golds, and oranges rivaled the best autumn colors I had ever seen in New England at Dartmouth. In Sangju, we were supposed to change to a bus to continue the trip to Mt. Songni.

Our train was late arriving in Sangju, so we missed the early evening bus and had to wait for a later one. The fifteen of us found a comfortable makoli chip near the bus depot and whiled away the hours until the next bus drinking many kettles of makoli. It was a primitive makoli chip with an outdoor *pyunso,* or "toilet," if you could call it that. At some point I went outside to use the toilet in the dark and found that it was essentially two slippery boards straddling a fairly deep pit. To do your business you inched out onto the boards several feet and squatted. The smell was horrific. The only light was a kerosene lantern, which you had to carry with you and balance on the boards. I finished my business and returned to my friends with a report of the potential dangers lurking at the outdoor toilet.

We had a fine time drinking. At some point our students and Professor Koo, from the philosophy department, started to discuss the "ideal Korean woman" of this age of rapid changes in Korea. All agreed that the gentle and obedient woman of Korea's past had disappeared. I wondered whether such women had ever existed in Korea. From what I had observed, women ran Korea today, behind the scenes, and had probably always done so. Our discussion, led by several of the female students, undertook the task of trying to define an ideal woman for modern Korea.

During the course of our discussion our students told us the treasured stories from Korea's history of three of the most famous heroines of Korean literature: Sim Chong, Choon Hyang, and Sassi Namjong. As the students pointed out, the three heroines represent a Korean male view from the past of the virtues of the ideal woman: noble character and humble beauty, with "noble" defined as resignation, chastity, obedience (to men), and courage.

I have already mentioned the legend of Choon Hyang. According to the story of Sim Chong, a loving daughter sacrificed herself in exchange for a large quantity of rice with which she hoped to restore the sight of her blind father. She jumped into the sea as a human sacrifice to the sea dragon, so that the rice could be transported safely. Sim Chong was brought to life again and became a queen. When she invited all blind persons to a royal feast in order to find her father, who eventually appeared still stricken with grief at his daughter's sacrifice, there was a dramatic reunion between father and daughter, which shocked his blind eyes into sight.

In the third story, which had slightly Biblical overtones, a married woman by the name of Sa was the legitimate wife of Yu Han-rim. Having no children of her own, she invited another woman, Miss Ko, to become the concubine of her husband to bear him sons. Over time the concubine falsely persuaded Yu that his wife was a bad person, and the faithful wife was expelled from the family, becoming homeless and destitute. Without resentment Sa quietly suffered her tribulations until eventually her husband realized the truth about the vile concubine and expelled her. Sa was restored to her husband, and they lived happily ever after.

Just as we were beginning to get into a good analysis of these stories, there was a terrible scream from outside, behind the makoli chip. It came from the direction of the outdoor toilet. We rushed outside in the dark. Barely visible in the darkness in the pit, covered with its contents, was one of our PCV members, who had gone out to the toilet a bit inebriated and slipped from the boards headlong into the pit. It was a serious situation.

The PCV (who shall remain nameless) managed to scramble out

of the pit, reeking with mellifluous scents. He was no longer welcome in the makoli chip. The hostesses managed to fill several buckets with water, and from a safe distance outside we drenched him repeatedly with cold water tossed from the buckets, until he was relatively free of excrement and stench. In the cool evening air the cold water was almost as unpleasant as the fall itself. The kind Korean women offered to clean his clothes, which he would be able to pick up on the way home. So after another coldwater shower and changing clothes, he managed to join us on the continuation of our trip to Mt. Songni by bus.

My PCV friend was traumatized, although even he could finally see the humor in the situation. Everyone in our group promised not to reveal his identity if we ever recounted the story of his evening swim. Our discussion of the "ideal Korean woman" was never continued on this trip, but if it had, we would have had to include as examples the compassionate women who helped him that evening.

The next day was one of the most beautiful autumn days I have ever seen anywhere. Its magnificence helped us put aside the memory of the previous night's adventure. The leaves of the azaleas and other bushes and trees in the mountains were scarlet, orange, and yellow beneath a deep blue sky. It was a cool day with no wind, so we were very comfortable hiking with only sweatshirts or light jackets.

The Sobaek Mountains comprise the largest range of mountains in South Korea, stretching southwest from north of Taebaek Mountain (5,121 feet) in Gang Won Province to the Kohung Peninsula near Yeosu. Several of Korea's highest mountains are in the range: Mt. Sobaek (4,760 ft), Mt. Dokyu (5,276 ft), Mt. Baegun (4,190 ft), and our destination, Mt. Songni (3,468 ft). My students and I had already climbed Mt. Chiri (6,283 ft) in the southwestern branch of the Sobaeks. We had chosen Mt. Songni for this expedition more for its rugged beauty than for its height, as well as because there was a famous temple nearby called Beopju, which I had never visited.

Besides the gorgeous weather, what I remember most about our climb of Mt. Songni were the incredible views from the summit and the number of hikers who were in the mountains that day, enjoying the autumn foliage, crisp air, and superb terrain. The well-worn trail to the summit was crowded with people of all ages—children, parents, and grandparents in every kind of clothes imaginable. Thousands of people were on that trail. It was not exactly an escape from the hustle and bustle of the city. Nevertheless, we all thoroughly enjoyed the five-hour hike to the top and the three-hour return, followed by a bulgogi dinner at a local restaurant at the base. It was my last hiking trip in Korea and probably one of my most pleasant.

After an uneventful night at a nearby yogwan, the next morning we explored Beopju Temple, which dates from the sixth century. It lay on the lower lopes of Mt. Songni, surrounded by granite peaks and forests resplendent in fiery autumn foliage. The most interesting and famous building in the temple complex was one of Korea's national treasures known as *Palsangjeun,* or the "hall of eight pictures." This wooden five-tiered pagoda, standing about seventy-five feet tall, was originally built at the time of the founding of Beopju Temple in 553. The Japanese burned the first structure, according to my students, but the monks told us that the current lovely building was reconstructed in 1626. Another major restoration had just been completed. The four interior walls of the first floor were adorned with the eight pictures that give the pagoda its name, depicting the life of Buddha. Palsangjeon was the oldest such structure in Korea.

Besides being an important religious structure, it reminded me of the hundreds of years of conflict between the Japanese and Koreans and the tension between Buddhism and other Korean religions, Confucianism, and governing authorities. For me it epitomized the beauty of Korean art forms as expressed in the graceful architectural lines of the pagoda and in the interior paintings of Buddha's life.

There was a huge stone statue of Buddha as well at Beopju Temple. It towered over the pagoda and other temple buildings, as though protecting the temple and the surrounding mountains. To walk and talk with my students and Peace Corps colleagues among Beopju Temple's ancient inspiring buildings under the blue October sky and amid beautiful mountains was a privilege.

After returning from our hiking expedition, I was plunged into a week of frantic activity at Kyungpook University. The English department of the Liberal Arts College was holding an English Night the first week in November, right after Halloween. My students were putting on Thornton Wilder's *The Happy Journey to Trenton and Camden,* which has always been a favorite play of mine and had the advantage of requiring no set and only six characters. I liked the way Wilder elevated regular daily human conversations between ordinary people to the level of universal human experience. My students also liked the play a lot, appreciated its message, and worked hard to make it a success. We spent hours and hours rehearsing. The final production was a resounding success, despite my clumsy coaching and directing.

During the first weekend in November I attended my last Peace Corps operations meeting in Seoul as the representative of North Gyeongsang Province. I was sad that it was my last such meeting. Over almost two years the quarterly meetings had provided an opportunity to get to know the Korean and American members of the Peace Corps staff in Seoul, whom I seldom saw otherwise, as well as PCVs from each of the other eight provinces. I realized, when I got to know them, that the Koreans who comprised Peace Corps/Korea's outstanding staff were extremely talented and personable. Peace Corps was fortunate to have such an exceptional staff.

Our discussions during these meetings ranged from problems PCVs were encountering to programmatic issues, security concerns, political issues, health issues, and the schedule of PCV groups' arrivals and departures for the upcoming year. It was a shock to realize that within months, groups K-VII and K-VIII would leave Korea and no longer be a subject of discussion—forgotten and relegated to the honey wagons of history.

After I returned to Daegu I discovered that in my absence an article I wrote for the Kyungpook University Press had caused quite a stir. My article reflected on the many wonderful things I had experienced at Kyungpook in the past two years but criticized the cheating on university exams that I had observed (not in my classes) and suggested that the recent withdrawal of some of the American troops in Korea was justified and a positive development for Korea. What was I thinking?

The Kyungpook administration confiscated most of the newspapers as soon as they started to be distributed. Nothing was said to me, and I didn't even hear about the fuss until several weeks afterward, when the USIS director told me jokingly about my faux pas. When I found out, I apologized to the head of the English department in the Liberal Arts College, Dean Kim Young-hee. He had been my first contact from the university when I originally arrived, had arranged for me to come to Kyungpook University, and had found the Na family for me to live with. I was upset that I might have caused him trouble. Dean Kim told me to forget about it and said that he agreed with what I had written. (Several years later I was delighted when Dean Kim wrote me that he had became president of Kyungpook University.)

During my years in Korea, the striking beauty of Korean music, dance, and paintings had tremendously impressed me, but it was not until my final months there that I encountered Korean ceramics. With several of my students I visited a small pottery company on the outskirts of Daegu, where reproductions of ancient Korean ceramics were being carefully crafted. The loveliest of these were the vases and bowls of a greenish-blue tinge, reproductions of the glazed celadon artworks of the Koryo Dynasty (935–1392). I fell in love with these astonishingly appealing examples of Korean celadon, which are by far the single most famous class of art objects in Korea.

The Chung family, with whom I had stayed in Honolulu, had several celadon pieces in their fine art collection. I was told that Korean celadon may be imitated today but cannot be duplicated, because the composition of the glaze and the firing techniques of the ancient Korean potters were lost by the time of the late Yi Dynasty (1392–1910). One of my biggest regrets after that visit to the Korean potters was that I came to know about Korean celadon and other similar works so late in my volunteer service. This was a terrible irony in that the excellent collection of Korean ceramics housed at the Kyungpook University museum was located on the floor below my office at the university. I didn't find it until my last months in Korea.

Shortly after my seduction by the beauty of Korean pottery, I received a letter from my good friend and former language teacher from Peace Corps training Kim Hae-shik. He wrote that he was a little homesick but was otherwise enjoying the University of Illinois. My cousin, Beth Hobbie Jones, and her husband, Ron, had been extremely kind to him, he wrote, as he settled in at graduate school. He had been selected from among the approximately forty Korean students at Illinois for a position in the linguistics department as a Korean language instructor—a part-time assistantship that paid well and waived tuition for him. He felt that he had been picked on the basis of his Peace Corps training experience. Hae-shik also wrote that he had met a charming Japanese girl in the library. (While professing an intense dislike for anything Japanese, most Korean men were fascinated by Japanese women.) I was pleased that he seemed to be adjusting to life in the United States and suspected that he would stay on, if he could. One of the things he liked most about America, he wrote, was central heating in classrooms and dormitories.

The charcoal-burning stoves were placed in our office and classrooms at Kyungpook University, as the weather turned quite chilly by mid-November. One good thing about chilly classes was that the cold kept you on your feet and moving around the classroom. Constant movement by the teacher was an effective way of keeping the attention of students, we had confirmed in Peace Corps training. As a result of excellent teachers in my childhood and at Dartmouth, as well as of the outstanding instructors in Hawaii, I knew that physical proximity between teacher and student in the classroom, as well as meeting students socially after classes, helped build a stronger teacher-student relationship and promote a better learning environment. We tried to train our students by our example as teachers in the classroom (as our marvelous Korean language instructors had shown us by example) to eschew the safety of the teacher's desk at the front of the class and to soften the demands for respect and distance maintained by most Korean teachers.

I could keep warm by moving around the classroom, but the students who sat furthest from the stove in our classroom were visibly shivering on some days. Despite the cold in late November, very few students missed classes. I found that my students did their homework and did it well. Except for a few lapses, they were attentive in class and most showed great improvement in their spoken English ability since they had walked into my classroom either one or almost two years before.

I can't take credit for their exceptional grammatical skills. The majority had been able to enter Kyungpook University because of their excellent grounding already in English grammar, honed in high-school and middle-school classes (some had previously been taught by PCVs) and in the private tutoring sessions that most students had undertaken after school. Additionally, my students were in the English department of one of Korea's best universities—the best university outside of Seoul, as I have mentioned. They were already elite students with impressive skills, interested in learning English fluently, when they entered Kyungpook. I was indeed fortunate to have had such highly intelligent and dedicated students.

At the Nas' home I saw Reverend Na less and less often, as his teaching in Seoul at the Seoul Theological Seminary consumed more and more of his time. Mrs. Na had a young girl from the countryside again helping her prepare meals and take care of the children. In Reverend Na's absence, I occasionally went out with Mrs. Na for a bulgogi dinner at the Dangchip at my insistence, which I thought she enjoyed. She had done so much for me during my volunteer service in Daegu. I doubted that, when the Na family had agreed to let me live with them almost two years ago, they had anticipated how long I would stay and how much trouble I inevitably turned out to be. They had been a wonderful, kind, and caring family for me. I owed them a lot.

As November sped by, I was incredibly busy. Besides the rounds of farewell dinners and parties with Korean friends, colleagues, and students, I arranged for continuing health insurance between the end of my Peace Corps service and the start of whatever I would be doing in 1971, packed and shipped off my trunk, applied to four law schools (including the completion of lengthy financial aid applications), arranged to take the LSAT at the American embassy in Seoul, and began to make travel arrangements for the trip back home. My ambitious travel plans included a brief visit to Tokyo, Kyoto, and Yokohama; travel by train from Nakhodka (adjacent to Vladivostok) across the Soviet Union to Leningrad through Moscow (the so-called Trans-Siberian Railway); a visit with a friend in Finland; several weeks in Uppsala, Sweden, with friends; and a visit with the French family I had lived with during my term abroad in college, when I studied at the University of Montpellier.

In the meantime, I made a quick farewell trip to Geoje Island to say goodbye to the Korean friends—especially Choi Hwa-wook and Han Jae-chul—assisting with the health project, as well as to the Sibleys, whom I considered in many ways my "American family" abroad. I was extremely sad to think that this might be my last visit with the people, rural villages, and lovely islands that now meant so much to me. Hwa-wook and Jae-chul promised to come to Seoul after Christmas for a last visit. As we toasted each other in the ship's cabin on the return trip from Geoje Island to Busan, I vowed to Captain Yi—the ferryboat captain—that I would return in the near future to see how Korea and the life of its southern coastal waters had changed.

On November 23 I headed for Seoul to begin the week of final medical exams and conferences that marked the end of our combined K-VII and K-VIII groups' service. The official date of the completion of our groups' Peace Corps Volunteer service was December 8. My draft board in Buffalo had given me permission to be out of the United States until just before my birthday in mid April, so I decided to extend my service for one additional month. Peace Corps Deputy Director Wayne Olson and his delightful wife, Yvonne, invited our groups to their home for a wonderful Thanksgiving dinner and party on November 26. It was a tremendously bittersweet occasion. My Peace Corps cohorts were such close friends by now. It was a joy to be with them and reminisce about all of our adventures during the past two years. At the same time, I wondered if I would ever again meet, and be part of, such a dedicated and mutually supportive group of young Americans.

During the end-of-service conference, we were required to write a one-page succinct statement of our Peace Corps experience. This turned out to be a very difficult task. How does one describe in a few sentences the experience that has completely changed your life? We were told to be very brief and perfunctory. My statement was as follows:

> After three and one half months of TESOL training at the University of Hawaii's Hilo Center and Honolulu campus in the autumn/winter of 1968, I came to Korea as a member of the eighth group of PCVs to work in Korea. For two years I have been working as a TESOL instructor at the Language Institute of Kyungpook National University, Daegu, Korea, teaching four levels of students (freshmen, sophomores, juniors, and seniors), as well as graduate students and secondary-school teachers in the university's "teacher retraining program," a program aiming to retrain previously qualified teachers in other fields for teaching English (TESOL). My students were in the English department of the Liberal Arts and Science College; most will become teachers of English language and literature in secondary schools or universities. My duties also included making tapes for the institute.

During my university's vacations (five weeks each year), I worked in a hospital construction project under the auspices of the Medical Commission of the World Council of Churches, on Geoje Island, off Korea's southern coast. Most of the work I did at the hospital involved heavy construction—making bricks and concrete forms, road building, etc.

I consider myself one of the most fortunate members of Korea 8, for my teaching situation, my students and friends, and the Korean family with whom I lived for two years were exceptionally satisfying. My Peace Corps experience more than fulfilled my expectations.

Left untold in my statement were the sounds of street vendors in the streets and markets of Daegu; the faces and voices of my beloved students and fellow teachers at Kyungpook University; the rhythm and exuberance of Korean drumming and dancing; the laughter and kindness of my Korean family; the rugged ranges of mountains; the nighttime glow of the ocean waters off the south coast; the beauty of Daegu women; the curving silhouettes of Korean rooflines against evening skies; the richness of the four-thousand-year-old Korean history and culture; the sweet taste of kimchee and bulgogi; the seductiveness of Korean celadon; and most of all, the vibrancy and spirit of the Korean people.

The remainder of the conference was filled with discussions about issues like how to improve the university-level TESOL program; how Peace Corps staff could better support PCVs in the program; medical matters; problems we would encounter upon our return home (such as reverse culture shock); and future hopes and aspirations of the members of groups K-VII and K-VIII. At the end of our final Peace Corps conference, I was enveloped in profound sadness at the thought of leaving Korea, Peace Corps, and all that the country and years of service had come to represent for me. I knew I would never be able to recapture the excitement of what I had been experiencing for two brief, fleeting years. The constant thrill of new sights, smells, tastes, sounds, people, and stimuli of all kinds would never be with me again, I sensed. Although there was also a feeling of satisfaction that I had done something worthwhile and perhaps contributed a tiny bit to the country and people that had welcomed me as a Peace Corps Volunteer, I knew that what I had received from Korea and its citizens in return had far outweighed my small contribution, if any.

After returning to the bitter cold of Daegu in early December, I redoubled my efforts to prepare for the LSAT. In the face of limited exposure to English periodicals of the past two years, I felt that my English reading, comprehension, and writing skills were pretty rusty. The LSAT was a formidable challenge, particularly because my mind had forgotten the peculiar way that American aptitude tests are designed. Many evenings of song and rounds of makoli and maekju seemed to help my preparations.

As the final weeks in Korea approached, I began to think more and more about returning home. It was odd that my most intense time of homesickness abroad occurred just before I left Korea. Thoughts of my family in Buffalo, American food, Western toilets, hot showers, and driving an automobile—some of the things I missed most during my volunteer service—became almost obsessive. I dreamt about these matters almost every night in December.

At Kyungpook University there were three fine farewell parties, including one sponsored by the university officially to thank Moe Cain, Russ Feldmeier, and me for our teaching. I was very lucky to have had two other PCVs like Moe and Russ teaching at the same university. They were good friends and provided the occasional sounding board and other support that I sometimes needed. We each received certificates of gratitude, or *kamsajang*, from Kyungpook, as well as several exquisite presents: Korean paintings, calligraphy, and Korean dolls.

The eight professors who had been in my conversation class for the entire two years took me out one evening for my last dinner at a favorite restaurant, where we talked and sang together until curfew was almost upon us. They also presented me with a kamsajang and a Korean painting. Each of these men and women was special to me in a different way, and they had been kind, helpful colleagues over the years. I still miss the fun and laughter we shared while discussing in our class the differences between American and Korean cultures as manifested in the *Reader's Digest* articles we read.

Perhaps the most poignant of the farewell parties was the lovely party that my students collectively arranged. I had become really good friends with many of them, although most were four to five years younger than I was. I had a very special friendship with one in particular. Miss Rhee Sook-hee, who had introduced me to the Buddhist temples near Daegu and Gyeongju and taught me so much about Korean culture, was one of my youngest, brightest, and kindest students. She seemed like a younger sister and confided in me more than any other Korean friend. It was very difficult to say goodbye to her. I still treasure my students' farewell gifts and especially the beautifully carved, small wooden vase that she gave me.

Over the years I have lost touch with all of my students, including Miss Rhee. They are lost but not forgotten. I often wonder what became of them and suspect that many of them became leaders in the amazing transformation of Korea—over a mere forty year period—from a war-ravaged, impoverished country in 1970 to its important status in the world in the first decades of the new millennium.

The week before Christmas I said a final farewell to my Kyungpook University students and faculty colleagues, to my English conversation class students, and to my favorite shopkeepers, vendors, bus drivers, tabang hostesses, and as many of my other day-to-day Korean acquaintances I could find. I was surprised by how emotional these goodbyes were for me. Even people I did not know well but had passed every day on the streets had been kind. I already missed their bows of greeting each day and deeply regretted that I would probably never see many of these good citizens of Korea again.

It was equally difficult to part with the caring Peace Corps staff in Daegu: Alice Lenarz, the PCV secretary in the Daegu office; Mr. Kwon Hwa-soon, the assistant regional director; and Regional Director Tim O'Brien and his wife, Hyon. All of the staff were like family to me by this time. They were wonderful people.

Among the last things I did was write a letter to the unknown PCV who would succeed me at Kyungpook University, outlining what I had done for two years and suggesting what needed to be finished. I wrote that I hoped that he or she would be as fortunate as I had been in the friends which I had made and in the experiences in Daegu that had changed me forever.

When I left Daegu on the Friday before Christmas, it was lightly snowing. The mountains surrounding the city were capped with snow, but in the city the ground was still bare. The path and steps down to the street from our snug house were slippery, as I lugged my suitcases down to a waiting taxi. I asked the driver to swing by the Kyungpook University campus on our way to the brand new bus station next to the East Daegu Station. Through the snow, I saluted the buildings where my office had been located and where I had spent so many fond classroom hours. With offices closed for the winter break and without students, the campus looked bleak in the snow, but the Korean flags snapped and fluttered beautifully in the wind as a kind of upbeat postlude to a Korean symphony on my last full day in Daegu.

My farewell to the Na family would await my final departure in January from Busan. I planned to return to Daegu only for part of one day in the New Year and then to go the airport in Busan to catch my flight to Japan en route home. The Nas wanted to accompany me to the airport then.

On my last trip north to Seoul as a PCV I took an "expressway bus" along the impressive new super-highway that had been completed between Busan and Seoul earlier in the year and officially opened in July. Beautifully landscaped and featuring several awesome bridges and tunnels, the expressway offered an attractive alternative to trains. Instead of a noisy train ride on a crowded railway car, I enjoyed a quiet, smooth ride in a luxurious bus. It was quite a different experience than the train I was used to and cost about the same. The bus had a video system playing Korean movies and music, a Western-style toilet in the rear, comfortable reclining seats, and lovely, uniformed hostesses serving hot and cold drinks. Wonderful!

I didn't watch the video, as I was still entranced by the mountains, rice paddies, villages, and rivers that flashed by the bus. As we proceeded north, the winter landscape changed from brown, barren fields and mountains to white-cloaked countryside. Although I had made this trip perhaps a dozen times already by train, I never tired of the changing scenery or of enjoying how light subtly played across the terraced paddies and mountains, creating shifting patterns of shadows, even under leaden winter skies.

In Seoul I stayed with PCV friends for almost two weeks. Some of the members of K-VII and K-VIII had left Korea in mid-December immediately after the completion of our end-of-service conference. They had rushed to get home for the Christmas holidays. I had thought about doing that, but the enticement of a few more weeks in Korea, the LSAT scheduled for December 20 in Seoul, and my wish to see a bit more of the world before I returned home all persuaded me to extend my period of service for a month and to take a leisurely route home afterward.

Peace Corps/Korea seemed happy to extend me, even though classes were over for the winter. At the Peace Corps office I met daily with members of the staff to discuss my experiences at Kyungpook and how the TESOL program could be improved for future groups. I also sorted the hundreds of slides that I had taken for Peace Corps/Korea and organized them into a brief presentation of the various health, TESOL, and other programs the first sixteen groups had been involved with.

There were enough members of my group still in Korea to visit and party with. They showed me Seoul's palaces, museums, and best shopping areas, including several new department stores that, except for the signs in Korean and the tremendous crush of patrons, were exactly like any department store at home. Despite cold weather in Seoul, I had a grand opportunity to explore Seoul and enjoy its delights. One afternoon, three of my best PCV friends—Mike Robinson, Jon Moody, and Brian Copp—joined me in a commemorative formal portrait in which we tried to pose in the Korean way: unsmiling and looking as if we were about to be executed.

On December 20 I went to the American embassy early in the morning and took the LSAT with about a dozen other people. I was the only PCV there. The rest of the examinees were either Korean or members of the American armed forces. I skipped a lot of questions and felt as though I had not done well on the test. My reading speed had seriously declined during my two years in Korea. On the other hand, I felt as though I did very well on that part of the exam that tested writing skills, such as grammar, punctuation, and style. It was an exhausting test for me. Considering that it probably would be determinative of whether or not I would become a lawyer, I had carefully tried to prepare for it but left the testing room pretty discouraged by the end of the eight-hour exam.

The following day was the winter solstice. The weather had turned pleasant in Seoul, with bright sunshine and temperatures approaching fifty degrees. I walked around in the crowds in the downtown area of

Seoul near Duksoo Palace and the Peace Corps office, enjoying the warmth of the sun on my face, the bustling people, the traffic jams of hundreds of buses and taxis, and the energy of the society I would soon be leaving. Daegu had changed enormously in the two years I had lived there, but the changes in Seoul were even more incredible, as new buildings were going up everywhere and entire neighborhoods were disappearing in the face of development. I wondered if I would be able to recognize Korea, in the event that I returned in ten years, for this society and its people were changing so fast, right before my eyes.

Professor Lee Woo-gun, My Good Friend and Colleague, at the
Language Institute, Kyungpook National University, Daegu, Korea,
March 1970

Woman who Left her Shoes on the Road, Geoje Island, Korea,
July 1970

My Students Marching in ROTC Drills, Kyungpook National
University, Daegu, Korea, October 1970

My Special Friend Shin Young-ei, Daegu, Korea, April 1969

# Chapter Fourteen—
# Departure from Korea

hristmas Day was quiet. While Korean Christians spent most of the day in their churches, I walked around Seoul enjoying the few decorations and thinking of Christmas at home. It was a day of contemplation in bright sunshine with no wind. In the evening, about thirty PCVs enjoyed a fine turkey dinner with the Peace Corps/Korea Director Don Hess, his charming wife Nancy, and their daughter at the Hess's home. I had a long talk with Don and found him to be a friendly, bright, and impressive country director. (He later became Peace Corps' fifth director in Washington.)

My good friends Choi Hwa-wook, Han Jae-chul, and Shin Young-ei joined me for dinner on December 27. Mr. Choi and Mr. Han had come north from the Geoje Island project to Seoul for the holidays. Miss Shin had come over from Inchon, where she was working as a nurse. We had a fond-farewell evening. I knew I would especially miss these exceptional friends.

On New Year's Eve I had a last Peace Corps party with many of the new PCVs in Seoul and some of the older ones. A fair number of PCVs from groups K-I through K-VI had either extended their service or had taken jobs in Korea after the completion of their service. Many felt more comfortable now in Seoul than they did at home. As the church bells rang out the old year and welcomed 1971 in downtown Seoul, about fifty PCVs and Peace Corps/Korea staff members celebrated Korea and Koreans in a downtown hotel. It was so hard to say goodbye.

Peace Corps gave each terminating PCV either a plane ticket home with several days per diem to cover lodging, food, and miscellaneous expenses or the equivalent amount in cash, based on the cost of the most direct flight home. I used the money to pay for the tickets and other costs that I would incur in my seven-week trip home. It was just enough money to cover the expenses of the much longer trip, providing I traveled by boat and train across Asia and Europe to London and then flew to New York, rather than by the much more expensive plane route across the Pacific. I had been making my travel arrangements for several months, through a travel agency in Tokyo, which arranged for the necessary tickets and visas. January and February were not the most ideal months to travel across Siberia and northern Europe, but I hoped for an adventure, and if the trip included cold and snowy weather, so much the better.

I thought of the contrast between my arrival in Korea two years before in January 1969 and my departure in January 1971. Seoul had been covered with snow then and had seemed almost medieval with its occasional ox-drawn cart. My eyes had been wide with surprise at the military presence, the astonishing numbers of people everywhere, and the pervasive poverty. As I prepared to leave, the weather was relatively warm for winter, with temperatures in the forties. The light snow that had fallen in December and January was already gone. Seoul seemed like a modern Western city compared to Daegu. Mercedes cars had replaced ox-drawn carts. I was so used to the military presence, crowds, and signs of lingering poverty that I didn't notice the soldiers, crush of people, and homeless people any longer.

People had also changed for me. High cheek-boned, squarish faces, smaller, heavy-lidded oval eyes, and black hair were normal, attractive features. As I passed store windows and looked at my reflection, my nose seemed enormous and my eyes seemed too big for my face. Westerners seemed to have huge noses with narrow, ape-like or fox-like features in some cases. The once-familiar faces of Westerners were no longer appealing. The once exotic faces of Koreans had become the familiar and comfortable.

On my last day in Seoul I decided to do something I had never before done in Korea. A new cultural center in Seoul had recently opened about two blocks from the Peace Corps office. As I was walking around downtown Seoul and passing the beautiful new building, I noticed that the Korean National Opera was performing *Madama Butterfly*, which was my favorite opera. A ticket was about five dollars. I could barely afford one but wanted to have a special last day in Korea's capital city, so I bought a ticket for that night's performance. I went by myself.

The singers of the Korean National Opera Company, the staging, and the orchestra were all superb. I particularly remember that the singer who played Cio-Cio San—the opera's tragic heroine Butterfly—had a magnificent voice and was stunningly beautiful. I enjoyed every second of the terrific performance. As Cio-Cio San killed herself behind a screen at the opera's end, her very young son—about to be taken from Japan to the United States by his natural father, Pinkerton, and his American wife—sat on the floor in the center front of the stage, slowing waving a small American flag. The curtain fell to resounding cheers from everyone, except me. I was too overcome with sadness and tears to move. I sat there crying until the theater emptied.

The next morning I took an expressway bus down to Daegu, concentrating on the countryside that the bus wound through. I wanted to remember every detail of the fields, terraced paddies, straw- and tile-roofed houses, stone walls, rivers, and ancient mountains of the Land of the Morning Calm. Even in the winter the landscape—home for four thousand years to a unique race—tugged at your heart.

The Na family met me in Daegu and joined me on a train to Busan. All of the children accompanied us. It was an overcast day with a biting wind when we took a taxi to the airport from the Busan train station. I was very sad to leave the Na family. They had been extremely kind and supportive for almost two years. Very few other PCVs in my group had stayed with the same family for their entire service. Words are inadequate to describe how very fortunate I was to have met Reverend Na and his wife and to have been able to live with them. I was very sincere when I told them I could not thank them enough.

At the airport I felt my thoughts turning toward home. I suddenly became eager to be on my way and put Korea behind me. I guess I knew I would return somehow before too much time had elapsed. At the same time I realized that the Korea I had known and come to love in so many ways would never be the same for me in the future. I would probably never feel so strongly again about the places and people that had captured part of my heart here. It was like leaving my home in Buffalo for college had been almost eight years before—sadness was overwhelmed by the excitement of the life ahead—except that I was leaving my Korean home and returning to my American home.

When I saw on the runway the Pan American plane that would carry me from Korea, homesickness washed over me. I thought of my family in Buffalo, classmates, friends, and teachers. I remembered the mundane that now seemed so important: hot showers, bathtubs, sit-down toilets, air conditioning, driving a car, and cold, safe drinking water from faucets. I recalled orange juice, bacon and eggs, doughnuts, ice cream, milk, freshly baked bread, milkshakes, hamburgers, French fries, and hotdogs. Most of all I remembered the serenity of walking streets at home, without stares, as just another American among many.

As I climbed up the steps leading to the open door of the plane, I asked myself whether I had achieved any of the three goals that had been drummed into our heads during Peace Corps training. Certainly goal number one (helping the people of interested countries in meeting their need for trained men and women) had been minimally realized, if at all. Koreans at Kyungpook University seemed perfectly capable of learning English, and teaching English, without assistance from young Americans. On Geoje Island the construction work I had done was quite insignificant, particularly in comparison to that of the hard-working Koreans who were my companions.

My service in Korea was like the one occasion when I helped row the stern-and-aft-oared small ferryboat between Chilcheon Island and Geoje Island. To be sure, I had helped some students get from one island to another, across the channel between the two islands, on their way to school. But the strong-armed old Korean ferryman had done much of the real work with the oar at the stern. What I did once, he did better and every day, year in and year out. If I was honest, I had to admit that I had accomplished very, very little in Korea.

Regarding goal number two (helping promote a better understanding of Americans on the part of the peoples served), there was no evidence that I could think of to support any belief that my being in Korea had helped Koreans understand Americans better. After all, for my two years in Korea there had been more than fifty thousand Americans serving in Korea in the military and another four hundred or so missionaries and diplomats, compared to several hundred PCVs in Korea, including me in the Language Institute of Kyungpook University. Why should I think that one person's two-year period of service had contributed to Koreans' better understanding of Americans? Honestly, I had been treated generously by Koreans, giving me their time, friendship, and countless days and evenings of pleasure, usually at their expense. I had given very, very little back in comparison. If I had left any impression at all on the Koreans I was acquainted with, it was probably that I was slow to reciprocate, stingy, not very smart, and insensitive.

Perhaps with goal number three (helping promote a better understanding of other peoples on the part of Americans) I had done better, in a small way. Personally, I had certainly learned a lot about Korea, its people, and its culture and even learned conversational Korean to some degree. My enthusiasm for this country and its splendid people, as well as what I learned about Koreans and their culture, had been conveyed in biweekly letters to my parents and friends at home, who had circulated them to more family and friends. Many members of my family at home had hosted Korean friends of mine, or other Koreans visiting or studying in the United States. My understanding and appreciation of Korea, although somewhat superficial, was undisputable. Some of what I had learned had been passed on to many other Americans.

The bottom line, however, was the strong feeling that I had failed in any significant degree "to tame the savageness of man and make gentle the life of this world," as Bobby Kennedy had urged in his eulogy for Martin Luther King, or to "make a difference—a difference that may create a condition for peace," as Peace Corps Director Vaughn had hoped.

The flight attendant slammed the plane's door shut on my tale of two cultures. The plane taxied down the runway, and we lifted off over the Busan harbor, across the Korea Strait, heading for Japan with Geoje Island visible in the distance off the starboard side of the plane. John Denver's song ran through my mind: "Leavin' on a jet plane, don't know when I'll be back again ..." Korea's mountains faded quickly in the distance.

Strait between Geoje Island and Chilcheon Island, Korea, May 1970

Buddha at Beopju Temple, North Chungcheong Province, Korea,
October 1970

Dancing Woman in a Makoli Chip, Daegu, Korea, November 1970

Farewell Portrait of PCVs (from left) Brian Copp, Chuck Hobbie,
Mike Robinson, and Jon Moody, Seoul, Korea, December 1970

# EPILOGUE

A newspaper I found on the plane informed me that in Vietnam, despite significant reductions in American military personnel in the past year, body bags were still flown home by the hundreds. At the end of 1970, US military personnel in Vietnam totaled 334,600, according to the article. I wondered how many of them loved Vietnam, even a little.

I spent two days in Tokyo. The second evening I attended a performance of *Madama Butterfly*, which coincidentally was playing at the Tokyo Opera. As in the Korean performance a week before, Puccini's wonderful story, lyrics, and music were very moving. This time I didn't cry. The Korean performance had been much better.

During my one week in lovely Kyoto, I visited shrines and temples draped in snow. I stayed with two former Korea PCVs who were living with a Japanese family in a traditional, cozy Japanese home that was elevated on bamboo posts and sat on the side of a mountain overlooking Kyoto. In the middle of my second night there I awoke to the sound of what I thought was a rising wind with blowing snow. Then I felt the swaying of the house and realized that I was experiencing an earthquake and a blizzard, both at the same time. Remembering the eruption of Mt. Kilauea and the Seoul blizzard at the beginning of my Peace Corps service, I felt there was a marvelous, natural symmetry at work.

From Kyoto I took a train to Yokohama, where I boarded a ship destined for Nakhodka, Russia. There were about fifty foreigners on the Russian ship—mostly Japanese, Australians, and one American (me). I remember the meals, which I found quite delicious, and the dancing of the Russian sailors, who performed for us each of our two nights at sea. The Aussies complained bitterly about the food. The weather was cold and blustery in the North Pacific between Japan and Russia, and it was a rough crossing.

Nakhodka was a port city slightly to the east of Vladivostok. It was the eastern terminus of the Trans-Siberian Railway. Most of the ship's passengers were also taking the train west to Moscow. By this time I had made several friends among the Australians, who were friendly and fun-loving men and women. I was shown to a sleeping coach, where I shared accommodations with six petite Japanese women, slightly older than I was. There were eight bunks—four stacked on each side of the sleeping compartment. My bunk was at the bottom nearest the door.

The train departed at midday. The cars were luxurious, with crimson, velvet upholstered chairs, fine china, and a small stove in each, which gave off prodigious amounts of heat. It was a comfortable slow trip across a desolate terrain covered with snow, which seemed to alternate between rugged mountains and flat prairies. The train moved about forty mph. During the days we stopped briefly at several small towns and could get off the train to stretch our legs, as long as we didn't leave the area of the station. The only people we saw were old women tightly bundled up in poor-quality coats and hats against the wind and cold. They were uncommunicative. "Bleak" is the one word that most readily comes to mind to describe those Siberian towns in winter.

I played Poker and Hearts with the Aussies every night until well past midnight and had a grand time. The first nights on the train I was perplexed that the Japanese women in my sleeping compartment were never there when I went to bed about one o'clock in the morning. They would steal into the compartment about half an hour after I had settled down, undress in the pitch dark, and go to bed without a sound. Then I realized that they were waiting for me to retire to bed first each night. So I changed my routine to go to bed early, lie in my bunk fully dressed but making fake snoring sounds, until each of the women had come to bed and started to snore, and then quietly get up and exit to play cards to my heart's content. This arrangement seemed to work very well for the remaining six nights on the train.

Occasionally, we saw Soviet military trains bristling with tanks and other armaments heading in the opposite direction. There had been recent escalating border clashes between Soviet and Chinese military personnel, we had heard, and the Russians were rapidly beefing up their military forces along parts of the Chinese border. Train after train chugged by. When these trains approached, the conductor would pull down the shades on that side of our train and announce that we were not supposed to observe the trains when they passed. Of course these actions sent us scurrying to our sleeping compartments, where we could lock the door and watch the military trains without interference.

It was a relief to finally arrive in Moscow in late January. I stayed at an old lavish hotel called the Moskva, where I was surprised by the relatively warm weather—daytime temperatures were close to sixty degrees for the three days I was in Moscow—and by the very tall prostitutes who lined the hotel lobby's walls with their fur hats and wraps. I had been warned by the American embassy in Seoul that most of these women were working for the Soviet's intelligence agencies, such as the KGB, so I avoided them carefully, although several of my Aussie friends did not seem to have received the same warning.

While in Moscow, I visited Lenin's Tomb in Red Square. A young Egyptian student studying at the University of Moscow approached me while I was standing in the long line that snaked across the square. He explained that this was his last day in Moscow after one year as an exchange student, that he wanted to see the tomb before he left, and that Americans were usually given expedited treatment, so that if I would allow him to accompany me into the tomb, he could arrange for us to avoid the hours-long wait in line. I agreed, and several minutes later he returned with a policeman, who escorted us to the front of the line.

That evening we shared a bottle of vodka together, before I left for a performance by the Bolshoi Ballet of Tchaikovsky's *Swan Lake*. The Egyptian student was a bit inebriated and talked effusively of his dislike for Moscow and for the Soviet Union. Unfortunately, I had also had too much to drink. Vodka was potent stuff. I enjoyed the ballet but had trouble focusing my eyes and seemed to see double images of the dancers, which made for quite a surrealistic—almost kaleidoscopic—effect at times.

The following evening I met a young American woman in the hotel lobby who introduced herself as a Fitzgerald—a cousin and secretary of Senator Theodore ("Ted") Kennedy. We went together to the Bolshoi

Opera to see *Madama Butterfly*. Having seen two other performances by different companies of the same opera in the past several weeks, I felt as though I was quite an opera expert, at least regarding *Madama Butterfly*. I enjoyed the performance, as always, but I was quite put off by the Wagnerian-like Russian singers and their attempts to mimic the movements of Asian women. Their voices were spectacular, but there was no question that the Korean *Madama Butterfly* was far superior to the Japanese and Russian versions.

At dinner in a nearby restaurant the next night, Miss Fitzgerald and I were surprised when a waiter (for whom we had waited patiently for over an hour) suddenly appeared and presented us with a bottle of vodka, courtesy of an elderly Russian woman at an adjoining table. We went over to ask her to join us and to thank her. She told us in heavily accented English that she was the aunt of the Canadian actor Lorne Greene—who played the role of Ben Cartwright in the television series *Bonanza*—and that she loved Canadians and Americans. She was a charming, friendly, and gracious woman.

After several days and nights in a drab and bleak Moscow, I took a train to Leningrad (now St. Petersburg), where again I met Miss Fitzgerald at the hotel. We visited the impressive Hermitage and the palace of Catherine the Great in Pushkin, located not far from Leningrad to the southeast. Both buildings and their contents were spectacular, although the palace was still under reconstruction. In one of the lavish rooms of the Hermitage, a little old lady furtively approached Miss Fitzgerald, after assuring that we were alone with her in the museum's room, and thrust a thick letter into her hands while making a prayerful gesture with her hands, as though to ask a favor. The letter was addressed to the United Nations in New York. The woman assumed her seat in a corner of the room as quickly and quietly as she had approached us. Miss Fitzgerald tucked the letter quickly into her handbag.

That evening we had dinner again together, since we were the only Americans at the hotel. Some students from the local university at another table invited us to join them and entertained us royally, insisting on paying for our dinners and on taking us to several clubs, where only foreign tourists and their guests could enter. I had a good time. The next morning, as I departed the hotel to catch a train to Helsinki, Finland, I offered to take the letter to New York and deliver it to the United

Nations. Miss Fitzgerald told me that one of the students had offered to take the letter himself and send it to the United Nations, so she had relinquished it to him. I was incredulous that she would do such a thing when it was hard to know whom to trust.

On the train to Finland in bright sunshine I shared a compartment with a friendly Swedish couple with whom I had an engaging conversation. He was the head of a Swedish international service organization similar to the Peace Corps and was extremely interested in my Peace Corps experience. In the midst of our long conversation, four North Korean soldiers in uniforms with red-starred hats entered the compartment and sat down facing us. They were friendly and spoke some English. We talked with them about their impressions of the Soviet Union, and they were all quite responsive, until they realized I was an American. Without a word, they stood up as one and quickly exited the compartment.

Shortly after that the train stopped at the Finnish border. Soviet soldiers in long, dark-green greatcoats with automatic rifles boarded the train, going from car to car and inspecting the compartments. At our compartment they ordered us to stand up, lifted the top of the seat on which we had been sitting, and demanded to know what was in the three packages, wrapped in plain paper, lying beneath our seats. The Swedes and I were dumbfounded. None of us had been aware of the packages. The soldiers became accusatory in their broken English and strident Russian. I was starting to get really worried, and my Swedish friends looked quite scared.

Suddenly there was a shout from outside the car and several huge soldiers in white parkas, carrying submachine guns, strode down the car and poked their heads into our compartment—Finnish soldiers. The Russian soldiers took the packages and exited immediately, to our great relief. I don't believe I was the only passenger who imagined that, as we crossed the border into Finland, it was as though a cloud had lifted from the train. People toasted each other with schnapps and broke into song. I realized that throughout the train trip through the Soviet Union, I had been quite stressed with an overall feeling of depression at the hopelessness and bleakness of life there. Many of my Aussie friends, who were still on the train, said that they would never return to the Soviet Union. I felt a renewed appreciation for my own country.

After several wonderful weeks in Helsinki with friends of my Aunt Kate's and in Uppsala, Sweden, with my Swedish friends, including Staffan, I had a delightful reunion with my French "family"—Madam Rénée Lévère and her son, Alain—in Montpellier, France. Then I spent several days in London before flying from England to New York. As the day of my arrival home got closer and closer, I became more and more eager to see my family and friends in Buffalo.

In New York I had to change flights. Since I had to wait several hours, I walked around Kennedy International Airport, mesmerized by the faces of the people in the airport. Ever since arriving in Helsinki I had felt as though I somehow knew the people I passed on the streets. At the New York airport the feeling of recognition was even more pronounced. I felt as though I had met most of the people in the airport before. This was a preposterous idea. Nevertheless, I seemed to recognize the faces all around me. Perhaps they were former classmates from Nichols High School in Buffalo, or from Dartmouth, or Wisconsin. Or were they neighbors from Buffalo's West Side, or Hanover, or Madison? It was the strangest feeling.

I finally realized that the faces all around me looked very much the same, with their big round eyes and large noses. I would have been hard put to identify even someone I knew well among the people around me. I also smelled a faint aroma of rancid butter—the smell that crowds of Westerners seemed to generate.

As we landed at the Buffalo airport on the flight from New York City, the plane circled to the west before approaching the airport, carrying me right over Holloway Bay and Point Albino on the Canadian shore of Lake Erie, where I had spent eighteen happy childhood summers. I looked down at the beach on the familiar bay, frozen lake, and woods, and then on the glorious Niagara River and downtown Buffalo with a fondness and longing that words cannot describe. I was home.

I recall several blissful initial weeks at home, basking in the joy of being with my family and reacquainting myself with American life and friends. I had more than two years of news and pop culture to catch up with, to say nothing of gorging myself on hot fudge sundaes, hamburgers, hotdogs, bacon, and other unhealthy foods. It was as though there was a "black hole" in my life in the United States, during which my stomach had been fasting and my mind had been blank as far as Americana was concerned. At the same time, several unexpected elements of so-called reverse culture shock hit me.

The first occurred when I walked outside or drove around my hometown. There were very few vehicles and almost no people anywhere. Buffalo's empty streets, seemingly almost completely deserted compared to Korea's streets, gave me an uneasy feeling that something terrible had just happened, or was about to happen, causing everybody to hide indoors. I missed the bustle and energy of Daegu's crowded alleys and boulevards.

I also missed the status that I was accorded in Korea, where I had been stared at, treated as an honored guest, and accorded respect as a university teacher. At home I was loved by my family but had no other status, except as a returned PCV. No one stared at me. No one noticed me, except the policeman who ticketed me on my first day home for exceeding the speed limit in Delaware Park—which had been lowered in my absence. My position in society was essentially meaningless. I was contributing to nothing. My ego was deflated.

Surprisingly, and perhaps ironically, the wealth of material goods and pleasures in the United States upset me. It was too easy to obtain the foods I had longed for in Korea. In the grocery stores at home there were six kinds of peanut butter, four brands of orange juice, and thousands of various delectable foods not available in Korea. There were five fast food restaurants within two minutes of my Buffalo home, hawking hamburgers, French fries, and milkshakes. For a hot shower or a relaxing bath I only had to turn a faucet handle. There were sit-down toilets in every building and home. If I wanted to go downtown, I hopped into my family's car. No more walking everywhere for me. The waste of food, water, and power was astonishing. It was all too much. My resulting depression was debilitating.

To top it all, at the end of March my draft board in Buffalo notified me of my induction into the US Army scheduled for mid-May. My draft number (#124) in the Selective Service lottery had been reached. The notice arrived just before my twenty-sixth birthday—the birthday after which by law I could not be drafted. My euphoria at being home with family and friends and my reverse culture shock quickly gave way to despair at the thought of returning to Asia to fight in Vietnam.

I immediately ordered a cord of unsplit wood from a local firewood supplier and spent three straight days splitting wood in my parents' basement. There is nothing better to nurture reflection than splitting wood. Perversely, I thought that at least I would be able to say that I had not "dodged" the military draft by joining the Peace Corps. In the following difficult weeks, the fact that my parents, siblings, so many family members, former teachers, my minister at St. John's Episcopal Church, and friends rallied to my emotional support touched me immeasurably.

I began a month of intense, anguished introspection. My opposition to the war was steadfast. My belief that I would be sent to Vietnam to fight, if I joined the American military, was equally firm. I was not a Conscientious Objector, as I believed that some wars were justified and certainly would have returned to Korea to fight to protect friends there from an invasion again from North Korea. My former classmates at Nichols High School and at Dartmouth College were also wrestling, or had already wrestled, with the issues of morality, duty to country, and duty to self that I was struggling to resolve. Some, like Bill Smoyer, had enlisted in various branches of the military, or enrolled in officer candidate schools. Some had fled to Canada. Some had been granted status as Conscientious Objectors. Some had rushed into marriage and immediately had children, which was an automatic deferment. A few had reported for induction and then refused to be inducted, incurring a conviction and a criminal penalty.

My twin cousins, Molly and Kitty Craig, were then working as volunteers in a program run by the Quaker church to counsel young men who were facing induction, like myself. At their urging I attended two weeks of sessions with dozens of young men. We learned about our options. I discovered that in Buffalo, if a young man refused to be inducted and thereby violated federal law, he would be arrested and eventually tried before Judge John T. Curtin. If convicted, such a felon would stand little chance of eventually being admitted to a bar as a lawyer, which was what I had hoped to become.

President Lyndon Johnson had appointed US District Court Judge Curtin to the federal bench in 1967. Born in Buffalo, Curtin served in the US Marine Corps during World War II from 1942 to 1945, achieving the rank of lieutenant colonel. He was known as a no-nonsense type of judge and a strong supporter of the US Armed Forces. But he was also extremely sympathetic to men convicted of refusing to be inducted. In fact, in the vast majority of the cases involving convictions for induction refusal, Judge Curtin imposed a five-year suspended sentence with expungement possible at the successful completion of the probationary period.

After weeks of soul searching, I decided to refuse to be inducted, despite the consequences. I talked with my elementary-school principal and teachers, several of my former high-school teachers, and with the headmaster of my high school. I had long discussions with Reverend Clare Backhurst, my minister at St. John's Episcopal Church in Buffalo. My parents, aunts and uncles, my brother and sister, cousins and friends—all were consulted. I felt that I had a duty to the United States, but I drew the line at including in that duty acts I believed to be morally repugnant. The bottom line for me was whether I could live with myself, assuming I survived a tour in Vietnam, if I was put in a position of having to kill Vietnamese or destroy a village in the war I considered unjust.

The Quaker classes were designed to teach us what to expect at the induction center when we reported for induction and what to do, and not to do, when arrested for refusing to step forward for induction. On the day of my induction, about fifty of the seventy young men who reported to the induction center had been in the Quaker classes with me and were prepared to refuse to be inducted. I felt that I was not alone, which was terribly reassuring. Lawyers stood by to represent us.

After several hours of processing, which included physical examinations and psychological consultations, we were called to a large central room where we all assembled for the induction ceremony—which would be the moment when most of us were going to refuse to step forward. I expected that it would be a moment that could change my life, probably for the worse. As we entered the room, my name was announced over the loudspeaker. I was instructed to return to the medical office.

There, a young doctor advised me that I was being temporarily rejected because my stool sample indicated that I had giardiasis, an infection of the small intestine caused by a waterborne microscopic organism or protozoa: Giardia lamblia. It usually causes bowel discomfort and diarrhea. I had no symptoms. My Peace Corps end-of-service physical examination in Seoul had cleared me of any medical issues, except the fungus on my back. I had picked up the organism on the way home.

The doctor gave me some medicine and instructed me to take it to get rid of the infection. I would be sent a new induction notice in several weeks, he told me, and sent me home. I silently turned, walked out of the medical office, and left the induction center. Then it hit me that I was free. Having already turned twenty-six several weeks before, I could not be given a new notice. A weight I had borne for half a decade was lifted from my shoulders. Strangely, I was not euphoric but rather wondered if I had experienced divine intervention or merely met a protozoan "friend" from the waters of Leningrad. I discarded the medicine unused. As far as I know, my friend still dwells with me. After all, I might need some help again someday.

By the end of 1971, forty-five thousand Americans had died in Vietnam. Thousands of others returned home horribly maimed, physically and mentally. I was grateful that I had walked through many Asian rice paddies but never with a weapon.

At some point between my departure from Busan in January and my May departure from the induction center in Buffalo, I realized that Korea's rice paddies represented for me a kind of symbolic bridge. Just as Freedom Bridge at Panmunjom was a tangible symbol of a gateway to freedom from oppression, my personal journey through and past Korean rice paddies in the Peace Corps was a path on which I had entered into the community of the world, leaving behind forever the person who had flown to Hilo in 1968. My primary guides on this path—to whom I will always be deeply appreciative—were the incredible Korean people I encountered in the brief time of my life spanning the Years of the Monkey, Rooster, and Dog.

Over the next five years I was on the Peace Corps training staff at the School for International Training in Putney, Vermont, preparing the nineteenth group of volunteers to go to Korea; joined the Peace Corps headquarters staff as a special services officer and then country desk officer for Korea and Thailand; and completed law school. In 1974, with Reverend Na presiding, I was married in Virginia to the enchanting Korean woman—Shin Young-ei—who captured my heart first in Daegu and later in Germany, where she had emigrated in 1972.

In subsequent years I returned to Korea often, sometimes with Young-ei, our son, Jason, and our daughter, Amy, watching Korea transform itself into a modern democracy and its trees mature into lush forests on once-barren mountains. But those years are another tale and a time of different animals.

Woman Dancing Farmer's Dance, Daegu, Korea, December 1970

Pulguk Temple, Gyeongju, Korea, April 1970

Street in Hachung, Geoje Island, Korea, October 1969

Mountains, North Gyeongsang Province, August 1970

Made in the USA
Lexington, KY
24 September 2011